Lecture Notes in Computer Scie␣

Edited by G. Goos, J. Hartmanis, and J. van ␣

T0238414

Springer
Berlin
Heidelberg
New York
Hong Kong
London
Milan
Paris
Tokyo

Jon Timmis   Peter Bentley   Emma Hart (Eds.)

Artificial
Immune Systems

Second International Conference, ICARIS 2003
Edinburgh, UK, September 1-3, 2003
Proceedings

 Springer

Series Editors

Gerhard Goos, Karlsruhe University, Germany
Juris Hartmanis, Cornell University, NY, USA
Jan van Leeuwen, Utrecht University, The Netherlands

Volume Editors

Jon Timmis
University of Kent, Computing Laboratory
Canterbury, Kent, CT2 7NF, UK
E-mail: J.Timmis@kent.ac.uk

Peter Bentley
University College London, Department of Computer Science
Gower Street, London, WC1E 6BT, UK
E-mail: P. Bentley@cs.ucl.ac.uk

Emma Hart
Napier University, School of Computing
10 Colinton Road, Edinburgh EH10 5DT, UK
E-mail: e.hart@napier.ac.uk

Cataloging-in-Publication Data applied for

A catalog record for this book is available from the Library of Congress.

Bibliographic information published by Die Deutsche Bibliothek
Die Deutsche Bibliothek lists this publication in the Deutsche Nationalbibliografie;
detailed bibliographic data is available in the Internet at <http://dnb.ddb.de>.

CR Subject Classification (1998): F.1, I.2, F.2, H.2.8, H.3, J.3

ISSN 0302-9743
ISBN 3-540-40766-9 Springer-Verlag Berlin Heidelberg New York

Springer-Verlag Berlin Heidelberg New York
a member of BertelsmannSpringer Science+Business Media GmbH

http://www.springer.de

© Springer-Verlag Berlin Heidelberg 2003
Printed in Germany

Typesetting: Camera-ready by author, data conversion by Olgun Computergraphik
Printed on acid-free paper   SPIN: 10931806   06/3142   5 4 3 2 1 0

Preface

In many ways, our immune systems are as complex as our brains. They learn, predict, remember and adapt, protecting us from the maelstrom of pathogens that infect us daily. Computer Science frequently takes inspiration from the seemingly endless capabilities of natural systems. It should therefore be no surprise that, like the field of Artificial Neural Networks inspired from brains, we now have a vigorous field of research known as Artificial Immune Systems (AIS), inspired by our own immune systems.

Although still relatively new, the previous 10 years has seen the paradigm of AIS rapidly establish itself as an important biological metaphor. Researchers all over the world fruitfully exploit "immunological ideas" in many different ways to provide mechanisms for tackling a wide variety of applications.

In this volume we present the proceedings of ICARIS 2003, the 2nd International Conference on Artificial Immune Systems. This was the second international conference entirely dedicated to the field, and followed the extremely successful first conference held in Canterbury, UK in 2002. The number and diversity of papers in this year's conference is a tribute to the ever-growing number of researchers in the area, and representative of the solid foundation of work that now exists in this area. The range of topics considered is wide. For example, at one end of the spectrum we see a selection of papers providing a necessary theoretical grounding for the field. At the other end, we have an exciting range of applications to real-world problems, covering, for example, job-shop scheduling and fault detection in refrigeration systems.

As last year, the conference was divided into two streams, technical and conceptual. The conceptual stream provided an important platform for determining the future direction of this domain, and the variety of papers published in this stream suggest an exciting future for the field. Also, this year we devoted a special session to the topic of "Immunocomputing," supported by the Commission of the European Communities Directorate-General Information Society IST Programme on Future and Emerging Technologies. This is a new computational paradigm that aims to implement the principles of information processing using proteins and immune networks in new kinds of computer algorithms and software, leading to the concept of a new kind of computer, the "immunocomputer." (Analogous to the widely spread neurocomputers, which are based on the models of neurons and neural networks.)

ICARIS 2003 could not have happened without the help of a large number of people. Thanks to Chris Osborne for providing the online registration system, to Simon Garret for UK publicity arrangements, to Dipankar Dasgupta for publicity in the US and to Andy Secker for helping out with the proceedings. Emma Hart took care of local arrangements, and was invaluably assisted and advised by Jennifer Willies. Finally, thanks are of course due to all of the program committee for ensuring that the material presented at the conference was of the highest quality. Forty-one papers were submitted for review, of which 26 were accepted.

We hope you enjoyed Edinburgh and ICARIS 2003, and we look forward to welcoming you again in the future to ICARIS 2004.

September 2003   Jon Timmis, Peter Bentley, Emma Hart
                                                                        Editors
                                                                  ICARIS 2003

Organizing Committee

Conference Chairs	Jon Timmis (University of Kent, UK)
	Peter Bentley (University College, London, UK)
Local Chair	Emma Hart (Napier University, UK)
Publicity Chairs	Simon Garrett (University of Wales, Aberystwyth, UK)
	Dipankar Dasgupta (University of Memphis, USA)
Local Organization	Jennifer Willies (Napier University, UK)

Program Committee

U. Aicklein	University of Bradford, UK
H. Bersini	Université Libre de Bruxelles, Belgium
L. Boggess	Mississippi State University, USA
S. Cayzer	Hewlett-Packard (Bristol) plc, UK
C. Coello Coello	CINVESTAV-IPN, Mexico
V. Cutello	University of Catania, Italy
R. Duncan	NCR (Scotland) plc, UK
L. de Castro	University of Campinas, Brazil
S. Forrest	University of New Mexico, USA
A. Freitas	University of Kent, UK
F. Gonzalez	University of Memphis, USA
Y. Ishida	Toyohashi University of Technology, Japan
C. Johnson	University of Kent, UK
J. Kim	King's College London, UK
T. Knight	University of Kent, UK
M. Neal	University of Wales, Aberystwyth, UK
N. Nikolaev	Goldsmiths College, UK
P. Ross	Napier University, UK
S. Stepney	University of York, UK
A. Tarakanov	St. Petersburg Institute, Russia
A. Tyrrell	University of York, UK
A. Watkins	University of Kent, UK
S. Wierzchon	Polish Academy of Sciences, Poland
F. Von Zuben	University of Campinas, Brazil

Special Session on Immunocomputing

Prof. Ioannis Antoniou	International Solvay Institutes for Physics and Chemistry, Brussels, Belgium
Prof. Costas Karanikas	Aristotle University of Thessaloniki, Thessaloniki, Greece
Dr. Yuri Melnikov	International Solvay Institutes for Physics and Chemistry, Brussels, Belgium
Dr. Alexander Tarakanov	International Solvay Institutes for Physics and Chemistry, Brussels, Belgium, and St. Petersburg Institute for Informatics and Automation, St. Petersburg, Russia

Sponsoring Institutions

EVONET
Hewlett-Packard plc

Table of Contents

Emerging Metaphors
(Conceptual Stream)

Augmentations of Artificial Immune System Algorithms
(Technical Stream)

Theory of Artificial Immune Systems
(Conceptual Stream)

Representations and Operators (Technical Stream)

Plenary Session

Use of an Artificial Immune System
for Job Shop Scheduling

Carlos A. Coello Coello, Daniel Cortés Rivera, and Nareli Cruz Cortés

CINVESTAV-IPN
Evolutionary Computation Group
Depto. de Ingeniería Eléctrica
Sección de Computación
Av. Instituto Politécnico Nacional No. 2508
Col. San Pedro Zacatenco
México, D. F. 07300
ccoello@cs.cinvestav.mx
{dcortes,nareli}@computacion.cs.cinvestav.mx

Abstract. In this paper, we propose an algorithm based on an artificial immune system to solve job shop scheduling problems. The approach uses clonal selection, hypermutations and a library of antibodies to construct solutions. It also uses a local selection mechanism that tries to eliminate gaps between jobs in order to improve solutions produced by the search mechanism of the algorithm. The proposed approach is compared with respect to GRASP (an enumerative approach) in several test problems taken from the specialized literature. Our results indicate that the proposed algorithm is highly competitive, being able to produce better solutions than GRASP in several cases, at a fraction of its computational cost.

1   Introduction

Scheduling problems arise in all areas. The purpose of scheduling is to allocate a set of (limited) resources to tasks over time [26]. Scheduling has been a very active research area during several years, both in the operations research and in the computer science literature [1, 2, 18]. Research on scheduling basically focuses on finding ways of assigning tasks (or jobs) to machines (i.e., the resources) such that certain criteria are met and certain objective (or objectives) function is optimized.

Several heuristics have been used for different types of scheduling problems (e.g., job shop, flowshop, production, etc.): evolutionary algorithms [8, 9], tabu search [4], and simulated annealing [7], among others. Note, however, that the use of artificial immune systems for the solution of scheduling problems of any type has been scarce (see for example [10, 14, 15]).

This paper introduces a new approach, which is based on an artificial immune system and the use of antibody libraries and is applied for optimizing job shop scheduling problems. The proposed approach is compared with respect to GRASP (Greedy Randomized Adaptive Search Procedure) in several test problems taken from the specialized literature. Our results indicate that the proposed approach is a viable alternative for solving efficiently job shop scheduling problems.

J. Timmis et al. (Eds.): ICARIS 2003, LNCS 2787, pp. 1–10, 2003.
© Springer-Verlag Berlin Heidelberg 2003

2   Statement of the Problem

In this paper, we will be dealing with the Job Shop Scheduling Problem (JSSP), in which the general objective is to minimize the time taken to finish the last job available (makespan). In other words, the goal is to find a schedule that has the minimum duration required to complete all the jobs [2]. More formally, we can say that in the JSSP, we have a set of n jobs $\{J_j\}_{1 \leq j \leq n}$, that have to be processed by a set of m machines $\{M_i\}_{1 \leq r \leq m}$. Each job has a sequence that depends on the existing precedence constraints. The processing of a job J_j in a machine M_r is called operation $O_j r$. The operation $O_j r$ requires the exclusive use of M_r for an uninterrupted period of time $p_j r$ (this is the processing time). A schedule is then a set of duration times for each operation $\{c_j r\}_{1 \leq j \leq n, 1 \leq r \leq m}$ that satisfies the previously indicated conditions. The total duration time required to complete all the jobs (makespan) will be called L. The goal is then to minimize L.

Garey and Johnson [19] showed that the JSSP is an **NP-hard** problem and within its class it is one of the least tractable problems [1]. To exemplify this statement is sufficient to mention that a 10×10 problem proposed in [21] remained without solution for over 20 years. Several enumerative algorithms based on *Branch & Bound* have been applied to JSSP. However, due to the high computation cost of these enumerative algorithms, some approximation approaches have also been developed. The most popular practical algorithm to date is the one based on *priority rules* and *active schedule generation* [17]. However, other algorithms, such as an approach called *shifting bottleneck* (SB) have been found to be very effective in practice [3]. Furthermore, a number of heuristics have also been used in the JSSP (e.g., genetic algorithms, tabu search, simulated annealing, etc.).

The only other attempt to solve the JSSP using an artificial immune system that we have found in the literature is the proposal of [14, 15]. In this case, the authors use an artificial immune system (adopting a traditional permutation representation) in which an antibody indirectly represents a schedule, and an antigen describes a set of expected arrival dates for each job in the shop. The schedules are considered to be dynamic in the sense that sudden changes in the environment require the generation of new schedules. The proposed approach compared favorably with respect to a genetic algorithm using problems taken from [20]. However, the authors do not provide enough information as to replicate their results (the problems and results obtained are not included in their papers).

3   Description of Our Approach

Our approach is based on two artificial immune system mechanisms:

1. The way in which the molecules called antibodies are created. An antibody is encoded in multiple gene segments distributed along a chromosome of the genome. These segments must be placed together to make one antibody. In order to make such a molecule (i.e., an antibody), the gene segments are concatenated (see Figure 1). Note that other authors have used this sort of encoding of the antibodies in their corresponding computational models (e.g., [16, 24, 25]).
2. The clonal selection principle.

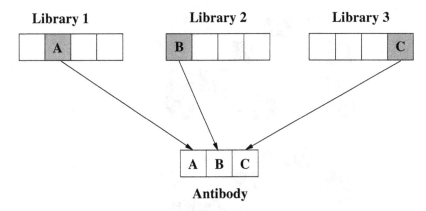

Fig. 1. Building antibody molecules from gene libraries (taken from [11]).

Table 1. A problem of size 6 × 4.

job	machine (time)
1	1(2) 2(2) 3(2) 4(2)
2	4(2) 3(2) 2(2) 1(2)
3	2(2) 1(2) 4(2) 3(2)
4	3(2) 4(2) 1(2) 2(2)
5	1(2) 2(2) 3(4) 4(1)
6	4(3) 2(3) 1(1) 3(1)

The approach proposed in this paper is a variation of CLONALG, which is an artificial immune system based on the clonal selection principle that has been used for optimization [23]. CLONALG uses two populations: one of antigens and another one of antibodies. When used for optimization, the main idea of CLONALG is to reproduce individuals with a high affinity, then apply mutation (or blind variation) and select the improved maturated progenies produced. Note that "affinity" in this case, is defined in terms of better objective function values rather than in terms of genotypic similarities (as, for example, in pattern recognition tasks), and the number of clones is the same for each antibody. This implies that CLONALG does not really use antigens when solving optimization problems, but, instead, the closeness of each antibody to the global optimum (measured in relative terms with respect to the set of solutions produced so far) defines the rate of hypermutation to be used. It is also worth noting that CLONALG does not use libraries to build antibodies as in our approach.

In order to apply an artificial immune system (or any other heuristic for that sake) to the JSSP, it is necessary to use a special representation. In our case, each element of the library represents the sequence of jobs processed by each of the machines. An antibody is then a chain with the job sequence processed by each of the machines (of length $m \times j$). An antigen is represented in the same way as an antibody. The representation adopted in this work is the so-called *permutations with repetitions* proposed in [27].

To illustrate this representation, we will consider the 6 × 4 problem (6 jobs and 4 machines) shown in Table 1.

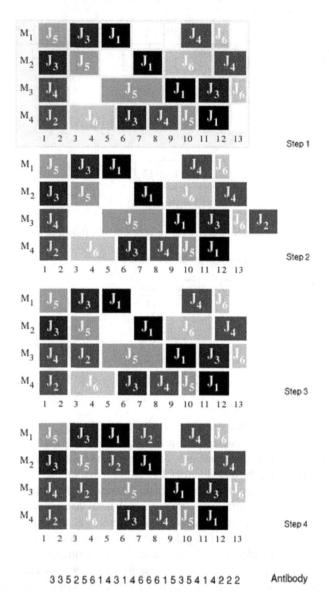

3 3 5 2 5 6 1 4 3 1 4 6 6 6 1 5 3 5 4 1 4 2 2 2   Antibody

Fig. 2. The graphical representation of a solution to the 6×4 problem shown in Table 1 using a Gantt diagram. The string at the bottom of the figure indicates the antibody that we are going to decode. See text for an explanation of the different steps included.

Input data include the information regarding the machine in which each job must be processed and the duration of this job in each machine. Gantt diagrams are a convenient tool to visualize the solutions obtained for a JSSP. An example of a Gantt diagram representing a solution to the 6×4 problem previously indicated is shown in Step 1 of Figure 2. Figure 2 also requires some further explanation:

- The string at the bottom of Figure 2 corresponds to the solution that we are going to decode.
- **Step 1:** This shows the decoding before reaching the second operation of job 2.
- **Step 2:** This shows the way in which job 2 would be placed if a normal decoding was adopted. Note that job 2 (J_2) is shown to the extreme right of machine 3 (M_3).
- **Step 3:** Our approach performs a local search to try to find gaps in the currrent schedule. Such gaps should comply with the precedence constraints imposed by the problem. In this case, the figure shows job 2 placed on one of these gaps for machine 3.
- **Step 4:** In this case, we apply the same local search procedure (i.e., finding available gaps) for the other machines. This step shows the optimum solution for this scheduling problem.

Our approach extends the algorithm (based on clonal selection theory) proposed in [22] using a local search mechanism that consists of placing jobs in each of the machines using the available time slots. Obviously, this mechanism has to be careful of not violating the constraints of the problem.

Algorithm 1 Our AIS for job shop scheduling.

Require: Input file (in the format adopted in [5]).
    Input parameters: #antigens, #libraries, mutation rate, random seed (optional)
    p - number of iterations
    i - counter
    Generate (randomly) an antibody library.
    Generate (randomly) an antigen (i.e., a sequence of jobs) and encode it.
    repeat
        Generate an antibody using components from the library.
        Decode the antibody and apply local search to improve it.
        if the antibody is better than the antigen **then**
            Make the antigen the same as the antibody
        end if
        Generate N clones of the antibody
        Mutate each of the clones generated
        Select the best segments produced to update the library
    until $i > p$
    Report the best solution found

Our approach is described in Algorithm 1. First, we randomly generate an antibody library. Such a library is really a set of strings that encode different job sequences for each machine. Then, we generate (also randomly) an antigen, which is a possible solution (i.e., a jobs sequence) to the problem. After that, we generate a single antibody by combining different segments taken from the library. The antibody is decoded and a local search algorithm is used to try to improve it by eliminating the larger gaps between jobs. At this point, the solution encoded by the antibody is compared to the solution encoded by the antigen. If the antibody encodes a better solution, then it replaces the antigen. So, the antigen will be keeping the best solution found along the process. In the following step, we generate N clones of the antibody (N is a parameter defined by the user) and we mutate each of them. From these mutated solutions, we select the best segments produced (i.e., the best jobs sequence for each machine) and we use them to update the library. Comparisons at this point are again made with respect to the antigen, but instead of comparing the entire solution, we only compare job sequences for each machine. Note that we do not select based on the complete solution which minimizes total makespan (such a solution is always located in the antigen), but we look for the best partial solutions to the problem to try to recombine them when building a new antibody. In order to define N (number of clones), we used an incremental approach: we started with 100,000 evaluations and we increased this value only if we considered that the results obtained were not too good. In the number of evaluations reported below for our algorithm, we do not include the cost of fine-tuning the parameter N.

Note that no affinity measure is used. This is mainly due to the representation adopted which allows repetitions. This makes it difficult to define a measure of similary between two sequences of jobs and therefore our choice of not adopting an affinity measure. Thus, we use instead the values of the objective function (minimize makespan) as the affinity measure in order to determine what solutions should be adopted to produce new ones.

4   Comparison of Results

We compared our AIS with respect to the GRASP approach proposed in [6]. We chose this reference for two main reasons: (1) it provides enough information (e.g., numerical results) as to allow a comparison, (2) GRASP is an enumerative approach which has traditionally been found to be very powerful in combinatorial optimization problems such as the job shop scheduling problem studied in this paper [13].

Table 2 shows a comparison of results between our AIS and GRASP, using several test problems taken from the OR-Library [5]. We chose a set of problems that we found to be difficult both for GRASP and for our approach. Note however that better results than those presented here are available in the literature (see for example [12, 27]). However, we decided to compare our approach with respect to [6], because in this reference, we found a more exhaustive table of results (i.e., a larger set of problems was studied by the authors).

All our tests were performed on a PC with an AMD Duron processor running at 1 GHz with 128 MB of RAM and using Red Hat Linux 7.3. Our approach was implemented in C++ and was compiled using the GNU g++ compiler.

The parameters of our approach are the following:

- **Number of libraries:** We adopted between 4 and 8. Note that each library is of the same length as the antibodies and the antigens.
- **Number of antigens:** We used only one antigen in the experiments reported in this paper. However, we experimented with different values (up to 8) and no significant differences were detected in the performance of our approach.
- **Mutation rate:** This value is a function of the antibodies length and it is defined such that 3 mutations take place for each string (i.e., antibody). We used exchange mutation. Thus, we perform a $flip(P_m)$ (the function $flip(P)$ returns true P percent of the times that it is invoked) for each position along the string (P_m is the mutation rate) and if the result is true, then we exchange the current value with another one (randomly chosen) from the same string.

– **Number of clones:** We adopted values between 100 and 1000 depending on the complexity of the problem (these values were empirically found for each problem).

Results are summarized in Table 2. We report the following information:

– **problem:** Name of the problem (as given in the OR-Library [5]).
– **size:** Size of the problem in the format: $m \times j$ (m = number of machines, j = number of jobs).
– **BKS:** Best known solution for each problem.
– **AIS:** Best solution obtained by our AIS (we performed 20 runs per problem).
– **GRASP:** Best solution obtained using GRASP, as reported in [6]. Note that in [6] no statistical values are available for GRASP.
– **AIS err(%):** Percentage of error (with respect to the best known solution) of our approach.
– **mean AIS:** Mean result of ALL the solutions produced by our approach on the 20 runs performed per problem.
– **sd AIS:** Standard deviation of ALL the solutions produced by our approach on the 20 runs performed per problem.
– **evaluations AIS:** Number of evaluations performed by our approach (expressed in millions).
– **iterations GRASP:** Number of iterations performed by GRASP, as reported in [6]. Note, however, that at each iteration, GRASP builds a valid solution, performs local search and updates the best current solution. This implies multiple evaluations for each iteration. In contrast, what we report for our approach is the total number of evaluations (rather than iterations) performed.

4.1 Discussion of Results

The first important aspect to discuss is the computational cost of the two approaches compared. In Table 2, we can clearly see that in all cases, our AIS performed less evaluations than GRASP. We attribute this lower computational cost of our AIS to the representation adopted, because the *permutations with repetitions* always generate feasible solutions, whereas GRASP uses an encoding based on graphs. In some cases, the differences in computational cost are remarkable. For example (keep in mind that an iteration of GRASP requires more than one evaluation as defined in our AIS):

– In problem **la03** (10×5), our AIS reaches the best known solution 75% of the time performing 5,000,000 evaluations of the objective function. In contrast, GRASP performs 50,000,000 iterations (ten times more than our AIS).
– In problem **la29** (20×10), the best known solution has a makespan of 1195. In this case, our AIS finds a solution with a makespan of 1248 performing 6.4 millions of evaluations, whereas GRASP finds a solution with a makespan of 1293 after performing 10.1 millions of iterations.
– In problem **abz7** (15×10), our AIS finds a better solution than GRASP (707 vs. 723) performing 6.4 millions of evaluations. GRASP required in this case 20.1 millions of iterations.

In general terms, we can see that our AIS was able to find the best known solution in 38.7% of the problems, whereas GRASP was able to converge to the best known solution

Table 2. Comparison of Results between AIS and GRASP. Note that in all problems we are minimizing makespan. AIS = Artificial Immune System, GRASP = Greedy Randomized Adaptive Search Procedure. The number of evaluations of our AIS and the number of iterations of GRASP are expressed in millions.

problem	size	BKS	AIS	GRASP	AIS err(%)	GRASP err(%)	mean AIS	sd AIS	evaluations AIS	iterations GRASP
abz5	10 × 10	1234	1238	1238	0.3	0.3	1469.7	86.0	5.0	20.1
abz7	15 × 20	667	707	723	6.0	8.4	839.3	33.3	6.4	20.1
abz8	15 × 20	670	743	729	10.9	8.8	858.5	31.1	5.0	20.1
abz9	15 × 20	691	750	758	8.5	9.7	883.5	30.82	5.0	20.1
ft10	10 × 10	930	941	938	1.2	0.9	1141.4	80.6	20.0	90.1
la01	10 × 5	666	666	666	0.0	0.0	775.6	57.3	0.01	0.1
la02	10 × 5	655	655	655	0.0	0.0	775.1	58.0	0.01	0.1
la03	10 × 5	597	597	604	0.0	1.2	700.1	50.0	10.0	50.1
la04	10 × 5	590	590	590	0.0	0.0	705.9	62.2	0.01	0.1
la05	10 × 5	593	593	593	0.0	0.0	616.5	30.7	0.01	0.1
la06	15 × 5	926	926	926	0.0	0.0	961.3	35.1	0.01	0.1
la07	15 × 5	890	890	890	0.0	0.0	961.1	44.2	0.01	0.1
la08	15 × 5	863	863	863	0.0	0.0	964.9	49.5	0.01	0.1
la09	15 × 5	951	951	951	0.0	0.0	1018.7	43.7	0.01	0.1
la10	15 × 5	958	958	958	0.0	0.0	981.9	34.3	2.0	50.1
la16	10 × 10	945	945	946	0.0	0.1	1100.2	67.5	2.0	20.1
la17	10 × 10	784	785	784	0.1	0.0	911.8	60.0	2.0	20.1
la18	10 × 10	848	848	848	0.0	0.0	1013.3	68.9	2.0	10.1
la19	10 × 10	842	848	842	0.7	0.0	1030.8	64.6	10.0	50.1
la20	10 × 10	902	907	907	0.6	0.6	1072.1	63.3	5.0	10.1
la25	15 × 10	902	1022	1028	4.6	5.2	1234.9	71.5	5.0	10.1
la28	20 × 10	1216	1277	1293	5.0	6.3	1554.7	66.6	5.0	10.1
la29	20 × 10	1195	1248	1293	4.4	8.2	1463.0	55.0	6.4	10.1
la35	30 × 10	1888	1903	1888	0.8	0.0	2179.4	72.6	5.0	10.1
la36	15 × 15	1268	1323	1334	4.3	5.2	1560.5	71.22	6.4	11.2
la38	15 × 15	1217	1274	1267	4.7	4.1	1548.4	61.6	6.4	11.2
la39	15 × 15	1233	1270	1290	3.0	4.6	1548.3	73.4	6.4	11.2
la40	15 × 15	1222	1258	1259	2.9	3.0	1537.4	69.3	6.4	11.2
orb02	10 × 10	888	894	889	0.7	0.1	1069.5	72.75	5.0	40.1
orb03	10 × 10	1005	1042	1021	3.7	1.6	1275.5	91.6	5.0	40.1
orb04	10 × 10	1005	1028	1031	2.3	2.6	1220.82	80.1	5.0	40.1

only in 35.4% of the problems. It is also interesting to note that both approaches have a similar performance for problems in which 5 machines are used regardless of the number of jobs. However, for larger problems, AIS finds better solutions than GRASP with a lower number of evaluations. Despite the noticeable differences in computational costs of the two algorithms, their percentages of error are very similar. AIS has an average percentage of error of 2.2%, whereas GRASP presents a 2.3%.

All of the previous led us to conclude that our approach is a viable alternative for solving job shop scheduling problems. Our results are not only competitive in terms of the makespan, but were obtained at a fraction of the computational cost required by GRASP.

5   Conclusions and Future Work

We have introduced a new approach based on an artificial immune system to solve job shop scheduling problems. The approach uses concepts from clonal selection theory (extending ideas from CLONALG [23]), and adopts a permutation representation that allows repetitions. The approach also incorporates a library of antibodies that is used to build new solutions to the problem. The comparison of results indicated that the proposed approach is highly competitive with respect to GRASP, even improving on its results some times.

As part of our future work, we plan to improve our procedure to initialize the antibody library by using an additional heuristic (e.g., a genetic algorithm). We also intend to add a mechanism that avoids the generation of duplicates (something that we do not have in the current version of our algorithm). It is also desirable to find a set of parameters that can be fixed for a larger family of problems as to eliminate the empirical fine-tuning that we currently perform. Additionally, we plan to define an affinity measure that can work with our encoding.

Finally, we also plan to work on a multiobjective version of job shop scheduling in which 3 objectives would be considered [1]: 1) makespan, 2) mean flowtime and 3) mean tardiness. This would allow us to generate trade-offs that the user could evaluate in order to decide what solution to choose.

Acknowledgments

The first author acknowledges support from NSF-CONACyT project No. 32999-A. The third author acknowledges support from CONACyT through a scholarship to pursue graduate studies at the Computer Science Section of the Electrical Engineering Department at CINVESTAV-IPN.

References

1. Tapan P. Bagchi. *MultiObjective Scheduling by Genetic Algorithms.* Kluwer Academic Publishers, New York, September 1999. ISBN 0-7923-8561-6.
2. Kenneth R. Baker. *Introduction to Sequencing and Scheduling.* John Wiley & Sons, New York, 1974.
3. J. Adams E. Balas and D. Zawack. The shifting bottleneck procedure for job shop scheduling. *Management science*, 34(3):391-401, 1988.
4. J.W. Barnes and J.B. Chambers. Solving the Job Shop Scheduling Problem using Tabu Search. *IIE Transactions*, 27(2):257–263, 1995.
5. J. E. Beasley. OR-Library: Distributing Test Problems by Electronic Mail. *Journal of the Operations Research Society*, 41(11):1069–1072, 1990.
6. S. Binato, W.J. Hery, D.M. Loewenstern, and M.G.C. Resende. A GRASP for Job Shop Scheduling. In Celso C. Ribeiro and Pierre Hansen, editors, *Essays and Surveys in Meta-heuristics*, pages 59–80. Kluwer Academic Publishers, Boston, 2001.
7. Olivier Catoni. Solving Scheduling Problems by Simulated Annealing. *SIAM Journal on Control and Optimization*, 36(5):1539–1575, September 1998.
8. R. Cheng, M. Gen, and Y. Tsujimura. A tutorial survey of job-shop scheduling problems using genetic algorithms: I. Representation. *Computers and Industrial Engineering*, 30:983–997, 1996.

9. R. Cheng, M. Gen, and Y. Tsujimura. A tutorial survey of job-shop scheduling problems using genetic algorithms: II. Hybrid genetic search strategies. *Computers and Industrial Engineering*, 36(2):343–364, 1999.

10. Xunxue Cui, Miao Li, and Tingjian Fang. Study of Population Diversity of Multiobjective Evolutionary Algorithm Based on Immune and Entropy Principles. In *Proceedings of the Congress on Evolutionary Computation 2001 (CEC'2001)*, volume 2, pages 1316–1321, Piscataway, New Jersey, May 2001. IEEE Service Center.

11. Leandro Nunes de Castro and Jon Timmis. *An Introduction to Artificial Immune Systems: A New Computational Intelligence Paradigm*. Springer-Verlag, 2002.

12. U. Dorndorf and E. Pesch. Evolution based learning in a job shop scheduling environment. *Computers & Operations Research*, 22:25–40, 1995.

13. T.A. Feo and M.G.C. Resende. Greedy Randomized Adaptive Search Procedures. *Journal of Global Optimization*, 6:109–133, 1995.

14. Emma Hart and Peter Ross. The Evolution and Analysis of a Potential Antibody Library for Use in Job-Shop Scheduling. In David Corne, Marco Dorigo, and Fred Glover, editors, *New Ideas in Optimization*, pages 185–202. McGraw-Hill, London, 1999.

15. Emma Hart, Peter Ross, and J. Nelson. Producing robust schedules via an artificial immune system. In *Proceedings of the 1998 IEEE International Conference on Evolutionary Computation (ICEC'98)*, pages 464–469, Anchorage, Alaska, 1998. IEEE Press.

16. R. Hightower, S. Forrest, and A. S. Perelson. The evolution of emergent organization in immune system gene libraries. In L. J. Eshelman, editor, *Proceedings of the 6th. International Conference on Genetic Algorithms*, pages 344–350. Morgan Kaufmann, 1995.

17. Albert Jones and Luis C. Rabelo. Survey of Job Shop Scheduling Techniques. NISTIR, National Institute of Standards and Technology, 1998.

18. E.G. Coffman Jr. *Computer and Job Shop Scheduling Theory*. John Wiley and Sons, 1976.

19. David S. Johnson Michael R. Garey. *Computers and Intractability: A Guide to the Theory of NP-Completeness (Series of Books in the Mathematical Sciences)*. W H Freeman & Co., June 1979. ISBN 0-7167-1045-5.

20. Thomas E. Morton and David W. Pentico. *Heuristic Scheduling Systems: With Applications to Production Systems and Project Management*. Wiley Series in Engineering & Technology Management. John Wiley & Sons, 1993.

21. J. F. Muth and G. L. Thompson, editors. *Industrial Scheduling*. Prentice Hall, Englewood Cliffs, New Jersey, 1963.

22. Leandro Nunes de Castro and Jonathan Timmis. *Artificial Immnue System: A New Computational Intelligence Approach*. Springer Verlang, Great Britain, September 2002. ISBN 1-8523-594-7.

23. Leandro Nunes de Castro and Fernando José Von Zuben. Learning and Optimization Using the Clonal Selection Principle. *IEEE Transactions on Evolutionary Computation*, 6(3):239–251, 2002.

24. Mihaela Oprea. *Antibody Repertories and Pathogen Recognition: The Role of Germline Diversity and Somatic Hypermutation*. PhD thesis, University of New Mexico, Albuquerque,NM, 1999.

25. A. Perelson, R. Hightower, and S. Forrest. Evolution and Somatic Learning in V-Region Genes. *Research in Immunology*, 147:202–208, 1996.

26. M. Pinedo. *Scheduling—Theory, Algorithms, and Systems*. Prentice Hall, Englewood Cliffs, 1995.

27. Takeshi Yamada and Ryohei Nakano. Job-shop scheduling. In A.M.S. Zalzala and P.J. Fleming, editors, *Genetic Algorithms in Engineering Systems*, IEE control engineering series, chapter 7, pages 134–160. The Institution of Electrical Engineers, 1997.

An Artificial Immune System
for Multimodality Image Alignment

Esma Bendiab, Souham Meshoul, and Mohamed Batouche

Computer Vision Group, LIRE Laboratory
Computer Science Department, Mentouri University
25000 Constantine, Algeria
Bendiab_e@yahoo.fr, {meshoul,batouche}@wissal.dz

Abstract. Alignment of multimodality images is the process that attempts to find the geometric transformation overlapping at best the common part of two images. The process requires the definition of a similarity measure and a search strategy. In the literature, several studies have shown the ability and effectiveness of entropy-based similarity measures to compare multimodality images. However, the employed search strategies are based on some optimization schemes which require a good initial guess. A combinatorial optimization method is critically needed to develop an effective search strategy. Artificial Immune Systems (AIS_s) have been proposed as a powerful addition to the canon of meta-heuristics. In this paper, we describe a framework which combines the use of an entropy-based measure with an AIS-based search strategy. We show how AIS_s have been tailored to explore efficiently the space of transformations. Experimental results are very encouraging and show the feasibility and effectiveness of the proposed approach.

1 Introduction

For many computer vision applications such as pattern recognition, 3D reconstruction and image data fusion, image alignment is an essential platform. Basically, image alignment or registration is the process that aims to find the geometric transformation that allows the best superposition of the common part of two images. A great deal of effort has been devoted to develop image registration methods. Good and comprehensive surveys have been proposed in the literature [1-3]. These methods fall into two broad categories: feature-based methods and intensity-based methods. For the first ones, homologous features are extracted from the images to be aligned and put into one to one correspondence. The geometric transformation parameters are then estimated from the obtained correspondences [4]. For the second ones, no feature extraction task is needed. They require the definition of a similarity measure and a search strategy. The similarity measure, as suggested by its name, is used to have a quantitative evaluation of how much two images or their parts are similar. The search strategy acts to describe how the search space i.e. the space of allowable transformations, is explored to find the best alignment. When the two images to be aligned are provided by two different imagery systems they contain different but complementary information. As a consequence, their fusion is a useful tool to get an evolved description of the scene under consideration. As the images are highly dissimilar, it is very hard to detect homologous features in both of them. That is why it is very hard to apply a

J. Timmis et al. (Eds.): ICARIS 2003, LNCS 2787, pp. 11–21, 2003.

feature-based method to align them. Intensity-based methods are more suitable in this case. Entropy-based measures like mutual information [5-8] have been shown in several studies to be the most appropriate and effective similarity measures to compare multimodality images. However the employed search strategies rely on some optimization schemes like hill climbing and gradient descent to avoid being trapped by local minima. The exploration of the search space is labor intensive and can be viewed as a combinatorial optimization task. As a consequence, a combinatorial optimization method is critically needed when developing a search strategy for multimodality alignment. Recently, there has been a boost of interest in applying naturally inspired optimization methods.

During the last decade and independently to computer vision, a new emerging area called artificial life is born. Artificial life is devoted to new field that researchers exploit to solve real world problems, using ideas gleaned from natural mechanisms. An artificial life approach to the image processing offers a chance to discover techniques perhaps more novels, more efficient or just unusual [9]. Neural networks, genetic algorithms, ant colonies and recently immune systems are paradigms from this area. Artificial immune systems have aroused great interest among researchers. This is motivated by the fact that natural mechanisms such as: recognition, identification and post processing by which the human body attains it immunity, suggest new ideas for patter recognition, learning, communication, adaptation, self organization, and distributed control [10]. Artificial immune systems have significantly contributed in the artificial intelligence field. Their applications range from network security, data mining, robotics, image classification to optimization.

In this paper, we suggest the use of an artificial immune system for solving the multi modality images alignment problem. In [11] authors have described a solution based on a genetic algorithm. Promising results were obtained however some limitations have been encountered especially those related to the algorithm convergence, the diversification and the exploration of the search process. Furthermore, recent work described the artificial immune systems as an approach that can overcome these restrictions [12]. This explains our motivation in using this new paradigm. We propose an intensity-based approach for multi modality image registration based on the maximization of the mutual information, as a similarity measure and an artificial immune system, with a real valued representation, as a search strategy.

The remainder of the paper is organized as follows: In Section 2, we formulate the problem to be solved. In section 3, we present a brief introduction to the natural immune system and an overview of artificial immune systems and related work. Section 4, is devoted to the description of the proposed approach. Experimental results and a comparison with an approach based on genetic algorithm are presented in section 5. Finally, conclusion and further work are drawn.

2 Problem Formulation

The addressed problem can be formulated as follow. Let two images I_1 and I_2 acquired from two different imagery systems, where I_1 is the sensed image and I_2 is the reference one. We have to find a geometric transformation T that correctly aligns the two images. T is a non-linear transformation defined by a set of parameters (a_0, a_1, a_2, a_3, b_0, b_1, b_2, b_3) such as:

$$x' = a_0 + a_1 x + a_2 y + a_3 xy$$
$$y' = b_0 + b_1 x + b_2 y + b_3 xy$$

Where (x', y') are coordinates of a point in I_1, and (x, y) are the coordinates of its corresponding point in I_2. We seek for parameters values in R^8 space that provide a best superposition of the two images. For this purpose, we need a measure that quantitatively evaluates the relationship between the two images when they are superimposed, and a search strategy.

- **Similarity Measure:**

Most of the existing similarity measures are based on the hypothesis of similarity between intensity values up to an unknown geometrical transformation. This assumption is very restrictive and makes methods inefficient in practice especially in multimodality alignment. The reason is that the acquired images are similar in structures but present very different characteristics. So, instead of expressing the sensed image as a function of the reference image, the idea is to predict the sensed image from the reference image. In information theory, predictability is closely related to an old concept introduced by Shannon, known as *Entropy*.

Formally, entropy summarizes the randomness of a certain random variable. Given a certain random variable represented by a probability distribution X i.e. a set of couples (x_i, p_i) where x_i is a value and $p_i = p(X=x_i)$ is the probability of occurrence of value x_i. Entropy of X denoted by $H(X)$ is defined as an expectation:

$$H(X) = - E_x [log(X)] = -\Sigma p_i \, log \, p_i$$

Entropy is defined in terms of the logarithm base 2. Intuitively, entropy measures the average information provided by a certain distribution. When dealing with two random variables represented by two probability distributions X and Y, we are interested by answering the question: how likely the two distributions are functionally dependent?. In total dependence case, a measurement of one distribution completely determines the other and hence removes any randomness about it, whereas knowledge of one does not help at all predict the other in total independence case. As a consequence, quantifying dependence is equivalent to quantifying randomness. So, entropy measure is a tool that allows evaluating the extent to which two distributions are dependent.

The joint distribution denoted by $P(X, Y)$ is a mathematical structure that relates the co-occurrence of events from distribution X and Y. It offers a complete description of a random behavior of X and Y. This can be evaluated by the joint entropy, given by:

$$H(X, Y) = - \Sigma \Sigma p(x,y) \, log \, p(x,y)$$

The mutual information MI is a measure of the reduction on the entropy of Y given X. It is defined as the difference between the sum of marginal entropies and the joint entropy:

$$MI(X, Y) = H(X) + H(Y) - H(X, Y)$$

The mutual information is equal to zero when X and Y are independent and it is maximized when they are totally dependent.

- **The Search Strategy**

According to mutual information definition, maximizing this measure seems to be a promising alternative to find good alignment of multimodality images. Therefore, we have to define an efficient search strategy in order to find the transformation T* by exploring the search space $\Im$ such that:

$$T^* = \text{argmax } (MI\ (I_2, T\ (I_1)))$$

$$T \in \Im$$

The search space $\Im$ in the case of our study is the set of non-linear transformations. For this purpose, we suggest a population-based optimization approach that exploits the evolutionary characteristics of artificial immune systems.

3   From Natural Immune System to Artificial Immune System

3.1   Natural Immune System

The immune system is the name of a collection of molecules, cells, and organs whose complex interaction forms an efficient system that is usually able to identify and protect an individual from both exogenous agents, called antigens and its own altered internal cells, which lead to disease.

The basic building blocks of the immune system are white cells or lymphocytes. A lymphocyte has about 10^5 receptors. In particular, B cells, special lymphocytes, have the responsibility of secreting receptors called antibodies. A special part of the antibody, called paratope, is used to identify other molecule. In other side, antigens have also receptors called epitope. Binding between a paratope   and an epitope is based on their complementary shapes that suppose the generation of an opposite structure that adjusts at best the antigenic receptor. The strength of this bind is termed affinity.

When a B cell recognizes an antigen i.e. its antibodies are strongly matched to the antigen, it clones itself producing identical copies. This B cells selection based on their antigenic affinity is called the clonal selection principle. The number of clones produced by a lymphocyte is proportional to its stimulation level. After the B cells proliferation, clones are not perfect. By allowing mutation the match could become better. So clones are subjected to somatic mutation called hypermutation, inversely proportional to their affinity. Therefore, the clones' affinity becomes better mature, leading to affinity maturation. Cells with low affinity or self-reactive receptors are subject to a process named negative selection, where they destroy their affinity by developing new receptors or by direct cells elimination. As a result of clonal expansion, an immune memory is built; some of the cloned cells differentiate into memory cells and the rest of clones become plasma cells. Thus, B cells remember the shape of the antigen during a probable intrusion. Theoretical insights of these concepts can be found in [13, 14].

3.2   Artificial Immune System

Artificial immune systems are adaptive systems inspired by the biologic immune system for solving different problems. Dasgupta [10] define them as a composition of intelligent methodologies, inspired by the natural immune system for the resolution of real world problems. In the AIS, a problem with unknown solution is treated as an antigen while problem solutions are modeled by antibodies. There are many successful AIS implementations [15-18]. Typically, antibody-antigen interactions coupled with the somatic mutation are the basis of a lot of AIS applications. Various models and algorithms have been suggested : negative selection algorithm for networks security [17] and the anomalies detection [19] immune network dynamics and the negative selection for image inspection and segmentation [15,20], the clonal selection theory and its applications in the pattern recognition [20], the machine learning [20,21] and the optimization [21-25].

Particularly, optimization problems have been the subject of lot of investigations. Hajela and Yoo [18] have proposed an approach based AIS devoted to solving optimization problems that improves the classical genetic algorithm. They argued their approach by the fact that capabilities of an immune system for accomplishing recognition and adaptation schemes can be used for improving both optimization problems and convergence in classical genetic algorithms. That is ensured by mechanisms avoiding the premature convergence in GAs while maintaining diversity. Later on, other optimization approaches based on AIS$_s$ have been developed.

Based on the clonal selection theory, the affinity maturation and the negative selection, the Clonalg algorithm (CLONal selection ALGorithm) has been developed and implemented by De Castro and Von Zuben [21,22], not only for accomplishing machine learning and pattern recognition tasks but also for solving optimization problems.

The proposed algorithm can be viewed as a multi-agent approach using competition and cooperation mechanisms. Individual antibodies are in competition in order to solve (optimize) the problem and the whole of the population cooperate given the final solution. The proposed algorithm has been successfully applied to a variety of problems like testing the learning capabilities and memory acquisition by a binary characters recognition system, multi modal optimization tasks and instance of the TSP for combinatorial optimization. In the next section, we describe how Clonalg algorithm has been tailored to our problem.

4   Description of the Proposed Framework

The proposed approach has been developed by taking inspiration from Clonalg. It assumes the existence of an antibodies folder that can be stimulated. Moreover no distinction between cells and theirs receptors is made.

The main immune aspects taken into account are:

- Maintenance of the memory cells;
- Selection and cloning of the most stimulated cells;
- Death of non-stimulated cells;
- Affinity maturation and re-selection of the higher affinity clones;
- Generation and maintenance of diversity;
- And hypermutation proportional to the cell affinity.

To adapt Clonalg our problem, we first need to define an appropriate representation scheme.

4.1   AIS Elements Representations

The representation scheme can be described by the following definitions of the key elements arising in AIS.

1. Antigen: It represents the problem to solve. In our context, it is the transformation T* which aligns at best the transformed sensed image and the reference one by maximizing their mutual information:

$$T^* = argmax \, (MI \, (I_2, \, T \, (I_1)))$$
$$T \in \mathcal{S}$$

2. Antibody: As a non-linear transformation T is a potential solution to the problem, an antibody can be viewed as a possible parameter combination (a_0, a_1, a_2, a_3, b_0, b_1, b_2, b_3). A population of antibodies is therefore a set of non-linear transformations. A real valued representation of genes is used to encode the transformation parameters. For the need of the mutation of real values, we associate to each vector another vector (a_{0s}, a_{1s}, a_{2s}, a_{3s}, b_{0s}, b_{1s}, b_{2s}, b_{3s}) representing the values of the standard deviation for each parameter (see figure 1).

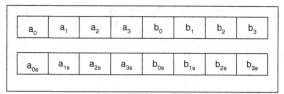

Fig. 1. Representation of a candidate solution: transformation.

3. Clone: solution's offspring. One clone has the same structure as a solution. It is also represented by a couple of real valued vectors.

4. Antigen-antibody affinity: According to the problem analysis, it seems obvious that the fitness function value of an antibody is closely related to mutual information value computed for the corresponding transformation. To compute mutual information value for a certain antibody (transformation) T relating the sensed image I_1 and the reference image I_2, we determine the joint distribution between I_2 and $T(I_1)$ by the computation of their joint histogram obtained by recording the occurrences of every pair of pixel values within I_2 and $T(I_1)$. From the joint histogram, we can deduce the marginal histograms X and Y corresponding to $T(I_1)$ and I_2 using formulas :

$$P(X)= \Sigma P(X,Y=y_i) \quad and \quad P(Y)= \Sigma P(Y, X=x_i)$$

From the joint and marginal histograms, we derive directly the entropies and the mutual information.

4.2   The Proposed Algorithm

The proposed algorithm proceeds as follows:

Step 1: Generation of a set (Ab) of candidate solutions, composed of the subset of memory cells (M) added to the remaining (Abr) population (Ab = Abr + M); It is the set of the potential transformations.

Step 2: Select the n best solutions of the population, based on the affinity measure MI.

Step 3: Clone (reproduce) these n best solutions of the population, giving rise to a temporary population of clones (C). The clone size is an increasing function of the mutual information;

$$N_c = \sum_{i=1}^{n} round\left(\frac{\beta * N}{i}\right)$$

Where N_c is the total amount of clones generated for the antigen, β is a multiplying factor and N is the total amount of antibodies. Each term of this sum corresponds to the size of each selected antibody.

Step 4: Submit the population of clones C to an hypermutation scheme, where the hypermutation is conversely proportional to the mutual information of the antibody. A maturated antibody population is generated C^*. We have chosen a Gaussian mutation with a real valued mutation.

Mutation: The mutation is an operator which changes the genetic information by modifying genes of the two vectors. For each gene of the first vector, a random number r in [0, 1] is generated. If r is smaller than a predefined mutation probability the value of the gene in the first vector is modified using its corresponding gene in the second vector which is taken as the standard deviation of a centered normal distribution, given by the formula:

$$a_i^* = a_i + K.X, \quad X \sim \aleph(0, a_{is})$$

Where:
a_i^* is the mutated value of the selected gene a_i, K is a weight factor used to improve convergence and X is a random variable. An acceptable convergence occurs for $Kmax = 60$.

The associated gene in the second vector is also modified according to a random variable normally distributed according to:

$$a_{is}^* = a_{is}.e^{X}, \quad X \sim \aleph(0, 0.5)$$

where:
a_{is}^* is the mutated value of the correspondent gene a_{is} in the standard deviation vector.

The mutation rate, α, is such that:

$$\alpha = \ell^{-\rho f}$$

Where:
ρ is a factor controlling the decay and F is antigenic affinity (the mutual information value). ρ and F are normalized to the range [0..1].

Step 5: Re-select the improved individuals from C^* to compose the memory set. Some members of the Ab set can be replaced by other improved members of C^*;

Step 6: Finally, replace d low affinity antibodies of the population, maintaining its diversity.

The proposed algorithm is an iterative process. Starting with an initial population of potential solutions, the process is repeated numerous times until a maximum number of iterations is reached.

5 Experimental Results

To evaluate the performance of the proposed algorithm, different pairs of images have been used. In figure 2, we show two examples of medical image pairs. These images are acquired from Magnetic Resonance Imagery system and Computed Tomography system. Results are illustrated in table 1.

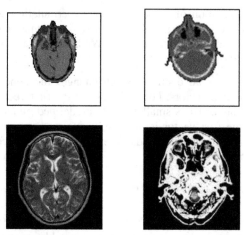

Fig. 2. Examples of image pairs.

Table 1. Results of the application of the proposed algorithm to both pairs of images.

Initial state.	Final state
Pair 1 : Marginal Entropy of (a) = 4.746. Marginal Entropy of (b) = 3.852. Joint Entropy of (a)and (b)= 7.494. MI (Mutual Information)= 1.104.	MI (Mutual Information) = 2.529. The best transformation parameters obtained are: a_0 = 3.506 , a_1= 0.891, a_2= 0.125, a_3= 0.002, b_0= 9.812 , b_1 = −0.157, b_2= 1.062, b_3= 0.013
Pair 2 : Marginal Entropy of (a) = 5.681. Marginal Entropy of (b)= 4.107. Joint entropy of (a) and (b)= 8.808. MI (Mutual Information) = 0.980.	MI (Mutual Information) = 1.735. The best transformation parameters obtained are: a_0 =1.235, a_1=0.992, a_2=-0.125, a_3=0.000 , b_0=1.214 , b_1=0.125, b_2=0.982 , b_3=0.001,

Convergence of the algorithm has been studied by monitoring the affinity function that is the mutual information during the search process. For this purpose, we have compared the results with those obtained from a genetic based algorithm [11].

For the case of genetic algorithm, the tunable parameter settings are as follows. The population size is set to 100 individuals. Mutation ant crossover rates are respectively set to Pm=0.01 and Pc=0.8. For the case the proposed algorithm, the population size is also set to 100 individuals. The parameters d and β are set respectively to 20% and 2. The number of antibodies to clone is set to 50. Both algorithms have been executed 20 times. Average values through iterations have been gathered and the obtained results are illustrated in figure 3.

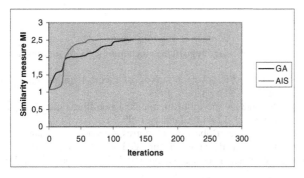

Fig. 3. Convergence of the proposed AIS algorithm and the classic GA-based algorithm.

The graph in figure 3 indicates that both strategies achieve the same quality solutions. Moreover, it is clear that the proposed algorithm reach different sets of local solutions which denotes a better-diversified search. This can be explained by the fact that the evolutionary searches of the two approaches proceed differently. Genetic algorithms tend to polarize the whole population of individuals towards the best solution whereas in the AIS-based algorithm, the mutation rate applied to an individual is a function of the individual affinity (MI value), contrary to a genetic algorithm that considers rates neglecting this affinity. In table 2, other statistics have been goatherd to get a closer insight into the performance of the algorithm.

Table 2. Results of the AIS based and classic GA based algorithms applied to pair1. Given are the best the best solution found (best MI), the average solution quality (Avg MI) and its percentage deviation from the optimum. Results are taken over 20 trials.

Algorithm	Best MI	Avg MI	Std
AIS	2,529	2,516	0.63 %
Classic GA	2.529	2.491	0.71 %

6 Conclusion

This paper described a search strategy that intends to achieve a good quality alignment for two multi modality images by maximizing their mutual information. The proposed strategy is a population-based approach for optimization based on an artificial immune system with a real valued representation.

The approach proposes an evolutionary search similar to a genetic-based approach but introduces new mechanisms like the somatic mutation and the clonal selection policy. Experiments on real images show not only the feasibility of the approach but also its ability to achieve good quality solutions. As ongoing work, it would be an interesting attempt to conduct an in-depth comparison with a more elaborate genetic algorithm using mutation rate control.

References

1. L.G. Brown, A survey of image registration techniques, ACM surveys, and 24(4): pp 325-376, December 1992.
2. J. B. A. Maintz, M. A. Viergever, A survey of medical image registration techniques, Medical Image Analysis, 2(1): pp 1-36, 1998.
3. H. Lester, S. R. Arridge, A survey of hierarchical non-linear medical image registration, Pattern Recognition, 32(1): 129-149, January 1999.
4. S. Meshoul, M. Batouche, Robust point correspondence for image registration using optimization with extremal dynamics, In proceedings of DAGM2002, L.Van Gool (Ed.) Lecture Notes in Computer Science2449, pp 330-337   Springer Verlag Berlin Hiedelberg 2002.
5. W. M. Wells, P. Viola, H. Asumi, S. Nakadjima, Multi-modal registration by maximization of mutual information, Medical Image Analysis, 1(1): 35-51, 1996.
6. F. Maes, A. Collignon, D. Vandermeulen, G. Marchal, P. Suetens, Multimodality Image Registration by Maximization of Mutual Information, IEEE Transactions on Medical Imaging, 16(2): 187-198, 1997.
7. Studholme, D.L.G.Hill, D.J.Hawkes, An overlap invariant entropy measure of 3D medical image alignement, Pattern Recognition 32(1999) 71-86.
8. C. Nikou, F. Heitz, J. P. Armspach, Robust voxel similarity metrics for the registration of dissimilar single and multimodal images, Pattern Recognition, 32(8): 1351-1368, 1999.
9. T. Carden. Image processing with artificial life. Artificial intelligence with mathematic 2001-2002.
10. D. Dasgupta, Artificial Immune Systems and Their Applications, Springer-Verlag. (Ed.) (1999).
11. S. Meshoul, M. Batouche, An evolutionary framework for multimodality image alignment, In proceedings of International Conference on Artificial Intelligence (ICAI'02). Las Vegas, Nevada, June 24-27, CSREA Press.
12. P. Hajela, J.S. Yoo, Immune Network Modelling in Design Optimization, Chapter in "New Ideas in Optimization" pp.203-215. McGraw-Hill, (ed) 1999.
13. L.N. De Castro, F.J. Von Zuben, Artificial immune systems: Part 1 – basic theory and applications, Technical Report 1. December 1999.
14. D. Dasgupta, N. Attoh Okine, Immunity-Based systems: A survey, In the proceeding of the IEEE International Conference on systems and cybernetics. October 1998.
15. L. N. De Castro, F. J. Von Zuben, Artificial immune systems: Part 2 – a survey of applications, Technical Report 2. February 2000.
16. L. N. De Castro, J. Timmis, Artificial Immune Systems: A New Computational Intelligence Approach, Springer-Verlag, London. (2002).
17. J. Hunt, J. Timmis, D. Cooke, M. Neal, C. King, Jisys: The development of an Artificial Immune System for real world applications, Applications of Artificial Immune Systems, D. Dasgupta Ed., pp.157-186, Springer—Verlag , 1999.
18. D. Dasgupta, Information Processing Mechanisms of the Immune System, A chapter in the book, New Ideas in Optimization. McGraw-Hill publication, 1999.
19. S. Srividhya, S. Ferat, AISIMAM – An Artificial Immune System Based Intelligent Multi Agent Model and its Application to a Mine Detection Problem, In proceeding of Icaris2002, first conference on artificial immune system.
20. L. N. De Castro, F. J. Von Zuben, An Evolutionary Immune Network for Data Clustering, Proc. of the IEEE Symposium on Neural Networks(2000), pp. 84-89.
21. L. N. De Castro, F.J. Von Zuben, Learning and Optimization Using the Clonal Selection Principle, IEEE transactions on Evolutionary Computation, Special Issue on Artificial Immune Systems, 2002.

22. L.N. De Castro, F.J. Von Zuben, The Clonal Selection Algorithm with Engineering Applications, In Workshop Proceedings of GECCO, pp. 36-37, Workshop on Artificial Immune Systems and Their Applications. Las Vegas. Nevada. USA, July 2000.
23. C.Xianbin, S.Zhang, X. Wang, Immune Optimization System Based on Immune Recognition, Hybrid Systems-Soft computing.2001.
24. C. Jang-sung, J. Hyun-Kyo, H. Song-Yop, A study on comparison of optimization Performances between immune algorithm and other   heuristic algorithms, IEEE transaction on magnetic Vol 34 n° 5 Sep 1998.pp 2972-2975.
25. A. Gaspar, P. Collard, Two Models of Immunization for time dependent Optimization, In the proceedings of IEEE International Conference on Systems, Man and Cybernetics (SMC), Nashville, October 8-11, 2000.

Bioinformatics Data Analysis
Using an Artificial Immune Network

George Barreto Bezerra and Leandro Nunes de Castro

State University of Campinas (Unicamp), CP. 6101, Campinas, SP, 13083-970, Brazil
Phone: +55 (19) 3788-3816 Fax: +55 (19) 3289-1395
{bezerra,lnunes}@dca.fee.unicamp.br

Abstract. This work describes a new proposal for gene expression data clustering based on a combination of an immune network, named aiNet, and the minimal spanning tree (MST). The aiNet is an AIS inspired by the immune network theory. Its main role is to perform data compression and to identify portions of the input space representative of a given data set. The output of aiNet is a set of antibodies that represent the data set in a simplified way. The MST is then built on this network, and clusters are determined by using a new method for detecting the inconsistent edges of the tree. An important advantage of this technique over the classical approaches, like hierarchical clustering, is that there is no need of previous knowledge about the number of clusters and their distributions. The hybrid algorithm was first applied to a benchmark data set to demonstrate its validity, and its results were compared with those produced by other approaches from the literature. Using the full yeast *S. cerevisiae* gene expression data set, it was possible to detect a strong interconnection of the genes, hindering the perception of inconsistencies that may lead to the separation of data into clusters.

1 Introduction and Motivation

Recent advances in biosciences, mainly in molecular biology and genomics, are leading to a revolution in the research in these areas. Due to the development of novel experimental techniques, biological data (like DNA and RNA sequencing, protein structural data and gene expression levels) are being produced at explosive rates. This results in an accumulation of huge quantities of information (data) lacking computational analysis. Moreover, all these data must be stored and made available efficiently in order to provide a wide accessibility to the scientific community. This new scenario has produced a necessity of specialists capable of treating the problems related to the management, storage and analysis of biological data, thus giving origin to a new field of science, called bioinformatics [1,13].

The problems in bioinformatics are generally characterized by very large sets of multivariate data, which present high levels of redundancy and noisy patterns. These properties make them extremely complex, and to perform data analysis by traditional computational tools becomes impracticable in most cases. As an alternative, bioinformatics researchers usually employ machine learning techniques, like neural networks [8] and evolutionary algorithms [14], to solve such problems. Machine learning techniques provide satisfactory performances in most cases because of their intrinsic features like robustness to noise and non-linear adaptiveness.

J. Timmis et al. (Eds.): ICARIS 2003, LNCS 2787, pp. 22–33, 2003.
© Springer-Verlag Berlin Heidelberg 2003

The high complexity and dimensionality of the problems in bioinformatics is an interesting challenge for testing and validating new computational intelligence techniques. Under this perspective, they also represent a great opportunity for exploring the capabilities of artificial immune systems (AIS), thus contributing to their development and consolidation as useful machine learning techniques. Besides, the application of AIS to bioinformatics may bring important contributions to the biological sciences, providing an alternative form of analyzing and interpreting the huge amount of data from molecular biology and genomics.

Gene expression data analysis is a recent problem in bioinformatics that is receiving increasingly more attention. The collection of gene expression data in large amounts has only become possible because of the development of a novel experimental technique, the DNA Microarrays [12,16], capable of measuring the expression levels of thousands of genes simultaneously. These data assume the form of very large matrices. The expression levels of a gene consist of indirect measures of the quantity of proteins it is producing, thus giving an indication of the biological state of a cell. Through the analysis of these data it is possible to determine the functional role of several genes, to study the way the expression levels reflect biological processes of interest (as in the case of diseases), to evaluate the effects of experimental treatments, and to design tools for diagnosis based on the regularity of expression patterns.

The microarray experiments usually produce very large quantities of gene expression data, thus making impracticable for the biologists to perform data inspection in a visual and intuitive manner. In order to perform knowledge extraction, a fundamental step in the analysis consists of identifying groups of genes that manifest similar expression profiles. This way, it is possible to explore the inherent structure of the data, thus discovering possible correlations among genes and revealing hidden patterns.

This problem is commonly known as gene expression data clustering, and it has already been treated by several different techniques. The commonly used approaches are hierarchical clustering [6], self-organizing maps (SOM) [9], principal component analysis (PCA) [18] and k-means clustering [10]. These techniques have been proving their practical usefulness when applied to gene expression data. However, their results depend on the regularity of the geometric shape of the clusters. Besides, most of them require previous knowledge about the number of clusters as an input parameter. The algorithm used in this paper is capable of identifying the clusters based on a local concept, using the minimal spanning tree [19]. The information is initially explored and compressed by aiNet [3,5], generating an antibody network that represents the data set in a simplified way. On the final architecture of the network, the MST is then applied, and the inconsistent edges of the tree are removed detecting the inherent clusters of aiNet, thus of the data set. The minimal spanning tree has already been used for gene expression data clustering [17], but it is important to stress that, in the present work, the MST is applied to the antibody network, and not directly to the raw data. Furthermore, the criterion to identify and remove inconsistent edges used here is completely different from the one used in [17].

There are several clustering techniques being applied to this problem, and their results may be quite different in some cases. However, there is no method commonly used for evaluating the quality of the clusters, and there is not a consensus among the specialists as to what is a good clustering. This is one of the reasons why so many techniques have been successfully employed to solve this problem. The final result of a clustering method must be analyzed and interpreted by a specialist in biosciences, who is interested, in most cases, in the similarity relationships among genes. Several co-regulated genes may exist under different conditions, thus it is up to the specialist to define which results are most relevant to the considered application. Under this perspective, it is sometimes more interesting to use clustering techniques that provide alternative points of view on the expression levels, for instance, different ordering of the genes. The most important contribution of this paper is to provide a new interpretation of the Yeast gene expression data. Furthermore, our intention is to propose a new and useful technique for clustering gene expression data, rather than to evaluate if the proposed hybrid algorithm has a superior performance when compared to other techniques presented in the literature.

2   The Hybrid Algorithm: aiNet and MST

The proposed algorithm has two main stages in the clustering process. The first one consists of applying the aiNet, an immune inspired algorithm introduced by de Castro and Von Zuben [3,5], to the whole gene expression data. In this first step, the raw data set is explored and compressed by the aiNet, generating an antibody network that extracts the most relevant information contained in the data for clustering tasks. In the second step of the analysis, the MST is built on the antibody network, and its *inconsistent edges* are then identified and removed, thus performing the network (data) separation into clusters. This section describes both parts of the algorithm and their overall importance in the whole clustering process.

2.1   aiNet (Artificial Immune NETwork)

The aiNet is an artificial immune system inspired by the immune network theory proposed by Niels Jerne in 1974 [11]. The main role of this algorithm is to perform a data compression by following some ideas from the immune network theory and the clonal selection principle [2]. This results in an antibody network that recognizes antigens (input data set) with certain (and adjustable) generality. By decreasing the data cardinality, aiNet reduces the problem complexity, filtering out outliers and using multiple prototypes for representing different clusters of data. AiNet also places the prototypes (network cells or antibodies) in regions of the input space relevant for the clustering of multivariate data in spaces of very high dimension, such as gene expression data.

The aiNet procedure can be divided in two main steps. The first one corresponds to the clonal selection principle and affinity maturation interactions, where the antibodies (Ab) suffer cloning and mutation in order to recognize the antigens (input patterns – Ag). This first stage of the aiNet adaptation procedure corresponds to the CLONALG (CLONal selection ALGorithm) algorithm, originally proposed by de Castro and Von Zuben [4]. The second step of aiNet includes the immune network interactions and introduction of diversity. It follows a basic principle of the network theory, which states that the immune cells are capable of recognizing each other. The affinity between the memory cells is determined, and those that present an affinity higher than a pre-defined threshold are suppressed, reducing the redundancy in the network architecture. After that, new individuals randomly generated are introduced in the population of immune cells, thus forcing the introduction of diversity. The aiNet adaptation procedure can be found in [3,5].

2.2 The Minimal Spanning Tree (MST)

The main objective of the aiNet is to compress information by creating an antibody network, placing prototypes in strategic portions of the data distribution that are relevant for clustering, thus reducing the problem complexity. The next step consists of defining a mechanism capable of detecting the inherent separations present in the spatial distribution of antibodies.

An interesting way of doing this is to use the minimal spanning tree to perform the network (data) separation into clusters. The MST is a tool from graph theory that proved to be a powerful artifice for data clustering [19]. Roughly, given a set of points (data), an MST is built by linking some of these points, and those links considered inconsistent are removed from the tree, resulting in a disconnected graph; that is, a set of sub-graphs. Each of the sub-graphs generated correspond to one cluster. This approach is quite powerful because it not only defines the members of each cluster, but it also automatically determines the number of clusters. This is a potentiality presented by very few alternatives.

There are several forms of evaluating the inconsistency of edges in an MST. The criterion to be used in this work has a particularly important property of exploring cluster boundaries by taking into account their relative densities and distances, thus preserving the inherent structure of the spatial distribution of the data. This criterion was originally proposed by Zahn (1971) [19], and can be described as follows. After building the MST for a given set of points, for each edge of the tree, its two end points are analyzed with a depth p. This means that the average (avg) and the standard deviation (σ) of the length of all edges which are within p steps of each end point are calculated. An edge is considered inconsistent if its length (l) is greater than the average plus d standard deviations. That is, if $l > (avg + d.\sigma)$, then the edge is considered inconsistent. There are several algorithms that can be used to generate the minimal spanning tree of a given set of points, and we chose to employ the Prim's algorithm [15].

This approach is more sophisticated than simply removing the longest edges of the tree, as proposed in [17], because it is adaptive to the cluster structure and it takes into account the relative density of each cluster. Fig. 1 illustrates a hypothetic case in which removing the longest MST-edge does not separate the clusters correctly, but in which the present criterion works well. This picture shows the presence of two clusters, one labeled (I) with a high density of data, and another labeled (II) with a low density of data. The separation between the two clusters, though identifiable by visual inspection, cannot be appropriately performed by removing the longest edge. The numbers next to the edges correspond to their length. Note that the longest edges have length 11, while the edge that should be pruned is edge AB of length 10. The average avg of nearby edges with depth $p = 2$ from node A is $avg = \frac{1}{4}(5 + 5 + 5 + 3) = 4.5$ and the standard deviation is $\sigma = 1$. Thus, the average plus two standard deviations is $avg + (d.\sigma) = 4.5 + 2{\times}1 = 6.5$. Hence, according to the criterion used here, and with the default parameters $p = 2$ and $d = 2$, the edge AB would be considered inconsistent, and the two clusters would be correctly identified.

This criterion makes the MST a *density search* clustering technique. It identifies clusters that are continuous regions of the space containing a relatively high density of points, separated from other such regions by other regions containing a relatively low density. Clusters described in this way are referred to as *natural clusters* [7]. This description is similar to the way we identify clusters visually, in bi- or three-dimensional spaces. Note that the inconsistency criterion used can be applied to data points in a space of any dimension. It is not necessary to visualize the MST in order to detect the edge(s) to be pruned. This is a necessary capability for gene expression data analysis, because these data are usually of very high dimension.

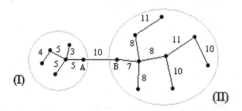

Fig. 1. Cluster identification using the minimal spanning tree.

3. Materials and Methods

3.1. Experimental Data and Similarity Metrics

The data set to be analyzed is composed of the expression levels of 2467 genes of the budding yeast *Saccharomyces cerevisiae*. It was obtained from [6], and is available on line at http://rana.lbl.gov/. The expression levels were measured in 8 different processes, totalizing 79 experiments. The values in the data table correspond to the transformed (log base 2) fluorescence ratio Cy5/Cy3. Due to difficulties in measuring, some values in the table are missing.

In the first part of the experiments, four clusters (68 genes in total) out of the ten previously detected in [6] were chosen for analysis. These clusters were the same used in the analysis performed in [17], and they are protein degradation (cluster C), glycolysis (cluster E), protein synthesis (cluster F), and chromatin structure (cluster H). Using this data set it is possible to make a comparison between the results presented by the proposed hybrid approach and those obtained by the other two approaches [6,17]. In the second part of the analysis, cluster B (spindle pole body assembly and function, with 11 genes), also obtained from [6], was used.

The similarity metric used was the correlation coefficient [6]. Thus, those genes with similar behavior in parallel are privileged, not giving emphasis to the magnitude of the values. Let G_i be the expression level of gene G in experiment i, for two genes X and Y, the similarity measure S in a total of N experiments can be computed as follows:

$$S(X,Y) = \frac{1}{N}\sum_{i=1}^{N}\left(\frac{X_i - X_{offset}}{\Phi_X}\right)\left(\frac{Y_i - Y_{offset}}{\Phi_Y}\right), \quad \Phi_G = \sqrt{\sum_{i=1}^{N}\frac{(G_i - G_{offset})^2}{N}}. \quad (1)$$

The value G_{offset} was chosen zero in all cases [6]. Missing values were omitted in the calculation of the similarity, and for these cases, N corresponds to the number of experiments that are actually included in the table. The data set was normalized between 0 and 1, thus the maximum value possible for S is 1, and the similarity does not assume any negative value. As the aiNet algorithm was implemented to work with distances (dissimilarity metric), the following equation was used for the calculation of the distance D between two genes [17]:

$$D(X,Y) = 1 - S(X,Y) \tag{2}$$

3.2 Setting of Parameters for aiNet

The aiNet has some parameters to be tuned in order to run the algorithm. The initial population of antibodies was generated by a random reordering of the elements in each column of the expression matrix (genes and its coordinates), rather than simply generating random numbers. This was done to create an initial approximation between the antibodies and the training data set, thus imposing some previous knowledge to the network. The following parameters were adopted: n = 4, qi = 0.2, it = 20, σ_p = 0.035, σ_s = 0.01, N_1 = number of antigens, and N_2 = 10. These were obtained after some preliminary tests with the algorithm, though no exhaustive search of parameters or sensitivity analysis was performed. The reader interested in the aiNet sensitivity to the tuning parameters should refer to [5]. However, it is important to stress that most of these parameters assume their default values suggested in [5], such as n, qi, and N2. The main parameter that required tuning was σ_s, and some comments about how its influence on the performance of the algorithm will be provided later.

4 Computational Analysis and Discussion

The tests were performed in two major steps. Initially, the proposed algorithm was applied to part of the gene expression data set of the yeast *Saccharomyces cerevisiae*, that represents clusters previously detected in [6]. This test was done with the objective of validating the method proposed through a comparison with the results obtained by classical tools available in the literature. Besides, this is an important step for adjusting the parameters of the algorithm, and many other researchers have applied their clustering proposals to these data before using more data or other sets of data. The second test was performed on all the data set of the yeast.

4.1 Validating the Method

An important aspect of our proposal is that the MST is built on the antibody network, and not directly on the data set. This characteristic has a major impact on the clustering process. This is because the data compression performed by the aiNet and the prototype positioning reduces the levels of noise and redundancy in the data set and discovers key portions of the input space for the detection and representation of clusters.

In [17] three different criteria for cutting the MST edges were proposed: 1) Remove long MST-edges; 2) An iterative algorithm based on cluster center optimization; and 3) A dynamic programming algorithm. In this work, it was claimed that these three methods obtained virtually identical results when applied to the same data set used here. We then first tried to reproduce the results obtained in [17] using the criterion of removing the long MST-edges. These results were further compared with those obtained by applying the method of cutting the tree proposed in this paper, when the MST is built directly on the raw data. The intention was to evaluate the performance of the local cutting criterion used in our analysis. This first part of the computational tests is described in Section 4.1.1. After that, the hybrid algorithm was applied to the same data set, and its results are described in Section 4.1.2.

4.1.1 Applying the MST to the Raw Data Set

Removing the longest edges of the MST is a very simple artifice to evaluate the inconsistency of the connections of the tree. It has the advantage of being easily implementable but it may be very time consuming when the number of data available is high. In this method those MST-edges with larger weights are removed one by one, starting from the longest edge, until an optimal cutting point that accurately identifies the clusters is reached. Each cluster is then formed by one remaining sub-graph linking the data points. The problem here is to define a threshold to identify when an edge is considered "long". This is equivalent to determining the number of clusters in the data, which corresponds to the quantity of inconsistent edges plus one. However, this is not a trivial task. Another problem of this approach is that it does not take into account the densities of the clusters, thus it may fail to correctly detect the inconsistent edges in several situations. This feature was demonstrated in the hypothetical case of Section 2.2. Moreover, this criterion is very sensitive to outliers. If a datum is placed considerably distant from the others, the length of the edge connecting it to the rest of the tree will be very large. Thus, removing this edge as a long one will not be sufficient for determining the presence of a cluster.

To assess the performance of this method, the minimal spanning tree was built on the raw data, corresponding to clusters C, E, F and H. The similarity measure used is the correlation coefficient (Equation (1)). The first method proposed in [17] did not perform well in this data set. The alternative was to use the information about the number of clusters (previously known in this case), thus removing the three longest edges, in order to find four sub-graphs (clusters). The results obtained demonstrated that cutting the longest edges of the MST is not a good criterion for evaluating the inconsistency of the edges of the minimal spanning tree. Only clusters E and H were correctly separated. Clusters C and F were identified as belonging to the same group, and the fourth cluster was formed by only one gene (TYE7), which is actually part of cluster E. The reason for this result is that the distance that separates gene TYE7 from cluster E in the MST is greater than the distance separating clusters C and F. The histogram of Fig. 2, where each bar represents the length of an edge of the MST, illustrates this situation. Note the prominence of the three longest edges.

Observe that if the gene TYE7 is removed from the data set, the problem will still persist, because in the MST there are other edges with a length greater than the distance between C and F. The removal of the longest edges does not take into account the independent distribution of each cluster in the space, thus it may lead to incorrect clustering. This criterion is incapable of perceiving that for clusters C and F, which have high density of genes, the distance between them is relatively large, thus evidencing an inherent separation. For cluster E, which has a low density, the distance separating its elements from gene TYE7, although larger than most connections of the tree, does not reveal an inconsistency.

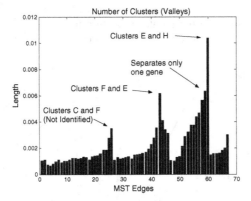

Fig. 2. Histogram of the connections of the MST. Prominence of the three longest edges that separate clusters F and E, E and H, and another one that separates only one gene. The edge that divides clusters C and F is relatively small when compared with the longest ones, and was not identified by the algorithm as being inconsistent.

In order to identify the clusters accurately it is necessary to adopt a local criterion that takes into account the relative density of the clusters. The method proposed in this paper has proved to be considerably efficient in this task. Using the default parameters $p = d = 2$ the algorithm was capable of detecting five inconsistent edges (six clusters) in the data set. The clusters C, F and H were correctly identified, and cluster E, although also separated from the others, was divided into two subgroups. The last cluster identified is formed by two genes (RPN5 and RPN8), which are originally from cluster C. This result shows that the algorithm detected not only the expected clusters, but two more inherent divisions in the data, one that partitions the cluster E into two and another that separates two genes from cluster C. These extra divisions are probably due the noise existent in the data set. Clusters formed by one or two genes were identified by the proposed method and considered outliers. It is important to stress that the proposed algorithm does not need the number of clusters as an input parameter.

4.1.2 Applying the Hybrid Algorithm (MST + aiNet)

The next step in the analysis is to use the aiNet to perform a data pre-processing, and then build the MST on the resulting antibody network, using again the cutting criterion described in this paper. As any other tool that involves probabilistic steps during processing, the hybrid algorithm had to be executed a number of times so that the results become statistically significant. Using again the default parameters $p = d = 2$, the performance obtained was remarkable, with an accurate data clustering in 100% of the ten executions performed. The average information compression was 34% and the maximum compression rate achieved was 44%. Outliers represented 2% of the genes in the totality of cases observed. Fig. 3(a) presents the dendrogram produced by a hierarchical clustering procedure applied directly on the raw data, and Fig. 3(b) shows the dendrogram obtained with the antibodies of the network.

Note in the dendrogram of Fig. 3(b) that the number of antibodies is much smaller than the number of genes in Fig. 3(a). Nevertheless, the structure of the clusters remains almost the same, with the exception of the introduction of one outlier, that was identified only by the hierarchical clustering, and not by the aiNet. Observe that cluster C was the one that suffered the greater reduction in the number of genes. This is because its data density is relatively higher than that of the other clusters.

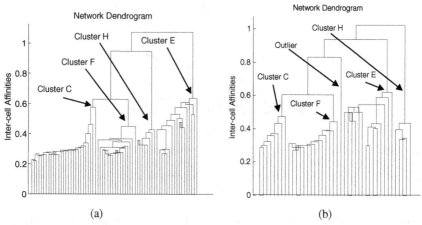

(a)   (b)

Fig. 3. Dendrograms. (a) Dendrogram built directly on the raw data. (b) Dendrogram built on the resultant aiNet.

The results demonstrated that the hybrid algorithm is capable of accurately separating the clusters analyzed. This is achieved through the exploration of the structure of the distribution of genes taking into account their relative density in the space, thus revealing a better performance than simply removing the longest edges of the tree. The proposed method for cutting the MST-edges proved to be efficient for clustering gene expression data. However, the data compression performed by the aiNet is crucial for reducing the noise in the data, leading to better results of the technique. The aiNet pre-processing is a fundamental step in more complex analyses as well, mainly when data sets are very large and have high levels of noise and redundancy. This is usually the case with bioinformatics data.

4.2   Analyzing the Whole Yeast Data Set

The next step is to analyze all the yeast gene expression data set, a total of 2,467 genes in 79 different experimental conditions. The parameters and distance measure used were the same as in the previous analysis. Surprisingly, no significant cluster was detected in the data set, not even the clusters C, E, F and H, correctly identified and separated previously, could be detected. Only groups containing some few genes were identified as being clusters by the algorithm, but they were considered no more than outliers, giving the relatively inexpressive number of genes that they contain when compared with the whole data set.

The reason for this result is that there is a strong interconnection of the genes in the data set. Between two groups with different expression profiles, there is a bridge formed by a series of genes with intermediate behavior, making the inconsistencies disappear. To illustrate, let us have a closer look in clusters B and C. These clusters were chosen because they are close, according to the ordered sequence of the genes presented in [6], thus facilitating the visualization of the effect to be demonstrated. Fig. 4(a) presents the histogram of the MST when constructed directly from the data composing the known clusters B and C, where each bar corresponds to an edge of the tree. This histogram gives a rough idea of the relative length of the MST edges, but it does not always provide an accurate visual identification of the inconsistent edges. It also suggests an inherent separation between the two clusters, because there is an edge of the tree with a length significantly larger than the others in its neighborhood. Applying the same inconsistency criterion, but now with the introduction of 50 genes with intermediate patterns to these clusters – this is possible because the genes were previously ordered in [6] – the histogram presented in Fig. 4(b) is obtained.

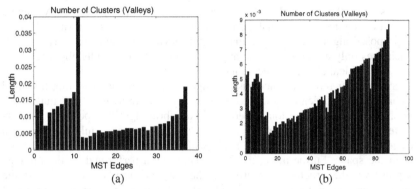

Fig. 4. Histograms of clusters B and C. (a) Clusters B and C. (b) Clusters B and C with the introduction of genes with intermediary expression patterns.

Note that the inconsistent edge disappears, indicating the existence of a single cluster. It is important to stress that the inconsistencies do not become more difficult to identify, they just disappear with the introduction of these genes. Fig. 5 illustrates, in two dimensions, what is happening to the clusters. Observe in Fig. 5(a) the existence of two perfectly separable groups of points, representing clusters B and C. With the introduction of the genes with intermediate profiles (Fig. 5(b)) there is no more visible (natural) separation between the clusters.

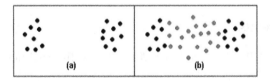

Fig. 5. Clusters perfectly separable (a). Clusters after the introduction of genes with intermediate behavior (b).

A similar situation occurs to all the data set. Hence, there is no way to define where one cluster begins and where it ends, unless a hierarchical approach is used. If there is a set of genes ordered according to their similarities in expression profiles, one can have completely different patterns in both extremes of the sequence, but the transition between them may still be extremely smooth. Any separation of its elements will be arbitrary. This result reveals that the data set analyzed presents a distribution of genes in the space that does not admit an inherent separation between its elements. There-fore, there is no *natural cluster* in the yeast data. In such cases, the most classical clustering techniques, such as hierarchical clustering, have the advantage that they allow the user to choose where to find clusters by specifying where to cut the dendro-gram. By contrast, it has the disadvantage of always providing results biased by the cutting point chosen by the user; there is no guarantee that the clusters suggested are reasonable, because there is no natural cluster.

5   Conclusion

This work assessed the potentiality of using a hybrid algorithm between an AIS and a graph theoretic technique to the analysis of gene expression data. The results obtained with the proposed algorithm were compared with those of the analysis performed in [17], which uses only a graph theoretic approach, and with the results obtained in [6] based on a hierarchical clustering technique.

The criterion for removing inconsistent edges of the minimal spanning tree used by the hybrid algorithm demonstrated to be more efficient in identifying natural clus-ters than simply removing the longest edges. The hybrid algorithm performs cluster-ing by interpreting and by preserving the key cluster features, while the approach proposed in [17] separates the data elements without taking into account the density of genes in the space. Furthermore, the data compression performed by the immune network preserves the structural properties of the clusters and plays a key role in the detection of important portions of the input space, being crucial for the analysis of complex data sets with high numbers of (noisy) data.

The hybrid algorithm was initially applied to part of the yeast gene expression data set, and then to the whole data set. The results obtained demonstrated that the aiNet provides a new interpretation of the data set analyzed, detecting a strong inter-connection of the genes. The yeast data does not have visible points of inconsistency that lead to the identification of clusters. Due to this feature, it may be more interest-ing to concentrate efforts to order the genes efficiently, as it was already performed in [9], rather than to cluster them. Any separation of the data will be forced, and will not preserve its inherent structure, thus the clustering techniques may present biased re-sults.

Acknowledgements

The authors thank CNPq (Profix n. 540396/01-1) for the financial support.

References

1. Baldi, P. & Brunak, S., (2001), *Bioinformatics - The Machine Learning Approach*, Second Edition, MIT Press, Cambridge, Massachussetts.
2. Burnet, F.M. (1959), *The Clonal Selection Theory of Acquired Immunity*, Cambridge University Press.
3. de Castro, L. N. & Von Zuben, F. J. (2001), "aiNet: An artificial Immune Network for Data Analysis", In Data Mining: A Heuristic Approach, H. A. Abbass, R. A. Saker, and C. S. Newton (Eds.), Idea Group Publishing, USA, Chapter XII, pp. 231-259.

4. de Castro, L.N. & Von Zuben, F.J. (2000a), "The Clonal Selection Algorithm with Engineering Applications", GECCO'00 Proc. of the Genetic and Evolutionary Computation Conference – Workshop Proceedings, pp. 36-37.
5. de Castro, L. N. & Von Zuben, F. J. (2000b), "An Evolutionary Immune Network for Data Clustering", Proc. of IEEE SBRN – Brazilian Symposium on Neural Networks, pp. 84-89.
6. Eisen, M. B., Spellman, P. T., Brow, P. O., & Botstein, D. (1998), "Cluster Analysis and Display of Genome-wide Expression Patterns", Proc. Natl. Acad. Sci, vol.95, pp. 14863-14868, USA.
7. Everitt, B. (1993), *Cluster Analysis*, Heinemann Educational Books.
8. Fausset, L. (1994), *Fundamentals of Neural Networks: Architectures, Algorithms and Applications*, Ed. Prentice-Hall, New Jersey, USA.
9. Gomes, L.C.T., Von Zuben, F.J. e Moscato, P. (2002), "Ordering Gene Expression Data Using One-Dimensional Self-Organizing Maps", Proc. of the 1st Brazilian Workshop on Bioinformatics, pp. 91-93, Gramado, RS, Brazil.
10. Herwig, R., Poustka, A.J., Mller, C., Bull, C., Lehrach, H. e O'Brien, J. (1999) "Large-scale clustering of cDNA-fingerprinting data", Genome Res., vol. 9, pp. 1093-1105.
11. Jerne, N. K. "Towards a Network Theory of the Immune System", Ann. Immunol. (Inst. Pasteur), 1974, pp. 373-389.
12. Lockhart, D.J. et al. (1996), "Expression monitoring by hybridization to high-density oligonucleotide arrays", Nature Biotechnology, vol. 14, pp. 1675-1680.
13. Luscombe, N.M., Greenbaum, D., Gerstein, M. (2001), "What is Bioinformatics? – A Proposed Definition and Overview of the Field", *Methods of Information in Medicine*, vol. 40, pp. 346-358.
14. Michalewicz, Z. (1999), *Genetic Algorithms + Data Structures = Evolution Programs*, Third Edition, Ed. Springer, Nova York, USA.
15. Prim, R. C. (1957), "Shortest Connection Networks and Some Generalizations", Bell Sys. Tech. Journal, 36, pp. 1389-1401.
16. Schena, M., et al. (1996), "Parallel human genome analysis: microarray-based expression monitoring of 1000 genes", Proc. Natl. Acad. Sci. USA, vol 93, pp. 10614-10619.
17. Xu, Y., Olman, V. & Xu, Dong (2002), "Minimum Spanning Trees for Gene Expression Data Clustering", Bioinformatics, vol. 18, pp. 536-545.
18. Yeung, K.Y., (2001), "Cluster Analysis of Gene Expression Data", Ph.D. Thesis, Computer Science, University of Washington, Seattle, WA, USA.
19. Zahn, C. T. (1971), "Graph-Theoretical Methods for Detecting and Describing Gestalt Clusters", IEEE Trans. on Computers, C-20(1), pp.68-86.

An Investigation of the Negative Selection Algorithm for Fault Detection in Refrigeration Systems

Dan W. Taylor[1,2] and David W. Corne[1]

[1] Department of Computer Science, University of Reading, Reading, UK
d.w.corne@reading.ac.uk
[2] JTL Systems Ltd, 41 Kingfisher Court, Hambridge Road, Newbury, UK
dan.taylor@jtl.co.uk

Abstract. Failure of refrigerated cabinets costs millions annually to supermarkets, and a large market exists for systems which can predict such failures. Previous work, now moving towards deployment, has used neural networks to predict volumes of alarms from refrigeration system controllers, and also to predict likely refrigerant gas loss. Here, we use in-cabinet temperature data, aiming to predict faults from the pattern of temperature over time. We argue that artificial immune systems (AIS) are particularly appropriate for this, and report a series of preliminary experiments which investigate parameter and strategy choices. We also investigate a 'differential' encoding scheme designed to highlight essential elements of in-cabinet temperature patterns. The results prove feasibility for AIS in this application, with good self-detection rates, and a promising fault-detection rate. The best configuration of those examined seems to be that which uses the novel differential encoding with r-bits matching.

1 Introduction

The role of a supermarket refrigerator is to keep food within a constant temperature range, ensuring the contents remain in a good condition. Consumers' health (and the reputation of the supermarket) depends upon the refrigerator's ability to perform this core task. There are, however, many other factors which affect the design of refrigeration systems: power usage must be minimised for financial and environmental reasons; maintenance must also be minimized to ensure that a refrigerated cabinet can remain in constant operation. Temperatures must be recorded regularly, to comply with public health legislation, and cabinets must be able to cope with continual disturbances caused by customers selecting their purchases.

For such reasons, supermarket refrigeration systems are far more complex than household refrigerators and other commercial refrigeration systems. In almost all supermarkets, refrigerant is pumped around the store via a pipe network. The evaporation of refrigerant removes heat from cabinets on the shop floor and the resultant gas is then compressed and pumped to condensers outside the building, where heat is expelled. Evaporators, the component in which refrigerant is allowed to evaporate to absorb heat, must be regularly defrosted to prevent a build-up of frost and ice caused by moisture in the atmosphere. Defrost often involves the application of heat to the evaporator from an electric heating element.

Embedded control systems within every refrigerator are used to control the evaporator and thus the temperature of the cold-space and to manage defrosts. Similar controllers in plant machinery govern the operation of compressors and condensers as load on the refrigeration system changes. These are linked to a central data management unit which co-ordinates the timings of defrosts and provides a mechanism for logging data. A PC is linked directly to the central data management unit to provide additional data logging, reporting and management functionality for maintenance engineers and store staff.

This highly complex system provides a rich source of data for experimentation with data mining, prediction and classification techniques for the prevention of faults. There exists a great demand for such prediction systems within the supermarket industry.

JTL Systems Ltd is a refrigeration controls manufacturer, based in the UK. JTL operate an Alarm Monitoring Centre (AMC), which monitors alarms raised by systems in supermarkets throughout the UK. AMC staff manage the dispatch of engineers and warn store staff of faults, based on the alarms they receive. The AMC currently monitors *c.* 40,000 controllers in *c.* 500 supermarkets, receiving *c.* 1.5 million alarms each year. Previous work by the authors has involved the development of systems to predict daily alarm volumes [1] and to detect the early symptoms of refrigerant leaks based on alarm data received at the monitoring centre [2]. Recent advances in connectivity within the JTL network have made the collection of temperature data from cabinets much quicker. It is now feasible to begin targeting faults on a cabinet by cabinet basis.

One of the most common cabinet level faults is *icing-up*, which occurs when defrosts are not sufficiently effective and a thick layer of ice builds up on the evaporator. The ice layer acts as an insulator around the evaporator, drastically lowering its efficiency until it is no longer capable of cooling the air in the cabinet. At this point the attention of an engineer will be required and the cabinet will need to be emptied and shut down for many hours. It is also possible that products within the cabinet will have reached an unsafe temperature and will need to be destroyed. A great financial loss will be incurred due to engineering expenses, stock losses and the hidden costs of lost trading from the cabinet.

There are thought to be characteristic patterns in temperature log data which are symptomatic of icing-up. These patterns can be recognised by human experts and used to detect problems before they become too serious. However, due to the sheer quantity of temperature log data it is impractical to monitor the system in this way. There is a definite need, therefore, for an automated system which is able to recognise the symptoms of icing up and raise an alarm to prevent stock being endangered and to allow timely preventative maintenance.

The task of recognising the symptoms of icing up in noisy real-world data is an ideal application for computational intelligence. The main problem with the development of such a system is the lack of data representing fault conditions. Though in excess of 4 billion temperature log data items are available to us, there is no feedback system in place to match temperature data to the occurrence of a fault. It is, therefore, extraordinarily hard to find a useful number of data patterns which are symptomatic of an iced up cabinet. Despite this, an abundance of data is available which is indicative of normal operation.

Artificial Immune Systems (AIS) are a relatively new paradigm in AI and have the distinct advantage of requiring only positive examples for training. This makes AIS an ideal technology to investigate in this application. The remainder of this paper details work carried out to investigate the use of AIS to detect the early symptoms of icing up in supermarket refrigerators. For completeness, Section 2 gives some brief background into the biological inspiration for AIS and also includes a brief review of relevant research in the field to date (readers familiar with AIS can skip this section, although section 2.2 does provide the introductory focus for the issue of matching, the strategy for which is an experimental variable later on in section 4). A more detailed exploration of the refrigeration data can be found in section 3. The results of experiments carried out to investigate the usefulness of AIS in this domain and to determine appropriate AIS configurations are included in section 4 and some conclusions and suggestions for further work can be found in section 5.

2   Immune Systems, Artificial and Otherwise

Artificial Immune Systems (AIS) have become an increasingly popular area for study by computer scientists in recent years. The term AIS refers to any computer system which is inspired by the natural immune system. This is by no means limited to computer models of the immune system which are used by biologists to gain a better understanding of the subject. Detailed reviews of the various AIS architectures which exist can be found in [3] and [4]. This section briefly outlines the operation of the human immune system, before detailing the nature of the *negative selection algorithm*, which forms the basis of experiments carried out later in the paper.

2.1   The Human Immune System

The immune system is a natural, distributed system which protects us from attack by foreign bodies known as *pathogens*. The job of the immune system is to monitor the body and make classifications as to whether the items it encounters are *self* or *non-self*. Everything which the immune system categorises as non-self, such as bacteria, cancer or tumour cells, must be destroyed. Everything which is a natural and healthy part of the body should be categorised as self and should remain untouched by the immune system. The term *antigen* is used to denote anything which the immune system is able to recognise. Antigens are essentially features which occur in both the body's cells and pathogens such as bacteria. The self/non-self categorisation is based on the antigenic patterns on the surface of cells.

The human immune system operates on two main levels. Innate immunity is the first and most simple line of defence. The innate immune system consists of basic, passive defences such as the skin, mucus membranes and other structures which help to keep foreign bodies out. When the innate immune system fails to keep a pathogen out of the body it is up to the acquired (or adaptive) immune system to destroy it [5]. Acquired immunity is based on a population of lymphocytes. Lymphocytes are cells which circulate around the tissues of the body in the blood stream. They are capable of recognising and responding to pathogens, initiating an immune response which destroys them.

Two types of lymphocyte exist, B-cells and T-cells. Both of these are able to respond to antigenic patterns, presented on the surface of pathogens. Receptors on the surface of lymphocytes chemically *match* antigenic material. *Helper* T-cells stimulate

B-cells to proliferate and destroy the pathogen. The magnitude of this immune response is proportional to the strength of the match between T-cell and pathogen.

On detection of a pathogen, B-cells undergo a process of *Clonal Expansion* and *Affinity Maturation*. During this process B-cells rapidly reproduce with high mutation rates (known as *hypermutation*). Those B-cells which more closely match the antigen are encouraged to reproduce more quickly, while those which do not match will reproduce more slowly. Thus, the population of B-cells which can correctly recognise and react to the pathogen in question is quickly increased in size. Clonal expansion refers to the rapid, single parent reproduction which takes place to produce a large population of targeted B-cells. Affinity maturation is the Darwinian process which increases, through mutation and the reward of closely matching lymphocytes, the strength of the match between pathogen and B-cells within the immune repertoire.

T-cells are produced in the bone marrow, but undergo a *Maturation* process in the thymus. Maturation involves the presentation of *Self* proteins to naïve T-cells. Any T-cell which matches a self protein is destroyed. This prevents the immune system attacking the body itself. Auto-immune diseases are caused by a breakdown in the maturation process which allows T-cells which match self to be allowed out of the thymus. The censoring process which destroys T-cells which match self patterns is known as *Negative Selection*.

2.2 Artificial Immune Systems and Negative Selection

The negative selection algorithm was first used by Forrest et al [6] as a means of detecting unknown or illegal strings for virus detection in computer systems. A population of detectors is created to perform the job of T-cells. These detectors are simple, fixed length binary strings. A simple rule is used to compare bits in two such strings and decide whether a match has occurred. Such a match is equivalent to a match between lymphocyte and antigen.

Every randomly generated candidate detector is compared to every pattern in the self set. The self set is analogous to the self proteins stored in the thymus in that it contains examples of self, against which detectors are tested. Any detector which matches any pattern in the self set is not included in the detector set. New patterns can then be gathered from the system which is being monitored. These patterns are translated into the appropriate binary form and compared to the detector set. If the tested pattern matches any detector in the detector set then it can be guaranteed that that pattern is non-self and action can be taken accordingly.

If an exact match were required by the matching rule, the detector set would need to contain detectors for every possible illegal string which could occur. This would lead to a huge computational overhead and an impractical algorithm. Instead, detection is probabilistic. Only r contiguous bits are required to be identical for a match to occur. The value of r is known as the matching threshold. E.g. the strings "01111010" and "01011011" match when the matching threshold is less than 5.

Much other work has concentrated on the use of artificial immune systems and the negative selection algorithm for virus detection and computer security [7] [8]. Work has also been done to use self/non-self discrimination to detect anomalies in time series data [9] [10] [11] [12]. This is of particular interest and relevance to us. Though work has been done to real-valued representation of time series data [13] [14], in most cases, in order to be used by negative selection based algorithms, data are transformed into a series of short binary strings. This is done by sequentially sampling the data in blocks of a given size. E.g. for a time series $\{t_0, t_1, \ldots t_n\}$ and a pattern length of 4, the first pattern would contain $P_0 = \{t_0, t_1, t_2, t_3\}$, the second would contain $P_1 = \{t_4, t_5, t_6, t_7\}$ and so on. Each value is converted and stored sequentially in a binary string which forms the final representation of the pattern.

The self set is constructed using data patterns which represent the normal operation of the system. Patterns should be long enough to capture any important system behaviours. The detector set is then generated and negative selection is used to ensure that no detector matches any self pattern. New data from the system can then be matched against these detectors to find anomalies. Work in this area has, to date, generally focussed on the use of simulated datasets such as Mackey-Glass time series and simulated cutting tool data.

In the anomaly detection systems created by Dasgupta, Forrest et al [9] [10] [11] the binary encoding detailed above is used. However, by encoding self and detector sets as binary strings we run the risk of destroying the semantic value of relationships between data items [12], as the r contiguous bits required to match can lie across word boundaries. It has been shown, however, that increasing the number of symbols used to represent patterns (i.e. using a decimal rather than binary encoding) greatly increases the required size of the detector set and, thus, increases the computational complexity of the algorithm [12].

Another, more simple, matching rule can be applied in situations where a greater number of symbols is required, for whatever reason. This matching rule is based on the Euclidean distance between the patterns in p dimensional space, where p is the number of data items in each pattern. A threshold, D, is chosen for the matching rule and patterns are said to match if the distance between them is less than this threshold value. Patterns then *cover* an area of problem space with radius D. We explore this and other matching scenarios later on in section 4.

3   Refrigeration Temperature Data

3.1   Data Visualisation Using 'aiVIS'

Extensive use was made of the aiVIS data visualisation technique [15] which is essentially a visualisation technique for artificial immune networks. aiVIS also provides an invaluable tool for visualising the topologies of complex data sets and has been shown to give better results than other techniques such as principle component analysis for this task.

Data patterns are represented as dots in a two dimensional display space. The position of each dot is initially chosen at random and bears no relation to the data within the pattern itself. A mutual repulsion between all dots exists, which is proportional to proximity and is limited to a given radius. A measure of similarity is used to compare data in the patterns which the dots represent, similar dots are attracted to a degree proportional to the similarity of the associated data patterns. Euclidean distance between patterns is normally used as the measure of similarity. When iteration begins, similar dots will move toward each other, while other dots will move apart. After a given number of iterations the forces of repulsion and attraction will balance and movement will decrease. Full details are available in [15].

The result of this simple algorithm is that data will automatically cluster itself spatially. The effect is similar to that seen in a self organising map [16]. Figure 1 shows the aiVIS display on initialisation and after a series of iterations. The data set being viewed is a 'healthy' refrigeration data set, as detailed below in section 3.2, which contains further discussion of this figure.

a)   b)

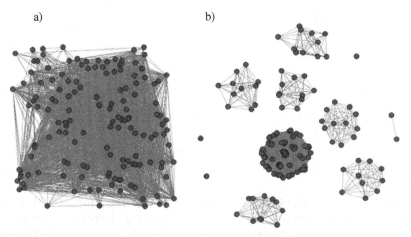

Fig. 1. aiVIS display of a) the initial random distribution of data patterns and b) the final clustered data set. See text in section 3.2.

3.2 Data Gathered from Sites

The operation of refrigerated cabinets in supermarkets is managed by an embedded controller. This controller uses temperatures, measured from various points around the cabinet, to control the flow of refrigerant through the evaporator and thus maintain a constant temperature. Each cabinet controller is linked, via a wired network, to the central data management unit, which it in turn linked to a PC. UK law demands that, in the interests of public health, the temperature of refrigerated food be logged at regular intervals throughout the day. The site PC maintains this logging database. Four temperatures from each cabinet are logged at 15 minute intervals, 96 times a day. Most stores will contain around 100 refrigerated cabinets.

Figure 2 shows a sample plot of temperature data from a freezer cabinet over two days. Note the large peaks in the data. These correspond to defrosts of the evaporator which normally take place every 6 to 8 hours.

Conversion of the temperature data to a form appropriate for AIS involved mapping the real-valued temperatures to the integers 0 to 9, hence corresponding to ten temperature levels. This was similar to [11] but in this case we do not perform the final step, converting the data to its binary representation.

Two data sets, A and B, are used for validation in the experiments presented in the next section. These contain appropriately encoded data from two ice cream cabinets at a particular supermarket. We use a fixed pattern length of 10 throughout, corresponding to a time period of 2.5 hours. When constructing self sets for the experiments presented in this paper no data from the cabinets associated with A and B were used.

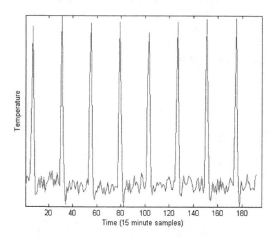

Fig. 2. Sample refrigeration temperature data showing transient defrost peaks.

Figure 1 shows an aiVIS visualisation of data set A. The left figure (1(a)) shows the initial situation before running the aiVIS clustering algorithm, while the right figure (1(b)) shows the result. The large central cluster corresponds to patterns with no defrost features (generally consisting of a series of very small values {0, 1}). The satellite clusters each correspond to a group of patterns with defrost peaks at particular points in the cycle.

3.3 Simulated Fault Data

As mentioned towards the end of section 1, the determination of temperature data which is known to correspond to an occurrence of icing-up is very difficult. For this reason, it was appropriate to create a simulated fault data set for testing purposes. One of the main symptoms of an iced-up cabinet is a slow or incomplete *defrost recovery*. Defrost recovery is the decrease in temperature after the defrost is over. This decrease should be as fast as possible to protect stock. If the evaporator is encased in ice it is less efficient, so more time will be taken to bring the temperature of the cabinet down. This can be easily simulated for a temperature value X at time t by summing a proportion of previous temperature values into the new value.

$$X_t = X_t + (0.5 \, X_{t-1}) + (0.25 \, X_{t-2}) \, . \tag{1}$$

This will cause an unusually long defrost recovery which should be detectable by our AIS. A set, F, of faulty data was created using this technique on real refrigeration data. Not all of the patterns in F would be clearly recognisable as non-self by our AIS as they correspond to periods between defrosts where fault is not readily apparent. F is a realistic approximation of data which might be recorded by the controller of an iced-up refrigerator. A good classifier would be expected to flag about 50% of these 2.5 hour long data patterns as non-self.

4 Experiments

This section gives details of the experiments performed to investigate suitable encoding schemes and matching rules for detecting icing up in refrigeration temperature data sets. The data set which is being examined for faults will henceforth be known as the *checking set*. The two healthy data sets, A and B, and the simulated faulty data set, F, detailed in the previous section are used throughout as checking sets. A variety of data sets are used to form self sets of various sizes and types. A and B are not used in any self set, neither are any data from the cabinets associated with A and B used when constructing self sets. In all cases, a *generate and test* approach is taken when constructing the detector set. Candidate detectors are generated at random before negative selection and insertion into the detector set as appropriate. Many, more efficient, detector set generation algorithms exist [17] but these are not evaluated here. Taking the mean classification rate over 10 experimental runs helps to address the issues associated with the evaluation of stochastic techniques.

Every experiment (i.e. every configuration of the AIS run on a particular dataset) was repeated ten times with different random seeds, and hence all results tabulated in this paper are mean values over ten independent runs, shown as a percentage to one decimal place. Every time a comparison between experimental results is alluded to in the following, the statement is justified (unless stated, or clear from context to be otherwise) by the result of a one-tailed t–test (assuming unequal variances) with p value below 0.01.

4.1 Experiments with Euclidean Matching Rule

Preliminary experiments, whose full details we omit, were done to help establish a good design for the generation of detector sets and setting of the matching threshold. Using detector sets of size 10,000 throughout, the design arrived at was a self set containing data from 13 different frozen food cabinets, and pattern lengths of 10 (a 2.5 hr time window), and a matching threshold $D = 10$. Table 1, using this configuration, shows performance on sets A, B and F.

Table 1. Baseline results for Euclidean Matching; 10,000 detectors, $D = 10$.

Data	% Self	% Non-self
A	98.6%	1.4%
B	99.9%	0.1%
F	65.7%	34.3%

Recall that datasets A and B both contain entirely self patterns (emerging from non iced up cabinets), and so an ideal classifier should detect 100% self and 0% non-self on these sets. The situation with set F is more complex. Strictly, the *ideal* classifier should find these all faulty, with 0% self and 100% non-self, but there is great variation in the 'faultiness' of the patterns in F. When between defrosts, the temperature curve of an iced-up cabinet is only subtly different from that of a normal cabinet. Hence we would regard 50% self / 50% non-self (roughly the number of patterns in F which include defrost 'activity') as a very good result for *F*.

4.2   Comparison of Euclidean and R-Bits Matching Rules

Using an appropriate detector set, preliminary experiments were done to select an r–bits threshold. After testing the values 3, 5, 7 and 10, we concluded that $r = 5$ provided the best balance between self-detection on healthy sets and non-self detection on F. Table 2 compares the best (from the small number tested above) configuration for Euclidean matching with this best configuration for r-bits matching, using the same detector set of 10,000 generated from a 13-cabinet self-set.

Table 2. Euclidean vs r-bit matching; 10,000 detectors, R = 5, D = 10.

Data	Euclidean		R-Bits	
	% self	% non-self	% self	% non-self
A	987%	1.3%	95.8%	4.2%
B	100.0%	0.0%	92.3%	7.7%
F	65.7%	34.3%	86.6%	13.5%

Both matching methods perform comparably on A and B, but the Euclidean rule gives a better non-self classification rate on F. The fact that the Euclidean matching rule performs better here is probably due to the fact that the decimal encoding makes the number of detectors required to *cover* the problem space much higher.

4.3   The R-Bits Matching Rule with Differentially Encoded Data

In attempt to decrease the size of the pattern space in a sensible way, and thus potentially increase the effectiveness of the R-bits matching rule, we experimented with a 'differential encoding' scheme. In conjunction with experts in the application area, our view is that the key elements of a faulty defrost temperature curve are not the precise pattern of real-valued temperatures, but the local 'ruggedness' of the temperature curve. The scheme we detail next is designed therefore to capture this structural element of the temperature pattern, while eschewing information which might otherwise lead either the Euclidean or R-bit matching rules astray. In close connection with this, the differential encoding allows us to use fewer symbols in our encoding scheme, decreasing the pattern space from 10^{10} for a decimal encoding to 10^3. The details are as follows. To construct a pattern in this encoding from a straightforward string of temperature values, we compare the temperature value at time t and at the previous sample point, t–1. We then use three symbols {0, 1, 2} to represent an upward slope, no change, and a downward slope respectively. The symbol we use for any given data value X at time t is given by:

$$Symbol = \begin{cases} 0 & if \ X_t < X_{t-1} \\ 1 & if \ X_t = X_{t-1} \\ 2 & if \ X_t > X_{t-1} \end{cases} \tag{2}$$

An important point of note regarding this encoding scheme is that the comparison of data values at time t and t–1 is performed after the data has been encoded into a decimal form as in the above experiments. If the comparison is made based on real valued data we find that much of the semantic value is lost due to very minor differences between X_t and X_{t-1}. Using this technique we encode changes in successive temperatures, rather than the temperatures themselves.

In preliminary experiments to determine a good value of r when using this encoding with r-bits matching, we found $r = 7$ to be the better choice. We then compared the best configurations for each of the following cases: Euclidean matching, r-bits (decimal encoding), and r-bits (differential encoding), and the results are in table 3. Experiments using the differential encoding and Euclidean matching rule were not performed because the selection of an appropriate matching threshold (D) to provide a fair comparison is very difficult. There is no clear way to find an appropriate value except by empirical means and space constraints prevent the inclusion of more results here. Future work may well approach this area.

Table 3. 10,000 detectors are used with D = 10 for Euclidean matching rule, R = 5 for R-bits matching as applied to decimally encoded data and R = 7 for R-bits matching as applied to differentially encoded data.

Data	Euclidean		R-bits (decimal)		R-bits (differential)	
	self	non-self	Self	non-self	Self	non-self
A	98.6%	1.4%	95.8%	4.2%	93.4%	6.6%
B	99.9%	0.1%	92.3%	7.7%	93.0%	7.0%
F	65.7%	34.3%	86.6%	13.5%	59.1%	40.9%

The best technique in terms of avoiding false non-self predictions in healthy data sets is the Euclidean matching rule with a decimal data encoding. However, better all round performance is given by the R-bits rule with a differential encoding. Though the rate of false non-self predictions is very slightly higher for this technique, the generated detector set is significantly more sensitive to non-self in the fault data.

5 Conclusions

We have summarised some extensive but early-stage investigations of the use of AIS to spot fault patterns in time series temperature data from supermarket freezer cabinets. The aim is to arrive at a fault detection system capable enough to be deployed on in-store PCs and/or at the JTL monitoring centre. Related work (in terms of the application) has examined the use of evolved neural networks to predict both future alarm totals [1] and refrigerant gas loss from controller alarms data [2], and this has recently been deployed commercially. Such commercial deployment is also a goal of this work, thereby exploiting the almost unique and continually maintained data sources available to JTL, and thereby being able to combat a major source of financial and customer concern to supermarkets.

AIS technology was therefore investigated here, owing to its promise and applicability in scenarios where 'healthy' data are plentiful but faulty data are very hard to come by. The key task is to detect the early symptoms of icing up in refrigerated cabinets in supermarkets. Experiments have allowed us to pinpoint a good design for seeding further development of an AIS system for this task. In particular, the r-bits matching rule, in conjunction with a specialised differential encoding of data, gives the best trade-off between a low rate of false positives on healthy data and an accurate classification rate on *faulty* data.

Our main finding is that we regard the feasibility of AIS on this application as proven, taking into account the following points, and the potential offered by many extensions which are now under way. We noted predictable and marked improvements in performance as more data were made available to construct the self set. In terms of the JTL application, this augurs well, since there are orders of magnitude more real data available to us than has been used in the experiments reported here. With an appropriate configuration, we know that we can produce a system which spots towards half of the faults at the cost of around 10% false positive rate. This is well beyond what can be achieved with, for example, artificial neural networks at present since we do not have negative data. Nevertheless, the fact that we can to some (unknown) extent construct suitable negative data leads to the possibility of using such in the training of neural networks and other supervised learning systems for this task. This, along with further investigation of encodings based on the differential one, are prioritised for future work, along with the employment of more advanced architectures for the AIS itself towards achieving better fault prediction rates without compromising on false positives.

References

1. Dan Taylor, David Corne, David Taylor and Jack Harkness "Predicting Alarms in Supermarket Refrigeration Systems Using Evolved Neural Networks and Evolved Rulesets", *Proceedings of the World Congress on Computational Intelligence (WCCI-2002)*, IEEE Press *(2002)*
2. Dan Taylor and David Corne "Refrigerant Leak Prediction in Supermarkets Using Evolved Neural Networks", *Proceedings of the 4th Asia Pacific Conference on Simulated Evolution and Learning (SEAL), (2002)*
3. Leandro N de Castro and Jon Timmis "Artificial Immune Systems: A Novel Paradigm to Pattern Recognition", *Artificial Neural Networks in Pattern Recognition*, University of Paisley *(2002)*
4. Dipankar Dasgupta and Nii Attoh-Okine "Immunity-Based Systems: A Survey", *Proceedings of the IEEE International Conference on Systems, Man and Cybernetics*, IEEE Press *(1997)*
5. C A Janeway "How the Immune System Recognizes Invaders", *Scientific American: 41-47, (1993)*
6. Stephanie Forrest, Alan   S Perelson, Lawrence Allen and Rajesh Cherukuri "Self-Nonself Discrimination in a Computer", *Proceedings of the IEEE Symposium on Research in Security and Privacy*, IEEE Press *(1994)*
7. Stephanie Forrest, S A Hofmeyr, A Somayaji and T A Longstaff "A Sense of Self for Unix Processes", *Proceedings of the IEEE Symposium on Research in Security and Privacy*, IEEE Press *(1996)*
8. Jeffery O Kephart "A Biologically Inspired Immune System for Computers", *Proceedings of the Fourth International Workshop on the Synthesis and Simulation of Living Systems, (1994)*
9. Dipankar Dasgupta "Using Immunological Principles in Anomaly Detection", *Proceedings of Artificial Neural Networks in Engineering (ANNIE), (1996)*

10. Dipankar Dasgupta and Stephanie Forrest "Tool Breakage Detection in Milling Operations using a Negative-Selection Algorithm", *Technical Report CS95-5*, Computer Science, University of New Mexico *(1995)*
11. Dipankar Dasgupta and Stephanie Forrest "Novelty Detection in Time Series Data Using Ideas from Immunology", *Proceedings of The 5th International Conference on Intelligent Systems, (1996)*
12. Shantanu Singh "Anomaly Detection Using Negative Selection Based on the R-Contiguous Matching Rule", *Proceedings of ICARIS 2002*, University of Kent at Canterbury Printing Unit *(2002)*
13. Fabio Gonzales and Dipankar Dasgupta "An Imunogenic Technique to Detect Anomalies in Network Traffic", *Proceedings of GECCO 2002*, Morgan Kaufmann Publishers *(2002)*
14. Fabio Gonzales and Dipankar Dasgupta "Neuro-immune and Self-Organising Map Approaches to Anomaly Detection: A Comparison", *Proceedings of ICARIS 2002*, University of Kent at Canterbury Printing Unit *(2002)*
15. Jon Timmis "aiVIS - Artificial Immune Network Visualisation", *EuroGraphics UK 2001 Conference Proceedings, (2001)*
16. T Kohonen "Self Organising Maps Second Edition" Springer *(1997)*
17. Modupe Ayara, Jon Timmis, Rogerio de Lemos, Leandro N de Castro and Ross Duncan, "Negative Selection: How to Generate Detectors", *Proceedings of ICARIS 2002*, University of Kent at Canterbury Printing Unit *(2002)*

A Role for Immunology
in "Next Generation" Robot Controllers

Emma Hart, Peter Ross, Andrew Webb, and Alistair Lawson

Napier University, Scotland, UK
{e.hart,p.ross,a.webb,al.lawson}@napier.ac.uk

Abstract. Much of current robot research is about learning tasks in which the task to be achieved is pre-specified, a suitable technology for the task is chosen and the learning process is then experimentally investigated. A more interesting research question is how can robot be provided with an architecture that would enable it to developmentally 'grow-up' and accomplish complex tasks by building on basic built-in capabilities. Previous work by the authors defined the requirements of a robot architecture that would enable this to happen – in this paper, we describe how some components of such an architecture can be achieved using an immune network model, and present preliminary results that show the plausibility of the suggested approach.

1   Introduction

A great deal of current research work in mobile robotics and autonomous systems is still focused on getting a robot to learn to do some task such as pushing an object to a known location or running as fast as possible over rough ground. The learning process may be supervised, unsupervised or a process of occasional reinforcement, but the whole aim in such work is to get the robot to achieve the task that was pre-defined by the researcher.

As a step towards achieving truly autonomous robots that can function productively for long periods in unpredictable environments, it is important to investigate how one might design robots that are capable of 'growing up' through experience. By this, we mean that the robot starts with only some basic skills such as an ability to move about and an ability to sense and react to the world , but in the course of time it develops genuinely new skills that were not entirely engineered into it at the start. In particular it should be capable of building some kind of hierarchy of skills, such that for each new skill s_{new} there is one or more sets of skills $S_1, S_2, \cdots S_n$ such that s_{new} is significantly more easily acquired if the robot has acquired all the members of some S_i than if it lacks at least one member of each of those sets. To achieve this requires a fundamental shift in thinking when designing robotic architectures compared to the type of systems prevalent in the literature today.

Previous work by the authors [1] attempted to lay out a research agenda by which this question could be answered and identified six essential ingredients of an architecture that can realise growing-up robots. These are: sensors, memory, data-abstraction, planning, motivation, and finally a developmental schedule.

J. Timmis et al. (Eds.): ICARIS 2003, LNCS 2787, pp. 46–56, 2003.

[1] provides an overview of existing developmental architectures in relation to the above features. In this paper, we argue that an immune-network model can form the central component of a new architecture, which in particular provides a convenient method for handling the first four requirements. The immune network model was first proposed by Jerne in [7], and suggested that antibodies not only recognise foreign antigens, but also are connected together in a large-scale network formed by chains of stimulation and suppression between communicating antibodies. Although still controversial in immunological circles, the model has been successfully adopted by many AIS practitioners, producing diverse applications from data-mining systems [16] to simple robot-control architectures [4,10,14].

In the next sections, we describe the proposed architecture in detail and provide results of some early experimentation. Although this in no way represents the complete architecture and is tested only in simulation, it does at least point to the plausibility of the model.

2   Previous Work

AIS ideas have already appeared in robotics research. Lee [9] proposed an AIS for realisation of cooperative strategies and group behaviour in collections of mobile robots, and Singh and Thayer [13,15] proposed another architecture for coordination and control of large scale distributed robot teams based on concepts from the immune system. Of more relevance to this research is the work of Ishiguro and Watanabe who introduce an immune-network for behaviour-arbitration in [4,17], for gait-control in walking robots [5] and also the work of [10] who also consider an immune network for decentralised autonomous navigation in a robot. In some senses, this work suffers from the same problems as other robotic approaches in that it results in a control module that is essentially static, i.e. successfully implements certain fixed behaviours, but would not permit a robot to 'grow-up' in the developmental sense outlined in the introduction. However, the overall approach contains many elements that can be incorporated into our proposed system and hence is briefly outlined here.

In [4,17], antibodies are formed into a network that successfully arbitrates between simple behaviours on a real robot; initially they handcrafted antibodies, in later work they evolved them. An antibody consists of a paratope defining a desirable condition and related motor-action, and an idiotope which identifies other antibodies to which the idiotope is connected. Connection between the idiotope of one antibody x and the paratope of an antibody y stimulates the antibody y, and links between antibodies in the network can either be evolved by a genetic algorithm [17] or formed via an on-line adaptation mechanism which provides reinforcement signal to links, [5]. The architecture which we propose must also handle behaviour arbitration, however we wish to construct it in such a way that its links also express *sequences* of actions, and thus paths in the network represent both a past history of robot actions (i.e. an episodic memory) and also provide information useful for planning.

A related line of research to AIS is that of the application of *classifier systems* to robot-control. Rules in a classifier system consist of conditions which are matched against the current state of the environment, and associated actions which are executed by the 'winning' rule. Such systems have been used to control a robot in simulation, for example [18] and also animats navigating in environments containing aliasing states, for example [8]. However, although these system generate control rules automatically, individual rules are distinct and there is no interaction between rules, therefore a pure classifier system approach cannot represent sequences of actions which is essential if the goals of this research are to be met. However, both the work of [18] and [8] partially informs the architecture proposed here, in particular in the chosen representation of antibodies in the network with regard to representing sensor information and motor actions.

Finally, [2] proposes a developmental mechanism which has some similarities to the proposed method, but it is not clear whether his system is scalable. His work, and its relation to our proposed model, is further discussed in section 3.1.

3   A New Architecture

Let us suppose that at the very start, the robot is driven by basic instincts such as a 'desire to avoid collisions' and a 'desire to seek novelty'. The robot should learn through experience, and the learned behaviours should gradually take over control from the instinct-driven initial system. The robot therefore needs to capture some minimal details of its experiences. In the proposed model, depicted in figure 1, this information is held as a collection of *rule-like associations* (RLAs). Each RLA is a node in a network and consists of a (partial) description C of sensory information, a robot action command A and a partial description of the sensory effects E of doing the action. After creation, an RLA therefore expresses some of the expected results of doing action A in a context C, and weighted network links express the sequencing information; a sub-path involving strongly positive weights would express an episode.

In immunological terminology, antibodies correspond to these RLAs, and antigens correspond to sensory data (not necessarily just raw data, see below); the C and E parts of an RLA can be regarded as paratope and epitope. Much as in Jerne's [7] immune-network hypothesis, connections are formed and adjusted by a process of *recognition* between the paratope of one antibody and the epitope of another, and result in stimulation and suppression of one antibody by another, according to a dynamical equation of the form given in equation 1, as first suggested by Farmer in [3]. In this equation, $a_i(t) \geq 0$ represents the strength or concentration of antibody i at time t, e_i represents the stimulation of antibody i by the antigen (current sensory information), the first summation term represents the total stimulation of the antibody i from the other antibodies in the network, the second summation term represents the suppression of antibody i from other antibodies in the network, and k_i is a natural decay factor.

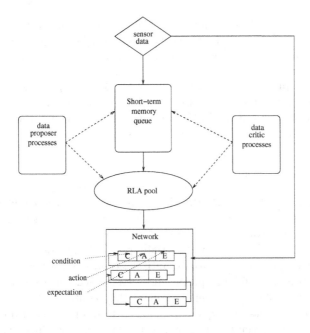

Fig. 1. A schematic representation of the proposed architecture

$$\frac{da_i(t)}{dt} = \left(e_i + \sum_{j=1}^{N} m_{ij}a_j(t) - \sum_{j=1}^{N} m'_{ji}a_j(t) - k_i \right) a_i(t) \qquad (1)$$

Immune system models require a mechanism by which recognition can occur. For example, AIS network models (e.g. [16]) often use the Euclidean distance in data-space between two data-items to signify recognition. In the proposed architecture, recognition between RLAs or antibodies serves the following purposes:

- individually, they can express a temporal association between RLAs – a strong positive connection between X and Y means that if RLA X fits the current situation then RLA Y is a possible candidate to describe the subsequent situation. Thus, individually, they can capture some aspects of episodic memory. Importantly, the boundaries of episodes can emerge from the dynamics of the network. That is, an episode ends when there is no clear winner as to the successor RLA.
- individually, they can (as inhibitory links) express a competition between different RLAs to account for the current situation.
- collectively, they can act as an attentional mechanism. The dynamics of the network can cause it to settle to a state in which some set of RLAs are reasonably active and the remainder are not; the active set represents the 'current memory context', as it were. In the set of linear differential equations in equation 1 above, the system can only have either a point attractor or a limit cycle depending on the values of the constants involved, but note that

the e_i would normally be time-dependent (the external data changes with robot activity) so the system should be capable of flipping between different attractors and limit cycles as the robot moves and the environment changes.

Clearly, this approach raises several questions. By what process(es) are RLAs created, and on what timescales? How are the connections between antibodies formed, and the strength of their affinities quantified? How will the dynamics of the network operate? We consider these questions next.

3.1   Generating RLAs

Although the aim of the architecture is to provide a framework in which the robot can grow-up, it seems reasonable to start with a system that has built-in basic behaviours, for example "explore", "avoid obstacles", "avoid boredom". We propose that this is handled by a partially pre-built network of RLAs, which then undergoes adaptation and growth until it becomes capable of allowing the robot to perform non-trivial and purposeful-seeming sequences of actions.

First, there is a short fixed-length queue that contains recent interesting sensory and motor events. The queue provides a form of short-term or working memory and distantly resembles human short-term memory which experimental studies have suggested is of bounded capacity (although expandable through lengthy training) and contains things that are fairly closely linked to the sensory input. For our initial purposes, 'interesting' means 'significantly changing'; for example if the robot is moving straight ahead across a vast empty space, the queue should not alter. The contents of this queue provide the raw material from which candidate RLAs can be built and then inserted into the network. Clearly the queue needs to contain some consequences of an action before this can happen, so RLAs can only get created at certain moments. The RLA pool can be viewed as containing fragments of experience. We propose RLAs of the following form:

```
RLA-3:
   condition: front-sensors = high
              and left-sensors = low
              and moving-average-of-front-sensors = low
      action: turn right
 expectation: left-sensors = high
  activation: 0.05
       links: 7/0.9, 453/-0.2, 64/1.2
```

Note that the condition does not fully describe the raw sensor data, and may refer to higher-level data constructs at later stages of the robots development. At the very start only raw sensor data will be available, but in real application, this will contain far too much information to be useful. So, abstractions will be proposed – for example, natural ones to suggest at the start would contain either thresholded or thresholded-moving-average versions of raw sensory information. We envisage that there will be some *data proposer and data critic processes* that suggest and evaluate new data abstractions built out of all existing data items (whether raw or already abstracted). Thus, the data universe will be dynamic. It is envisaged that the RLA proposer processes will gradually generate RLAs representing higher and higher levels of knowledge, thus representing the robot 'growing-up' in terms of its capabilities to understand its world. Thus, for example, an early set of RLAs composed of raw sensor data indicating that a robots left and front sensors are high, might eventually be replaced by an RLA representing the concept 'corner', with an associated action to turn right. Note that this thinking has some similarities with the work of Drescher [2] who introduced a general learning and concept-building mechanism called the *schema mechanism* in order to reproduce aspects of Piagetian cognitive development [11] during infancy. In this mechanism, the world is initially represented only in terms of very simple motor and sensor elements. Crucially however, the mechanism can define new, abstract, actions and invent novel concepts by constructing new state elements to describe aspects of the world that the existing repertoire of representations fails to express. Eventually, representations are discovered which can represent an object independently of how it is currently perceived and may be far removed from the original description.

Newly-formed RLAs will be presented to the network, where they will survive by being found to be useful and continue to survive only by continuing to be useful. Conversely, RLAs will be removed from the network if their stimulation falls below some threshold value. Data proposer processes are likely to be based on clustering techniques, for example k-means clustering or self-organising maps. Recent work by Prem *et al* in relation to this architecture shows promising results in using the ISO-map technique [12] for finding abstractions in time-series of sensor data generated by a real-robot. Data critic processes are likely to be based on checking whether data items have become redundant.

3.2   Quantifying Recognition between RLAs

As already stated, there is no straightforward way of quantifying the extent to which one RLA in the network should recognise another. As already mentioned in section 2, [10,17] tackled this problem by using a genetic algorithm, but this method has significant disadvantages if the goals of the new architecture are to be achieved. Firstly, use of a GA is likely to be too computationally expensive and slow in a real robotic environment, and furthermore, the connection strengths between antibodies could possibly change over time as the robot learns more about its environment, which would require the use of a continuously running GA. This type of process does not really have an analogy in the biological immune system in which connection strengths are determined by physical binding processes which do not alter over time, but there is an obvious analogy with the kind of Hebbian learning processes occurring in neural networks in which connection strengths are continuously adjusted over time.

However, [5] describes use an on-line adaption mechanism in an immune-network for achieving behaviour-arbitration – in this mechanism, affinity values are adaptively modified until the required behaviour emerges. This type of approach familiar to reinforcement learning appears to be more promising when using real robots, and hence will be adopted in this architecture.

3.3   Network Dynamics

As mentioned in section 3.1, the RLA pool can be thought of as containing fragments of experience which may become incorporated into the network. Initially, the network should consist of instinct driven behaviours but over time, these should be replaced by more sophisticated behaviours – however, it seems reasonable that the network should still maintain some record of these instinctive behaviours, as they may be useful at points in the future, and hence can override other behaviours given the right conditions.

Biological and neurological studies tell us that the network cannot be infinitely large; the brain has a finite volume in which neurons can exist, and similarly the immune system cannot physically contain an infinite number of antibodies (and anyway, the number of different types of antibodies is limited by the diversity of the DNA from which they can be formed) hence it seems logical and practical that the size of the network must somehow be bounded. Various mechanisms for achieving this can be found in the literature; plausible ones would seem to be based on the notion of a competition for resources, where RLAs would have to prove their worth to be allowed to remain in the network else be replaced by others. The natural decay constant k_i of the antibody would aid this process but further 'cell-death' mechanisms need to be investigated.

3.4   The Emergence of Planning

Planning-like behaviour should emerge from the network: this could occur as a dynamic cascade of internal events. For example, a goal is represented as an antigen which is injected into the system. As in the immunological system, the network must respond to this antigen - the antigen (goal) remains in the system until it is satisfied. At any point in time, the external environment will consist of multiple and changing data items, representing goals, sensory information and (perhaps) maps and internal memory states; the resulting course of action is results from a chain of RLAs firing, determined by the dynamically changing concentrations of the antibodies. Thus, the network effectively records chains of events that can allow a desired goal to be achieved. This may lead to the emergence of more complex behaviours.

Alternatively, a more classical planning approach could be taken. The RLAs associate expectations with states, therefore in theory a *virtual* antigen could be injected into the system, representing some potential goal or action, and the dynamical equations applied to determine what would be the result of such an action. By comparing the results of a number of such virtual experiments, a 'plan' could then be selected. The network thus provides a blackboard for 'thought' experiments by the robot.

4   An Initial, Partial Implementation of the Ideas

This section describes an experiment performed as a proof of concept for the architecture, though clearly it is only a basic skeleton of the proposed system. We used Olivier Michel's simulation (http://diwww.epfl.ch/lami/team/michel/khep-sim/) of a Khepera robot. This robot has six forward-looking IR sensors and two backward-looking ones. Each returns a value between 0 (nothing sensed) and 1023 (object very close), but disturbed by significant noise. The robot has two wheels controlled by stepped motors, each wheel can be commanded to go forward or backward, by an integer amount in the range 0 to 10. The robot's world is bounded and contains user-configurable internal obstacles. We used just the default world for this experiment and the robot actions were limited to moving forward at speed 4 (ie both motors), or turning left or right by 45 or by 90 degrees – that is, five possible actions.

In order to perform a proof-of-concept demonstration, a set of 32 *hand-crafted* RLAs were produced, using the representation described below. It should be emphasised however that in the final system all RLAs should be generated automatically by the system – methods for achieving this are currently under investigation. The concentrations of each antibody were initially all set to a value of 0.1, and initially, there were no links in the network (that is, all link weights were 0).

As previously mentioned, antigens should capture the essence of the current sensory experience of the robot. In this initial model, an antigen consists of a binary string representing 2 types of sensory information; the first captures the current sensory data, the second attempts to maintain some record of the recent history of the robots experience. In both cases, rather than deal only with raw sensory data, we describe the sensory information in a binary string of total length 24 bits. The first 8 bits represent thresholded sensor values from each of the robots eight sensors (1=over the threshold, 0=under the threshold). A moving average of each sensor value is also maintained over 5 timesteps, and each of these values is converted into a 2-bit value (00=0-255, 01=256-511, 10=512-767, 11=768-1023) resulting in a further 16 bits.

Antibodies consisted of a binary string with 3 parts. The first 24 bits representing the condition part of the RLA corresponds to the current sensory information, and thus has the same form as the antigens. The 2nd part denotes a motor action, and the final part, the paratope, represents the expectation of the sensory conditions that should prevail following execution of the action, and therefore again consists of 24 bits. In this case however, the bits can contain 'don't care' symbols.

The algorithm described below was run over a period of 100,000 timesteps which took about 9 minutes using the Khepera simulator on a 1GHz PC.

1. Initialise a pool of antibodies with a concentration of 0.1. At this stage, all connections have a strength of 0.0
2. At time t:
   - Present an antigen representing sensory current conditions to the network

  - Apply equation 1 to update the concentration of all antibodies in the network
  - Select the antibody with highest concentration and execute its action - call this antibody x
3. At time $t + 1$:
  - Get the current antigen
  - If the match between the current antigen and the expectation of the previously selected antibody x is greater than some threshold, update the links between x and all antibodies whose condition part matches the expectation of x, by an amount δ_1 proportional to the strength of the match
  - *else* if the expectation was incorrect, decrease the strength of all links emanating from x by an amount δ_2.
4. Goto step (1)

The matching algorithm is simple; it does a bit-by-bit comparison and accumulates a 'match score'. A bit-comparison involing a 'don't care' scores $+1$; if there is no 'don't care', then equality is worth $+2$ and inequality is worth -2. Thus the score can range between -48 and $+48$, and the threshold we use is 80% of maximum. In this experiment, we chose $\delta_1 = \delta_2 = 0.01$ but this clearly influences stability and speed of adaptability, and needs further experiment.

4.1   Results

After running the algorithm for an initial learning phase of 100000 iterations, the RLAs chosen by the algorithm were recorded. A flow diagram showing the sequences of surviving RLAs is shown in figure 2. Note that this is not the immune network topology, but is instead used to illustrate how the different sensory experiences are captured when using the immune network approach. As an example, the RLA sequence 0, 1, 5, 6, 8, 0 captures the sequence of events that occur when the robot meets an obstacle head-on and turns to avoid it. This sequence could be interpreted as: 'sensing clear space, go forward, obstacle looming in front, go forward, obstacle ahead, turn right, obstacle to the left, turn right, obstacle more to the left, turn right, sensing clear space, go forward' and so on.

The remaining RLAs appear to capture some episodes (sequences of sensory events) in a reasonably stable manner, thus the robot could be said to have a long-term memory that maintains a record of the relationships between sensory situations, actions performed and the effects of those actions.

5   Conclusion

In this paper we have proposed a robot control architecture based on an AIS that should be capable of capturing at least some aspects of 'growing up' through experience. An initial experiment showed that it seemed to be capable of capturing some episodes of experience. However, a lot more remains to be done and

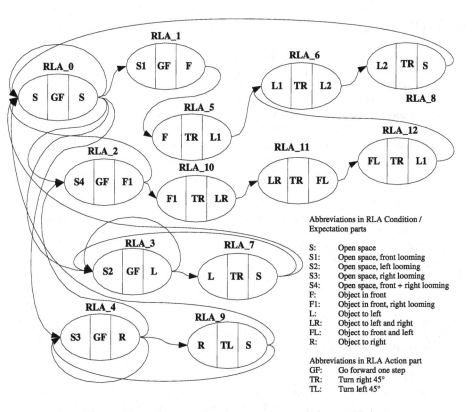

Fig. 2. Flow diagram showing sequences of chosen RLAs

in particular we have not yet done any experimental investigation of the idea of changing the data universe dynamically, nor have we done much exploration of the sensitivity of the system to the many choices involved. Clearly, much work also needs to be performed in investigating the scalability of the system. Furthermore, it is well known in robotics research that simulated systems rarely transfer seamlessly to the real-world, therefore we fully intend to transfer this architecture to a real-robot (see [6]).

However, we do believe that what we have sketched out represents a very fruitful line of work, both in terms of studying robot development and in terms of studying AISs. Too much research in AISs still relies on overly-simplistic metaphors. We claim that the problems of robot development provide an excellent context for studying AIS issues such as sophisticated matching algorithms, the dynamics of network models, the problems of handling a continually-evolving representation and even the computational tractability of AISs.

Acknowledgements

This work is supported by the European Union funded IST programme, grant no. IST-2000-29225.

References

1. Anonymous for reviewing purposes. Requirements for getting a robot to grow-up. In *Proceedings of the European Conference on Artificial Life, ECAL 2003*, 2003.
2. G. Drescher. *Made-Up Minds: A Constructivist Approach to Artificial Intelligence.* MIT Press, 1991.
3. J.D Farmer, H Packard N, and A.H Perelson. The immune system, adaption and machine learning. *Physica D*, 22:187–204, 1986.
4. A. Ishiguro, T. Kondo, Y. Watanabe, Y. Shirai, and H. Uchikawa. Immunoid: a robot with a decentralized consensus-making mechanism based on the immune system. In *Proceedings of ICMAS Workshop on Immunity-based Systems*, pages 82–92, 1996.
5. A. Ishiguro, S. Kuboshiki, S. Ichikawa, and Y. Uchikawa. Gait-control of hexapod walking robots using mutual coupled immune networks. *Advanced Robotics*, 10(2):179–196, 1996.
6. IST-2000-29225. Systemic intelligence for growing up artefacts that live. http://www.ist-signal.org.
7. N.K Jerne. The immune system. *Scientific American*, 229(1):52:60, 1973.
8. Pier Luca Lanzi. An analysis of the memory mechanism of XCSM. In *Genetic Programming 1998: Proceedings of the Third Annual Confere nce*, pages 643–65. Morgan Kaufman, 1998.
9. D. Lee, H. Jun, and K. Sim. Artifical immune system for realisation of cooperative strategies and group behaviour in collective autonomous mobile robots. In *Proceedings of Fourth Internation Symposium on Artifical Life and Robotics*, pages 232–235, 1999.
10. R. Michelan and F.J. von Zuben. Decentralized control system for autonomous navigation based on an evolved artificial immune system. In C.L. Giles et al, editor, *Proceedings of CEC-02*, pages 1021–1026. IEEE Press, 2002.
11. J. Piaget. *The Origins of Intelligence in Children.* Norton, N.Y., 1952.
12. E. Prem and P. Poelz. Concept acquistion using isomap on sensorimotor experiences of a mobile robot. In *Proceedings of International Workshop on Epigenetic Robotics*, Boston, August 2003. to appear.
13. Surya Singh and Scott Thayer. Immunology directed methods for distributed robotics: A novel, immunity-based architecture for robust control and coordination. In *Proceedings of SPIE: Mobile Robots XVI*, volume 4573, November 2001.
14. Surya Singh and Scott Thayer. A foundation for kilorobotic exploration. In *Proceedings of the Congress on Evolutionary Computation at the 2002 IEEE World Congress on Computational Intelligence*, May 2002.
15. Surya Singh and Scott Thayer. Kilorobot search and rescue using an immunologically inspired approach. In *Distributed Autonomous Robotic Systems*, volume 5. Springer-Verlag, June 2002.
16. Jon Timmis and Mark Neal. A resource limited artificial immune system for data analysis. *Knowledge Based Systems*, 14(3-4):121–130, June 2001.
17. Y. Watanabe, A. Ishiguro, Y. Shiraio, and Y. Uchikawa. Emergent construction of behaviour arbitration mechanism based on the immune system. *Advanced Robotics*, 12(3):227–242, 1998.
18. A. Webb, E. Hart, P. Ross, and A. Lawson. Controlling a simulated khepera with an xcs classifier system. In *Proceedings of 7th European Conference on A-Life*. Springer-Verlag, 2003. to appear.

Immunologic Control Framework for Automated Material Handling

Henry Y.K. Lau and Vicky W.K. Wong

Department of Industrial and Manufacturing Systems Engineering
The University of Hong Kong
Pokfulam Road, Hong Kong, PRC
hyklau@hku.hk, vickywong@hkusua.hku.hk

Abstract. An Artificial Immune System (AIS) paradigm, which is an engineering analogue to the human immune system, is adopted to deliver the performance and robustness required by a multi-vehicle based delivery system in an automated warehouse. AIS offers a number of profound features and solutions, including the ability to detect changes, coordinate vehicle activities for goals achievement and adapt to new information encountered, to the control of such distributed material handling systems. By adopting some of these mechanisms of AIS adapted to specify and implement the behaviour of warehouse delivery vehicles, an architecture that defines the control framework is developed. This control framework improves the efficiency of a multi-agent system as demonstrated by computer simulations presented.

1 Introduction

The human immune system is a multi-agent distributed system with distributed memory and a mechanism for learning behaviours. It has evolved to be self-organising without the intervention of any central controller. The properties of self-organisation and distribution impart a high degree of robustness that has created great interest in implementing engineering systems based on its properties. This adopted engineering analogue is called Artificial Immune System (AIS).

AIS has been studied widely in the fields of Artificial Intelligence (AI) due to its deep inspiration to the engineering sciences. The essences of human immune system properties are imitated to perform complicated tasks, for example, learning strategies, adaptive control, memory managements and self-organisation. These special properties of the immune system have adopted in solving problem in various engineering disciplines. They include autonomous agents systems [1], distributed intrusion detection system [2], mine detection system [3], fault tolerance systems [4] and artificial intelligent-based systems [5], [6] and [7].

This paper details a control framework that has the ability to manage, coordinate and schedule a fleet of autonomous guided vehicles (AGVs) deployed in an automated warehouse which takes the inspiration from the highly distributed multi-agent based properties found in the immune system. The AGV-based systems deployed in most existing warehouses are based on centralized controlled systems that are integrated with the rest of the material handling system. Certain limitations can be found

J. Timmis et al. (Eds.): ICARIS 2003, LNCS 2787, pp. 57–68, 2003.
© Springer-Verlag Berlin Heidelberg 2003

on such a centralized system, for example, some form of guidance is essential to navigate the vehicles, communication within the system is limited to information transferral via a central controller and tasks for an AGV must be well defined in advance in the system planning stage. Due to these limitations, these AGVs that are used for material handling in a warehouse cannot be regarded as fully autonomous. To achieve fully automated warehousing, a control framework for dispatching material handling tasks, specifying individual AGV behaviours, controlling information exchange between AGVs and accomplishing delivery tasks automatically is necessary.

The control framework presents in this paper addresses how individual AGV with different utilities and capabilities can be exploited through altering their behaviour to achieve goals in a dynamic working environment. Through the studies of the immune system characteristics, AGVs can be thought of as independent agents that carry information, search the solution space and exhibit robust behaviours. Hence, a framework that achieves superior performance in terms of flexibility, scalability, robustness and self-organisation from a multi-agent system implementing a flexible delivery system for a possible warehouse of the future can be developed.

2   An Overview of Human Immune System

The human immune system is a complex functional system consisting of diverse organs, tissues innate cells and acquired cells distributed throughout most of our body. These components are interrelated and acted in a highly coordinated and specific manner when they recognize, eliminate and remember foreign macromolecules and cell [8]. The main mechanism of the immune system is to distinguish self from non-self so as to protect a human body by recognition of, and defence against foreign antigens such as virus and bacteria.

Protection against infection of a human body is classified to innate immunity, inborn and unchanging, and acquired immunity, developed during the lifetime of a person. Innate immunity provides resistance to a variety of antigens during their first exposure to a human body. This general defence mechanism is known as primary immune response which is slower and less protective. In the meantime, the antigen-specific acquired immune system is activated to eliminate the antigen by its element such as antibody and immune cell [9]. Among all the immune cells, lymphocytes are the main antigen killer in the immune system. They have special binding areas, known as receptors, which can structurally determine and react with specific foreign antigens. The two important types of lymphocytes are B-cells and T-cells. B-cells have direct interactions with the antigens during the elimination process. On the other hand, T-cells act as mediators in the control of immune responses by providing specific cells capable of helping or suppressing these responses. When an antigen binds to the immune cell surface receptors, this interaction sensitizes the proliferation and differentiation of the population of immune cells specific for that individual antigen. This is known as Clonal selection. After the elimination of the antigen, some of the immune cells become memory cells for action on the reoccurrence of the same antigen in the future. Due to this immunologic memory, the next time when the individual encounters the same antigen a much faster and stronger immune response is resulted which is known as secondary immune response.

Six major characteristics of the human immune system can be identified from the study of the immunity mechanisms. They are specificity, inducibility, diversity, memory, distinguishing self from non-self and self-regulation [8]. Among these functionalities, the immune system is able to explore a very high dimensional space with efficiency. The distributed memory without the intervention of a central controller is a strong contender for a solution to the distributed warehouse problem. AGVs can be thought of as independent agents that carry information and search the solution space for robust behaviours.

3   Artificial Immune System for Distributed Control

Ongoing research projects that are related to multi-agent systems have established the emerging benefits of AIS. Even though the application of the AIS paradigm to AGVs control in warehousing operation is a relative new field of research, a huge variety of AIS-based distributed multi-agent studies have proven the feasibility and applicability of adopting this biological theory to the proposed control framework.

Meshref and VanLandingham [1] had illustrated a Distributed Autonomous Robotics System (DARS) application based on AIS - the dog and sheep problem. With the use of an immune system approach, a noticeable improvement in solving the problem such as a minimization of total time taken for dogs to herd a sheep is shown. Dasgupta [6] had examined various recognition and response mechanisms of the immune system to develop a generic framework for multi-agent decision support system. The framework enumerated different types of agents with various modes and behaviours that facilitated the interaction and communication between agents. Sathyanath and Sahin [3] had developed a generic Artificial Immune System based Intelligent Multi Agent Model (AISMAM) to solve agent-based applications. The model draws an analogy between the immune system and agent methodologies and aims to apply the immune system principles to the agents so as to perform a global goal in a distributed manner. An Immunology-derived Distributed Autonomous Robotics Architecture (IDARA) was presented by Singh and Thayer [10] for the coordination and control of large scale distributed robot teams in a dynamic environment. This algorithmic architecture was derived from a more general picture of the immune system so that heterogeneous robots with unique talents could be fully exploited. Hunt and Cooke [7] introduced an Adaptive, Distributed Learning System which is based on both the generic mechanisms used to construct antibodies and on the influence of the immune network. The combination of these two special features results in a self-organising and highly distributed learning system. Kim and Bently [11] had reviewed and assessed the analogue between the human immune system and network intrusion detection system. A number of significant features and mechanisms of the human immune system had been identified which established the basis for building an effective network-based intrusion detection system.

4   An Immunologic Control Framework

Building on the findings from these foregoing researches, an immunologic control framework is proposed for the control of multiple AGVs that operate in a modern warehouse. In contrast to most existing material handling systems that are managed by centralized control systems, the control framework proposed is based on a fully distributed schema in organising groups of agents in a dynamic environment. The design of the control framework is based on the human immune system mechanism. The immune system is a special type of multi-agent system where each agent or the immune system element has specific behaviour patterns and functions for a particular antigen. The agents' overall behaviours depend on the environment as well as individual behaviour. These characteristics are adopted by the AGVs that operate in a warehouse, and the overall system is to operate in a fully autonomous manner. An AGV has a specific set of capabilities for determining their fundamental intelligence or talents. Each AGV has the ability to gain additional capabilities through communications among each other or via explorations in the environment. In this paper, focuses are put on the study of individual AGV's behaviours as well as the overall system behaviour of a group of AGVs in achieving typical material handling goals under the proposed control framework.

One of the major advances of the proposed control framework over a traditional AGV control system for material handling is the adoption of a behavioural-based, distributed network for controlling AGVs. In fact the operation of individual AGV need not be predefined in the planning stage but can be altered dynamically to adapt corresponding working environment. This consideration allows an AGV to respond quickly to the changing environment with appropriate responses by adjusting its internal capabilities. In order to develop a control framework to such a dynamic distributed system, mechanisms of the immune network, which is also a highly distributed multi-agent system, are imitated. The proposed framework inherits the following characteristics and capabilities that are offered by a human immune system when carrying out control actions for multiple AGVs:

- Self-organisation: AGVs independently determine responses to solve a task. Through the autonomous decision-making and communication capabilities, the non-deterministic and distributed system is developed with a fully decentralized control.
- Adaptability: Each AGV contains a list of capabilities that can be modified over time. By manipulating the capability list, AGVs are able to achieve various goals. AGVs adjust their behaviours when tackling a problem with the best response in the shortest time. New knowledge and functionality can be added to the list of capabilities in coping with the variations on tasks and environment.
- Robustness: Failure of any AGV to execute an operation will not cripple the overall system. The control framework is designed to be fully decentralized and flexible. No full dependency is fixed between a task and an AGV.
- Specificity: The specific response allows AGVs to tackle specific problem by manipulation of their own capability lists.
- Diversity: AGVs contains different kinds of capabilities to deal with various problems.

4.1 The Control Framework

In the human immune system, two major classes of immune cells or lymphocytes are found, namely, the B-cells and T-cells. They circulate throughout our body to protect us against invasions from foreign antigens. Taking this property from the immune system, the proposed control framework defines a set of AGVs as a swamp of immune cells where Master AGVs and Slave AGVs correspond to the T-cell and B-cell respectively. The allocated tasks in a warehouse are regarded as antigens. Both the AGVs and tasks have different characteristics. Each AGV has a list of default capabilities that defines its ability to deal with different sets of work. On the other hand, every task is specified by a complexity function that describes the requirements necessary for an AGV to complete the job.

The overall architecture of the control framework is presented in Figure 1. The control framework provides a set of rules that guides and determines the behaviour of individual AGV in respond to the changing environment. By following these rules, an AGV is able to determine their internal behaviour in relation to surrounding environment. This property of self-organisation makes the control framework both adaptable and robust. Through manipulations of the rules, the unknown events and dynamic variations in the workplace can be investigated effectively.

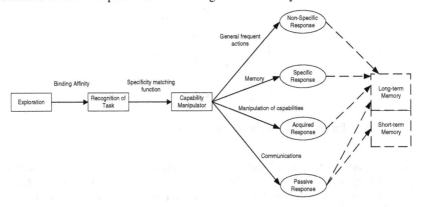

Fig. 1. The architecture of the control framework for individual AGV

4.2 Capabilities and Behaviours of AGVs

The basic actions an AGV performs are sensing the environment and communicating with each other. These abilities are quantified by the sensory circle and communication circle parameters. An AGV is able to detect its surrounding environment within the range specified by the sensory circle. Each AGV is also capable of exchange information with one another that are in close proximity defined by the communication circle. These are the two basic parameters common to all the AGVs. The behaviours specify in a capability list determines the intelligence of an AGV in tackling tasks. The set of behaviours may differ from different AGVs and change from time to time.

In the proposed framework, the Master AGVs assume a more powerful set of capabilities than the Slave AGVs. This follows the concept of humoral immunity and cell-mediated immunity of the immune system. In humoral immunity, the B-cells, being the key players, produce antibodies to bind and eliminate the foreign invaders. When an antigen is unreachable by antibodies, the T-cells who react specifically are then activated to destroy the antigen. This response to antigens constitutes the cell-mediated immunity. Following this mechanism, the Slave AGVs that have sets of capabilities that are general to problem solving at the initial stage whereas Master AGVs have more advanced capabilities for tackling more specific tasks. The Slave AGVs in this respect are responsible for tackling all the tasks in a non-specific manner similar to the primary response of the immune system. Capabilities increase as the Slave AGVs and the Master AGVs go through more explorations of the environment and operations on the task to give a more rapid and effective secondary response when a similar task is reencountered. Here, capabilities are categorized into four main groups and they are responsible for generating different responses to tackle different tasks. An example of the capability set in relation to the context of material handling is given in Figure 2.

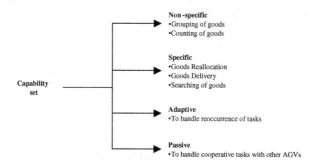

Fig. 2. Entries to a capability list for material handling operations

As aforementioned, the general capabilities of Slave AGVs are defined at the initial stage and they may improve their knowledge through communication with the Master AGVs. The permission to knowledge transfer is determined entirely by the Master AGVs. They may pass information as a form of short-term memory for immediate problem solving or a form of long-term memory handling tasks that reoccur. A memory function is used to determine if the new capabilities are required for a Slave AGV.

Besides capabilities, different behavioural states have been identified to describe the strategies of AGVs. The AGVs decide their behaviours by perception of the environment. In different stages of an operation cycle, AGVs switch from one state to another state. This also signals an AGV's strategy towards a particular task to other AGVs. Figures 3 and 4 show the state transition diagrams defining the changes of behaviours of an AGV when tackling a task with and without the help of other AGVs respectively. The two state transition diagrams provide a formal means to express the semantics about their behavioural sets [12]. The allowable behavioural states are defined as follows:

- Explore: explore environment and search for tasks randomly.
- Agitate: a task has been found and approach the targeted task.
- Acquire: tackle the task.
- Idle: wait for help after a request has been sent.

Master AGVs in general have a higher priority in handling tasks to environment explorations than Slave AGVs. Similar to the human immune system, both the T-cells and B-cells have the ability to activate each other for assistance in antigens eliminations; the Master and Slave AGVs of our control framework can also request help from each other. Priorities in task tackling are given to Master AGVs when a request has been signalled by both of them. This means that Master AGVs can request help and activate Slave AGVs who are in the Explore state and Agitate state within their communication circle. On the contrary, Slave AGVs can only send request signals and are not able to activate any Master AGVs for help. Slave AGVs who required help from others need to wait if there are no Master AGVs are available in the Explore state in their proximity.

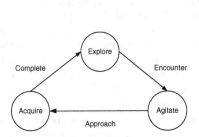

Fig. 3. Task tackling without help

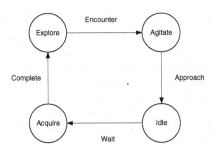

Fig. 4. Task tackling with help

4.3   Operational Scheme of the Control Framework

In our control framework, AGVs are regarded as the self where tasks are regarded as non-self. The AGVs start the operation cycle by exploring the environment by undergoing pseudo-random motions. Such exploration actually allows the AGVs to identify non-self and thus approach tasks. This mechanism for distinguishing between self and non-self is the prime function of the immune system. B-cells and T-cells recognize and respond to antigens by their receptors. The sensing ability of the AGVs is equivalent to the immunity cell's receptor. Instead of pattern-recognizing antigens, AGVs use binding affinity to recognize and approach tasks. The binding affinity is quantified by the distance between an AGV and a specific task, AGV familiarity with task and frequency of task occurrences. These factors for attracting AGVs are mainly driven by the equivalent first instinct towards the non-self. Once a task is detected by an AGV, binding affinity is calculated without any consideration of their capabilities. Hence, a specificity matching function is employed to check on the AGVs capabilities in handling the targeted task.

To determine whether an AGV is capable of tackling a specific task, the specificity matching function is used to match between AGV's capabilities along with the task requirements. This function generates or highlights the capabilities of the AGVs in relation to the complexity function of the tasks. Comparisons are made on these two parameters in order to examine how well AGVs can handle and solve a problem. The results of this comparison are eventually used to generate grading for each of the four responses specified in the capability list.

Through the proposed control framework architecture as illustrated in Figure 1, four types of responses are generated through the capability manipulator. Non-specific response uses binary match to determine whether an antigen is a general task that should offer a quick and reactive response. Same as acquired response, binary match is used to check whether the antigen has been encountered before. For a specific response, a manipulation function is required to verify necessary capabilities in relation to that particular task in order to grade on the success of the specific response. A passive response is an action in responds to other AGVs requests where the activated AGV is assumed to have no suitable capability towards the requested job. This cooperative work depends entirely on information transferred from the initiating AGVs.

Different kinds of knowledge are generated or acquired by AGVs from the four types of responses described above. Basic knowledge that generates frequent and nonspecific responses is located in long-term memory. New knowledge acquired or transferred to the AGV will either go to short-term or long-term memory. Knowledge put in long-term memory is added to the acquired response for the next occurrence of the same problem. This mechanism is equivalent to the secondary response of the immune system. Information or knowledge that passed to an AGV for immediate problem solving during cooperation is put in short-term memory. Immunologic memory is a consequence of Clonal selection where immune cells proliferate and differentiate into memory cell for a more rapid and intense secondary response. For the proposed control framework, memory is proliferated by communications among AGVs. Knowledge and capabilities are spread throughout the whole system when AGVs cooperate and communicate with each other. Hence, a robust and adaptive multi-agent system is resulted. A summary of the analogies between the proposed control framework and immune system is tabulated in Table 1.

Table 1. Relationships between the proposed control framework and the immune system

HUMAN IMMUNE SYSTEM	AGVS CONTROL FRAMEWORK
B-cell	Slave AGV
T-cell	Master AGV
Receptor of immune cell	Sensors of AGV
Primary response	Non-specific response
Secondary response	Acquired response
Specific response	Specific response
Vaccination	Passive response
Immunologic memory	Long-term and short-term memory

5 Simulation Study

The feasibility and performance of the control framework is demonstrated via a simulation study involving material handling operations by a fleet of AGVs. The goal of the AGVs is to search and handle parcels located over the workplace (Figure 5). In particular, a special constraint is put to the material handling task such that a group of four AGVs are required to deal with one parcel so as to highlight the cooperative feature of the control framework. A 50x50 unit square workspace is used in the simulation study. We adopt two initial configurations of the AGV depot, one where all AGVs are initially placed at a single depot located at the centre of the workspace

(Centre Depot), and the other configuration where equal numbers of AGVs are separately located at four depots located along the edge of the workspace (Edge Depots). Each AGV has a sensory circle of radius equal to 6 units and a communication circle of radius equal to 5 units. AGVs are allowed to move freely within the workspace and transfer information concerning only the parcel locations to other AGVs. The received information is stored in the AGVs' local memory.

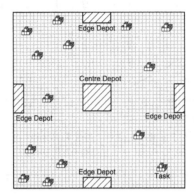

Fig. 5. Layout of the simulation workplace

To evaluate the performance of a fully distributed AGV system based on our proposed control framework, two cases, one based on a centralized control scheme and the other using the AIS-based control as proposed are studied. For the Centralized Control case, AGVs are grouped under the command of some leaders. Each group has a group leader to coordinate its members. The members follow the commands of their group leader and approach the specific tasks that their leader has targeted. This grouping behaviour of the Centralized Control system follows the global planning strategy of modular robot as suggested by [13] and [14]. The other case uses the AIS-based Control framework representing a fully distributed system. Each AGV has their autonomy in searching parcels and handling tasks. No leaders are imposed. AGVs are coordinated via simple information communication and they cooperate to achieve goals by altering their behaviours to adapt the changing environment.

5.1   Simulation Results

In both cases, an increasing number of AGVs is deployed. Figures 6 and 7 show the results of comparing a centralized and AIS-based control framework. The figures show the time taken for the system to delivery all the pre-defined parcels in the workspace with a centrally located and edge located depots. In these figures, the dotted lines represent the results of the Centralized Control and the solid line represents the results of the AIS-based Control. A considerable reduction of the number of time steps that is taken by each AGV to achieve a task is obtained as the number of AGVs increases in the AIS-based Control for both configurations of the depots. On the other hand, there is not much improvement as the number of AGVs increases for the Centralized Control. In this respect, the proposed framework shows a significant enhancement in time required to complete tasks. In the context of this study, an improvement of about 80% in efficiency is achieved in the AIS-based Control as compared to the Centralized Control. This proves the effectiveness of the control framework in coordinating and operating a multi-agent delivery system.

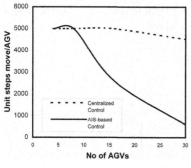 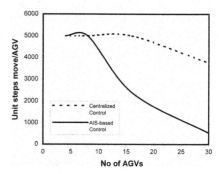

Fig. 6. Results of AGVs located at the centre depot initially

Fig. 7. Results of AGVs located at the edges depots initially

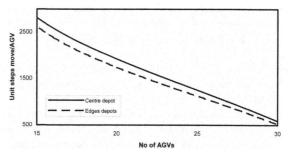

Fig. 8. Results of AGVs located at the centre depot vs. the edge depots of AIS-based Control

Figure 8 further compares the results of the AIS-based Control with different depot configurations. The solid line in this case represents a system where the AGVs are being located at a single centre depot whereas the dotted line represents a system where the AGVs are located at four edges depots. According to this comparison, the AIS-based Control system shows a rather similar trend in the number of steps taken by AGVs. Only a slight improvement in performance is obtained for AGVs located at the edges depots was observed. As the performance in terms of efficiency and flexibility of the proposed control framework is primarily based on the autonomy and adaptability of its AGVs, other physical factors, such as the initial location of AGVs, are not significant in affecting the system overall performance.

5.2 Discussion

The significant decrease in time steps as demonstrated by the AIS-based Control compared to Centralized Control as the number of AGVs deployed is increased is mainly due to the non-deterministic and fully decentralized organisation of AGVs. The AGVs under the control of the AIS-based Control are able to determine responses independently without the presence of any central controller. AGVs have autonomy in decision-making and communicating with each other. Unlike the AIS-based Control, AGVs of the Centralized Control required coordination by each group leader in order to complete a task. This dependency on group leaders, in communication and decision-making, degrades the efficiency and performance of the Centralized Control considerably. When only a few numbers of AGVs are participated in the system, more time is needed for them to search and handle all the tasks. As the number of AGVs is increased, the amount of communications required through the leaders significantly increased and this consumed most of the time for completing a task. Hence, the number of time steps required to complete all the jobs in the workplace for such a Centralized Control is almost the same, as shown in Figures 6 and 7, which is almost independent to the number of AGVs involved in the system.

6 Conclusion

This paper presents a control framework based on the immune system to deploy fleets of AGVs for material handling in an automated warehouse. The control framework allows AGVs to be self-organised in determining their own internal behaviours. AGVs are thought of as independent agents with basic intelligence that explore their workspace to achieve goals. The fully distributed control framework enhances the robustness of the overall system where individual AGV adapts and accommodates the dynamics working environment. Such responses that are exhibited by the AGVs are similar to the non-specific and specific responses of the human immune system. The AGVs that are controlled by the proposed framework have the ability to memorized tasks that have occurred before so as to carry out a more efficient and rapid secondary response. This task-memory capability also permits AGVs to propagate information to others. The effectiveness of proposed control framework is demonstrated by simulation studies that are described in Section 5.

The current focus of the control framework is on individual AGV behaviours. By having self-organisation, an adaptive and distributed system is obtained which is robust and flexible in tackling task that may even be unstructured. In addition to behaviour definition for AGVs for goal achievement, the framework defines the mechanism for communications between AGVs. The current focus of our research is to enhance the efficiency of the framework through the development of a formal model of inter-AGV communication by taking reference from the Clonal selection mechanism.

References

1. Meshref, H. and VanLandingham, H.: Artificial Immune Systems: Application to Autonomous Agents. Systems, Man, and Cybernetics, 2000 IEEE International Conference, Vol. 1 (2000) 61-66.
2. Gopalakrishna, R. and Spafford, E.: A Framework for Distributed Intrusion Detection using Interest Driven Cooperating Agents. Fourth International Symposium on Recent Advances in Intrusion Detection, RAID 2001, (October 2001).
3. Sathyanath, S. and Sahin, F.: AISIMAM – An Artificial Immune System Based Intelligent Multi Agent Model and its Application to a Mine Detection Problem. ICARIS, Session I (2002) 22-31.

4. Bradley, D. W. and Tyrrell, A. M.: Immunotronics – novel finite state machine architecture with built-in self-test using self-nonself differentiation. IEEE Tran. Evolutionary Computation, Vol. 6(3) (2002) 227-238.
5. Tarakanov, A. and Skormin, V. A.: Pattern recognition by immunocomputing. Proc. Congress Evolutionary Computation, CEC'02, Vol. 1 (2002) 938-943.
6. Dasgupta, D.: An Artificial Immune System as a Multi-Agent Decision Support System. IEEE International Conference On Systems, Man, and Cybernetics, San Diego (1998).
7. Hunt, J. E. and Cooke, D. E.: An Adaptive, Distributed Learning System based on the Immune System. Proc. Of the IEEE International Conference on Systems Man and Cybernetics, (1995) 2494-2499.
8. Elgert, K. D.: Immunology: understanding the immune system. New York: Wiley-Liss (1996).
9. Sheehan, C.: Clinical immunology: principles and laboratory diagnosis. 2nd edn. Philadelphia : Lippincott (1997).
10. Singh, S. and Thayer, S.: Immunology Directed Methods for Distributed Robotics: A Novel, Immunity-Based Architecture for Robust Control & Coordination. Proceedings of SPIE: Mobile Robots XVI, Vol. 4573 (November 2001).
11. Kim, J. and Bentley, P.: The Human Immune System and Network Intrusion Detection. 7th European Conference on Intelligent Techniques and Soft Computing (EUFIT '99), Aachen, Germany, (1999).
12. Arkin, R. C. and MacKenzie, D.: Temporal Coordination of Perceptual Algorithms for Mobile Robot Navigation. IEEE Transactions on Robotics and Automation, Vol. 10(3) (Jun 1994) 276-286.
13. Yoshida, E., Murata, S., Kamimura, A., Tomita, K., Kurokawa, H. and Kokaji, S.: Reconfiguration Planning for a Self-assembling Modular Robot. Proceedings of the 4th IEEE International Symposium on Assembly and Task Planning (2001) 276 –281.
14. Kamimura, A., Murata, S., Yoshida, E., Kurokawa, H., Tomita, K. and Kokaji, S.: Self-reconfigurable modular robot - experiments on reconfiguration and locomotion. Proceedings of 2001 IEEE/RSJ International Conference on Intelligent Robots and Systems Vol. 1 (2001) 606-612.

An Immune Learning Classifier Network for Autonomous Navigation

Patrícia A. Vargas, Leandro N. de Castro,
Roberto Michelan, and Fernando J. Von Zuben

Department of Computer Engineering and Industrial Automation (DCA)
State University of Campinas (Unicamp)
Campinas, São Paulo, Brazil C. P. 6101, 13083-970
{pvargas,lnunes,rmichela,vonzuben}@dca.fee.unicamp.br

Abstract. This paper proposes a non-parametric hybrid system for autonomous navigation combining the strengths of learning classifier systems, evolutionary algorithms, and an immune network model. The system proposed is basically an immune network of classifiers, named CLARINET. CLARINET has three degrees of freedom: the attributes that define the network cells (classifiers) are dynamically adjusted to a changing environment; the network connections are evolved using an evolutionary algorithm; and the concentration of network nodes is varied following a continuous dynamic model of an immune network. CLARINET is described in detail, and the resultant hybrid system demonstrated effectiveness and robustness in the experiments performed, involving the computational simulation of robotic autonomous navigation.

1 Introduction

Watanabe et al. [12] investigated an autonomous control system for a mobile robot based on the immune network theory. In their original proposal, the antibodies and the connections are either arbitrarily defined or provided by a constructive approach based on local decision-making, as if the range of complex global behaviours to be expressed by the immune network could usually be designed in a step-by-step manner. In autonomous navigation, the emergence of a global co-ordination of elementary modules of behaviour can not be adequately synthesised by means of a constructive approach [11]. Therefore, important questions arise here: How to automatically determine the antibodies to be used in the network? And how they are going to be connected?

Michelan and Von Zuben [10] proposed an evolutionary mechanism for solving one of these problems; that of determining an appropriate network structure. However, their proposal still lacks a mechanism for automatically determining the antecedent and consequent parts of the condition-action rules, represented as antibodies in the immune network and directly associated with elementary modules of behaviour.

This work proposes an immune learning classifier network, named CLARINET, to simultaneously determine the antibodies and the network structure used to control the autonomous robot. CLARINET is based upon the hybridisation of three computational intelligence techniques: a standard learning classifier system (LCS), as intro-

J. Timmis et al. (Eds.): ICARIS 2003, LNCS 2787, pp. 69–80, 2003.

duced by Holland [6], an immune network model [2], and an evolutionary algorithm to evolve the network structure, as proposed by Michelan and Von Zuben [10].

The literature associated with LCS is full of initiatives to implement control devices for autonomous navigation [3]. Due to the multitude of tasks and restrictions associated with the navigation problem, the hybrid solution provided by CLARINET is capable of incorporating the advantages of both approaches; that is, the learning ability of learning classifier systems, and the pattern recognition, network structure and adaptation capabilities of artificial immune networks.

This work is organised as follows. Sections 2 and 3 provide a brief theoretical background about the learning classifier system and the immune network model to be considered. Section 4 describes the CLARINET in detail, and Sections 5 and 6 present the case study and some preliminary simulation results. Section 7 provides a general discussion about the proposed hybrid system, its outcomes and possible extensions.

2   Learning Classifier Systems

The *learning classifier systems* (LCS) were introduced by J. Holland in the mid 1970s [6]. Basically, they refer to methods and principles for creating and updating rules, named *classifiers,* which encode potential actions to be taken by an agent under specific environmental conditions [1]. There have been a number of variants to the standard (original) LCS introduced by Holland. This section provides a brief description of the standard learning classifier system to be used in this work.

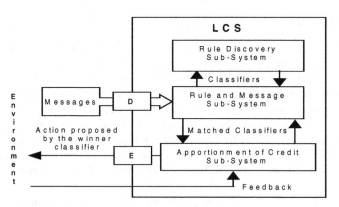

Fig. 1. Simplified flow of the interaction of a learning classifier system with the environment. D: detectors; E: effectors.

The learning classifier system communicates with the environment through its message detectors. These detectors are responsible for the reception and proper encoding of the messages received by the system. The system acts on the environment through its effectors, which decode the actions proposed by the system. The appropriate reward applied to the active classifier is determined by the nature of the outcome of each action, that is, the feedback from the environment. Fig. 1 summarises the interaction of a LCS with the environment, depicting the main component parts of a learning classifier system.

A classifier is composed of an antecedent and a consequent part, similarly to a rule with a condition and an action part. Associated with each classifier there is a value named strength used to express the energy of the classifier during the adaptive process. It is the matching of the antecedent part of the classifier with the messages received from the environment that defines which classifiers will compete to act on the environment. This competition is based on the strength of the selected classifiers.

The process of interaction between the LCS and the environment continues for one epoch of iteration, defined as a sequence of actions adopted by the learning classifier system between two consecutive executions of the adaptive phase. At the end of each epoch, the learning classifier system takes part in an adaptive phase. At this stage, some evolutionary operators, such as crossover and mutation, are applied to produce the next generation of classifiers. Basically, a genetic algorithm is used to evolve the set of classifiers, taking the strengths as the fitness value. The generated offspring classifiers are introduced into the population at the next generation, replacing the weakest individuals (the ones with the lowest strength).

The learning classifier system previously described corresponds to the standard framework proposed by Holland [6], which has been adopted in this work. However, there have been a number of variants to the standard LCS (see [8] and [9] for further details).

3 A Model Derived from the Immune Network Theory

Basically, the immune network theory suggests that the immune system is composed of sets of cells and molecules dynamically connected with each other through molecular structures.

In the immune network theory, originally proposed by N. Jerne [7], antibodies are capable of recognising not only antigens, but also other antibodies. This way, antibodies were assumed to have molecular patterns on their surfaces, named *idiotopes*, which play the role of antigens and could thus be recognised by other antibodies.

Another important concept is the network *metadynamics*, which corresponds to the insertion of new cells and molecules into the network, and death followed by removal of not stimulated cells from the network. The network metadynamics models an inherent tendency of the immune system, also expressed by other mechanisms in living organisms, to be always producing new components (e.g., cells and molecules) and removing useless ones from the organism.

To determine if one of the generated cells is going to be allowed to enter the network, it is necessary to determine the sensitivity (stimulation and suppression) level of each new cell with relation to the cells already in the network. Several immune network models were devised to account for how the cells and molecules of the immune system vary their concentration level and molecular structure; processes known as the network *dynamics*.

These models usually assume an attribute string to represent the cells and molecules of the network, and use ordinary differential equations (ODEs), difference equations or iterative procedures of adaptation to control the network dynamics and metadynamics. The model adopted in this paper to govern the network behaviour is a variation of the one proposed by Farmer et al. [4].

In this model, the immune cells and molecules (antibodies) are represented by binary attribute strings of fixed length. Only B-cells and antibodies are modelled, and as each B-cell has a single type of antibody on its surface, no distinction is made between a network cell and its antibody. Equation (1) is used to control the dynamics of the network model used in this paper. Based on this equation, the concentration a_i of each antibody is determined by considering the similarity of each antibody with the current antigen, the connections among antibodies (that can be stimulatory or suppressive), and the natural death of antibodies.

$$\frac{da_i(t+1)}{dt} = \left(\sum_{j=1}^{N} m_{ji} a_j(t) - \sum_{k=1}^{N} m_{ik} a_k(t) + m_i - k_i \right) a_i(t) \tag{1}$$

$$a_i(t+1) = \frac{1}{1+\exp(0.5 - a_i(t+1))} \tag{2}$$

where N is the number of antibodies that compose the network; m_i is the affinity between the antibody i and a given antigen; m_{ji} represents the stimulatory effect of antibody j into antibody i; m_{ik} represents the suppressive effect of antibody k into antibody i and k_i is the natural death rate of antibody i.

Equation (2) is a squashing function used to impose boundaries on the concentration level of each antibody.

4   An Immune Learning Classifier Network: CLARINET

Learning classifier systems have for long been demonstrated to be capable of generating appropriate rules for an agent in a complex environment. However, the number of rules is not usually automatically determined by the system (see [8] and [9] for some classifier systems with dynamical rule sets), and neither is the degree of interdependence between these rules. On the other side, some immune network models employ cells and molecules with pre-defined structures and adjust mainly the network connections (architecture) and their concentration level. The CLARINET to be introduced in this section combines many of the interesting features of both approaches.

In CLARINET, the network cells correspond to the classifiers of a learning classifier system, as illustrated in Fig. 2.

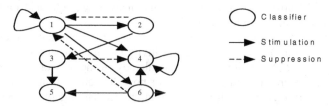

Fig. 2. Example of a network of classifiers. (For clarity, not all-possible connections are illustrated.)

The learning classifier system adaptation procedure allows the network cells (classifiers) to automatically adjust their structures to the environmental stimulation. The immune network approach to the LCS, in turn, allows classifiers to directly communicate with each other. The dynamics of the immune network will allow successful classifiers (those that were selected to post their messages) to have their concentration levels varied; a process that identifies those classifiers that are being useful for dealing with the current environment situation. CLARINET will be described focusing on its two most important features: 1) the classifiers (basic components); and 2) how they adapt to the environment (network dynamics and metadynamics).

4.1 Basic Components

The cells that compose CLARINET have two parts: a paratope, corresponding to a classifier (antecedent/consequent rule); and an idiotope, that indicates to which other network cells (classifiers) it is connected. Fig. 3 illustrates the structure of a network cell, or classifier, in CLARINET.

The antecedent part of the network cell can be further decomposed into two subparts, a tag and a condition. The tag serves as an identifier, thus identifying classifiers that match only messages with the same tag. The condition part is encoded as a string from a ternary alphabet {1,0,#}, and the consequent part has a binary encoding. The connections correspond to which other network classifiers a given classifier is linked with. For instance, assuming that the classifier illustrated in Fig. 3 is classifier 1, from Fig. 2 it is possible to note that it is linked with itself and classifiers 2, 4, and 6.

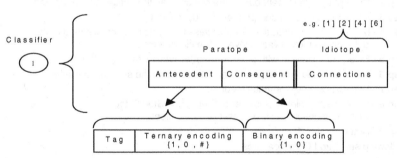

Fig. 3. Structure of the extended classifier that corresponds to a cell in the network of classifiers. Its structure is equivalent to an antibody in the immune network, including its paratope and idiotope. The antecedent portion can be decomposed into two parts: tag and condition. Assuming this classifier corresponds to cell number 1 in Fig. 2, it is thus connected with itself and with classifiers 2, 4 and 6 (see Fig.2).

4.2 Network Dynamics and Metadynamics

The dynamics of CLARINET follows the immune network model described in Section 3, and is a result of the mutual interactions of the classifiers, now taken as the immune cells. In the whole process, there are two kinds of matching. One match occurs between the classifiers and the environmental messages, based on a standard bit to bit comparison. Another match corresponds to the recognition between antibodies and antigens, as described in Section 3. Thus, the network dynamics can be summarised as follows. After the messages are received from the environment, the classifiers that best match the environmental messages provide inputs (that correspond to antigens) to the network of classifiers. These antigens, represented by the antecedent part of the matched classifiers, disturb the network thus causing a variation in the concentration level of a distinct set of classifiers, namely the ones that match (recognise) the antigens (Eqs. (1) and (2), Section 3).

The classifier that will have its action posted on the environment is the one whose activation level is the highest. This is determined by multiplying its strength by its concentration level (Eq. (2)). This is a very important operation performed by CLARINET, because it explicitly accounts for the mutual behaviour of the LCS with the immune network. Both conceptual systems, merged into a hybrid system, co-operate to determine the most suitable action to be posted on the environment.

The basic adaptation procedure of CLARINET is summarised in Fig. 4. Note that the classifier network receives inputs from the environment through its detectors, provides actions and receives feedback from the environment. The network structure allows the reinforcement of the activated classifier, the classifiers that are connected to it via network links, and the so-called antigenic classifier (that will be discussed later). Important differences between CLARINET and each individual system can be observed in the internal message processing of the input stimuli and output messages, and in the apportionment of credit performed (see Fig. 5).

Step 0 –Detect environmental messages.

Step 1 –Choose the classifier that best matches the environmental message(s)* (Fig. 5).

Step 2 –Present the antecedent part of the classifier as the antigen to the network.

Step 3 –Apply Equations (1) and (2) (network dynamics).

Step 4 –Multiply the concentration of each classifier by its respective strength, thus determining the activation level of the classifiers.

Step 5 –Select the classifier with the maximum activation level (see Fig. 5).

Step 6 –Apply the action (consequent part) contained in the selected classifier.

Step 7 –Receive the environmental feedback.

Step 8 –Reinforce the winner classifier of Step 1 and Step 6, together with the classifiers that are connected to it via network connections.

Step 9 –Return to step 1.

* following standard LCS procedures.

Fig. 4. Basic algorithm of the immune learning classifier network (CLARINET).

The internal message processing is performed in two phases. In Phase 1, the standard procedures of a learning classifier system are employed (Section 2). That is, the classifier that best matches the environmental messages is selected and corresponds to an *antigenic classifier*. It is called antigenic because its antecedent part is presented as an input to the network, thus playing the role of an antigen for the immune network (Fig. 5). Not only the messages, but also the classifiers have tags to govern the matching process (Section 4.1).

The main aspect that should be highlighted in Phase 1 is the fact that all the antigens, in the form of environmental messages, are previously processed by the classifiers. Only the "most reactive" antigen is selected to be posted to the immune learning classifier network. Therefore the classifier plays a role of dynamic filtering, giving rise to the antigenic classifier (see Fig. 5).

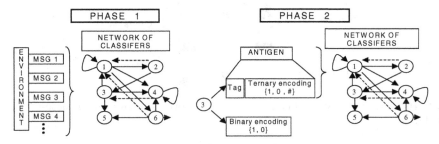

Fig. 5. Example of Phase 1 and Phase 2 of the internal message processing of CLARINET, showing the antigenic classifier (number 3), with its antecedent part (working as an antigen) decomposed into two sub-parts, a tag and a condition. As illustrated in Fig. 3, the condition part is encoded as a string from a ternary alphabet {1, 0, #}, and the consequent part has a binary encoding. Classifier 3 is the antigenic classifier and classifier 4 is the activated classifier. Solid arrows indicate stimulatory connections and dashed arrows are suppressive.

In Phase 2, the activation level of a classifier is determined by multiplying its strength by its concentration level. The concentration level of a classifier is calculated using Equation 1 (Section 3.2). The activated classifier, i.e. the one with the highest activation level, will have its action posted on the environment.

Note that in the example of Fig. 5 (Phase 1 and 2), despite the fact that the antigenic classifier (number 3) was the classifier that best matched the environmental messages, it was not allowed to act on the environment. This happened because the network dynamics determined that classifier 4 should be the activated classifier. However, the same classifier that best matched the environmental message could also be the one selected to act on the environment. This will depend on the connections between the classifiers of the network, thus on their activation level.

The apportionment of credit incorporates a reward or punishment value proportional to the strength of the activated and the antigenic classifier, and to the classifiers that are connected to it via network links (Step 8, Fig. 4). This creates a cascade of reinforcements that is an outcome of the feedback from the environment.

5 Case Study: Robot Autonomous Navigation

The problem studied here was equivalent to the one studied by Watanabe et al. [12] and Michelan and Von Zuben [10], in which a robot has to collect garbage without running out of energy. The robot must also recharge its internal energy at the base before the energy is over (self-sufficiency). The robot and an illustrative environment for the autonomous navigation problem are described in Fig. 6.

The robot receives information from the environment, such as the distance from garbage, by means of a set of sensors. An initial amount of energy is provided to the robot, and one of its sensors is capable of measuring its energy level. As the robot has to be self-sufficient, one aspect to be accounted for is the dynamics of the energy consumption of the robot. This requires a gradual context switching, i.e., the robot needs to gradually shift between its objectives in order to maintain its integrity.

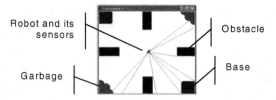

Fig. 6. The robot, its sensors and the environment with two bases, two garbage deposits and four obstacles.

Energy dynamics is the measure of the energy level of the robot, which varies at each iteration. This energy level depends upon four parameters: the energy level at the previous iteration, $E(t-1)$; the energy consumption at each iteration, E_m; the additional energy consumed when the robot carries garbage, E_g; and the energy lost when it collides with any obstacle, E_c. The energy level of the robot at each iteration t, $E(t)$, is given by the following expression:

$$E(t) = E(t-1) - E_m - k_1 E_g - k_2 E_c, \tag{3}$$

where,

$$k_1 = \begin{cases} 1 & \text{if carrying garbage} \\ 0 & \text{otherwise} \end{cases} \quad \text{and} \quad k_2 = \begin{cases} 1 & \text{if the robot collides with wall/garbage} \\ 0 & \text{otherwise} \end{cases}$$

At each time step, the energy level of the robot is reduced by a fixed amount of energy E_m. Constants k_1 and k_2 indicate that this energy level will be reduced only if the robot is currently carrying garbage and/or if it collides with some obstacle.

In the simulations to be presented, the following values are set to the energy parameters: $E_m = 1$, $E_g = 3$ and $E_c = 5$. These values indicate that the robot collision results in energy consumption greater than when it is simply carrying garbage.

5.1 Problem Representation and Modelling

The robot sensors receive the environmental stimuli (including its internal energy level), and transform them into a *message* related to the current *state* of the robot, e.g. *obstacle on the right* and/or *low energy level*. The robot contains a set of *state/action* (or *condition/action*) rules that will be matched against the information received from the sensors in order to decide an appropriate action to take. Fig. 7 illustrates part of the structure adopted by CLARINET for autonomous navigation. The current state of the robot, read from its sensors, corresponds to the environmental messages.

As illustrated in Fig. 5, the antigenic classifier will be used as an antigen to stimulate the network of classifiers. Then, the activated classifier, determined by the product of the classifier concentration by its strength, will be used as a response to the antigen, thus corresponding to the action to be taken. Four different actions were used to compose the action part of the classifiers [12]: F (move forward), R (turn right), L (turn left) and E (explore).

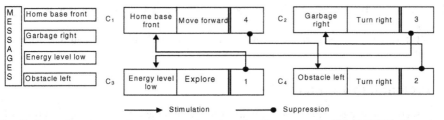

Fig. 7. Example of part of an immune learning classifier network (CLARINET) for robot autonomous navigation.

5.2 Action Selection

The problem of deciding what action to take (or behaviour to adopt) is now the problem of matching the information collected from the antigenic classifier, with the condition parts of the classifiers. This process of choosing an action to be performed is based on the concentration level of each network classifier multiplied by the strength of each network classifier, which will determine the activation level of each classifier.

As proposed in the immune network theory, the idiotope of each antibody is capable of recognising the paratope of another antibody, and vice-versa. These recognition events allow the immune network to select antibodies from the whole antibody repertoire. In the immune system, two parameters influence the selection of a cell to become an effector or a memory cell: 1) its concentration level; and 2) its affinity with an antigen and other cells in the network. As a result of the interaction, every antibody in the network will have its concentration level altered according to the differential equation proposed by Farmer et al. [4] and discussed in Section 3.

5.3 Network Dynamics

After the antigen is presented to the network, all classifiers will undergo a process of stimulation and/or suppression, through its network connections, altering their concentration level in order to specify a single action to be taken by the robot, i.e. a single classifier will have its action performed.

The connections in the network are evolved using a genetic algorithm, similarly to the proposal of Michelan and Von Zuben [10]. The same crossover operators and mutation are applied. However, these operators are applied to each portion of each network cell separately (the antecedent part, the consequent part and the connections). Only network cells (classifiers) with the same tag are allowed to suffer crossover. The crossover operator is applied to 10% of the population, following the standard evolutionary process of the rule discovery sub-system of the LCS: at the end of each epoch of iterations (500 iterations). The mutation rate chosen is 1%.

5.4 Network Evolution

The reinforcement learning mechanism initially starts with all classifiers and network connections (idiotopes) randomly generated. Then it alters the strength of the classifiers using *reinforcement signals*. Two types of reinforcement signals are used: 1) a *reward signal*, and 2) a *penalty signal*.

Reward: robot recharges with low energy level; and robot catches garbage with high energy level.

Penalty: robot catches garbage with low energy level; and robot collides with an obstacle.

6 Preliminary Results

This section presents some preliminary results obtained with the application of CLARINET to the simulation of an autonomous navigation system. A flexible simulation environment was developed and adapted to a garbage-collecting problem to evaluate CLARINET.

In order to assess the overall behaviour of the system, the robot was first navigated in the environment illustrated in Fig. 8(a). This sort of experiment was an attempt to provide a first source of evaluation of CLARINET. Some preliminary tests have been performed, where the robot should reach a steady behaviour. This corresponds to a sequence of actions that guide the robot to a trajectory leading to the accomplishment of the various conflicting objectives (collecting garbage without running out of energy and avoiding collisions with obstacles). As will be noticed from the simulations performed, the shortest trajectory is usually found between the garbage and the base, while a minimal energy level is maintained.

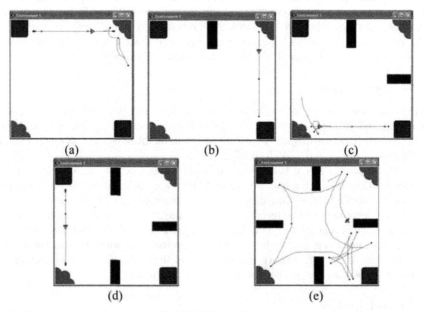

Fig. 8. Performance evaluation of CLARINET. (a) The first environment with no obstacles (only with the walls, bases and garbage). (b) The second environment with one obstacle inserted. (c) Third environment with two obstacles. (d) Fourth environment with three obstacles. (e) Fifth environment with four obstacles.

The experiments presented in Fig. 8 followed a particular protocol. The obstacles were inserted one by one, from time to time, based on the steady behaviour of the robot. That is, after the robot reached a steady behaviour in a given configuration of the environment, we intervened in the environment by inserting a new obstacle, thus creating a new scenario. This procedure was performed until the four obstacles depicted in Fig. 8(e) were inserted. The reasons for this intervention were twofold: 1) to avoid monotony; and 2) to study the behaviour of the robot when a new situation is faced. These forced changes in the environment serve the purpose of assessing the capability of CLARINET to adapt to dynamically changing environment.

In this first experiment, the robot starts its navigation task without any previous knowledge. All the 100 network cells, together with their connections, in the order of 70%, were randomly created (the number of nodes, associated with the population size, is kept unaltered).

Following the protocol described previously, Fig. 8(a) shows the initial environment with no obstacles. The robot found a trajectory that guided it from the garbage to the base and vice-versa, achieving a steady behaviour after 21,200 iterations on average. As expected, this behaviour was achieved after almost fully exploring the environment, and thus after many collisions. The simulated robot needs some time to learn to navigate in the environment without colliding with walls and obstacles, and without running out of energy. Fig. 8(a) depicts the last 250 steps of the robot after learning to properly navigate in the environment.

After this initial learning period, the obstacles were inserted one by one, just after a steady behaviour was achieved by CLARINET. After the inclusion of an obstacle (Fig. 8(b)) the robot automatically found an alternative trajectory to cope with its conflicting objectives. It is interesting to observe that the robot switched the base used for recharging. It chose the easiest (shortest) route from the garbage to the home base. In the third and fourth scenarios, Figs. 8(c) and (d), the robot always chose the more parsimonious solution; it switched the bases for recharging so as to use the shortest route from the garbage to the base. The number of iterations required by the robot to switch to another steady behaviour was 7,000 iterations, on average.

In all the experiments described so far, the robot was able to promptly react to changes in the environment, represented by the insertion of new obstacles from time to time. CLARINET provides the autonomous robot with the necessary ability (plasticity) to cope with new scenarios while managing its conflicting objectives (task accomplishment and energy maintenance). Note in Fig. 8(e) that even when the robot faced the fifth environment with four obstacles it was capable of finding a novel trajectory to cope with the new, and more complex, scenario. Observe that all the behaviours adopted previously had to be discarded, and a new one was generated.

7   Conclusions and Future Trends

This work proposed the use of a hybrid system, named CLARINET, combining the strengths of a learning classifier system (LCS) a continuous immune network model and an evolutionary algorithm. The application of the immune network without the classifier system is restricted to low-complex environments that can be appropriately navigated by a simple and small network easily designed by hand, or constructively [12]. In more complex situations, CLARINET is an appropriate alternative.

Preliminary simulation results indicated that the proposed hybrid system performs well in complex and dynamic environments. However, much research has to be performed to fully validate CLARINET, including the consideration of several other environmental settings and the practical implementation in real robots. Both extensions are under preparation, and conclusive results are due to come in the near future.

It is also interesting to compare CLARINET with the immune network model of Michelan and Von Zuben [10], and with learning classifier systems when applied separately. Nevertheless, even if these individual systems perform as well as CLARINET, they do not have its plasticity. As CLARINET is highly non-parametric, it is much closer to the non-parametric borderline [5] than all the other systems previously developed, though being more computationally intensive.

The activation level of a classifier is determined by the multiplication of its *strength* by its *concentration level*. This measure explicitly accounts for the hybrid behaviour of the learning classifier system with the immune network model. This is a very important operation performed by CLARINET, when considering time-varying conditions for autonomous navigation.

In summary, CLARINET allows classifiers to directly communicate with each other, thus resulting in an emergent behaviour characterised by the cooperation and competition between classifiers in order to define a set of rules and network connections that correspond to an elaborate and diverse internal model of the environment.

Acknowledgments

The authors would like to thank CAPES and CNPq for the financial support.

References

1. Booker, L. B., Goldberg, D. E. & Holland, J. H. (1989). Classifier Systems and Genetic Algorithms. Artificial Intelligence, vol. 40, pp. 235-282.
2. de Castro, L. N. & Timmis, J. I. (2002). Artificial Immune Systems: A New Computational Intelligence Approach, Springer-Verlag: London.
3. Dorigo, M. & Colombetti, M. (1997). Robot Shaping: An Experiment in Behavior Engineering (Intelligent Robotics and Autonomous Agents), MIT Press.
4. Farmer, J. D., Packard, N. H. & Perelson, A. S. (1986). "The Immune System, Adaptation and Machine Learning", Physica 22D, pp. 187-204.
5. Härdle, W. (1990) Applied Nonparametric Regression. Cambridge University Press.
6. Holland, J. H. (1992). Adaptation in Natural and Artificial Systems: an Introductory Analysis with Applications to Biology, Control, and Artificial Intelligence. The MIT Press, Ann Arbor, MI.91.
7. Jerne, N. K. (1974). "Towards a Network Theory of the Immune System", Ann. Immunol. (Int. Pasteur) 125C, pp. 373-389.
8. Lanzi, P. L., Stolzmann, W. & Wilson, S. W., editors (2000). Learning Classifier Systems. From Foundations to Applications, volume 1813 of LNAI. Springer-Verlag, Berlin.
9. Lanzi, P. L., Stolzmann, W. & Wilson, S. W., editors (2001). Advances in Learning Classifier Systems, volume 1996 of LNAI. Springer-Verlag, Berlin.
10. Michelan, R. & Von Zuben, F.J. (2002). Decentralized Control System for Autonomous Navigation based on an Evolved Artificial Immune Network. Proc. of the CEC'2002, vol. 2, pp. 1021-1026.
11. Nolfi, S. & Floreano, D. (2000) Evolutionary Robotics: The Biology, Intelligence, and Technology of Self-Organizing Machines. The MIT Press.
12. Watanabe, Y., Ishiguro, A. & Uchikawa, H. (1999). "Decentralized Behaviour Arbitration Mechanism for Autonomous Mobile Robot Using Immune Network", In D. Dasgupta (Editor), Artificial Immune Systems and their Applications, Springer.

Software Vaccination: An Artificial Immune System Approach to Mutation Testing

Peter May, Keith Mander, and Jon Timmis

Computing Laboratory
University of Kent
Canterbury, Kent, CT2 7NF.
Tel: +44 (0)1227 764000
{psm4,kcm,jt6}@kent.ac.uk

Abstract. Over time programming languages develop, paradigms evolve, development teams change. The effect of this is that test suites wear out, therefore these also need to evolve. Mutation testing is an effective fault-based testing approach, but it is computationally expensive. Any evolutionary based approach to this process needs to simultaneously manage execution costs. In this conceptual paper we adopt immune systems as a metaphor for the basis of an alternative mutation testing system. It is envisaged that through monitoring of the development environment, a minimal set of effective mutations and test cases can be developed - a 'vaccine' - that can be applied to the software development process to protect it from errors - from infections.

1 Introduction

Mutation testing is a powerful but computationally expensive fault-based unit testing method [16,17,20,21]. It aims to iteratively derive a minimal set of test cases in order to deliver confidence in the system under test (SUT). A program can be described as a sequence of lexemes, and by focussing on deriving tests that cause simple mutations (single lexeme changes, for example) of the SUT to produce incorrect outputs, the fault finding capabilities of the tests themselves can be demonstrated. The percentage of these mutations detected producing incorrect outputs, gives an indication to the relative adequacy of the tests. The quality of the test data is related to their error detecting capabilities, which in turn can be used to improve the SUT itself.

Unfortunately, mutation testing has significant problems. Completely automating the mutation testing procedure is a difficult task. At some stage, the correctness of a program's output has to be determined, which is not easily established automatically [20]. Additionally, mutation testing systems are slow; considerable time is required to execute tests on all mutant programs [21]. This is compounded by traditional mutation systems being interpretive. Furthermore, subtle changes in a program's behaviour are also possible because the SUT is not being executed on its intended operational environment [21]. In general, such unit testing techniques are considered in industry, as too expensive to apply with

J. Timmis et al. (Eds.): ICARIS 2003, LNCS 2787, pp. 81–92, 2003.

any conviction [16]. Offutt and Untch [20] postulate three main reasons for industries failure to use mutation testing techniques: no economic incentive to use rigorous testing methodologies; failure to successfully integrate unit testing into the development cycle; and difficulties with automating testing. The focus of this paper is to present a new approach to mutation testing that it is proposed will help overcome these obstacles.

The human immune system is capable of protecting a body by identifying, learning, adapting and defending against invading organisms. Artificial immune systems (AIS) are adaptive systems, inspired from immunology, and applied to problem solving [4]. They utilise models, principles and theories of the human immune system as metaphors to help develop new systems (for example, computer network security [8]). One advantage of the human immune system is that it can be taught to recognise new infections by the use of vaccines. A vaccine allows the body to develop antibodies to quicken the response to an infection by a particular pathogen. A useful analogy can be drawn from this; the SUT is comparable to a body we wish to protect from infections - from faults. A vaccination is required that can protect the software development process from such faults.

In section 2 we provide background information on mutation testing. This is complemented by a new view of mutation testing in section 3. Artificial immune systems are discussed in section 4, followed by the combination of the two disciplines in section 5.

2   Mutation Testing

Mutation testing is a process that is used to improve the quality of test data. A useful side effect to this is that the code under observation is tested. Proposed by DeMillo et. al. [14], it is based on the coupling effect: test data capable of distinguishing programs that differ by a simple error (a single lexeme difference for example) are sensitive to the point that they are implicitly capable of distinguishing more complex errors [14]. Empirical evidence to support this claim has been demonstrated by Offutt et. al. [17]. In relation to this effect, a competent programmer [7] can be viewed as someone who creates programs close to being correct. If a competent programmer creates an incorrect program, the correct version may differ by a small amount, perhaps a single program lexeme. It is these premises that mutation testing takes advantage of.

Initially mutation testing creates mutant programs (*mutants*) by use of mutation operators (*mutagens*). Mutagens alter the semantics of a program by, for example, replacing one logical operator with another. The mutants created by these mutagens differ from the original program by a small amount - a single lexeme for example. The coupling effect implies that if testing can distinguish small errors, it will implicity be able to discern complex errors too. An aim of mutation testing is therefore to find test cases that can detect the small errors found in our mutants. For this reason, mutation testing techniques have also been used to quantify the effectiveness of test data.

The process of mutation testing works in the following way. First, we assume that the outputs obtained from executing the original program with the test data are the desired outputs even if the program itself contains an error. If this assumption is incorrect, then the original program must be corrected before mutation testing can continue. Second, we consider each mutant. If a mutant program is tested and its output differs from those of the original program, then the test data has successfully detected a fault in that mutant. The fault-containing mutant detected is of no value (because it cannot be a correct version of an incorrect original) and is killed. The test case that detected this fault, however, is useful (because it can distinguish correct versions from incorrect versions of the program) and can be kept.

Third, once all the mutants have been tested with the current set of tests, those that remain alive are indistinguishable (in that they produce the same output) from the original program. Some of these mutants may be semantically equivalent to the original because they produce the same output as the original for every possible test case. No test data will distinguish them from the original, and so equivalent mutants must be discounted before proceeding further. This is traditionally done by manually examining the code, although partial solutions to automating this have been described [18].

Once every mutant has been tested, and equivalents discounted, a certain proportion of them will have been killed. Known as the *Mutation Score* (MS), this proportion gives an indication of the quality of the test data used to test the program. A competent programmer can usually detect 50-70% of mutants with the initial test set they give [1]. Increasing this percentage to as near to 100% as possible will increase confidence in our test data. Consequently, as our program passes these tests, we can be increasingly confident that it is correct.

Non-equivalent mutants that are not killed - the so-called "live" mutants - produce the same output as the original program and may correspond to a correct program in the case that the original has an error. These mutants require more thorough test data to distinguish them and show whether they are faulty. This is where the testers' attention can now focus by attempting to devise new test data that will find more faults (to kill more mutants).

Unfortunately, mutation testing suffers from a few problems. In particular, considerable time has to be invested in executing tests on all the mutations in addition to the original program. It has been shown that for simple mutants (mutants with one simple error), the number of mutations possible is of order n^2, where n is the number of lines [6]. Further to this, finding mutations that are likely to represent possible errors also presents problems. Research into this field usually focuses on one of three strategies: *do fewer*, *do smarter* or *do faster* [20].

A "do fewer" approach involves reducing the number of mutations produced and executed without affecting the performance of mutation testing. *N-Selective mutation* [19] is a good example of this. The Mothra [12] mutation system applies 22 mutagens to programs. N-Selective mutation omits the N mutagens that produce the greatest number of mutants. The theory behind this is that a very

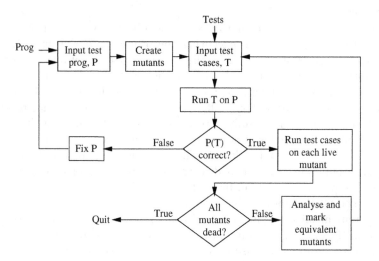

Fig. 1. Outline of the traditional mutation testing procedure. Reprinted from [20]

large proportion of the mutants produced from these prolific mutagens will be detected and killed by test data designed to kill mutations from other less-prolific mutagens. Empirical evidence supporting this assertion is demonstrated in [19].

Weak mutation [9] is a good example of a "do smarter" technique. Systems such as Mothra execute mutants until termination, before comparing the outputs; this is known as *strong mutation*. The alternative to this is to compare the internal states of the mutant and original after the mutated portion of code has been executed. As soon as a difference is detected, the mutant can be killed.

One problem associated with mutation testing is the time needed to execute mutants. Most mutation systems interpret mutant programs [20]. Whilst making it easier to control program execution, such systems are slow, difficult to construct and cannot easily emulate the operational environment. A "do faster" method, such as Mutant Schema Generation (MSG) [21], endeavours to overcome this by encoding all mutants into one program, a *metamutant*. This is compiled once, which improves execution speed and allows the mutants to run in the operational environment.

3   A New View of Mutation Testing

The traditional view of mutation testing (outlined above) uses the mutation score (the percentage of non-equivalent mutants killed by test data) as a measure of the goodness of the test data sets. But high mutation scores can also be obtained if the mutagens produce mutants that are so inappropriate that they would be distinguishable from the original almost irrespective of the test data used. Thus a high mutation score needs to be a function of both the quality of the test data and the appropriateness of the mutagens. As programming languages and paradigms evolve, the appropriateness of the mutagens becomes an increasingly significant issue. Beizer [2] has observed that test suites wear out; test methods do too.

A fundamental assumption of traditional mutation testing is that mutations reflect the typical errors that a competent programmer may make. While Mothra's mutagens were appropriate at the time, it is unlikely that they will continue to be appropriate to all languages in all situations. With good quality test data, the quality of mutations may not be so important; only a minimal set of mutations need to be applied. A "do fewer" approach such as N-selective mutation testing would be adequate. As the quality of the test data decreases though, the quality of the mutations needs to increase to help improve the test data. A minimal set of appropriate mutagens is required.

Further, while the competent programmer hypothesis states that programmers create programs close to being correct, appropriate mutations need also to be ones that reflect errors made by particular programmers (or programming teams). Obviously, this will differ between programmers, languages used, and applications. Therefore, a system that can learn appropriate mutagens for a particular team and development is required; these can be used to improve the quality of the mutagens. Good quality mutagens also allow mutation testing to improve the test data. By reflecting the most likely errors produced by a competent programmer, the test data and mutagens can be tailored to distinguish these faults. This provides the basis of a method for evolving higher quality mutation testing.

Combining these two requirements together results in a system that has a useful analogy. The program being developed can be viewed as a human who we wish to protect from infections - from errors. We wish to find some form of vaccination that can be applied to the system. A high quality test set coupled with high quality mutagens will provide the necessary 'vaccine' to improve the health of the software development process.

4   Immune Systems

Biology offers many interesting solutions to problems that can be applied to a variety of different applications in the computing field. One such metaphor that has had increasing interest is that of the human immune system. It provides features such as learning, memory, pattern recognition, predator-prey relationships, and mutation abilities. Qualities, such as these, are often particularly desirable and so immunological ideas are utilised to help develop various computing systems [5].

De Castro and Timmis [4] define artificial immune systems (AIS) to be adaptive systems, inspired by theoretical immunology and observed immune functions, principles and models, which are applied to problem solving. They are systems developed using the human immune system as inspiration, rather than creating a comprehensive model, in an attempt to capture some or all of the features it provides. In most instances however, only a few principles from immunology are used [4].

4.1 Human Immune System

The human immune system is designed to protect our bodies from infectious organisms, or *pathogens*, such as viruses and bacteria. It is composed of two main components, *B-cell* and *T-cell* lymphocytes (white blood cells), that work together to recognise invading microbes, or *antigens*. The strength of the interaction between these cells is defined as their *affinity*. In particular, B-cells produce single specificity receptors (*antibodies*) that are cable of binding to complementary matched antigens, found presented on the surface of pathogens.

The immune system combines two forms of immunity: *innate* and *adaptive*. Innate immunity provides an initial response to certain invading pathogens where as the adaptive immune system is more sophisticated, allowing it to direct its attack against antigen that cannot be removed by the innate system. In addition, this allows new antigens to be learnt and memorised in order to prompt a faster immune response to future encounters. An antigenic interaction with substantial affinity to cause recognition, triggers an adaptive immune response. One such response is the *Clonal Selection Theory* [3]. A B-cell receptor recognising an antigen is cloned proportional to, and mutated inversely proportional to, its affinity. This large number of clones is used to fight the pathogen. To memorise new antigen and quicken responses against a repeat infection, some clones form long-lived memory cells, entering into a memory pool.

4.2 Artificial Immune Systems

Artificial immune systems are adaptive systems applied to problem solving, that are inspired by theoretical and observed immunology [4]. From this biological metaphor, they hope to extract and utilise the features that natural immune systems possess. Features such as recognition, learning, memory and predator-prey response patterns.

To be considered an AIS a system must embody three central principles: (i) a basic model of an immune component, (ii) be designed by encompassing ideas from theoretical and/or experimental immunology, and (iii) be aimed at problem solving [4]. Simply using immunological terminology is not sufficient; a fundamental idea or model is required, which is typically antibody-antigen interactions coupled with antibody mutation (*somatic hypermutation*) [4].

A generalised framework for engineering artificial immune systems can be derived from studying other biologically inspired algorithms. The aim is to create a bridge from the application domain, or problem area, to a solution. Such a framework consists of three layers: (i) representations for the components of the system, (ii) measures of affinity between component interactions, and (iii) immune algorithms regulating system dynamics [4]. Starting at the problem domain, a representation of the system components is made. For instance, details of how to represent a particular element as an antibody. A suitable representation will give rise to a selection of appropriate affinity measures, such as Euclidean distance; this forms the second layer. Utilising these two layers, a third layer controlling the system dynamics can be adopted. For example, clonal selection, immune network theory, or negative selection algorithms. The combination of these layers provides an elegant bridge from problem to solution.

4.3 Genetic Algorithm and Bacteriological Approaches

Baudry et. al. [1] describe two significant approaches to optimising test cases. Their initial implementation focusses on the use of genetic algorithms. A population of individuals, each representing a set of test cases, undergo a standard GA algorithm to improve the quality of a member. The results obtained from this experiment show potential; using a 10% mutation rate, the mutation score rose to the 85-90% range.

They then compared this work to a bacteriological algorithm (BA) approach. The two main differences being that BAs maintain a memory set consisting of the best individual per generation, and that each individual of the population is an atomic unit; it cannot be divided. This means that individuals (*bacterium*) can only be reproduced and mutated, and so the problem becomes how to adapt a population, not an individual. This method resulted in a mutation score of 95%. These results are especially promising and demonstrate the potential that can be achieved by hybridising mutation testing with biological metaphors.

However, their work only focussed on optimising test cases for a specific subset of systems; namely those systems that translate input data from one format to another, i.e. a parser or compiler. They did not address the simultaneous optimisation of mutagens. Fortunately, AIS provide two distinct populations - predator and prey. Both populations evolve in an attempt to survive with respect to the other. This is intrinsic behaviour of immune systems. Additionally, there are subtle differences in the algorithms. Clonal selection does not perform crossover, unlike a GA, and reproduction and mutation are relative to the fitness of an individual, unlike a BA. Using the notion of an immune systems, it is proposed to create a 'vaccine' that can be applied to software development to protect it from errors.

5 Vaccination: Improving the Health of Software Development

Figure 2 demonstrates the effective paths through which AIS techniques can be applied to mutation testing.

This figure indicates two undesirable regions. The bottom left quadrant denotes the situation where we have worthless test data (we do not distinguish correct programs from incorrect ones), and are doing no effective mutation testing (to improve the test data); an ineffective state. Conversely, the top right quadrant is too expensive. We have perfect test data (distinguishing all programs) and yet we are also testing all mutations. The ideal situation for the system would be to have a minimal high quality test set (to distinguish correct programs) coupled with a minimal amount of well focussed mutation testing (to overcome problems associated with test suites wearing out); the top left quadrant. The 'vaccine' therefore consists of:

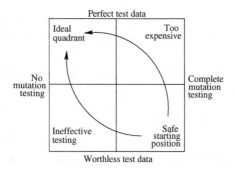

Fig. 2. The Mutation Testing/AIS approach

Table 1. Mapping between mutation testing and immunology

Mutation Testing	Immune Systems
Program	B-cells
Mutants	Antibodies
Test Data	Antigens
Producing and testing mutants	Clonal Selection
Evolving test data	Clonal Selection

- The smallest set of test cases that kill the largest proportion of mutants,
- The smallest set of mutagens that deliver the largest set of consistently living mutants.

Initially, it is difficult to know if we are located in the top left quadrant. The only safe starting point is to assume we are positioned in the bottom right, allowing test data and mutagen quality to improve.

5.1   General System Outline
The system is developed in three layers, detailed below, with the mapping summarised in table 1.

Layer 1: Representation for the System Components. In biological terms, the system being developed that we wish to protect, is analogous to the body. Code under test will therefore be represented as a B-cell, and mutations of this code will correspond to antibodies. When test cases are applied in mutation testing, they kill a percentage of mutants producing different outputs from the original program; test cases are harmful to the system, and so are termed antigens.

Layer 2: Affinity Measures between Component Interactions. In the proposed system, the components that interact are, like in the human immune system, antibodies and antigens; or mutants and test data. The survival of an antibody (mutant) is determined by its stimulation level. Test data executed on a mutant will produce a specific output. When compared to the output from the original program, a scale can be introduced detailing how suitable (how close its outputs are to the originals) one mutant is compared to the others - a stimulation level. This is the antibodies (mutants) affinity measure. Conversely though, an antigen is also fighting for survival. It is in competition to defeat the immune system's defences. Antigens themselves will constantly evolve to kill antibodies; test data will evolve to kill as many mutants as possible. This mutation score forms the affinity measure for the test data (antigens).

Layer 3: Immune Algorithms Regulating System Dynamics. Antigens (test data) applied to the system cause it to respond, similar to antigenic recognition in the clonal selection algorithm. Using the antibody stimulation level (comparative correctness of a mutants outputs to others) as an affinity measure, a selection of antibodies (mutants) will undergo clonal selection; they will clone proportional to, and mutate inversely proportional to their affinity. This process can be seen as a local search, refining the mutagens (via refining mutants) that constantly produce living mutants. The appropriate mutants can be added to the immune memory, allowing a set of mutagens to be determined, forming half the vaccination.

The evolution of the antigenic set (test data set) is also of concern. When test cases (antigens) are applied to the system, they cause a certain percentage of mutants (antibodies) to be killed. This affinity can be used in a similar clonal selection process to the antibody set, to reproduce and mutate the test data. Tests that constantly kill mutant programs form good quality tests and are added to the test set immune memory, forming the second half of the vaccination.

These clonal selection processes can be iteratively repeated until a suitable 'vaccine' is derived.

Outline of Software Vaccination Procedure. The process by which the vaccine will be obtained, can be envisaged to work as follows. For simplicity, a single program, P, is considered as opposed to a system.

1. *Initialisation:* Mutate program P to create a set of initial mutants, P'
2. *Antigen Presentation:* Execute test data on P'
   (a) *Affinity Evaluation:* Evaluate how well the mutant survives the test data
   (b) *Clonal Selection:* Clone high affinity mutants proportional to their affinities
   (c) *Affinity Maturation:* Mutate a selection of the clones inversely proportional to their affinities
   (d) *Memory:* Add the appropriate mutants to a memory set
3. *Test Data Adaption:* Execute test data on P'
   (a) *Affinity Evaluation:* Evaluate the percentage of mutants a test case kills
   (b) *Clonal Selection:* Clone high affinity test cases proportional to their affinities
   (c) *Affinity Maturation:* Mutate the clones inversely proportional to their affinities
   (d) *Memory:* Add the best test cases to a memory set
4. *Cycle:* Repeat steps 2 and 3 until a suitable vaccine is developed.

This process evolves two populations with a shared fitness landscape, where each population inhibits the growth of the other; a competitive co-evolution approach. It is to our knowledge, that such application to this problem domain (evolving programs and test data) is unique, in particular with the AIS metaphor. Some similarities can be drawn to genetic programming (GP) in respect the evolution of programs, although this is not typically co-evolutionary; one limited example is using a co-evolutionary GP to optimise intertwined spiral coverage [11]. The proposed AIS mutation system is also similar to a competitive co-evolutionary GA approach. Antibodies and memory cells allow AIS to maintain a diverse set of solutions, which is an advantage given the dynamic nature of programming languages, paradigms and programmers. It is theorised that this advantage will improve performance in the mutation system over a GA based approach.

5.2   Practical Issues

The initialisation and antigenic presentation stages described above will require considerable execution time. This is a problem associated with mutation testing in general (the time necessary to generate and execute mutants). Currently this is a conceptual paper, and so proof of the concept is still required. Our efforts have initially consisted of generating a Java system based on Mutant Schema Generation (MSG) [21]. This process creates a *metamutant* from a simple, single file Java program, that contains all possible mutations, and so only needs to be compiled once, allowing mutants to be selected at runtime.

The basis to MSG is that a programs syntactic tree can be altered so that mutagen functions replace certain nodes. In Java, for example, replacing i=3+4; with i=arithOp(3,4,+);. The plus in this example could be replaced by a bit string that selects an appropriate operation to perform from a list. Passing this bit string to the program at runtime will select the mutation that is to be applied. With all mutations compiled into the same source file, each mutant program is now referenced by a long bit string. In AIS terms, each bit string (or mutant) is an antibody. This makes the task a search problem; find the smallest set of bit strings that constantly remain living.

An additional problem is how to determine the affinity of a program. Some measure is required as to how well a program works with test data; how close its outputs are to the original program outputs. Currently mutation testing is dichotomous - mutants live or die. For an immune system approach, a scale needs to be introduced that allows for mutants to survive even if their outputs are not identical to the original's. This will encourage mutants that may require an additional mutation, for example, to be candidate solutions.

Further, some process is required, given a set of living mutants, to determine what are the appropriate mutagens for the vaccine. The living mutants will, hopefully, have common mutations in them, as these represent the errors that the programmers commonly make. Some procedure for clustering these together and deriving the common mutagens is needed.

6   Conclusion

Mutation testing suffers from a number of problems, in particular generation and execution time of many mutant programs. Traditional research has focused on three areas: do fewer, do faster, do smarter [20]. An initial proposal for an adaptive mutation testing system has been discussed. This attempts to combine all three areas.

The immune systems provides a good metaphor for such a system. It has features such as learning, memory, pattern recognition, and predator-prey response patterns. Features that make it particulary suitable for the mutation testing domain.

This metaphor has been used to create a system that initially works outside the main software development cycle, monitoring a team over time, to create a 'vaccine'. This will deliver a minimal high quality test set coupled with a minimal amount of well focussed mutation testing (via high quality mutagens), that can be 'injected' into the software development cycle, resulting in an adaptive do fewer, do faster, do smarter testing phase.

A number of problems present themselves. Firstly, the clonal selection portion of immune systems requires proliferation of B-cells proportional to their affinity. As B-cells are analogous to programs, and antigens to test data, some measure of affinity (how well a program executes with specific test data) is required between the two. How is this achieved? Secondly, given a mutated program that represents a possible error, how do we select the associated mutation operator that generated it?

To summarise, we believe the application of artificial immune systems to mutation testing seems a plausible concept, allowing a 'vaccine' to be developed to improve the health of the software development process.

Acknowledgements

The authors would like to thank the two anonymous reviewers for their valuable comments.

References

1. B. Baudry, F. Fleurey, J.-M. Jézéquel, and Y. Le Traon, "Genes and Bacteria for Automated Test Cases Optimization in the .NET Environment", presented at ISSRE 02 (Int. Symposium on Software Reliability Engineering), Annaplois, MD, USA, 2002.
2. B. Beizer, "Software Testing Techniques", Van Nostrand Reinhold, 1990.
3. F.M. Burnet, "The Clonal Selection Theory of Acquired Immunity", Cambridge University Press, 1959.
4. L.N. de Castro, and J. Timmis, "Artificial Immune Systems: A New Computational Intelligence Approach", Springer, 2002.
5. L.N. de Castro, and F.J. Von Zuben, "The Clonal Selection Algorithm with Engineering Applications", Workshop Proceedings of GECCO, pp. 36-37, Las Vegas, USA, July 2000.

6. R.A. DeMillo, "Completely Validated Software: Test Adequacy and Program Mutation", Proceedings of the Eleventh International Conference on Software Engineering, Pittsburgh, Pennsylvania, USA, 1989.
7. R.G. Hamlet, "Testing Programs with the Aid of a Compiler", IEEE Transactions on Software Engineering, 3(4), July 1977.
8. S.A. Hofmeyr, and S. Forrest, "Architecture for an Artificial Immune System", Evolutionary Computation, 7, pp. 45-68, 2000.
9. W.E. Howden, "Weak Mutation Testing and Completeness of Test Sets", IEEE Transactions on Software Engineering, 8, pp. 371-379, July 1982.
10. N.K. Jerne, "Towards A Network Theory of the Immune System", Annals of Immunology, 125C, pp. 373-389, 1974.
11. H. Juille, and J.B. Pollack, "Co-evolving Intertwined Spirals", Proceedings of the Fifth Annual Conference on Evolutionary Programming, pp. 461-468, 1996.
12. K.N. King, and A.J. Offut, "A Fortran Language System for Mutation-Based Software Testing", Software - Practice and Experience, 21(7), pp. 685-718, July 1991.
13. A.P. Mathur, "Performance, Effectiveness, and Reliability Issues in Software Testing", Proceedings of the Fifteenth Annual International Computer Software and Applications Conference, pp. 604-605, Tokyo, Japan, September 1991.
14. R. DeMillo, R. Lipton, and F. Sayward, "Hints on Test Data Selection: Help For The Practicing Programmer", IEEE Computer. Vol. 11(4), pp. 34-41, 1978.
15. M. Mitchell, "An Introduction to Genetic Algorithms", The MIT Press, 1998.
16. A.J. Offutt, "A Practical System for Mutation Testing: Help for the Common Programmer", Proceedings of the International Test Conference, pp. 824-830, 1994.
17. A.J. Offut, A. Lee, G. Rothermel, R.H.Untch, and C. Zapf, "An experimental determination of sufficient mutant operators", ACM Transactions on Software Engineering Methodology, 5(2), pp. 99-118, April 1996.
18. A.J. Offutt, J. Pan, "Automatically Detecting Equivalent Mutants and Infeasible Paths", The Journal of Software Testing, Verification, and Reliability, 7(3), pp. 165-192, September 1997.
19. A.J. Offut, G. Rothermel, and C. Zapf, "An experimental evaluation of selective mutation", Proceedings of the Fifteenth International Conference on Software Engineering, pp. 100-107, Baltimore, MD. May 1993.
20. A.J. Offutt, and R.H. Untch, "Mutation 2000: Uniting the Orthogonal", Mutation Testing for the New Century, W.E. Wong (Ed.) Kluwer 2001.
21. R.H. Untch, A.J. Offutt, and M.J. Harrold, "Mutation Analysis Using Mutant Schemata", Proceedings of the 1993 International Symposium on Software Testing and Analysis, (Cambridge MA.), pp. 139-148, June 1993.

Memory and Selectivity
in Evolving Scale-Free Immune Networks

P. Tieri[1,2], S. Valensin[1,2], C. Franceschi[1,2], C. Morandi[3], and G.C. Castellani[1,3]

[1] "L.Galvani" Interdipartimental Center for Biophysics,
Bioinformatics and Biocomplexity University of Bologna,
Bologna 40100, Italy
[2] Department of Experimental Pathology, University of Bologna,
Bologna 40100, Italy
[3] DIMORFIPA, University of Bologna, Ozzano E 40100, Italy
`gasto@alma.unibo.it`

Abstract. In this paper we examine the impact of graph theory and more particularly the scale-free topology on Immune Network models. In the case of a simple but not trivial model we analyze network performances as long term selectivity properties, its computational capabilities as memory capacity, and relation with Neural Networks. A more advanced Immune Network model is conceptualized and it is developed a scaffold for further mathematical investigation.

1 Introduction

Network models and related equations represent a topic of growing interest in modern interdisciplinary research. One of the present challenges is a better understanding of how microscopic relations between and within network elements can lead to macroscopic phenomena such as adaptation, learning and memory, and how genetic and environmental information fluxes interact. Modern graph theory (small-world models, scale-free networks theory) is one of the most effective and advantageous mathematical technique applied for understanding the evolution of network systems and to comprehend the basic principles of their structural organisation and evolution. Our work is focussed on the application of such technique to the formalisation of Immune System (IS) molecular-cellular networks in order to depict their topological features and attributes affecting their functionality. This approach, proceeding from the formalisation of elements of the network and their interactions as nodes and links, respectively, allows to structure a topology whose characterising features can be derived from analytical and numerical solutions. Various IS network topologies have been envisaged by us as relevant by both, an immunological and a structural point of view, that exploit different mechanisms of IS element interacting features, and show a progressively increase of immune complexity. In fact, a network model being reasonably adherent to the real IS should include combinations of ingredients like weighted links, fast evolving connections, interchange and average life span of nodes, appropriate number of nodes, topologically different functions of nodes,

J. Timmis et al. (Eds.): ICARIS 2003, LNCS 2787, pp. 93–101, 2003.

and some more, which are all factors that rise the mathematical analysis complexity. Thus, our aim is to proceed by deploying models at increasing levels of structural and mathematical complexity. At present, two different types of IS networks are under our investigation, having two different levels of analysis completion. The first is a growing, scale-free, idiotypic-inspired immune network (IN) model. The second is a network of heterogeneous immune cells constituting the nodes linked by soluble molecular mediators (cytokines and chemokines) that in the real IS appoint a molecular field by means of which immune cells indirectly communicate. In this paper we focus on a well known IS network model [25,11,4] whose activation function is based on microscopic and experimental data. This is a simplified model, that nevertheless allows to capture some fundamental features of the IS network properties. This work deals with the IS *connectivity* problem [7,26], and its extension to scale-free topology. The analysis on immune network can be extended also to the so called BCM (Bienenstock, Cooper and Munro) neural network model (BCM NN)[2,19,8] showing a interesting degree of similarity between their selectivity properties in term of stability of "learning rule" solutions. The relation between immune and nervous system looks very intriguing since both systems can be described, from a mathematical-systemic point of view, by similar equations based on a "network" structure [16,20]. Recent studies suggest that the similarity between the two systems is not purely formal [17]. Among others, a surprising result was [1] that some fundamental molecules for learning and memory in the nervous system (like CaMK II and Calcineurin) play a fundamental role also in the IS, leading to a new scenario in which molecules and pathways are shared by the two systems and conserved during evolution. One point of difference between IN and NN models is that for the IN we dont have a explicit learning so that we can think the connectivity changes as a prototipical learning rule or, more generally, as a physiological change that mark the IS behaviour and development throughout individual life. The major aim of this paper is a better understanding of the development of memory in immune network models when the network size is growing in a scale-free way. This study is motivated by the increased availability of experimental data on the evolution of the immune memory during lifespan (from birth to older age), that shows an age related increase in the ratio between memory and virgin cells [6] as well as by computational applications of immune networks in problems of feature extraction, dimensionality reduction and nonlinear separability.

2   Idiotypic-Inspired Scale-Free Immune Network

The IS network model that we consider describes the dynamics of a system of interacting lymphocyte clones. This interaction is described by the following system of nonlinear differential equations:

$$\frac{dC_i}{dt} = S_i + C_i(p_i f_i(h_i) - \mu_i) \qquad i = 1, \ldots, n, \tag{1}$$

where C_i is the concentration of the $i{-}th$ clone (that obviously must be taken as nonnegative: $C_i \geq 0$, $\forall i$), n is the number of clones, S_i is the influx term

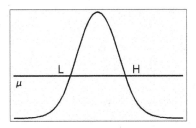

Fig. 1. Semilogarithmic plot of the bell-shaped dose-response curve. The points L and H represent respectively the low and high stable states for the clone concentration, given a specific value for μ, represented by the horizontal line.

(number of clones produced per unit of time), μ_i is the decay term (related to the death rate of the cells), p_i is the proliferation rate, while the function $f_i(h_i)$ describes the activation of the $i-th$ clone. We assume that $f_i(h_i)$ is given by a biphasic dose-response curve (Fig. 1), modeled by the following equation [3]:

$$f_i(h_i) = \frac{\theta_{2_i} h_i}{(\theta_{1_i} + h_i)(\theta_{2_i} + h_i)} \qquad i = 1, \ldots, n. \tag{2}$$

The parameters θ_{1_i} and θ_{2_i} represent two threshold values ($0 < \theta_{1_i} < \theta_{2_i}$), respectively for proliferation and for suppression, while the argument h_i represents the influence of the other clones on the $i-th$ clone, defined as follows:

$$h_i = \sum_{j=1}^{n} \alpha_{ij} C_j \qquad i = 1, \ldots, n. \tag{3}$$

The coefficients α_{ij} of the $\mathcal{A}$ matrix quantify the interactions between the i-th clone and the other ones; here we assume the symmetry property introduced by Hoffmann [18]: $\alpha_{ij} = \alpha_{ji}$, $i \neq j$, $\alpha_{ii} = 0$, since each clone does not interact with itself. Moreover, for the sake of simplicity, we assume that all the interactions have the same strength, $\alpha_{ij} = \alpha$. A further assumption is that the parameters p_i, μ_i, θ_{1_i}, θ_{2_i} and S_i have the same values for all the clones. In this way we have a simplified system[1]:

$$\frac{dC_i}{dt} = S + C_i(pf(h_i) - \mu) \qquad i = 1, \ldots, n. \tag{4}$$

For $n = 2$ this system is similar to one previously analysed [12,4], while the case with $S = 0$ is equivalent to the model analysed by Neumann and Weisbuch [23] with a "window automaton" proliferation function.

---

[1] System (4) admits the permutations over the indices $\{1, \ldots, n\}$ as a symmetry group, then solutions belonging to the same equivalence class by the group share the same dynamical properties (for instance stability). Hereafter, when treating some specific solutions, it is implicitly understood that our remarks about it are extended to all the elements of the equivalence class.

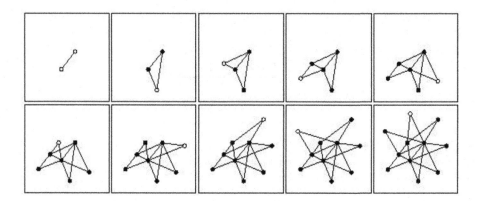

Fig. 2. Birth of a scale free graph.

The choice of the numerical values of the parameters in numerical computations, was performed on the basis of experimental data: $\alpha = 1$, $p = 2$, $\theta_1 = 0.1$, $\theta_2 = 10$, and $\mu = 0.1$ [12].

Following the classification proposed by [12,23,25,4], based on linear stability analysis, the only asymptotically stable states are those having only one clone at high (H) concentration: $(H, L, \ldots, L$ and all permutations). We will refer to these solutions (observed for the completely connected network) as *highly selective* solutions. The IN is, in this case, able to recognize or memorize only one antigenic specificity at a time.

2.1   Preliminary Results

We have generated scale-free graphs by the growth process described in [31] and depicted in Fig (2) using the adjacency matrices as connectivity matrix for the IN model. The scale free mechanism is based on two assumptions: the network size grows and new edges are added to the network at each time step following a preferencial attachement rule that states that the probability for a new node to be connected to the existing nodes is proportional to the number of their connections (the most connected nodes have the maximun probability to be connected). In our preliminary analysis the equation (4) has been numerically integrated, and in the case of nonsingular adjacency matrix a comparison between analytical and numerical solutions has been performed [4], while in the general case of singular adjacency matrix the analytical solution is in progress.

The numerical results show that by increasing the network size the number of stable states remains relatively constant. In particular we found that the most probable number of stable states is 3. These stable states are not selective for only one clonal specificity, as in the completely connected case, but they exhibit selectivity for more than one specificity. This result was expected on the basis our past studies that showed that the memory capacity of IN models changes drastically as function of the connectivity. This preliminary result that need to be confirmed, would suggest that it is possible to control the number of stable solutions as well as their selectivity properties, or in other word their capacity of recognizing foreign patterns.

3   Towards More Realistic Immune Network Models

Graph theory has already been successfully exploited for studies of the topological and connective features of existing real world networks [27,28], like for example citations of scientific papers and networks of collaborations [29], WWW and Internet [30,32], biological networks as neural networks, metabolic reactions network [33], genome and protein network [34], ecological and food webs, world web of human contacts [35], and languages [36], telephone call graphs, power grids, nets of small electronic components etc. As far as we know (beyond the "undistinguishable clones" hypothesis), a similar approach has never been applied before to the study of realistic IS network peculiarities [37]. A scale-up line of attack should be applied to take into consideration the facing problems, firstly dealing with the main basic attributes of the IS elements and successively arriving, step by step, to more realistic immunologic configurations (i.e. mirroring concepts more adherent to the real IS characteristics like weighted links, fast evolving connections, interchange and average life span of nodes, a more appropriate number of nodes, topologically different functions of nodes, among others).

The first phase of this strategy can consist in the representation and formalisation procedure of a "small scale" system (some tens of elements) in which nodes represent IS cells and links represent the immune role of cytokines and chemokines. In this simplified representation of the IS, cells (nodes) will be distinguished in "source cell type" (secreting cytokines and chemokines) and "target cell type" (on which secreted cytokines and chemokines act).

We propose this first oversimplified visualization of a part of the network of "communication" among the main types of IS cells. The graph (Fig 3) shows the network of heterogeneous immune cells constituting the nodes linked by soluble molecular mediators. Data are extracted and adapted from [40]. "Sources" (left side) and "targets" cells (right side) are linked by the various cytokine and chemokine signalling molecules. A source cell secretes different kinds of mediators that can act upon one or more target cells as well as on the source cell itself. The topology of this graph can be depicted by its "adjacency matrix". The matrix of sources and mediators and the matrix of mediators and targets can be multiplied to obtain a square adjacency matrix showing how cells communicates with each others. Relevant coefficients related to the network topology are: the *mean degree* of the network, i.e. the average number of the nearest connected neighbours of a node; the *degree distribution*; the *clustering coefficient of the network*, i.e. the probability of one edge between two nearest neighbours of a randomly chosen node; the *characteristic path length*, i.e. the average of the shortest paths -number of steps- necessary to go from any two vertices calculated on all pairs of vertices of the network. This last coefficient can be calculated both

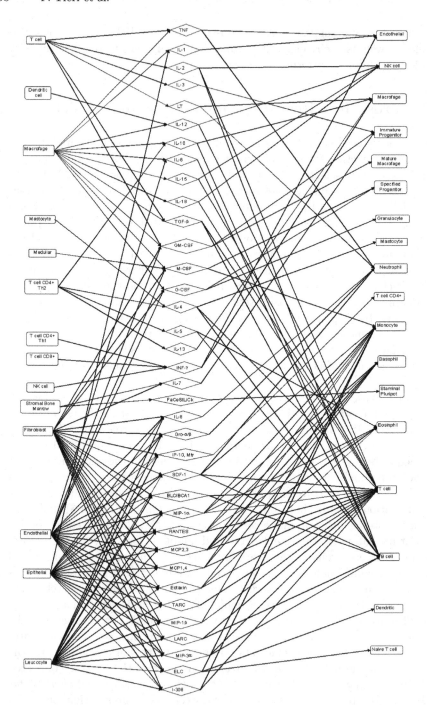

Fig. 3. Graph representing the complex cytokine-mediated cell interaction within IS. Diamonds represent cytochines and chemokines, source cells are on the left side, while target cells are on the right side.

with and without considering edge directions. We consider 26 types of cells, among which 14 are sources, 18 are targets, and 6 are both source and target. 36 types of chemical mediators are secreted. Among sources, T cells (and T CD4+ Th2 in particular), endothelial cells, epithelial cells, fibroblasts and macrofages are the most connected sources, while B cells, T cells, monocytes, basophils, neutrophils, eosinophils are the most linked targets. A complete mathematical formalization of the proposed model is in progress as well as a fine tuning of the model itself.

4 Conclusion

This analysis is one of the first attempts to characterize a key property as the long term memory specificity in a evolving IN. We are confident that these preliminary results can be exported to the BCM NN model, where the effect of replacing an input pattern global mean with local mean has been investigated. A remaining interesting question is the relation between memory properties in BCM NN model and moving average procedures. The numerical results obtained for the NN model suggest that the memory size and selectivity (in terms of recognized pattern) strongly depend on network topology, and that in a scale-free context these two properties can be separated so that we can control the "composition" of immune response in term of pattern of activity. Once an IS-representing small scale graph is fully and coherently formalised, its topological characterising features can be derived from analytical and numerical solutions. Our attack strategy foresees later on a migration to medium scale (10^3 -10^5 nodes-elements) representation, in which we will try to take into consideration the weights of the links, the direction of action flows, the fast evolving connections, interchange and average life span of nodes, topologically different functions of nodes and other peculiar more realistically detailed attributes of IS elements. The resulting complex graph will be again mathematically analysed in order to derive all the necessary measures and eventually a "mesoscale" model, that will serve as a first basis for IT architecture design. Indeed in approaching a more realistic formalisation of the IS network we will face problems relative to the complexity of the interrelationships among cells, due to: i. the diverse mechanisms of interaction (biochemical signalling, signal duration, chemical concentration, cascade activation and secretion, activation thresholds, i.e. the quantity of activated receptors per time unit, sterical recognition of peptides and antigens by surface receptors, locality of the interaction, migration of the cell in another immune district, systemic effects); ii. the miscellaneous nature of each cell type; iii. their rapid mobility; iv. the evanescence and alteration of the biochemical connection among cells; v. the different function, weight and relevance of each exchanged signal.

Acknowledgments

This work has been supported by Italian MIUR COFIN 2001 grant "Human Immunosenescence: an integrated experimental and theoretical approach" to C.F. and a Bologna University grant (ex 60 %) to G.C.C.

References

1. J. D. Bui, S. Calbo, K. Hayden-Martinez, L. P. Kane, P. Gardner, and S. M. Hedrick. A role for camkii in t cell memory. *Cell*, 10 (2000):457–467.
2. E. L. Bienenstock, L. N. Cooper, and P. W. Munro. Theory for the development of neuron selectivity: orientation specificity and binocular interaction in visual cortex. *J. Neurosci.*, 2:(1982)32–48.
3. F. Celada. The cellular basis of immunological memory. *Immunol. Rev.*, 110: (1971)63–87.
4. G. C. Castellani, C. Giberti, C. Franceschi, and F. Bersani. Stable state analysis of an immune network model. *Int. J. Chaos Bif.*, 8(6):(1998) 1285–1301.
5. G. C Castellani, N. Intrator, H. Shouval, and L. Cooper. Solution of the bcm learning rule in a network of lateral interacting nonlinear neurons. *Network*, 10: (1999) 111–121.
6. A. Cossarizza, C. Ortolani, R. Paganelli, D. Barbieri, D. Monti, P. Sansoni, U. Fagiolo, G. Castellani, F. Bersani, M. Londei, and C. Franceschi. Cd45 isoforms expression on cd4+ and cd8+ t cells throughout life, from newborns to centenarians: Implications for t cell memory. *Mechanisms of Aging and Development*, 86:(1996)173–195.
7. A. Coutinho. Beyond clonal selection and network. *Immunol. Rev.*, 110:(1989)63–87.
8. GC. Castellani, EM. Quinlan, LN Cooper, and HZ. Shouval. A biophysical model of bidirectional synaptic plasticity: Dependence on ampa and nmda receptors. *PNAS*, 98(22): (2001) 12772–12777.
9. L. N. Cooper and C. L. Scofield. Mean-field theory of a neural network. *PNAS*, 85:(1988) 1973–1977.
10. S. M. Dudek and M. F. Bear. Homosynaptic long-term depression in area CA1 of hippocampus and the effects on NMDA receptor blockade. *PNAS*, 89: (1992) 4363–4367.
11. R. J. De Boer. Symmetric idiotypic networks: Connectance and switching stability and suppression. *Bull. Math. Biol.*, 55:(1993) 745–780.
12. R. J. De Boer, I.G. Kewrekidis, and A.S. Perelson. Immune network behaviour from stationary states to limit cycle oscillations. *Bull. Math. Biol.*, 55:(1993) 745–780.
13. R. J. De Boer and A. Perelson. Size and connectivity as emergent properties of a developing immune network. *J. Theor. Biol.*, 149:(1991)381–424.
14. C. Franceschi, S. Valensin, M. Bonafé, P. Paolisso, A. Yashin, and G. De Benedictis. The network and the remodelling theories of aging. *Exp. Gerontol.*, 35:879–896, 2000.
15. C. Franceschi, S. Valensin, F. Fagnoni, C. Barbi, and M. Bonafé. Biomarkers of immunosenescence: the challenge of heterogeneity and the role of antigenic load. *Exp. Gerontol.*, 34:(1999) 911–921.
16. G. W. Hoffmann, T.A. Kion, R.B. Forsyth, K.G. Soga, and A. CooperWillis. The n-dimensional network. In A.S. Perelson, editor, *Theoretical Immunology, Part 2*, page 291. Addison-Wesley, 1988.
17. K. Hayden-Martinez, L. P. Kane, and S. M. Hedrick. Effects of a constitutively active form of calcineurin on t cell activation and thymic selection. *J. Immunol.*, 165:(2000) 3713–3721.
18. G. W. Hoffmann. A neural network model based on the analogy with the immune system. *J. Theor. Biol.*, 122:(1986) 33–67.

19. N. Intrator and L. N Cooper. Objective function formulation of the BCM theory of visual cortical plasticity: Statistical connections, stability conditions. *Neural Networks*, 5:(1992) 3–17.
20. N. K. Jerne. Towards a network theory of immune system. *Annu. Immunol.*, 125:(1974)373–389.
21. A. Kirkwood, H. K. Lee, and M. F. Bear. Co-regulation of long-term potentiation and experience-dependent synaptic plasticity in visual cortex by age and experience. *Nature*, 25;375(6529):(1995) 328–331.
22. J. A. Lisman. A mechanism for the hebb and the anti-hebb processes underlying learning and memory. *PNAS*, 86:(1989) 9574–9578.
23. A.U. Neumann and G. Weisbuch. Window automata analysis of population dynamics in the immune system. *Bull. Math. Biol.*, 54:(1992) 21–44.
24. A.S. Perelson. Immune network theory. *Immunol. Rev.*, 110:(1989) 5–36.
25. A.S. Perelson. Mathematical approaches in immunology. In S. I. Andersson, editor, *Theory & Control of Dynamical Systems*, pages 200–230. World Scientific, 1992.
26. J. Stewart and F. J. Varela. Exploring the meaning of connectivity in the immune network. *Immunol. Rev.*, 110:(1989) 37–61.
27. S.H. Strogatz: Exploring complex networks. *Nature*, 410 (2001) 268–276.
28. D.J.Watts, S.H. Strogatz: Collective dynamics of "small-world" networks. *Nature*, 393 (1998) 440-442.
29. M.E.J. Newman: Scientific collaboration networks. I. Network construction and fundamental results, and II. Shortest paths, weighted network and centrality. *Physical Review E*, 64 (2001) 016131–016132.
30. A.L. Barabasi, R. Albert: Emergence of scaling in random networks. *Science*, 286 (1999) 509-512.
31. A.L. Barabasi, R. Albert: Statistical mechanics of complex networks, *Rev of Mod Phys*, 74, 2002 48-94
32. R. Albert: Diameter of the World-Wide Web. *Nature*, 401 (1980) 130-131.
33. H. Jeong, B.Tombor, R.Albert, Z.N.Oltvai and A.L.Barabasi et al.: The large scale organization of metabolic networks. *Nature*, 407 (2000) 651-654.
34. H.Jeong, S.P.Mason, A.L.Barabasi and Z.L.Oltvai.: Lethality and centrality in proteins network. *Nature*,411 (2001) 41-42.
35. F.Liljeros: The web of human sexual contacts. *Nature*, 411 (2001) 907-908.
36. R. Ferrer i Cancho, R.V. Sole: Least effort and the origins of scaling in human language. *Proc Natl Acad Sci U S A* , 100 (2003) 788-791.
37. Editorial article: Making connections. *Nature Immunology* , 3 (2002) 883.
38. S.H. Yook,H. Jeong, A.L. Barabasi,Y. Tu: Weighted evolving networks *Physical Review Letters*, 86 (2001) 5835–5838
39. P. Kourilsky, P. Truffa-Bachi: Cytokine fields and the polarization of the immune response. Trends Immunol **22** ,(2001) 502-509.
40. A.K. Abbas, A.H. Lichtman, J.S. Pober: Cellular and Molecular Immunology. Saunders (2000) 4th ed.

Biomolecular Immunocomputing

Larisa Goncharova[1], Yuri Melnikov[2,*], and Alexander O. Tarakanov[2,3]

[1] Institute Pasteur of St. Petersburg Mira 14, St. Petersburg 197101, Russia
goncharova_lara@mail.ru
[2] International Solvay Institutes for Physics and Chemistry, Campus Plaine, ULB,
CP 231, Bd. du Triomphe, Brussels 1050, Belgium
imelniko@ulb.ac.be
[3] St. Petersburg Institute for Informatics, Russian Academy of Sciences 14-line 39,
St. Petersburg 199178, Russia
tar@iias.spb.su

Abstract. The paper proposes a new application of biomolecular computing to processing of ex vivo fragment of computer controlled immune system. Our approach involves two basic components: the immunocomputing computational paradigm and a protein biochip to provide a direct interface between the immune system and the computer hardware.

Keywords: Biocomputing, immunocomputing, biochip

1   Introduction

Nowadays the notion of biocomputing is conventionally used for a specific approach to various computational problems (e.g. traveling salesman, simulation of artificial neural networks, control of mobile robots, etc.) by using biological elements (e.g., DNA molecules, light-sensitive protein rhodopsin, biopolymers, etc.).

For example (Adleman, 1998), the tools of molecular biology are used to address the directed Hamiltonian path problem. A small graph is encoded by DNA molecules, and computational "operations" are performed with standard protocols and enzymes. Another relevant work has been devoted to the development of computer memory based on bacterial protein rhodopsin (Sienko et al., 2003). Investigation of chemical-based reaction-diffusion media for image processing, control of autonomous robots, and graph optimization are also under development now (Adamatzky, 2001).

On the other hand, current need for biocomputing emerges from the several developments in molecular immunology, such as immune networks theory (Jerne, 1974), cytokine networks, immune synapse, psycho-neuro-immune modulation (Ader et al., 2001), and rapidly emerging biochip technology (Cheng, Kricka, 2001). This technology brings together computer chips with biomedical assays and laser-based detectors.

---

[*] Corresponding author

J. Timmis et al. (Eds.): ICARIS 2003, LNCS 2787, pp. 102–110, 2003.
© Springer-Verlag Berlin Heidelberg 2003

Nowadays there is raising a great interest in innovative approaches to the developments in science and technology for the design of a three-dimensional (3D) ex vivo human immune system (DARPA, 2002). This system would be used for testing new vaccine constructs and immunomodulators that provide superior protection against threat agents. The program seeks to develop reliable methodologies that will accelerate the scientific and technological development of 3D tissue engineering.

According to this program, such engineering should be adaptable and capable of utilizing computer-aided design or computer-aided machine technologies (CAD/CAM) to meet the anatomic requirements of the construct. In addition, it is expected that a strong mathematical modeling component will be included wherever necessary.

Therefore, our paper could contribute to these studies by the development of both a strong mathematical basis and a technology for biochip-based biomolecular controllers of ex vivo immune system. Moreover, to the best of our knowledge, no biochips for implementing the immunocomputing are under development now.

2 Theoretical Foundations

2.1 Immunocomputing

According to (Dasgupta, 1999; de Castro, Timmis, 2002; Tarakanov et al., 2003), conventional computing approaches (e.g. differential equations, artificial neural networks, genetic algorithms, cellular automata, etc.) are insufficient to provide a realistic computational model of key biomolecular mechanisms of the immune system.

Recent breakthrough in this direction has been achieved within the EU project IST-2000-26016 "Immunocomputing" (IC). A new kind of computing has been developed by implementing the principles of information processing by proteins and immune networks.

We have developed a rigorous mathematical basis of IC and its applications to several specific real-life problems. We have introduced new mathematical abstractions of Formal Protein (FP) and Formal Immune Network (FIN). We have provided a rigorous proof that a FIN is able to learn, to recognize, to solve problems and to represent languages based on the theory of linguistic valence. We have presented some applied results, such as computing of ecological atlases, monitoring of most dangerous infections, detecting critical situations in near Earth space, information security, etc. These results allow speaking about the hardware implementation of the IC in so-called immunochip. We have developed several versions of the software emulator of the immunochip. Currently we are developing a working hardware prototype of the immunochip, which is a special electronic scheme for ultra-selective recognition of patterns. This would demonstrate the possibility of hardware implementation of an immunocomputer units.

Therefore, next breakthrough in this direction can be expected in few years from now and would lead to the creation of a first functional immunocomputer.

This immunocomputer could be based on the extension of our IC approach and the development of special protein biochip for IC.

2.2   Cytokine Networks

Cytokines is a group of biologically active mediator molecules that provide the intercellular interactions within the immune system. They are the central regulators of leukocyte growth and differentiation, being produced by a wide variety of cell types, targeting various cell subsets and exhibiting numerous biological activities. An increasing volume of data perceived by a human suggests a relationship between cytokine levels in human body fluids and disease pathogenesis (inflammation, in particular). The cytokine maladjustment is believed to play a role in the remodelling of the immune system in old age. Up to now more than 100 different human cytokines are identified. It is an established fact that they are not produced individually and they do not function individually, which brings additional difficulties for the investigation of their role and functioning.

New concept of cytokines as a network modulating and switching several cascades of immune reactions adjoins with the concept considering such molecules as a field or a milieu, which local properties mediate immune response (Kourilsky, Truffa-Bachi, 2001). Nevertheless, these two different concepts could both correspond successfully to different kinds of the immune mechanisms and match experimental data. That is not an exclusive case in molecular biology, because the same protein can have different functions in different conditions. However, the network properties of cytokines seem to be in better agreement with the IC as well as with modern experimental data.

Therefore, cytokines play one of the central roles in the immune regulation as well as in the neuro-immune-endocrine modulation (Ader et al., 2001). However, no mathematical or computational models of those important phenomena have yet been available in the field of AIS. Our goal is to provide a novel approach to mathematical modelling, software implementation and simulation of the ex vivo immune modulation by cytokines.

The corresponding simulator will be implemented as a modified version of the previously developed software emulator of the immunochip, and will include user-friendly interface and 3D visualization scheme for the immune dynamics (Tarakanov et al., 2003). The developing simulator will be tested and adjusted using immunoassay data from a midi-variant of a biochip matrix. This matrix will be designed through a modification of the previously developed macro-variant (Tarakanov et al., 2002).

2.3   Modulated Formal Immune Network

Definition. Define one-dimensional integer-valued modulated formal immune network (mFIN) as a tuple

$$mFIN(n, h) =< n, h, w, B - cells >,$$

where

$$B - cell =< P, S >,$$

P is the Formal Protein (FP, see e.g. Tarakanov et al., 2003) considered as the receptor of the B-cell and the antibody secreted by the B-cell;

S is the state indicator of the B-cell: $S = \{rec, pro, del\}$, where rec is the recognition, pro is the proliferation, and del is the deletion of the cell.

n is the number of types of FPs: $P = \{0, 1, \ldots, n-1\}$;
h is the integer threshold of binding: $0 \le h \le n-1$;
w is the integer binding energy between the FPs:

$$w_{ij} = min(|i - j|, n - |i - j|)$$

Rules of Behaviour. Let $\{B_k\}$ be a current set (population) of B-cells with $S_k = rec$ for $k = 1, \ldots, m$:

$$B_1, \ldots, B_k, \ldots, B_m.$$

For $1 < k < m$ any cell B_k has two nearest neighbors: *east* B_{k-1} and *west* B_{k+1}, while B_1 has only west and B_m only east neighbor.

The following rules are applied to the series over the population, and any rule is applied simultaneously over all B-cells of the population.

(Rule-Mod): Any cell B_k sends modulators P_k to the nearest neighbors, according to Tab. 1, where the modulators are shown on top of the B-cells.

Table 1. Modulators of B-cells

P_2	$\ldots$	P_{k-1}, P_{k+1}	$\ldots$	P_{m-1}
B_1	$\ldots$	B_k	$\ldots$	B_m

(Rule-Sel): Any cell B_k selects the modulator $P* = \{P_{k-1}, P_{k+1}\}$ with the maximal binding energy to its receptor:

$$w* = max\{w(P_k, P_{k-1}), w(P_k, P_{k+1})\}.$$

(Rule-Del): If $w_k \ge h$ then $S_k = pro$ else $S_k = del$.

(Rule-Div): If $S_k = pro$ then cell B_k divides into two neighboring copies B_k, B_k. Their type

$$P = \{P_k, (P_k \pm 1) mod(n)\}$$

is selected in the way to maximize the binding energy $w(P, P*)$, and $S_k = rec$.

(Rule-Shi): If $S_k = del$ then the population shifts left to fill the gap.

(Rule-Int): Any external modulator (antigen, cytokine, etc.) of type $P = \{0, 1, \ldots, n-1\}$ can intrude the network at step S1

Table 2. Binding energies between FPs

Types	0	1	2	3
0	0	1	2	1
1	1	0	1	2
2	2	1	0	1
3	1	2	1	0

Example. Consider $mFIN(4,1)$ with $P = \{0, 1, 2, 3\}$. Then the binding energies between the FPs are shown in Tab. 2. According to Tab.2 for the threshold $h = 1$, any two FPs bind if they have different types.

Consider the initial population $\{1,3\}$. According to the rules of behavior, the evolution of such mFIN is as follows:

$$\{1,3\} \to \{1,1,3,3\} \to \{1,3\} \to \{1,1,3,3\} \to ... \tag{1}$$

Therefore, a stable mode is obtained within the mFIN, where B-cells modulate one another. This mode can be treated as a model of the dynamical immune memory.

Consider an external modulator of type $P = 0$, which is applied to the first B-cell of any population. Than the evolution of the mFIN changes as follows:

$$\{1,3\} \to \{1,1,3,3\} \to \{2,2,1,1,3,3\} \to \{2,2,3,3,0,0,1,1,3,3\} \to$$

$$\{2,2,3,3,0,0,1,1,3,3\} \to \{2,2,3,3,0,0,2,2,3,3,0,0,...\} \to$$

$$\{2,2,1,1,0,0,2,2,1,1,3,3,...\} \to \{2,2,3,3,0,0,2,2,3,3,0,0,...\} \to .... \tag{2}$$

If one considers the modulator $P = 0$ as an antigen, them such changes of the stable mode (1) can be treated as a model of the primary immune response.

Now assume that the modulator has been eliminated from the mFIN after the last population in (2). Then the further evolution of the mFIN will be as follows:

$$\{2,2,3,3,0,0,2,2,3,3,0,0,..\} \to \{1,1,0,0,2,2,1,1,0,0,2,2,...\} \to$$

$$\{2,2,3,3,0,0,2,2,3,3,0,0,...\} \to \{1,1,0,0,2,2,1,1,0,0,2,2,...\} \to .... \tag{3}$$

Therefore, such mFIN has obtained a new stable mode (3), which contains both the best antigen binding cells $B = 2$ and the "internal image" $B = 0$ of the antigen.

2.4   Remarks

Note an essential difference between the mFIN and cellular automata. This difference is due to dynamical topology of mFIN. Namely, reaction-diffusion feature of mMIN is a byproduct of propagation of modulators and their interaction with cells.

Note also an essential difference between the mFIN and the immune algorithms proposed by (de Castro, Timmis, 2002). These algorithms represent a special case of genetic algorithms, because immune cells are coded by bit strings and "mutate" by random rules. On the contrary, the cells of the mFIN are coded by real-valued vectors and their behavior is deterministic.

As a result, the features of 1D mFIN (dynamical immune memory, primary and secondary immune responses, etc.) can be described by a row of theorems. However, if 1D mFIN still yields to a pure mathematics, 2D mFIN and especially 3D mFIN are already much more fuzzy. Investigation of their properties is practically impossible without computer modeling. At the same time, these mFINs seem to be the most appropriate mathematical models of modern 2D biochip microarrays and of the 3D immune system, correspondingly. Therefore, the proposed rigorous mathematical approach could be appropriate for the creation of a computer controlled fragment of 3D ex vivo immune system.

3   Experimental Prototype

3.1   General Description

Our objective is to develop a table-top experimental prototype of a computer controlled fragment of the immune cells system (in vitro). The prototype will implement mathematical and computational models of ex vivo immune system fragment based on novel theoretical foundations of the immunocomputer via immune (cytokine) networks. This prototype is expected to perceive the current status of the fragment, to compute and implement biomolecular control actions, and to correct the immune status of the fragment, if necessary. The prototype is expected to recognize at least 90% cases of abnormal immune status of the fragment, and to provide at least 80% of its successful correction, manipulating by at least 10 types of cytokines.

The prototype may serve as a basis for the development and the production of biochip-based autonomous intelligent controllers of the immunity. Such controllers will form an important part of ex vivo human immune system, which would be used for testing new vaccine constructs and immunomodulators.

The prototype may also be used in medical diagnostics to detect cytokine status of the immune system and, possibly, to measure C-reactive protein, which functions are rather close to those of cytokines. Besides, the increased level of this protein serves as a marker of the increased risk of severe cardiovascular diseases.

In long term perspective the prototype may serve as a proof-of-concept of the functional immunocomputer, based on emerging computational paradigm of the IC.

The expected scientific innovations are as follows:

- New mathematical approach to biocomputing based on the notion of formal immune network.

- New biophysical approach to biocomputing based on protein biochip, which provide direct interface between the natural immune network and computer hardware.
- New field of application of biocomputing – cytokine immune networks.

We expect to obtain the following technological innovations:

- First experimental prototype of computer controlled fragment of the immune cell system (in vitro). Such prototype will impose to the fragment the main functions of ex vivo immune system, i.e. it will provide its maintaining, differentiating, regulating, and correction of invalid behavior, if necessary.
- Novel approach to the creation of the protein biochip for the immunocomputing. The approach unifies streptavidin-biotin technology with biochip technology, thus giving rise to the universality in applications both to proteins and DNA, ultra sensitivity, miniaturization, and the ability to analyze large amount of complex samples simultaneously.
- New generation of clinical diagnostic assays based on the application of the developed prototype to medical diagnostics. This generation of intelligent autonomous assays would provide a direct interface between the immune system and computer hardware.

The immunocomputer prototype will include the following main components:

- Mathematical basis of the ex vivo immune system fragment focused on the possibility to control the immune system by cytokines, as a further development of the IC approach.
- Software for a PC compatible computer with user-friendly interface.
- Immunochip controller prototype.
- Pre-activated biochip prototype serving as a sensor (input) of the immuno-computer.
- In vitro fragment of the immune cells system to be analyzed by the immuno-computer.
- Liquid delivery system (to provide the reagents loading, diluting, mixing and dispensing with high accuracy) and scanning detector system (to provide sure detection of the results of the biochip reactions) as actuators of the immunocomputer.

Several parts of this work have been described in our previous publications (Gutnikov, Melnikov, 2003; Tarakanov et al., 2002, 2003). Consider now the ex vivo fragment of the immune system as a key part of the prototype.

3.2   Ex Vivo Fragment of the Immune System

The fragment will include ex vivo complex of human T cells during their differentiation into the subsets of CD4+ T helper cells Th1 and Th2, thus producing regulatory cytokines. At the same time, the process may be influenced and partly directed be exogenous cytokines that originate from outside the fragment. The fragment will allow to study expression and regulation activity of such cytokines as interferon IFN-γ, IFN-α, IFN-β, tumor necrosis factor TNF-α, interleukins IL-1, IL-2, IL-4, IL12, IL-5, IL-6, IL-10, IL-13, etc. The naive T cells will undergo a series of precise proliferation and differentiation events that will result in the generation of immune T cells with appropriate functional capabilities. All cytokines used in the study will be recombinant human proteins. Follow-up of specific T cell clones ex vivo will be achieved.

The procedure, allowing the establishment of human T cell lines with polarized cytokine production, and the exact composition of the appropriate cytokines cocktails for T cells differentiation and/or maintenance of T cell lines will be developed. This would result in selecting the optimal ex vivo system format for the examination and the control of the cytokine factors that are needed at different stages of T cells life.

The computer controlled fragment of ex vivo immune cells system will deepen our knowledge and understanding of the diversification of cytokine profiles in primary T cells, the maintenance of established cytokine expression patterns in differentiated T cells, and possibly of the molecular mechanisms involved in cytokine gene regulation.

Besides, the differentiation of CD4+ T-helper cells into Th1 or Th2 l subsets has profound effects on the outcome of autoimmune diseases, infectious diseases and graft rejection. Thus, understanding of the mechanism underlying Th cell differentiation and molecular events controlling T cell development, is essential for therapeutic manipulation of the cytokine phenotype in disease conditions and may allow the selective manipulation of Th subsets in vivo.

Acknowledgement

This work was supported by the European Commission under the project IST-2000-26016 Immunocomputing.

References

1. Adamatzky, A.: Computing in Nonlinear Media and Automata Collectives. Institute of Physics Publishing (2001)
2. Ader, R., Felten, D.L., Cohen, N. (eds): Psychoneuroimmunology. Academic Press (2001)
3. Adleman, L.M.: Computing with DNA. Scientific American 279(2) (1998) 54-61
4. Antoniou, I., Calude, C.S., Dinneen, M.J. (eds): Unconventional Models of Computation. DIMACS: Series in Discrete Mathematics and Theoretical Computer Science (2000)
5. de Castro, L.N., Timmis, J. Artificial Immune Systems: A New Computational Intelligence Approach. Springer, New York (2002)
6. Cheng, J, Kricka, L.J. (eds.): Biochip Technology. Harwood Academic Publishers, Philadelphia (2001)
7. DARPA BAA 01-42 Addendum 8. Special Focus Area: Engineered Tissue Constructs (2002)

8. Dasgupta, D. (ed.) Artificial Immune Systems and Their Applications. Springer, Berlin (1999)
9. Gutnikov, S, Melnikov, Yu.: A simple non-linear model of immune response. Chaos, Solitons, and Fractals 16 (2003) 125
10. Jerne, N.K. Toward a network theory of the immune system. Ann. Immunol. 125C Paris (1974) 373-389
11. Kourilsky, P., Truffa-Bachi, P.: Cytokine fields and the polarization of the immune response, Trends in Immunology 22 (2001) 502-509
12. Sienko, T., Adamatzky, A., Rambidi, N. (eds): Molecular Computing. MIT Press (2003) (in press)
13. Tarakanov, A., Goncharova, L., Gupalova, T., Kvachev, S., Sukhorukov, A.: Immunocomputing for bioarrays. 1st Int. Conf. on Artificial Immune Systems ICARIS-2002. Univ. of Kent at Canterbury (2002) 32-40
14. Tarakanov, A.O., Skormin, V.A., Sokolova, S.P.: Immunocomputing: Principles and Applications. Springer, New York (2003) (in press)

Signal Processing by an Immune Type Tree Transform[*]

Nikolaos D. Atreas[1], Costas G. Karanikas[2], and Alexander O. Tarakanov[3,4]

[1] Depts. of Mathematics, Aristotle University of Thessaloniki, Greece
natreas@auth.gr
[2] Depts. of Informatics, Aristotle University of Thessaloniki, Greece
karanika@auth.gr
[3] St. Petersburg Institute for Informatics and Automation, Russian Academy of Sciences
[4] International Solvay Institutes for Physics and Chemistry, Brussels, Belgium
sasha_tar@hotmail.com

Abstract. The paper makes an attempt to introduce a new approach for detection of local singularities in signals, including one-dimensional time series and two-dimensional images. Inspired by a mode of antigen processing in the immune system, our approach is based on the rigorous mathematical methods of Discrete Tree Transform (DTT) and Singular Value Decomposition (SVD). The approach has successfully been applied to detect local singularities in human electrocardiogram (ECG), as well as to enhance the detection of bound complexes of human immunoglobulin in biochip-like bio-membranes.

1 Introduction

Antigen processing is an important operation used by the immune system to provide total success of recognition and destruction of any non-self intruder. Summarily, the operation can be considered as cutting the antigen to pieces. Also called as antigenic peptides (peptide is a small protein), they usually represent local singularities of the antigen. After the processing, the antigenic peptides are represented on the surface of so called antigen presenting cells. It can be said that the antigen presenting cells show the singularities of the processed antigen to another immune cells for successful recognition of the whole antigen.

It is also known that the primary structure of any protein, represents a string in an alphabet of 20 amino-acids (e.g., see [10]). On the other hand, DTT and a p-adic sampling Theorem have recently been introduced in [1] and [5] acting on a collection of strings over an alphabet of p letters, where $p>1$. Being a special case of the Wavelet Transform (e.g., see [4]), DDT possesses an ability to focus at local singularities of the explored strings, (i.e. to explore the main frequencies of a periodic signal (see [3]), or the diversity of the fractal dimension (as in [4])), just like the antigen processing focuses on the local singularities of the proteins.

The above analogy prompts a new approach to application of DTT for one-dimensional signal processing. Moreover, according to [8], two-dimensional image can be reduced to two one-dimensional "antigens". Thus, the approach can also be useful for image processing.

---

[*] This work was supported by the European Commission under the EU project IST-2000-26016 Immunocomputing.

J. Timmis et al. (Eds.): ICARIS 2003, LNCS 2787, pp. 111–119, 2003.

The rest of the paper is organized as follows. Section 2 defines the binary DTT of any non-negative data and discusses some of its properties. Section 3 describes the algorithm for edge detection of time series. Section 4 presents applications of the approach to the detection of local singularities in human electrocardiogram and to enhancing of the detection of bound complexes of human immunoglobulin in biochip-like bio-membranes.

2 Mathematical Description of Dyadic DTT

Let $T_0 = \{t_1, .., t_S\}$ be a data consisting of S non-negative observations, where $S>1$. Let N be an integer such that $2^{N-1} < S \le 2^N$. Note that any data set can be done non-negative. For example, if $D = \{d_1, .., d_S\}$ contains negative values, then $T_0 = \{d_1 + d_{min}, .., d_S + d_{min}\}$ is non-negative, where $d_{min} = min\{d_1, .., d_S\}$.

Definition 1. The *dyadic extension* of T_0 is the following data:

$$T = \begin{cases} t_k, & 1 \le k \le S \\ t_S, & S < k \le 2^N. \end{cases} \quad (1)$$

It is obvious that $N = [log_2(S)]$ for any $S>1$, where $[x]$ is the biggest integer which is smaller than x and $T = T_0$ for $S = 2^N$.

Definition 2. The *binary tree expansion* of a non-negative data collection T is determined as follows:

$$\left\{ R_{n,k}(T) = \sum_{r=(k-1)2^{N-n}+1}^{k2^{N-n}} t_r, \quad k = 1,...,2^n, \quad n = 0,...,N \right\}.$$

For any $n = 1, .., N$, this definition implies that:

$$R_{n,2k-1}(T) + R_{n,2k}(T) = R_{n-1,k}(T), \quad k = 1,...,2^{n-1}. \quad (2)$$

Note that a *tree* is a standard data structure used in computer science and elsewhere for organizing information. Information in a tree is stored in *nodes*, starting with a root node and ending with terminal nodes called *leaves*. Nodes are linked to other nodes through *branches*. Leaves are nodes without any branches. Obviously, the following collection:

$$\left\{ R_{n,k}(T), \quad k = 1,...,2^n, \quad n = 0,...,N \right\}$$

has a binary tree structure with $N+1$ generations, such that: $R_{0,1}(T)$ corresponds to the initial node of the tree; each $R_{n,k}(T)$, $n = 1, .., N-1$ corresponds to the k node of the n-generation and $R_{N,k}(T)$ is the k branch (or leaf) of the last generation.

Definition 3. The *walks* $a_{n,k}(T)$ are the following real numbers:

$$a_{n,k}(T) = \begin{cases} 0, & R_{n-1,\left[\frac{k}{2}\right]}(T) = 0 \\ \dfrac{R_{n,k}(T)}{R_{n-1,\left[\frac{k}{2}\right]}(T)}, & R_{n-1,\left[\frac{k}{2}\right]}(T) \neq 0 \end{cases},$$

$$n = 1,..,N, \quad k = 1,..,2^n.$$

Definition 4. The *n-multiresolution* projection of T is the following collection:

$$\left\{ \frac{R_{n,\left[\frac{k-1}{2^{N-n}}\right]+1}(T)}{2^{N-n}}, k = 1,...,2^N \right\}, n = 0,..,N .$$

Definition 5. The Discrete Tree Transform (DTT) of T is the map:

$$T \to \{ a_{n,k}(T) : \ n = 1,...,N, \ k = 1,...,2^n \}.$$

The following Proposition gives one of the main properties of DTT (see [5]).

Proposition 1. The DTT of $T = \{ t_1,...,t_{2^N} \}$ satisfies to the multiplication formula:

$$R_{n,k}(T) = a_{n,k}(T)a_{n-1,[k/2]}(T)...a_{1,[k/2^{n-1}]}(T)R_{0,1}(T),$$

$$n = 1,..,N, \ k = 1,..,2^n.$$

Note that $R_{N,k}(T) = t_k$. Thus, for $n=N$, the last formula reconstructs the initial data set (leaves of the tree), while for $n<N$ it reconstructs the branches of the tree.
DTT gives also useful measure of data's variability.

Definition 6. The *tree variability* $V_n(T)$ of data T is the collection of numbers:

$$V_n(T) = \{ \omega_{n,k}(T) \}, \ \omega_{n,k}(T) = \frac{R_{n,k}(T) - R_{n,k+1}(T)}{2^{N-n}},$$

$$n = 1,..,N, \ k = 1,..,2^n - 1.$$

Definition 7. The norm of $V_n(T)$ is defined to be:

$$\| V_n(T) \| = \frac{1}{(2^N - 1)} \sum_{k=1}^{2^n - 1} |\omega_{n,k}(T)|, \ n = 1,..,N.$$

As a consequence of Definition 7, the norm of T_0 is:

$$\|V(T_0)\| = \frac{1}{S-1} \sum_{k=1}^{S-1} |t_k - t_{k+1}|. \tag{3}$$

Assuming that T is non trivial, we can prove below that the variability norm is a strictly increasing sequence.

Proposition 2. Let $T = \{t_1,...,t_{2N}\}$ such that $t_i \neq t_j$ for some i,j and $1 \leq n < m < N$, then:

$$\|V_n(T)\| < \|V_m(T)\| < \|V_N(T)\|.$$

3 Processing of Time Series

Consider edge detection as a processing to detect local singularities greater than some threshold. Consider the following problems of edge detection for (one-dimensional) time series:

1. Find measure of data variability and select the suitable threshold of variability.
2. Replace the original data by another one with the chosen variability.
3. Determine the important extreme points.

Using DTT processing, the problems can be solved by the following way: For problem 1, denote the tree variability of T and use Lemma 1 below to get the edge index n_0.

Definition 8. The *b-processing* of $T = \{t_1,...,t_{2N}\}$ is any data $Q(T) = \{t'_1,...,t'_{2N}\}$ such that:

$$\begin{cases} |t'_k - t'_{k+1}| = |t_k - t_{k+1}|, & if \quad |t_k - t_{k+1}| > b \\ |t'_k - t'_{k+1}| = 0, & if \quad |t_k - t_{k+1}| \leq b \end{cases},$$

$$k = 1,.,2^{N-1}.$$

Lemma 1. Let $\|V(T_0)\|$ be as in (3). Then for any $\|V(T_0)\|$-processing $Q(T) = \{t'_1,...,t'_{2N}\}$ of data $T = \{t_1,...,t_{2N}\}$ we obtain:

$$\|V(T_0)\| > \|V_N(T)\| > \|V_N(Q(T))\|. \tag{4}$$

There exists also a unique index n_0 such that for $1 < n_0 < N$ the following expression is minimal:

$$\left\| \|V_{n_0}(T)\| - \|V_N(Q(T))\| \right\| \tag{5}$$

Note that T is associated with the variability norms $V_n(T)$, $n=1,..,N$. These norms give the average variability of T over all (multiresolution) projections of T. Thus, call the index (5) as *edge index* of any data T.

For problem 2, get the n_0-projection of T. For problem 3, apply Proposition 3 (below) on the n_0-projection of T.

Proposition 3. If n_0 is the edge index and $a_{n,k}(T)$ are the walks, then the following set determines the position of the relevant extreme points of the n_0-projection of T:

$$J_k(T) = \left\{ k : sign\left(a(n_0,2k) - \frac{1}{2} \right) sign\left(a(n_0,2k+1) - \frac{1}{2} \right) = -1, \quad k = 1,...,2^{n_0-1} - 1 \right\}.$$

The following algorithm gives the rigorous solutions of the above problems.

1. Given a data $T_0 = \{t_1,..,t_S\}$, choose an integer N such that $2^{N-1} < S \leq 2^N$ and define the 2^N-dyadic extension of $T = \{t_1, t_2,...,t_{S-1}, t_S, t_S,...,t_S\}$.

2. Estimate $\|V(T_0)\|$ and $\{\|V_n(T)\|, n = 1,...,N\}$.

3. Find the $\|V(T_0)\|$-processing data $Q(T)$.

4. Use the $\|V(T_0)\|$-processing data to get the index $n_0 < N$.

5. Find the set $J_k(T)$ as in Proposition 3.

6. The set $\left\{ t_{\alpha(s)} : a(s) = 2^{N-n}s, \ s \in J_k(T) \right\}$ determines the singularities (local minima and maxima) of the original data T.

4 Applications

4.1 Electrocardiogram

We have applied DTT processing to a human ECG of $2^{10} = 1024$ observations (Fig. 1). According to Fig. 2, the processing successfully determines all singularities of ECG via the 8-projection of the original data.

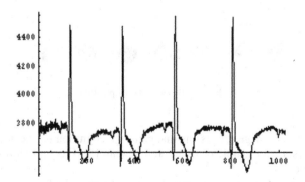

Fig. 1. The original ECG

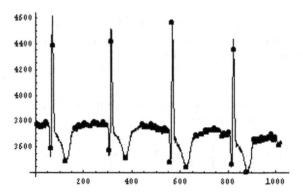

Fig. 2. The detected singularities of ECG

4.2 Immunoassays

We have applied DTT processing to enhance the detection of bound complexes of human immunoglobulin-G (IgG) with protein-G (pG), in biochip-like bio-membranes. The detection is based on a software implementation of our immunocomputing approach to pattern recognition [9]. Inspired by principles of antibody-antigen recognition in the natural immune system, our software solves problems of distinguishing background ("self") from patterns ("non-self") and processing the patterns. We have applied our software to a prototype of a protein biochip for immunoassay-based diagnostics [8].

We obtain bioarray as a nitrocellulose strip (bio-membrane) with the rows and columns of IgG. Detailed description of the biological part of the work can be found in [8]. We scan bioarrays by a custom scanner to make them available for processing on any usual Personal Computer (PC). Figure 3 shows an example of the scanned bioarray.

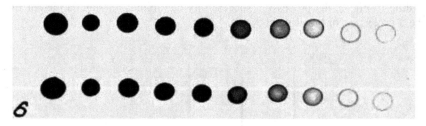

Fig. 3. Bioarray #6 of pG-IgG

The software for image processing and pattern recognition has been developed as a version of the software emulator of an immunochip [7]. Figure 4 shows a screenshot of the emulator.

Bioarray image is represented initially as a matrix M_A of dimension $n_L \times n_R$. According to the "key and lock" principle of antibody-antigen recognizing in the immune system, we consider the matrix M_A as a collection of "antigens-locks". To compute "antibodies-keys", we form an inverse matrix M of the same dimension:

$$M = 255 - M_A.$$

We represent this matrix in the following form:

$$M \cong sLR^T, \; L^TL = 1, \, R^TR = 1, \tag{6}$$

where s is first singular value; L and R are first left and right singular vectors of the matrix M. It is known (see e.g., [9]) that representation (6) corresponds to the first term of the so-called Singular Value Decomposition (SVD). Such SVD exists for any rectangular matrix over the field of real values and can be computed by an evolutionary like iterative scheme [10].

According to [9], unit vectors L, R can be considered as a mathematical model of "antibodies-probes", while $w=-s$ is their binding energy within so-called Formal Immune Network (FIN). By such a way, using our immunocomputing approach, we reduce two-dimensional input "antigen" M_A to two one-dimensional "antibodies" L, R. These "antibodies" represent a kind of "internal image" of the "antigen", generated by FIN. Figures 4 and 5 show the profiles of such "antibodies" in the right-hand screen.

Thus, using decomposition (6), we reduce the problem of detecting spots in the input image M_A to simpler task of finding local minima of one-dimensional functions L, R. The emulator determines these minima as "paratopes" (antigen binding parts of antibody), according to an analogy of "antigen processing" by the natural immune system.

Such "paratopes" of the left singular vector L correspond to the rows of the bioarray. For example, if vector L has two "paratopes" (as in two upper graphics of right-hand screen in Fig. 4), then the bioarray has two rows of spots (as in left-hand screen in Fig. 4). Analogously, the emulator finds all "paratopes" of the right singular vector R. They correspond to the columns of spots of the bioarray. For example, if vector R has eight "paratopes" (as in two lower graphics of right-hand screen in Fig. 4), then the bioarray has eight columns of spots (as in left-hand screen of Fig. 4).

As a result, the emulator detects roughly positions of all spots of the bioarray as the squares (see left-hand screen in Fig. 4). Comparing Fig. 3 and Fig. 4, one can notice, that four spots have been undetected in right-hand part of the bioarray #6. To enhance the detection, we apply DTT processing of "paratopes". Figure 5 shows an example of enhanced detection of spots by using this processing. Smooth curves in right-hand screen of Fig. 5 show initial profile of the "paratopes", while the corresponding stepped curves below show the processed profile. Note that all undetected spots of bioarray #6 in Fig. 4 have been detected in left-hand screen of Fig. 5 by using of DTT processing.

5 Conclusions

The proposed approach to signal processing is inspired by a mode of biomolecular computing, when immune cells chop unknown antigen to its local singularities and expose them to the immune system. Analogously, our approach represents unknown signal as a tree of data, and chop the branches of the tree to detect local singularities of the signal. The approach is based on the rigorous mathematical methods of DTT and SVD. The first method is implemented to process one-dimensional time series, while the second one reduces two-dimensional images to the previous case of two one-dimensional signals. The approach proved to be useful by its successful application to real-world data of human ECG and immunoassays. It's worth noting, that the approach can naturally be extended to process three-dimensional shapes (e.g., like in [6]), as corresponding extension of SVD has been proposed in [10].

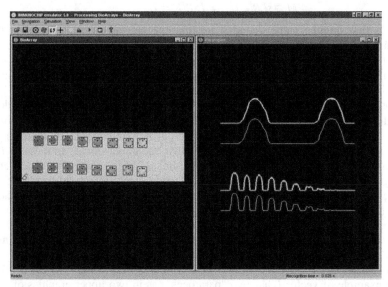

Fig. 4. Immunochip emulator for detection of bound complexes IgG-pG

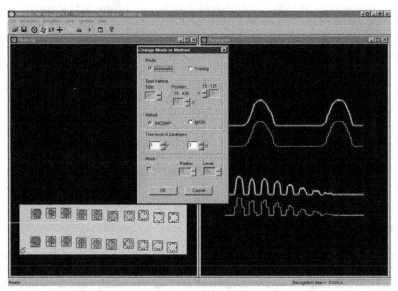

Fig. 5. Enhanced detection of IgG-pG complexes by DTT processing

References

1. Atreas, N., Karanikas, C.: Sampling formulas for spectral wavelet analysis on spaces of periodic sequences in base p>1 for computational applications of immune type. Applied Comp. Harm. Anal. (2003, submitted)
2. Atreas, N., Karanikas, C.: Detectors for Pattern Recognition on Periodic Forests of Data (2003, preprint)
3. Bisbas, A., Karanikas, C.: A New Entropy Formula for the Diversity of Strings and its Relation with the Dimension of Known Fractals (2003, preprint)
4. Daubechies, I.: Ten lectures on wavelets. CBMS-NSF Regional Conferences Series in Applied Mathematics. SIAM Philadelphia (1992)
5. Karanikas, C., Proios, G.: A discrete transform for pattern recognition of immune type based on the tree structure of data. Chaos, Solitions and Fractals (to appear in 2003)
6. Tarakanov, A., Adamatzky, A.: Virtual clothing in hybrid cellular automata. Kybernetes (Int. J. of Systems & Cybernetics) 31 (7/8) (2002) 1059-1072
7. Tarakanov, A., Dasgupta, D.: An immunochip architecture and its emulation. NASA/DoD Conf. on Evolvable Hardware (EH-2002). Alexandria, Virginia (2002) 261-265
8. Tarakanov, A., Goncharova, L, Gupalova, T., Kvachev, S., Sukhorukov, A.: Immunocomputing for bioarrays. 1st Int. Conf. on Artificial Immune Systems (ICARIS-2002). University of Kent at Canterbury, UK (2002) 32-40
9. Tarakanov, A., Skormin, V.: Pattern recognition by immunocomputing. World Congress on Computational Intelligence (CEC-2002), Vol. 1. Honolulu, Hawaii (2002) 938-943
10. Tarakanov, A.O., Skormin, V.A., Sokolova, S.P.: Immunocomputing: Principles and Applications. Springer-Verlag, New York (2003)

Index Design by Immunocomputing

Ludmilla Sokolova

St. Petersburg Institute for Informatics and Automation, Russian Academy of Sciences
14-line 39, St. Petersburg 199178, Russia
Lucy@sokolova.fsnet.co.uk

Abstract. This paper presents the concept of applying indices, data fusion and mathematical models using immunocomputing approach. The application of indices by immunocomputing can reduce large quantities of variable data relating to a complex interacting dynamic system, into a single general value or index that represents all of those factors (data fusion) to achieve a solution to a practical problem. To illustrate the concept, this article provides examples of mathematical models showing the identification of intrusions into computer networks and the occurrence of plague in Kazakhstan.

Keywords: Intrusion index, plague risk index, immunocomputing

1 Introduction

An index of a complex multi-dimensional dynamic system is essentially a general value that integrates a large number of special factors or variables called indicators. In some cases such an index is the only way to represent clearly the current state of a system and its dynamics, from which it is possible to estimate activity and try to predict risks and trends. For example, indices of business activity such as the Dow-Jones or NASDAQ indices are widely used in economics and finance. Some indices can be computed rather simply, as an average of a series of definite variables. The Standard and Poor's Index, for example, applies a value to the average performance of 500 stocks on the New York Stock Exchange over the course of a day. The Retail Price Index, as another example, measures the average increases in price of a standard range of foodstuffs across the UK. Analogous indices are of great importance in other fields as well as economics. The World Health Organisation for example calls the Mark of General Health Status an indicator or index. However, indices used in the field of ecology [7], are much more complex and not easy to create.

The application of immunocomputing techniques to indices that have been enhanced by mathematical models is a very effective method of reducing large quantities of complex, dynamic, discrete data to an easily understood index from which assessments can be made for important practical applications. These indices provide a fusion of data, i.e. integrating multi-dimensional heterogeneous data into one number. This is illustrated below using an index that can detect the risk of intrusions into computer networks and a plague risk index that can clearly indicate the risk of plague infection in a given area.

J. Timmis et al. (Eds.): ICARIS 2003, LNCS 2787, pp. 120–127, 2003.

2 Mathematical Model and Its Applications

Using an Immunocomputing approach, the following mathematical model is proposed to calculate an index for complex multi-dimensional system as follows:

Let $x_1, .., x_n$ be indicators of a complex multi-dimensional system. Let $X = [x_1, .., x_n]^T$ be a column-vector of this system record, where "^{T}" is a transposing symbol. Consider a training matrix $M = [X_1,..,X_m]^T$ of dimension $m \times n$, where $X_1,..X_m$ are records of the complex system state with known behavior: normal ("self") or abnormal ("non-self"). Using an Immunocomputing approach [11], consider the Singular Value Decomposition (SVD) of this matrix:

$$M = s_1 L_1 R_1^T + ... + s_r L_r R_r^T, \tag{1}$$

where r is the rank of the matrix, $s_1,..,s_r$ are singular values, $L_1,..,L_r$ are left singular vectors, and $R_1,..,R_r$ are right singular vectors. These singular values and vectors satisfy the following bindings:

$$s_1 \geq s_2 \geq ... s_p \geq 0, \; s_i = L_i^T A R_i, \; R_i^T R_i = 1, \; L_i^T L_i = 1, i = 1,..,r.$$

Select any right vector R_k as an "antibody-probe". Consider any state of the complex system which is presented by vector Z, and define its "abnormal energy" as follows:

$$w(Z) = \frac{1}{s_k} Z^T R_k. \tag{2}$$

Consider the following useful properties of the abnormal energy.

Let Z be the i-th string of the matrix M: $Z = X_i, i=1,..,m$. Then the abnormal energy of Z is exactly i-th component of the left singular vector L_k : $w = L_{k,i}$. This proposition follows from the known property of the singular vector [8]:

$$MR_k = s_k L_k.$$

Mathematically, the abnormal energy represents a linear combination of the input vector Z with coefficients given by the right singular vector R_k.

Physically, according to [11], the abnormal energy can be considered as a special case of "binding energy" between two "formal proteins": R_k and Z. Therefore, abnormal energy can be considered as a one-dimensional shape space model of an artificial immune system [5, 6].

Based on the abnormal energy (2), an "index for a complex multi-dimensional system" of vector Z is defined by the following empirical formula:

$$I(Z) = Entier(c_0 + c_1 w), \tag{3}$$

where c_0 and c_1 are coefficients.

Let any threshold I_h be given. Consider that $I \leq I_h$ correspond to normal behavior of a complex multi-dimensional system, while $I > I_h$ detects the abnormal behaviour.

It is worth noting that the values of the coefficients c_0 and c_1, as well as the number k of the right singular vector in equation (2) and the threshold I_h have to be selected according to the specific application. The selection can be made either empirically or using a formal method. This situation corresponds to supervised learning in pattern recognition [11].

The proposed algorithm has been used to calculate an intrusion index into computer networks and a plague risk index for landscape-ecological region of the Akdala plane presented bellow.

2.1 An Intrusion Index

Consider a numerical experiment with a fragment of the database [4]. The fragment contains connection records obtained from a model of a local area network provided by the US Air Force.

The database fragment contains 106 records of network connections: $X_1, ., X_{106}$. The records correspond to the normal behavior ('normal') of the network connections and to several types of intrusions, as in the first column of Table 1, where types of intrusions correspond to the designations of [4].

The fragment utilizes 33 indicators $x_1, ., x_{33}$ for any network connection, including x_1 – lengths (number of seconds) of the connection, x_2 – number of data bytes sent from source to destination, x_3 – number of data bytes sent from destination to source, ... , x_{26} – % of connections to the same destination host and the same service as the current connection in the past two seconds, ... , x_{33} – % of connections that have errors. An example of the connection record vector X_2 for intrusion of 'apache2' type is given below:

$$X_2 = [906, 57964, 0, 0, 0, 0, 1, 0, 0, 0, 0, 0, 0, 0, 2, 2, 0, 0, 1, 1, 1, 0, 0, 255,$$
$$253, 0.99, 0.01, 0,0, 0, 0, 0.01, 0.01]^T.$$

As shown in the previous section, form the training matrix $M=[X_1, ., X_{106}]^T$ with a dimension 106×33, and compute its SVD (1). According to the visual representation of clusters of binding energies for this example, as in [11], select the 5-th right singular vector R_5 as an "antibody-probe" for equation (2).

The components of this vector are given below:

$$R_5 = [0.0883, 0.0000, -0.0013, 0.0000, 0.0038, 0.0011, -0.0002, 0.0022,$$
$$0.0006, 0.0035, 0.0011, 0.0005, 0.0007, 0.0001, 0.0856, -0.0104,$$
$$0.0003, 0.0004, 0.0019, 0.0019, -0.0008, 0.0023, -0.0001, 0.4163,$$
$$-0.9008, -0.0037, 0.0011, -0.0002, -0.0002, -0.0000, 0.0003, 0.0007,$$
$$0.0023]^T.$$

According to the computed singular value $s_5 = 927$, consider $c_0=1000$. According to the computed values of intrusion energy (2) for the strings of the training matrix M, consider $c_1=250$, to avoid negative values of the intrusion index. Consider strings of this matrix as a set of test vectors Z. Table 1 gives values of the intrusion index, computed by (3).

Note that normal behavior of the network connection corresponds to relatively low values of the intrusion index: {3, 34, 63, 82, 118, 119, 236, 252}. Thus we can select the intrusion threshold as $I_h=100$. According to Table 1, any connection with $I \leq 100$ strictly corresponds to normal behavior, while any connection with $I>100$ can be considered as an intrusion.

Note that some normal connections with an intrusion index {118, 119, 236, 252} will be detected as intrusions. Such examples are treated as "false positive" in pattern recognition. However, more importantly the intrusion index gives no "false negative" examples, i.e. no intrusion have an index of less than 100. Therefore the proposed intrusion index can be a useful tool for the detection of intrusions.

Table 1. Computed values of the intrusion index

Intrusion type	Protocol type	Service	Intrusion Index
Normal	udp	private	3, 34, 63, 82, 118, 119, 236, 252
apache2	tcp	http	199, 204-206
buffer_overflow	tcp	telnet	349, 364, 368
guess_password	tcp	pop_3	361, 363
Ipsweep	icmp	eco_i	175, 182, 222, 224, 227, 239, 242, 249, 250
Multihop	tcp	telnet	253, 346, 364, 366,
Named	tcp	domain	228, 250, 251, 254, 268, 335, 431
Phf	tcp	http	241
Pod	icmp	ecr_i	234-250, 364
Portsweep	tcp	private	364
Saint	tcp	private	366-374
Sendmail	tcp	smtp	250, 272, 355, 362, 364
Snmpgetattack	udp	private	117-120
Udpstorm	udp	private	251
Xlock	tcp	X11	164, 246, 262, 301, 359, 370
Xsnoop	tcp	X11	348, 364

2.2 A Plague Risk Index

Natural plague foci have existed from ancient times and have been responsible for the deaths of many people. The second pandemic lasted from the 14-th to the 17-th centuries. The effects of this natural and human disaster changed the population of Europe profoundly, perhaps more so than any other event. For this reason, alone, the Black Death should be ranked as the greatest biological-environmental event in history. For the last 150 years the plague outbreaks have occurred regularly in different parts of the world.

Plague foci in the world covering vast territories are characterized by different regulation mechanisms at the population species and community (biocenotic) levels. The plague epizootic process is a complex multi-component dynamic system including the particular subsystems of the plague epizootic triad: carrier – vector - agent. The carriers are urban or rural warm-blooded animals (such as large gerbils, marmots, camels and so on). The vectors are fleas, which occur on the carriers. The transmission of infection can be through direct contact, ingestion, or droplet spread. The agents are plague microbes. The first stage of Plague is Bubonic Plague. The human immune system activates and makes every effort to destroy the infection. The mortality during this stage is about 30-40 %. The second stage is Pneumonic Plague, which is transmitted through droplet spread. The mortality is 100%.

The epizootic period is characterized [1, 2, 3] by a high susceptibility to infection of the carrier population, high density of carrier population, high numbers of vectors. The accumulations of the causative agents of plague increase its virulence. The rise is a specific response to the size of the carrier population. A decline in vector numbers and carrier density leads to a decline in the virulence of plague strains. The interepizootic period is characterized by: a rise of vector numbers, a rise of the density of the carrier population, an increase in the susceptibility to infection, a high specific response, rarity of density of carrier population and sporadic cases of plague among the carrier population.

For the first time, mathematical models have now been obtained [9] which show the dynamics of interactive carrier –vector relationship on population level in the plague triad. It is suggested that a new qualitative approach to predicting epizootic processes in natural plague foci [14] is now available using an Immunocomputing approach for its solution.

The aforementioned mathematical model to calculate a Plague risk index (PRI) for the landscape-ecological region - Akdala plane is proposed as follows: the database fragment contains 22 records of the space-time series with known behaviour: normal ("self") or epizootic ("non-self") from 1975 to 1997 years: $X_1,.,X_{22}$. The fragment utilises 45 indicators $x_1,.,x_{45}$. These indicators characterise the plague triad state such as: x_1 - number of rodents per square (in autumn), x_2 - (in spring), x_3 - number of infected rodents per square (in autumn), x_4 - (in spring),..., x_{40} - total atmospheric precipitates (September), x_{41} - average height of the snow blanket (January), x_{43} - average height of the snow blanket (March), x_{44} – average height of the snow blanket (November), x_{45} – average height of the snow blanket (December).

An example of the connection record vectors X_1, X_2, which characterized the plague triad states in 1975 year and in 1976 year, is given below:

$$X_1 = [3.3, 1.3, 5.2, 8.7, 33.9, 1.3, ..., 5.0, 0.3, 0.0, 4.5]^{T}.$$

$$X_2 = [0.7, 1.1, 29.6, 0.6, 3.1, 2.1,.,0.1, 4.7, 4.4, 3.7]^{T}.$$

The annual (spring, autumn) space-time dynamics of the plague numbers: numbers of careers, numbers of fleas, numbers of infected sectors are represented in Figure 1. For identifying the state of the epizootic process we use four classes: Class 1 - the period of depression prior to the epizootic process. Class 2 - the ascending branch of the epizootic process. Class 3 – the descending branch of the epizootic process. Class 4 – the depression after the epizootic process. The states of the epizootic triad on the ascending branch and the descending branch of the epizootic processes are different. The records correspond to the normal behaviour ('self') - Classes 1 and 4, and to the epizootic process ('non-self') – Classes 2 and 3.

The value of the Plague Risk Index (PRI) was calculated using the algorithm described above. In compliance with Figure 1, assign a dimensioned risk multiplier of $v=125$. The results of the calculations are shown in the table 2. The comparison of findings with Figure 1 shows that the suggested PRI reveals sharp peaks indicating major increases in the populations of carriers and vectors in 1979 and 1988. It is worth noting that after those peaks there were epizootic outbreaks in 1979 and 1989. Thus the PRI as a concept has been vindicated because the high values shown in the PRI have predicted an epizootic outbreak.

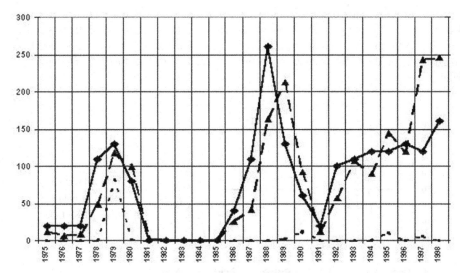

Fig. 1. Annual space-time dynamics of the plague numbers: numbers of careers (rhombus), numbers of fleas (triangles), numbers of infected sectors (points)

Table 2. Plague Risk Index according to the monitoring results of Akdala plain

m	YEAR	Y	PRI	RISK of EPIZOOTIC
1	1976	0.106	13	
2	1977	0.101	13	
3	1978	0.184	23	
4	**1979**	**0.560**	**70**	**High!!!**
5	1980	0.504	63	
6	1981	0.416	52	
7	1982	0.208	26	
8	1983	0.01	12	
9	1984	0.112	14	
10	1985	0.247	31	
11	1986	0.184	23	
12	1987	0.296	37	Mid
13	**1988**	**0.680**	**85**	**High!!!**
14	1989	0.496	62	
15	**1990**	**0.408**	**51**	**High**
16	1991	0.280	35	Mid
17	1992	0.168	21	
18	**1993**	**0.52**	**65**	**High**
19	1994	0.576	72	**High**
20	1995	0.480	60	**High**
21	1996	0.344	43	
22	1997	0.248	31	
22	1997	0.115	14	

Based on the results of the computation of the *PRI* values that are presented in the Table 2, we can select the *PRI* threshold as $PRI_t=50$. Any values with $PRI \leq 50$ strictly correspond to normal behavior, while any values with $PRI>50$ can be considered as an epizootic process. The diagrams for infected sectors, PRI_t and *PRI* are presented in Figure 2.

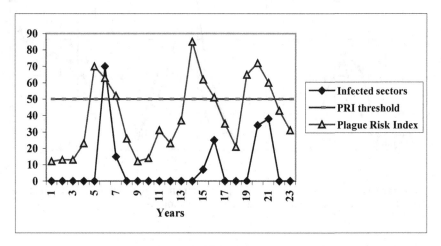

Fig.2 Interrelation of PRI with epizootic processes

The results of the computation shown in Figure 2, show that the calculated algorithm based on an Immunocomputing approach solves prediction tasks with the required degree of accuracy.

3   Conclusion

The application of indices using an Immunocomputing can reduce large quantities of variable data relating to a complex multi-dimensional interacting dynamic system, into a single general value or index that represents all of these factors (data fusion). From such an index it is possible to make assessments and predict the behaviour of the system by applying a mathematical model to the index. Examples of this are given above for (1) predicting the outbreak of natural plague and (2) the computation of indices for the identification of intrusions into computer networks.

In conclusion, the application of immunocomputing techniques to indices that have been enhanced using techniques of data fusion and mathematical models is a very effective method of reducing large quantities of complex, dynamic, discrete data to an easily understood index from which assessments can be made for an important practical application.

Acknowledgements

The author acknowledges the support of EOARD within the ISTC Project 2200p "Development of mathematical models of immune networks intended for information security assurance", EU Commission under INCO-contract # ICA2-CT-2000-10048 "The plague of Central Asia an epidemiological study focusing on space-time dynamics".

References

1. Ageyev V.S. Parasitic contacts of rodents in the river valleys of the desert zone of Kazakhstan and their significance in the plague epizootology, Saratov (1975), pp. 3-19 (in Russian)
2. Aikimbayev A.M., et al. Epidemiological Plague surveillance in the Ural-Emba and Ustyurt Autonomous Foci. Almaty, Gylym (1994) (in Russian)
3. Aubakirov S.A., et al. Instruction on Landscape-Epizootic Regionalization of Natural Plague Foci in Central Asia and Kazakhstan. Almaty, Gylym (1990) (in Russian)
4. Bay, S.D. The UCI KDD Archive [http://kdd.ics.uci.edu]. Irvine, CA: University of California, Dept. of Information and Computer Science (1999)
5. De Boer, R.J., Segel, L.A., Perelson, A.S. Pattern formation in one and two-dimensional shape space models of the immune system. J. Theoret. Biol. 155 (1992) 295-333
6. De Castro, L.N., Timmis, J. Artificial Immune Systems: A New Computational Intelligence Paradigm. Springer, New York (2002)
7. Kuznetsov, V.I., Milyaev, V.B. Tarakanov, A.O. Mathematical basis of complex ecological evaluation. St.Petersburg University Press (1999)
8. Horn, R., Johnson, Ch. Matrix Analysis. Cambridge University Press (1986)
9. Marshall E.C., Frigessi A., Stenseth N.C., Holden M., Ageyev V.S. and Klassovsky N.L. Plague in Kazakhstan: a Bayesian model for the temporal dynamics of a vector-transmitted infections disease. Oslo, University of Oslo (2001)
10. Sokolova S.P., Sokolova L.A. Immunocomputing for Complex Interval Objects.// Pros.1st International Conference on Artificial Immune Systems (ICARIS – 2002), - University of Kent at Canterbury, UK, (2002), pp.222-230
11. Tarakanov, A.O., Skormin, V.A., Sokolova, S.P. Immunocomputing: Principles and Applications. Springer, New York (2003, in press)
12. Tarakanov A.O. Formal peptide as a basic agent of immune networks: from natural prototype to mathematical theory and applications. // Proc. of the 1st Int. Workshop of Central and Eastern Europe on Multi-Agent Systems (CEEMAS'99), St. Petersburg, Russia, 1999, pp. 281-292.
13. Tarakanov A., Dasgupta D. A formal model of an artificial immune system. // BioSystems, 2000, 55 (1-3), pp. 151-158.
14. Tarakanov A., Sokolova S., Abramov B., Aikimbayev A. Immunocomputing of the natural plague foci. // Proc. of the Genetic and Evolutionary Computation Conference (GECCO-2000), Workshop on Artificial Immune Systems. – Las Vegas, USA, 2000, pp. 38-41.

Immune-Based Framework for Exploratory Bio-information Retrieval from the Semantic Web

Doheon Lee[1,*], Jungja Kim[2], Mina Jeong[2], Yonggwan Won[2],
Seon Hee Park[3], and Kwang-Hyung Lee[1]

[1] Dept. of BioSystems/AITrc, KAIST, Daejeon, Korea
[2] Dept. of Computer Engineering, Chonnam Nat'l Univ., Gwangju, Korea
[3] Computer and Software Research Lab., ETRI, Daejeon, Korea

Abstract. This paper proposes an immune-based framework for adaptive query expansion in the semantic web, where exploratory queries, common in biological information retrieval, can be answered more effectively. The proposed technique has a metaphor with negative selection and clonal expansion in immune systems. This work is differentiated from the previous query expansion techniques by its data-driven adaptation. It utilizes target databases as well as the ontology to expand queries. This data-driven adaptive feature is especially important in exploratory information retrieval where the querying intention itself can be dynamically changed by relevance feedback.

1 Introduction

The semantic web is a collaborative effort to make the web information machine-understandable. By associating semantic descriptions with web information elements, computer programs such as web robots can access the web in more meaningful ways. For example, suppose that an XML (eXtensible Markup Language) document has 'Title' and 'Author' elements. Without extra information, the XML document alone can indicate at best those two elements are components of a certain information unit [1]. If we associate an RDF (Resource Description Framework) description such that 'Author Publishes Title' with the XML document, a web robot can infer that those two elements are semantically related to each other by 'Publishes' relationship. If we associate a different description such that 'Author Has Title' with the same document, it leads different interpretation. Since this sort of semantic treatment is an essential ingredient to leverage the web as an information thesaurus, there have been fast growing interest and efforts to develop semantic web frameworks and RDF-based ontology systems recently [2][3][4].

Currently, we have over 500 bio-databases available in the Internet [5], and tons of bio-information repositories containing experimental summaries, published papers, and white papers. It is quite common that information requests arising in biology laboratories can be answered by integrating different but related information from such disparate sources. Thus, there have been many research and development endeavors to achieve integrated information retrieval systems, whichever they are virtual integration or data warehousing-based [6][7]. In the database community, the integration of heterogeneous data sources has been a longstanding but still a difficult

---

* To whom correspondence should be addressed

J. Timmis et al. (Eds.): ICARIS 2003, LNCS 2787, pp. 128–135, 2003.

issue. One of the most practical approaches is to pursue standardization as far as possible both in syntax and semantics so that information systems understand and exchange different information effectively. Despite that so many proposals have come and gone, XML and RDF-based semantic web is the most promising solution for that purpose now. XML facilitates to organize the information in a syntactically standardized way, and RDF makes it possible to fill the gaps between syntax and semantics.

Though information retrieval from bio-information repositories shares many common characteristics with traditional information retrieval domains such as library index systems and web search engines, it reveals at least two significant differences. Firstly, it is much harder to formulate the user query precisely at once since complex domain knowledge is heavily involved [10]. Rather, most users rely on interactive query reformulation based on relevance feedback [11]. Even if the users are well-trained to select proper terms to describe their queries, the severe diversity of biological terms from various disciplines causes significant amount of false positives and false negatives. More noticeable point is that the querying intention itself can be dynamically changed by relevance feedback. The second difference alleviates the problem. There are a lot of active standardization efforts on biological ontology construction [7][8][9], and more and more autonomous bio-information repositories have begun to accept the necessity and usefulness of such ontologies.

To remedy the hardness of precise query formulation, query expansion or query generalization techniques have been studied actively especially in the Internet-based information retrieval [12][13][14][15][16]. Though there have been many proposals for query expansion, they have common trade-offs. If queries are expanded too broadly, they retrieve too many false positives, and suffer unnecessary access cost. If queries are expanded too narrowly, they end up with many false negatives. Thus, the key issue of query expansion is how to expand queries to focus only on relevant information. To challenge this issue, it is necessary to expand queries in an adaptive manner, which means queries are expanded based on the result feedback. Recently, query expansion techniques for bio-databases focusing on vagueness of query expressions have been proposed [10][17]. However, they are not adaptive in the sense that they do not utilize relevance feedback. We have found a procedure of adaptive query expansion can have strong analogy with negative selection and clonal expansion principle in natural immune systems. Based on this observation, this paper proposes an adaptive query expansion technique for explorative bio-information retrieval from the semantic web in the framework of artificial immune systems. This approach can be regarded to belong to the information immune systems, which utilize the immune metaphor to filter unnecessary information glut [18].

Section 2 explains the metaphor between the proposed technique and immune principles, and Section 3 presents the proposed technique along with illustrative examples. Section 4 proposes a semantic web-based system architecture for implementing the proposed technique, and Section 5 concludes.

2 Immune Metaphor for Query Expansion

Let us remind the procedure of natural immune systems briefly to provide common terminology in this paper [19][20]. We will use the term 'antibodies' instead of 'B cells', and omit unnecessary biological details to focus on fundamental principles. (i)

In a primary lymphoid such as bone marrows, a large variety of immature antibodies are produced by combinatorial recombination of gene segments; (ii) Those antibodies who can bind with self-antigens are eliminated, i.e. negative selection; (iii) Mature antibodies circulate the body, and bind with foreign antigens; (iv) The foreign antigen-bound antibodies proliferate, and undergo hypermutation to produce more effective antibodies, i.e. clonal expansion; (v) Some of those antibodies differentiate to memory cells to cope with future infection, while the others become effector cells that can immediately bind with another instances of foreign antigens.

Our proposed information retrieval procedure follows similar steps. (i) Given a user query q_0, the procedure produces a set of queries Q_0 by expanding q_0 based on given ontologies; (ii) If the user-side querying system maintains a set of rules to avoid unnecessary information, the matching queries in Q_0 will be removed; (iii) The resulting Q_0 will be distributed to local information repositories through the Internet; Some of queries in Q_0 matches with data units in each local repository; (iv) Those matched queries are reported to the user-side querying system; Then subsequent query expansion is applied each query set from each local repository based on the given ontologies; (v) The matched queries are integrated into the knowledge-base to facilitate effective query expansion in another query processing. Table 1 shows an immune metaphor for our information retrieval technique.

Table 1. Immune metaphor for the proposed adaptive query expansion

	Natural Immune Systems	Adaptive Query Expansion
(i)	Gene recombination	Initial query expansion
(ii)	Elimination of improper antibodies	Elimination of uninteresting queries
(iii)	Binding to foreign antigens	Matching with data in local repositories
(iv)	Proliferation	Subsequent query expansion
(v)	Memory cells	Storing useful queries

3 Adaptive Query Expansion Procedure

To apply the adaptive query expansion, we suppose that local bio-information repositories provide RDF/XML signatures representing their respective information. Table 2 shows an example.

Table 2. Part of database signatures from local information repositories

No.	Substance	Relation	Process
d_1	Metabolic Enzyme	Related-to	Stomach Cancer
d_2	p53	Related-to	Cell cycle
d_3	E. coli	Exhibit	Chemotaxis
d_4	GPCR	Mediate	Signal Transduction
d_5	Metabolic Enzyme	Activate	Stomach Cancer

Though actual information repositories contain much more signatures than depicted in Table 2, it is given just for illustration. Actual representation of the signatures is supposed to be in RDF/XML. Figure 1 shows the appearance of such representation for the first and second rows of Table 2 as examples.

```
<rdf:RDF>
    <info:unit rdf:about="http://mydata.org/dbsig#d1">
        <info:substance> Metabolic Enzyme </info:substance>
        <info:relation> Related-to </info:relation>
        <info:process> Stomach Cancer </info:process>
    </info:unit>
    <info:unit rdf:about="http://mydata.org/dbsig#d2">
        <info:substance> p53 </info:substance>
        <info:relation> Related-to </info:relation>
        <info:process> Cell Cycle </info:process>
    </info:unit>
</rdf:RDF>
```

Fig. 1. RDF-XML representation of signatures in local information repositories

Also suppose that we have ontology as in Figure 2. Arrows and tildes represent 'isa' and 'synonym-of' relationships respectively.

```
Bio-molecule => Protein | Nucleic Acid | Compound
Protein => Cytoplasmic Protein | Nucleus Protein
Cytoplasmic Protein => Metabolic Enzyme | Protein Synthesis
    Factor
Disease => Infection Disease | Cancer | …
Cancer => Prostate Cancer | Stomach Cancer | Lung Cancer | …
Stomach Cancer ~ Gastric Cancer
Related-to => Activate | Repress
```

Fig. 2. Ontology example for adaptive query expansion

There are a lot of ongoing efforts to construct ontologies for various biological domains including genomics, proteomics, and medicine. Figure 3 shows a part of the ontology in Figure 2 in the form of RDF/XML as in the Gene Ontology [9].

Now, let us suppose that we have an initial query q_0 such as "Find information about cytoplasmic proteins related to stomach cancer." It is a typical query example in biology laboratories where stomach cancer is studied in the molecular level. Such queries have exploratory intention in nature. Though the query indicates cytoplasmic proteins and stomach cancer specifically, neighbor information such about intestinal cancer or membrane proteins could be also useful to the query submitters. It would become much more important if there are significant interactions between cytoplasmic proteins and membrane proteins in stomach cancer development.

Thus, query expansion to encompass such neighbor information is quite useful in exploratory query processing. By referring to the given ontology, the initial query q_0 can be expanded to a query set Q_0 as in Figure 4.

This query expansion is done by substituting terms in the initial query with direct descendent or direct ancestor terms in the given ontology one by one. As this illustrative example contains a few data and unrealistically small ontology, the expansion might look trivial work. However, it can come up with much more expanded queries in actual situations where the amount of data is huge and the size of ontology is realistic. For example, the current gene ontology in [9] contains over 70,000 terms. It can be mapped into gene recombination to produce a diversity of antibodies in the framework of the immune metaphor. As V/J/D regions of the antibodies are selected from gene segment libraries, this query expansion is done using ontology libraries.

```
<rdf:RDF>
    <go:term rdf:about="http://www.ontology.org/go#0001">
        <go:accession>GO:0001</go:accession>
        <go:name>Bio-Molecule</go:name>
    </go:term>
    <go:term rdf:about="http://www.ontology.org/go#0002">
        <go:accession>GO:0002</go:accession>
        <go:name>Protein</go:name>
        <go:isa rdf:resource="http://www.ontology.org/go#0001">
    </go:term>
    <go:term rdf:about="http://www.ontology.org/go#0234">
        <go:accession>GO:0234</go:accession>
        <go:name>Stomach Cancer</go:name>
        <go:synonym>Gastric Cancer</go:synonym>
    </go:term>
</rdf:RDF>
```

Fig. 3. RDF/XML representation of ontology

- q_{01}: Cytoplasmic Proteins, Related-to, Stomach Cancer (=q_0)
- q_{02}: Metabolic Enzyme, Related-to, Stomach Cancer
- q_{03}: Protein Synthesis Factor, Related-to, Stomach Cancer
- q_{04}: Metabolic Enzyme, Repress, Stomach Cancer

Fig. 4. Q_0: Expanded queries from the initial query q_0

Let us further suppose that the user is not interested in metabolic enzymes repressing stomach cancer development. Then, the user can specify this constraint as his/her own preference information. According to the specified user constraint, one of the expanded queries q_{04} is eliminated from the query set before distributed to local information repositories. This pre-screening can be mapped into negative selection to remove such antibodies that bind with self-antigens.

Among the expanded queries in Figure 4, only q_{02} is matched with data d_1 in Table 2. In the immune metaphor, this can be regarded as an antibody binds with a foreign antigen. The matched query q_{02} is further expanded by referring to the ontology as in Figure 5.

- q_{11}: Metabolic Enzyme, Activate, Stomach Cancer
- q_{12}: Metabolic Enzyme, Repress, Stomach Cancer

Fig. 5. Q_1: Expanded queries from the matched query, q_{02}

Again, q_{11} is matched with data d_5 in Table 3. After keeping the matched result, q_{11} is further expanded again by referring to the ontology as in Figure 6.

- q_{21}: Metabolic Enzyme, Activate, Gastric Cancer

Fig. 6. Q_2: Expanded queries from the matched query, q_{11}

This iterative process will continue until the user is satisfied with the result up to the point, or no more additional information can be retrieved.

4 Semantic Web-Based System Architecture

The proposed immune-based information retrieval system is aiming at web-based distributed information systems where each local information unit is characterizing its own information content in terms of RDF/XML signatures. Figure 7 depicts a system architecture enabling the proposed information retrieval procedure.

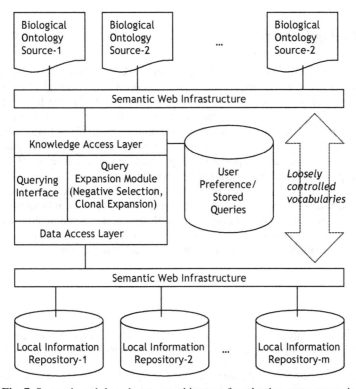

Fig. 7. Semantic web-based system architecture for adaptive query expansion

There are a variety of biological ontology sources available through Internet, which includes Molecular Biology Ontology (MBO), Gene Ontology (GO), and TAMBIS Ontology (TaO) [8]. Since most of them provide RDF-based representation to facilitate machine processing, they are already prepared to join the semantic web community. In addition, most of major bio-databases already support XML-based representation, and are on the way to support RDF.

As explained in Section 3, Query Expansion Module has negative selection sub-module to pre-screen unnecessary queries after each expansion. For such negative selection, semantic rules describing unnecessary information should be stored in the User Preference database. It also has clonal expansion sub-module to expand useful queries. Instead of maintaining local ontology for query expansion, we propose to utilize online ontology sources since the ontology itself is growing fast. Furthermore, we can expect that data elements in local information repositories are controlled loosely by major ontology sources since those information repositories begin to refer to major ontology sources. This loose relationship between local information repositories and major ontology sources play an important role for improving the information retrieval effectiveness. Selected queries from each expansion step can be stored in the Stored Queries database to be used directly in the next query processing. This feature can be mapped into memory cells in the immune metaphor.

5   Concluding Remarks

This paper has proposed an immune-based framework for adaptive query expansion in the semantic web, where exploratory queries, common in biological information retrieval, can be answered more effectively. The proposed technique has a metaphor with negative selection and clonal expansion in immune systems. This work is differentiated from the previous query expansion techniques by its data-driven adaptation. It utilizes target databases as well as the ontology to expand queries. This data-driven adaptive feature is especially important in exploratory information retrieval where the intention of querying itself can be changed by result feedback.

We are going to implement the proposed system using mobile agent technology. Since the information retrieval procedure has inherent parallelism, it fit quite properly into mobile agents. Mobile agents equipped with standard communication capability with ontology sources can navigate through the semantic web, proliferate upon their own matching situations, and extract relevant information to the users.

References

1. K. Sall, XML Family of Specifications: A Practical Guide, Addison-Wesley, 2002
2. T. Berners-Lee, J. Hendler, and O. Lassila, "The Semantic Web," Scientific American, May 2001
3. C. Bussler, D. Fensel, and A. Maedche, "A Conceptual Architecture for Semantic Web Enabled Web Services," SIGMOD Record, 31(4), pp. 24-29, 2002
4. S. Decker, et al, "The Semantic Web: the Roles of XML and RDF," IEEE Internet Computing, 4(5), pp. 63-73, 2000
5. C. Discala, et al, "DBcat: a Catalog of 500 Biological Databases," Nucleic Acids Research, 28, pp. 8-9, 2000
6. D. Buttler, et al, "Querying Multiple Bioinformatics Data Sources: Can Semantic Web Research Help?" SIGMOD Record, 31(4), pp. 59-64, 2002

7. C. Goble, et al, "Transparent Access to Multiple Bioinformatics Information Sources," IBM Systems Journal, 40(2), pp. 532-551, 2001
8. I. Yeh, P. Karp, N. Noy, and R. Altman, "Knowledge Acquisition, Consistency Checking, and Concurrency Control for Gene Ontology (GO)," Bioinformatics, 19(2), pp. 241-248, 2003
9. The Gene Ontology Consortium, "Gene Ontology: Tool for the Unification of Biology," Nature Genetics, 25, pp. 398-416, 2000
10. Y. Chen, D. Che, and K. Aberer, "On the Efficient Evaluation of Relaxed Queries in Biological Databases," Proc. of ACM Conference on Information and Knowledge Management, McLean, 2002, pp. 227-236
11. G. Salton and C. Buckley, "Improving Retrieval Performance by Relevance Feedback," J. of American Society for Information Science, 41, pp. 288-297, 1990
12. H. Joho, et al, "Hierarchical Presentation of Expansion Terms," Proc. of ACM Symposium on Applied Computing, Madrid, 2002, pp. 645-649
13. Y. Kanza, W. Nutt, and Y. Sagiv. "Queries with Incomplete Answers over Semistructured Data", Proc. of ACM PODS, Philadelphia, May, 1999.
14. T. Gaasterland. "Cooperative Answering through Controlled Query Relaxation", IEEE Expert, 12(5), pp. 48–59, 1997
15. M. Mitra, A. Singhal, and C. Buckley. "Improving Automatic Query Expansion," Proc. of ACM SIGIR, Melbourne, Aug. 1998
16. A. Motro. "Query Generalization: A Method for Interpreting Null Answers", Proc. of Expert Database Systems Workshop, Kiawah Island, Oct. 1984
17. D. Che, Y. Chen, K. Aberer, "A Query System in a Biological Database," Proc. of 11th International Conference on Scientific and Statistical Database Management, Cleveland, 1999, pp. 158-168
18. D. Chao and S. Forrest, "Information Immune Systems," Proc. of the 1st Int'l Conf. on Artificial Immune Systems, 2002
19. L. de Castro and J. Timmis, Artificial Immune Systems: A New Computational Intelligence Approach, Springer, 2002
20. D. Dasgupta, Artificial Immune Systems and Their Applications, Springer, 1998

An Artificial Immune System Approach to Semantic Document Classification

Julie Greensmith and Steve Cayzer

Hewlett-Packard Labs, Stoke Gifford,
Bristol, UK
BS34, 8QZ
Julie.Greensmith@hp.com, Steve.Cayzer@hp.com
http://www.hpl.hp.com/research/bicas/

Abstract. AIRS, a resource limited artificial immune classifier system, has performed well on elementary classification tasks. This paper proposes the use of this system for the more complex task of hierarchical, multi-class document classification. This information can then be applied to the realm of taxonomy mapping, an active research area with far reaching implications. Our motivation comes from the use of a personal semantic structure for ease of navigation within a set of Internet based documents.

1 Introduction

The explosion of information available on the Internet makes it increasingly difficult to navigate. The notion that intelligent annotations to Internet pages should be added is one possible way to approach this problem. Indeed, the underlying idea behind the Semantic Web is to introduce "an extension of the current web in which information is given well-defined meaning, better enabling computers and people to work in cooperation" [2]. The classification of such Internet documents into taxonomies is one method of enabling the end user to derive information more effectively through the use of defined 'semantics'. However, such manual annotation of pages is time consuming and for it to work successfully would require the majority of pages to contain such annotation. This would not only mean extra work during the creation of the pages, but would also have to be applied to many existing documents, and many amateur web authors would not have the time, or indeed the patience, to perform such a chore.

One solution which alleviates the problem involves applying a taxonomic structure to web documents in a post-hoc manner, independently of their authors, making searching for relevant content on the Internet a less daunting and more efficient task. As with many other problems involving classification or decision-making in a complex, distributed system, solutions have been inspired by a variety of biological metaphors. One idea in particular appeals as a potential candidate to perform this task, namely *artificial immune systems*. This is inspired by the ability of the human immune system to effectively distinguish

J. Timmis et al. (Eds.): ICARIS 2003, LNCS 2787, pp. 136–146, 2003.

between proteins, hence acting as a natural classification system. The modelling of such a system for a functionally similar task is a seemingly logical step.

Indeed, artificial immune systems (AIS) have demonstrable potential for success within this domain, since powerful classifier systems have been developed and evaluated as described in previous work from Watkins & Boggess [24] and Twycross & Cayzer [23]. This paper outlines the use of such a system within the field of Internet document classification. The reader will be introduced to the variety of methods and tools associated with the classification task and the use of taxonomies, in addition to the use of an AIS in the novel area of document classification. The paper is organised as follows: Section 2 introduces relevant information regarding artificial immune systems, feature extraction/representation, classifier systems and taxonomies; Section 3 discusses the work already performed and the research that will be carried out; the final sections include a summary and references.

2 Context

This section introduces the important concepts employed in this area of research. Basic immune system principles are summarised, with particular attention paid to the components that are specifically relevant to our system. The relevant algorithms and mechanisms are explained and related to the task of document classification. Following this, the techniques involved in document classification are examined including feature representation, similarity metrics and the utilisation of a taxonomic structure within this context.

2.1 Immune Systems

At a high level of abstraction, the immune system can be subdivided into two components: *innate* and *acquired*. The acquired component is of particular interest due to the adaptive nature of some of its constituents, that are thought to perform a biological classification task. B-Lymphocytes or B-Cells are one such constituent and within the immune system are responsible for the production of *antibodies* and the development of *memory cells*. An overview of the immune system can be found in many immunology texts, for example Janeway *et al.* [10]

Antibodies are proteins that are produced from B-Cells, in response to the detection of a foreign protein or antigen. The antibodies produced from B-Cells can perform complementary pattern matching with a corresponding antigen, initiating a series of events, resulting in the destruction of the invading pathogen. Each segment of antibody is encoded by a widely separated gene library which is subject to alternate splicing, therefore a wide variety of subtly different proteins can be produced. The pattern matching ability of a B-Cell antibody is *resource limited*. During the maturation period, if an antibody does not successfully match any given antigen proteins, then the resources for the replication of that antibody are removed (Fig. 1). It is thought that the energy used in the complementary antigen-antibody binding is a measure of an *affinity threshold*. Once a B-Cell

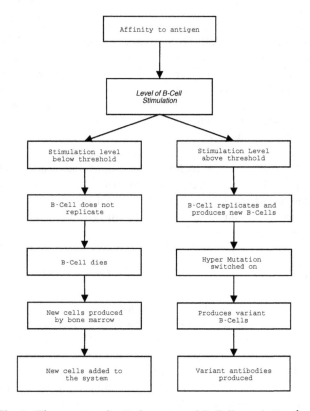

Fig. 1. The resource limited process of B-Cell regulation [10]

has exceeded this threshold, the cell is cloned and daughter cells are produced as a slightly mutated version (*hypermutation*). This can improve the antibody-antigen binding as the newly formed antibody may have a higher antigen affinity than the original cell.

Memory cells, formed as a result of this clonal selection process, are B-Cells that are successful with respect to antigen matching. These cells are longer-lived than normal B-Cells and are thus available (perhaps many years later) when a similar antigen challenge is encountered. Under that circumstance, a rapid secondary response can be initiated.

In addition to the action of B-Cells, the adaptive immune response is also facilitated through the use of T-Cells, which aid in the destruction of pathogens and the generation of memory cells. However, the action of T-Cells is not used in our system and so is not explained in this paper.

2.2 AIRS – A Resource Limited Immune Classifier System

Artificial immune systems do not attempt to be an accurate representation of the immune system, but use relevant mechanisms of action and concepts in order to create a robust, decentralised, adaptive system which are used in a variety of classification tasks. In the case of the system we will focus on, AIRS, inspiration has been derived from B-Cells.

AIRS is a particular type of artificial immune system, specifically designed for supervised classification tasks [24]. The system contains a population of B-Cells which respond to virtual antigens derived from the input data. A concentration of identical B-Cells is represented as an *artificial recognition ball* (ARB). Initial populations of both ARBs and memory cells are created from the training data. In order to achieve successful classification, training data must be presented to the system. Each item of training data is encoded as a single antigen, and AIRS responds to the antigen based on the closest matching existing memory cell, which gives rise to the creation of ARBs. The ARBs are then allocated resources based on the success achieved with respect to the antigen matching, i.e. proportional to antigen affinity. At this point, ARBs that are unsuccessful are removed from the system. This value for affinity is used to determine the number of clones produced by that particular ARB. This process is repeated until the average affinity for all of the ARBs is above a pre-determined stimulation threshold. The best matching ARB for a class of antigen is then promoted to a become a *candidate memory cell*. If the affinity of the candidate memory cell is greater than that of the closest memory cell, then the candidate memory cell is placed in the 'pool' of memory cells used in future classifications. This process has similarities with other clustering methods, e.g. k-means [7].

Once the system has been trained in this manner, it is applied to a set of test data. In this, the created memory cells are used as *class prototypes*. A k-nearest neighbour approach is used in order to determine the best match between memory cell and test antigen. The position of the antigen within the space is represented and compared with surrounding memory cells. A radius is established which encompasses a specified amount of neighbours, 'k'. Within this radius, the class of antigen is given by the class of the majority of nearest neighbours .The scenario of a tie is dealt with in various different ways as discussed in [11].

In order to use the AIRS system in the domain of document classification, the system needs no major modification. The system will already work with a variety of feature representations and similarity metrics. Some modification of the configuration file is likely to be required to tune the system for the current task. This includes the correct amount of training data needed to seed the program initially, and the thresholds for resource allocation and mutation rate of the artificial memory cells. The most significant task however involves extracting the information from the documents and placing the information in the correct representation for the system to use.

2.3   Text Classification

Text classification is a relatively well explored area (for an overview see [1]) with a number of potential approaches. In this section, we outline the relevant details of our text classification task, and how we intend to tackle semantic classification.

Note that we have not (yet) comitted to any single method; rather, we outline the overall issues in this section and describe some candidate solutions.

Successful classification of the documents relies on attributes of the document, also known as *features*, to be extracted. The weighting and selection of such features has to be deduced, and represented in a way that can be used by the classifier system. This is the process of compilation of *feature vectors*. Features can be *textual*, in the form of extracted words, or *semantic*: for example, a position within a meaningful structure such as a taxonomy.

AIRS also requires the definition of a *similarity measure*, that is, a metric that tells us how 'close' a document is to a memory cell, using the features defined above. Once the representation scheme and similarity metric are fixed, AIRS can be used essentially without modification to perform semantic classification.

Classification Using Textual Features: The extraction of text based features is a relatively trivial task, and simply involves extracting the words from the document. The selection of the important features after this extraction has been performed is more complicated. This stage is necessary in order to reduce the dimensionality of the feature vector, so the classifier is not confused by irrelevant terms and to reduce the computational expense. Methods used in feature selection include information gain [20] which is a statistical entropy based measure, and singular value decomposition [3] which is a matrix compression algorithm. In this instance, information gain will be used in order to determine the important words derived in a class of documents (based on a training set of pages). From this information, the 'gain' derived from each word with respect to the usefulness of the word in the classification of the document can be used as a metric. The presence or absence of the words within a class can be translated into a feature vector, and can then be represented in a variety of different ways. However information gain requires the dataset to be static as it depends upon the presence of all the words contained within the entire document collection.

Once the important features have been selected, then the data must be represented in a way that is suitable for use by the classifier system. There are a number of methods that can be implemented in order to provide this representation. Boolean vectors are utilised in Twycross & Cayzer [23] where a 0 or a 1 is used to represent the absence or presence of an important term within a feature vector, and is an effective way of representing the information to the system. Alternatively, term-frequency, inverse document frequency *(tfidf)* vectors can be used. This method takes into account the amount of times a term occurs in a document, and the amount of times that word appears more than once within a collection of documents. The latter is inverted to give a high value for an important word that occurs several times within a document, but is only present within the minority of documents [22]. The resulting vectors have to be normalised to achieve similarity of size. We will investigate both binary and vectorial features in our classification work. Note that we are concerned here with static classification tasks. A possible future extension would involve the use of dynamic document collections, for which alternate representations, capable of incremental update [15] would be more suitable.

AIRS' default choice of similarity measure is Euclidean, which we intend to use as a baseline. The problem with this method is that it regards all attributes as equally important. In reality, the importance of an attribute is likely to depend both on the attribute in question and on the region of feature space in which the memory cell resides. Therefore, we expect the task to benefit from more refined similarity measures, such as those involving wildcards [23], variable thresholds [17] or even variable weights for each attribute.

Classification Using Semantic Features: Taxonomies describe a structured way in which various information and classifications can be viewed, with each branch of the taxonomic tree having some relationship with the parent and siblings. They are a simple version of an ontology, which has been described as a "formal specification of a shared conceptualisation" [8]. That is, ontologies are concerned with methods for knowledge representation, and taxonomies are one such method. Taxonomic structures can in the first instance provide a useful classification of documents which are placed into the appropriate taxonomic location. However, it would be useful to classify a document according to multiple, user defined taxonomies. This would provide the user with a *personalised semantic structure* which would be both more comfortable and intuitive. This area of research has been prompted by the need to examine the classification of document within a hierarchical structure without the reliance of rigid logic techniques, to provide a system that has more flexible and ultimately more meaningful navigation experience. In order to achieve a classification based on this multiple mapping it must also be appreciated that the positioning of a document in one taxonomy can also be a feature of that document i.e. a *semantic feature*.

The representation of such a feature is fairly simple - we can use string descriptors such as '/computers/languages/java' and '1.3.6', or alternatively an index into an externally referenced taxonomic scheme. The more complex issue is that of computing taxonomic similarity. Here we have a range of approaches to choose from, for example a 'probability of the least subsumer' measure [13] or an upwards cotopy [13]. A discussion of the issues surrounding taxonomic similarity measures within the context of AIS can be found in [14].

2.4   Related Work

The classifier system used in this particular instance relies on the adaptive nature of the immune system and its ability to remember encountered antigens in a content addressable manner. However, there are many techniques available for classification. Such methods include the Naive Bayesian classifiers, nearest neighbour, decision trees and neural networks. Naive Bayesian classifiers are a common example of a probabilistic classifier, that is that the probability that a vector represented collection of weighted terms from a document belongs to a class of document types [22]. The k-nearest neighbours approach (as used by AIRS) relies on the assumption that in the feature space, if a document x is closest to k documents, then it belongs to the class of the majority of those documents [7]. The application of a neural net to perform classification is less common than the use of Naive Bayesian classifiers, but can be useful, especially where weighted terms are involved.

Classification of web documents has already been performed by a series of different research groups. Indeed, there is a web toolkit, Rainbow [12] available, which allows the user to experiment with Naive Bayes, k-nearest neighbour, tfidf, and probabilistic indexing techniques. A more recent and relevant example is the work of Twycross & Cayzer [23] who used a co-evolutionary AIS for the classification of web documents. We are extending the AIS beyond 2-class problems to classification tasks that are multiclass and hierarchical. Ceci et al [5] compare a Naive Bayes and centroid based technique for just such a hierarchical document classification task, finding that the Naive Bayes approach is generally better. This is interesting, because there is evidence that an immune approach can outperform Naive Bayes for document classification tasks [23]. In fact, we are testing AIRS on a similar corpus to that used by Ceci, but we also plan to perform an ontology transformation using semantic features.

3   Using AIRS as a Semantic Classifier

3.1   Validation of AIRS

The evaluation of the AIRS system has to date formed the major component of the work performed toward this project. This validation is performed in order to ensure that the system can perform supervised classification based upon known test database information. The ability of an artificial immune system to achieve the necessary classification task is derived from the fact that the system relies on the local interactions between individual antigens and antibodies. This in turn makes the system robust and gives it the ability to handle situations where traditional techniques might not be able to cope. Previous tests using this system [11] indicate the performance in classification of multiple class data to be exemplary. The ability of the system to remember previous actions in a content addressable manner, irrespective of centralised control makes it an ideal learning paradigm [9].

The initial testing and validation of the system used a voting dataset obtained from the UCI repository [4]. This dataset is an attractive one to use for many reasons. Firstly, this is a popular dataset, providing us with many figures against which we can compare the performance of AIRS. Secondly, a co-evolutionary AIS system [23] has already provided exemplary performance on this dataset. We have chosen AIRS rather than the co-evolutionary model for our document classification task due to the proven ability of the former on multi-class data. A comparable performance on this simpler task will give us confidence that we are not choosing an inferior classifier architecture. Thirdly, AIRS has not yet been tested on the voting dataset, and so the results will be interesting on their own merit.

The voting dataset contains votes from the 1984 US Congress on 16 different issues, and from the voting pattern, the senators are classified as democrat or republican accordingly. The information was extracted from this source in a

16-D vector, with equal weighting to each vote. The representation of the features was based on a system of a score of 0 for a 'no' and 1 for 'yes', and 2 for 'abstain'. As there are an equal number of features for every potential antigen, there was no need to normalise the data. In order to complete the process, 10% of the voting dataset was excluded from the dataset and used as the test data, and was repeated several times with different parts of the dataset comprising the test file. This gave a cross-validation of the system. On successful compilation of the AIRS code (using g++ version 2.94), the classifier was run and various statistical outputs were collected. Although a full analysis has not been performed, initial indications are promising, showing a classification accuracy in excess of 95%, which compares well with tests performed using a Naive Bayesian classification system (90%) and the co-evolutionary artificial immune system (97%) developed by Twycross & Cayzer [23]. Note that this result was obtained using a naive feature representation with a Euclidean similarity metric. Intuitively, one would expect to improve performance through the use of techniques like wildcards. Nevertheless, it is encouraging that AIRS appears to offer competent performance levels using only its default configuration.

3.2   Taxonomic Classification

Once the validation results have been analysed, the focus of the project will turn to the classification of actual web documents. This will involve the extraction of the information from the documents into feature vectors, the selection of appropriate features and the representation using feature vectors. The preparation of the feature vectors is a multistage process, including extraction of all of the words, followed by parsing of the documents to remove 'fluff words' and HTML tags. In order to further reduce the dimensionality of the document, a Porter Stemming Algorithm [18] is to be implemented which reduced the words in the document to their stem, e.g. 'classifier' and 'classification' would be reduced to 'classi'. Further dimensionality reduction will be achieved through the use of an information gain algorithm which will provide a measure of the k-most informative words within a class of document. The absence or presence of a word within a document can be represented as either a boolean value or as some frequency dependent vector (which would be normalised), both of which will be in suitable format for the use of the AIRS system. From this point the documents will be classified into an established taxonomic structure e.g. provided by Yahoo!. This is not only a useful task in its own right, it also provides an interesting test of the AIRS system's extensibility. Not only is the classification task concerned with documents (hence the textual features), it also requires multi-class output. The classification structure achieved is hierarchical which is a novel domain for the use of AIRS.

3.3   AIRS as a Tool for Personalised Semantic Structure

The subjectivity of the placing of the documents within this structure is a serious issue, as classification schemas, derived by human or machine annotation, can be inconsistent and often there is no 'correct' answer. This fact is not ignored and consequently, the process is adapted to include the additional option of multiple taxonomy mapping. In general, work performed regarding ontology mapping is on a one-to-one mapping basis, as demonstrated in [6] and reviewed by [21]. This implies that the positioning of a document in one taxonomy determines the placing of a document in an alternative taxonomy. However, we think that it is more effective to use *both* the features extracted from the document *in addition to* the position in an initial taxonomy in order to create the personalised semantic structure.

We start with a set of documents that have been pre-classified into a taxonomic structure. To derive the placing of the documents in an alternative taxonomy, a selection of documents from this original taxonomy are used as training data. The features of the training items are derived from the textual features of the documents, and the semantic feature (position) within the original taxonomy. Once the training has been performed with this information, AIRS classifies test documents using textual features and the semantic feature of the original taxonomy, into the new taxonomy. The success of this technique would have implications in a number of other parallel problems, such as data integration and machine translation.

We hope to use AIRS as a more effective searching and navigational tool for use on the Internet, through using a robust and adaptable technique, which gives the user the choice on the semantic structure of the taxonomy of the web documents. Additionally the application of this system in a context where the collection of pages is constantly changing would be an interesting test of the extensibility of the system as a whole. Indeed, there is evidence that AIRS is well suited for a dynamic environment [16]. The internet is, of course, inherently dynamic, and so extending document classification in this way is an important issue. The interesting question for us is not how can the AIRS work as a classifier, but rather how far can we push the system into performing increasingly complex tasks. As quoted in Marwah & Boggess [11], "..since AIRS is a very recent classifier, there are many possible areas for the exploration of the algorithm", and this seems like an excellent opportunity to do just that.

4   Summary

As the amount of information on the Internet increases, more meaningful and powerful navigational tools must be developed. An artificial immune system that has previously performed well in other classification tasks, will be used to classify web documents into a taxonomic structure. This structure will necessarily be subjective, therefore the information can be mapped to alternative taxonomies in order to provide the user with a personalised semantic structure. This not only attempts to introduce a bio-inspired technique to the development of the semantic web, but will test some of the boundaries involved in using an artificial immune system in the domain of document classification.

References

1. R. Baeza-Yates and B. Ribeiro-Neto. Modern *Information Retrieval*. ACM Press, New York, 1999.
2. Tim Berners-Lee, James Hendler, and Ora Lassila. The Semantic Web. *Scientific American*, 284(5):34–43, May 2001.
3. Daniel Billsus and Michael J. Pazzani. Learning collaborative information filters. In *Proc. 15th International Conf. on Machine Learning*, pages 46-54. Morgan Kaufmann, San Francisco, CA, 1998.
4. C.L. Blake and C.J. Merz. UCI repository of machine learning databases (available at http://www.ics.uci.edu/~mlearn/mlrepository.html), 1998.
5. Michelangelo Ceci, Floriana Esposito, Michele Lapi, and Donata Malerba. Automated classification of web documents into a web hierarchy. In *Proceedings of the international IIS: IIPWM2003*, pages 59-68, Zakopane, Poland, June 2003. Springer.
6. AnHai Doan, Pedro Domingos, and Alon Y. Halevy. Reconciling Schemas of disparate data sources: A machine-learning approach. In *SIGMOD Conference*, 2001.
7. AA Freitas. *Data Mining und Knowledge Discovery with Evolutionary Algorithms*. Spinger-Verlag, Berlin, 2002. Page 34.
8. T. R. Gruber. Towards Principles for the Design of Ontologies Used for Knowledge Sharing. In N. Guarino and R. Poli, editors, *Formal Ontology in Conceptual Analysis and Knowledge Representation*, Deventer, The Netherlands, 1993. Kluwer Academic Publishers.
9. John E. Hunt and Denise E. Cooke. Learning using an artificial immune System. *Journal of Network und Computer Applications*, 19(2):189–212, 1996.
10. Charles A. Janeway, Paul Travers, Mark Walport, and Mark Shlomchik. *Immunobiology The Immune System in Health and Disease*. New York : Garland ; Edinburgh: Churchill Livingstone., 2001.
11. Gaurav Marwah and Lois Boggess. Artificial immune systems for classification: Some issues. In *Proceedings of the 1st International Conference on Artificial Immune Systems (ICARIS)*, pages 149–153, Canterbury, UK, September 2002.
12. Andrew McCallum. Rainbow (available at http://www-2.cs.cmu.edu/ mccallum/bow/rainbow/), 1998.
13. A. Mdche and S. Staab. Measuring similarity between ontologies. In *Proc. Of the European Conference on Knowledge Acquisition and Management - EKAW-2002*, Madrid, Spain, October 1-4, October 2002. Springer.
14. T Morrison and U Aickelin. An artificial immune system as a recommender for web sites. In *Proceedings of the 1st International Conference on Artificial Immune Systems (ICARIS)*, pages 161–169, Canterbury, UK, September 2002.
15. Nikolaos Nanas. An adaptive, evolutionary user profile for knowledge management. KMI-TR-114, http://kmi.open.ac.uk/publications/techreports-text.cfm.
16. M Neal. An artificial immune system for continuous analysis of time-varying data. In *Proceedings of the 1st International Conference on Artificial Immune Systems (ICARIS)*, volume 1, pages 76–85, Canterbury, UK, September 2002.
17. Nasraoui O., Gonzalez F., and Dasgupta D. The fuzzy artificial immune system: Motivations, basic concepts, and application to clustering and web profiling. In *IEEE International Conf. on Fuzzy Systems (IEEE-FUZZY 2002)*, pages 711–716, May 2002. Part of the World Congress on Computational Intelligence (WCCI) held in Honolulu, HI, USA, May 12-17, 2002.

18. M.F Porter. An algorithm for suffix stripping. *Program*, 14(3):130–137, 1980. reprinted in Sparck Jones, Karen, and Peter Willet, 1997, Readings in Information Retrieval, San Francisco: Morgan Kaufmann, ISBN 1-55860-454-4.

19. P.W.Lord, R.D. Stevens, A. Brass, and C.A.Goble. Semantic similarity measures as tools for exploring the Gene Ontology. In *Pacific Symposium on Biocomputing*, pages 601–612, 2003.

20. J. Ross Quinlan. Induction of decision trees. *Machine Learning*, 1:81–106, 1986.

21. Erhard Rahm and Philip A. Bernstein. A survey of approaches to automatic schema matching. *VLDB Journal: Very Large Data Bases*, 10(4):334–350, 2001.

22. Fabrizio Sebastiani. Machine learning in automated text categorization. *ACM Computing Surveys (CSUR)*, 34(1):1–47, 2002.

23. Jamie Twycross and Steve Cayzer. An immune-based approach to document classification. In *Proceedings of the international IIS: IIPWM2003*, pages 33–48, Zakopane, Poland, June 2003. Springer.

24. Andrew B. Watkins and Lois C. Boggess. A Resource Limited Artificial Immune Classifier. In *Proceedings of Congress on Evolutionary Computation*, pages 926–931. IEEE, May 2002. Part of the 2002 IEEE World Congress on Computational Intelligence held in Honolulu, HI, USA, May 12-17, 2002.

Danger Theory: The Link between AIS and IDS?

U. Aickelin[1], P. Bentley[2], S. Cayzer[3], J. Kim[4], and J. McLeod[5]

[1] University of Bradford
U.Aickelin@bradford.ac.uk
[2] University College London
P.Bentley@cs.ucl.ac.uk
[3] HP Labs Bristol
Steve_Cayzer@hplb.hpl.hp.com
[4] King's College London
Jungwon@dcs.kcl.ac.uk
[5] University of the West of England
Julie.Mcleod@uwe.ac.uk

Abstract. We present ideas about creating a next generation Intrusion Detection System (IDS) based on the latest immunological theories. The central challenge with computer security is determining the difference between normal and potentially harmful activity. For half a century, developers have protected their systems by coding rules that identify and block specific events. However, the nature of current and future threats in conjunction with ever larger IT systems urgently requires the development of automated and adaptive defensive tools. A promising solution is emerging in the form of Artificial Immune Systems (AIS): The Human Immune System (HIS) can detect and defend against harmful and previously unseen invaders, so can we not build a similar Intrusion Detection System (IDS) for our computers? Presumably, those systems would then have the same beneficial properties as HIS like error tolerance, adaptation and self-monitoring. Current AIS have been successful on test systems, but the algorithms rely on self-nonself discrimination, as stipulated in classical immunology. However, immunologist are increasingly finding fault with traditional self-nonself thinking and a new 'Danger Theory' (DT) is emerging. This new theory suggests that the immune system reacts to threats based on the correlation of various (danger) signals and it provides a method of 'grounding' the immune response, i.e. linking it directly to the attacker. Little is currently understood of the precise nature and correlation of these signals and the theory is a topic of hot debate. It is the aim of this research to investigate this correlation and to translate the DT into the realms of computer security, thereby creating AIS that are no longer limited by self-nonself discrimination. It should be noted that we do not intend to defend this controversial theory per se, although as a deliverable this project will add to the body of knowledge in this area. Rather we are interested in its merits for scaling up AIS applications by overcoming self-nonself discrimination problems.

1 Introduction

The key to the next generation Intrusion Detection System (IDS) ([9], [25], [26]) that we are planning to build is the combination of recent Artificial Immune System (AIS) / Danger Theory (DT) models ([1], [4], [5], [32]) with our growing understanding of cellular components involved with cell death ([3], [11], [31]). In particular, the differ-

J. Timmis et al. (Eds.): ICARIS 2003, LNCS 2787, pp. 147–155, 2003.
© Springer-Verlag Berlin Heidelberg 2003

ence between necrotic ('bad') and apoptotic ('good' or 'planned') cell death, with respect to Antigen Presenting Cells (APCs) activation, is important in our proposed IDS. In the Human Immune System (HIS) apoptosis has a suppressive effect and necrosis a stimulatory immunological effect, although they might not actually be as distinct as currently thought.

In the IDS context, we propose to use the correlation of these two effects as a basis of 'danger signals'. A variety of contextual clues may be essential for a meaningful danger signal, and immunological studies will provide a framework of ideas as to how 'danger' is assessed in the HIS. In the IDS context, the danger signals should show up after limited attack to minimise damage and therefore have to be quickly and automatically measurable. Once the danger signal has been transmitted, the AIS should react to those artificial antigens that are 'near' the emitter of the danger signal. This allows the AIS to pay special attention to dangerous components and would have the advantage of detecting rapidly spreading viruses or scanning intrusions fast and at an early stage preventing serious damage.

2   AIS and Intrusion Detection

Alongside intrusion prevention techniques such as encryption and firewalls, IDS are another significant method used to safeguard computer systems. The main goal of IDS is to detect unauthorised use, misuse and abuse of computer systems by both system insiders and external intruders. Most current IDS define suspicious signatures based on known intrusions and probes [25]. The obvious limit of this type of IDS is its failure of detecting previously unknown intrusions. In contrast, the HIS adaptively generates new immune cells so that it is able to detect previously unknown and rapidly evolving harmful antigens [28].

In order to provide viable IDS, AIS must build a set of detectors that accurately match antigens. In current AIS based IDS ([9], [12], [19], [13]), both network connections and detectors are modelled as strings. Detectors are randomly created and then undergo a maturation phase where they are presented with good, i.e. self, connections. If the detectors match any of these they are eliminated otherwise they become mature. These mature detectors start to monitor new connections during their lifetime. If these mature detectors match anything else, exceeding a certain threshold value, they become activated. This is then reported to a human operator who decides whether there is a true anomaly. If so, the detectors are promoted to memory detectors with an indefinite life span and minimum activation threshold (immunisation) [27].

An approach such as the above is known as negative selection as only those detectors (antibodies) that do not match live on [13]. However, this appealing approach shows scaling problems when it is applied to real network traffic [26]. As the systems to be protected grow larger and larger so does self and nonself. Hence, it becomes more and more problematic to find a set of detectors that provides adequate coverage, whilst being computationally efficient. It is inefficient, to map the entire self or nonself universe, particularly as they will be changing over time and only a minority of nonself is harmful, whilst some self might cause damage (e.g. internal attack). This situation is further aggravated by the fact that the labels self and nonself are often ambiguous and even with expert knowledge they are not always applied correctly [24].

2.1 The Danger Theory

We now examine the biological basis for the self-nonself metaphor, and the alternative DT hypothesis. The HIS is commonly thought to work at two levels: innate immunity including external barriers (skin, mucus), and the acquired or adaptive immune system [28]. As part of the latter level, B-Lymphocytes secrete specific antibodies that recognise and react to stimuli. It is this matching between antibodies and antigens that lies at the heart of the HIS and most AIS implementations.

The central tenet of the immune system is the ability to respond to foreign invaders or 'antigens' whilst not reacting to 'self' molecules. In order to undertake this role the immune system needs to be able to discern differences between foreign, and possibly pathogenic, invaders and non-foreign molecules. It is currently believed that this occurs through the utilisation of the Major Histocompatability Complex (MHC). This complex is unique to each individual and therefore provides a marker of 'self'. In addition, the cells within the immune system are matured by becoming tolerised to self-molecules. Together, through the MHC and tolerance, the HIS is able to recognise foreign invaders and send the requisite signals to the key effector cells involved with the immune response.

The DT debates this and argues that there must be discrimination happening that goes beyond the self-nonself distinction because the HIS only discriminates 'some self' from 'some nonself'. It could therefore be proposed that it is not the 'foreignness' of the invaders that is important for immune recognition, but the relative 'danger' of these invaders. This theory was first proposed in 1994 [29] to explain current anomalies in our understanding of how the immune system recognises foreign invaders. For instance, there is no immune reaction to foreign bacteria in the gut or to food. Conversely, some auto-reactive processes exist, e.g. against self-molecules expressed by stressed cells. Furthermore, the human body (self) changes over its lifetime. Therefore, why do defences against nonself learned early in life not become auto-reactive later?

The DT suggests that foreign invaders, which are dangerous, will induce the generation of cellular molecules (danger signals) by initiating cellular stress or cell death [30]. These molecules are recognised by APCs, critical cells in the initiation of an immune response, which become activated leading to protective immune interactions. Overall there are two classes of danger signal; those which are generated endogenously i.e. by the body itself, and exogenous signals which are derived from invading organisms e.g. bacteria [16]. Evidence is accruing as to the existence of myriad endogenous danger signals including cell receptors, intracellular molecules and cytokines. A commonality is their ability to activate APCs and thus drive an immune response.

We believe that the DT will provide a more suitable biological metaphor for IDS than the traditional self-nonself viewpoint, regardless whether the theory holds for the HIS, something that is currently hotly debated amongst immunologists ([37], [21], [39]). In particular, the DT provides a way of grounding the response, i.e. linking it directly to the attacker and it removes the necessity to map self or nonself [1]. In our model, self-nonself discrimination will still be useful but it is no longer essential. This is because nonself no longer causes a response. Instead, danger signals will trigger a reaction. Actually, the response is more complicated than this, since it is believed that the APCs integrate necrotic ('danger') and apoptotic ('safe') signals in order to regulate the immune response. We intend to examine this integrative activity experimentally, which should provide useful inspiration for IDS.

2.2 The DT in the Context of the HIS

One of the central themes of the DT is the generation of danger signals through cellular stress or cell death. Cell death can occur in two ways; necrosis and apoptosis, and although both terminate in cell death, the intracellular pathways of each process are very distinct. Necrosis involves the unregulated death of a cell following cell stress and results in total cell lysis and subsequent inflammation due to the cell debris. Apoptosis, on the other hand, is a very regulated form of cell death with defined intracellular pathways and regulators [23]. Physiologically, apoptosis is utilised by the body to maintain tissue homeostasis and is vital in regulating the immune response. Once apoptosis is initiated extracellular receptors on the cell signal to phagocytic cells, e.g. APCs to remove the dying cell from the system.

Apoptosis can be initiated in a number of ways including; cytokine deprivation, death receptors e.g. CD95 and UV irradiation each having unique intracellular signalling profiles [17]. Interestingly, recent work has suggested that apoptotic pathways may not be as distinct from necrosis as previously assumed [20] and indeed may be inter-related. In both cases phagocytosis of the dying cell occurs and studies suggests that the APCs receive signals from the dying cells that affects activation state of the APCs themselves [35]. These results are of particular interest since they support the concept of danger signals, with the APCs being a rheostat responding to 'input' signals from cells undergoing necrosis, tipping the immune balance towards a pro-inflammatory state, which is an 'output' signal.

Evidence to support the critical role of cell death signals in APC activation has shown that APCs, which have phagocytosed necrotic cells, generate pro-inflammatory cytokines e.g. interleukin (IL) –1, interferon (IFN) and necrotic cells have been found to activate APCs in a vital step towards an immune response ([35], [15]). Of particular interest is the finding that cells undergoing apoptosis, rather than being invisible to the APCs, may actually help regulate the APCs response to necrotic cell debris. Studies [14] have shown that apoptotic cells actively down-regulate the APC activity by generating anti-inflammatory cytokines e.g. TGF and PGE2, although in other cases this has not been observed [35].

In a further complexity to the balance, reports have shown that necrotic and apoptotic cells work together to affect the APC activation and subsequent immune response [35]. Therefore a balance between cell death, either necrotic or apoptotic, would appear to be critical to the final immunological outcome. Here, we seek to understand how the APCs react to the balance of 'input' signals from apoptotic and necrotic cell death with an aim to determine and simplify the danger signal 'output'.

Previous studies have observed alterations in the generation of pro- and anti-inflammatory cytokines e.g. IL-1, IFN, TGF-ß and PGE2 following APC incubation with necrotic or apoptotic cells respectively [14]. In addition, activation-related receptors e.g. MHC and CD80/86 have been reported to be upregulated in the presence of necrotic cells [15]. We intend to extend and confirm these studies using proteomics, which will allow the pan-identification of novel, key proteins within the APC which are influenced by the presence of dying cells or 'danger signals'.

Hence, the aims of the immunological investigation can be summarised as:

- To identify and investigate key APC-derived signals in response to co-culture with necrotic or apoptotic cells.
- To undertake functional analysis of the identified key signals in affecting the activation state of immune cells.
- To manipulate the co-culture system and derived signals upon results from the AIS / IDS studies.

2.3 Intrusion Detection Systems –Current State of the Art

An important and recent research issue for IDS is how to find true intrusion alerts from thousands alerts generated [19]. Existing IDS employ various types of sensors that monitor low-level system events. Those sensors report anomalies of network traffic patterns, unusual terminations of UNIX processes, memory usages, the attempts to access unauthorised files, etc. [24]. Although these reports are useful signals of real intrusions, they are often mixed with false alerts and their unmanageable volume forces a security officer to ignore most alerts [18]. Moreover, the low level of alerts makes it hard for a security officer to identify advancing intrusions that usually consist of different stages of attack sequences. For instance, hackers often use a number of preparatory stages (raising low-level alerts) before actual hacking [18]. Hence, the correlations between intrusion alerts from different attack stages provide more convincing attack scenarios than detecting an intrusion scenario based on low-level alerts from individual stages.

To correlate IDS alerts for detection of an intrusion scenario, recent studies have employed two different approaches: a probabilistic approach ([8], [36], [38]) and an expert system approach ([6], [7], [10], [33], [34]). The probabilistic approach represents known intrusion scenarios as Bayesian networks. The nodes of Bayesian networks are IDS alerts and the posterior likelihood between nodes is updated as new alerts are collected. The updated likelihood can lead to conclusions about a specific intrusion scenario occurring or not. The expert system approach initially builds possible intrusion scenarios by identifying low-level alerts. These alerts consist of prerequisites and consequences, and they are represented as hypergraphs ([33], [34]) or specification language forms ([6], [10], [18]). Known intrusion scenarios are detected by observing the low-level alerts at each stage. These approaches have the following problems [7]:

- Handling unobserved low-level alerts that comprise an intrusion scenario.
- Handling optional prerequisite actions and intrusion scenario variations.

The common trait of these problems is that the IDS can fail to detect an intrusion if an incomplete set of alerts comprising an intrusion scenario is reported. In handling this problem, the probabilistic approach is somewhat more advantageous because in theory it allows the IDS to correlate missing or mutated alerts. However, the similarities alone can fail to identify a causal relationship between prerequisite actions and actual attacks if pairs of prerequisite actions and actual attacks do not appear frequently enough to be reported. Attackers often do not repeat the same actions in order to disguise their attempts. Thus, the current probabilistic approach fails to detect intrusions that do not show strong similarities between alert features but have causal relationships leading to final attacks ([8], [36], [38]).

3   A DT-Inspired Approach to Intrusion Detection

We propose AIS based on DT ideas that can handle the above IDS alert correlation problems. As outline previously, the DT explains the immune response of the human body by the interaction between APCs and various signals. The immune response of each APC is determined by the generation of danger signals through cellular stress or death. In particular, the balance and correlation between different signals depending on different causes appears to be critical to the immunological outcome. Proposed wet experiments of this project focus on understanding how the APCs react to the balance of different types of signals, and how this reaction leads to an overall immune response. Similarly, our IDS investigation will centre on understanding how intrusion scenarios would be detected by reacting to the balance of various types of alerts. In the HIS, APCs activate according to the balance of apoptotic and necrotic cells and this activation leads to protective immune responses. Similarly, the sensors in IDS report various low-level alerts and the correlation of these alerts will lead to the construction of an intrusion scenario.

3.1   Apoptotic versus Necrotic Alerts

We believe that various IDS alerts can be categorised into two groups: apoptotic type of alerts and necrotic type of alerts. Apoptotic alerts correspond to 'normal' cell death – hence, low-level alerts that could result from legitimate actions but could also be the prerequisites for an attack. Necrotic (unregulated cell death) alerts on the other hand relate to actual damage caused by a successful attack. An intrusion scenario consists of several actions, divided into prerequisite stages and actual attack stages [7]. For instance, in the case of Distributed Denial of Service (DDOS) intrusions, intruders initially look for vulnerable *Sadmind* services by executing the *Ping Sadmind* process [33]. This would be an apoptotic alert, relating to a prerequisite action. Just as apoptosis is vital in regulating the human immune response, apoptotic types of alerts are vital in detecting an intrusion scenario (since it indicates the prerequisite actions within an actual intrusion scenario) Necrotic alerts, or actual attack alerts are raised when the IDS observes system damage caused by the DDOS. Just as necrosis involves the unregulated cell death, necrotic types of alerts would be those generated from the unexpected system outcomes.

In our opinion, a better understanding how the APCs react to the balance of apoptotic and necrotic cells would help us to propose a new approach to correlate apoptotic and necrotic type of alerts generated from sensors. If the DT can explain the key proteins leading to necrotic and apoptotic signals, DT-based AIS would also be able to identify key *types* of apoptotic and necrotic alerts revealing the degree of alert correlation. In this way, DT-based AIS will correlate key types of alerts rather than specific alerts, and this will allow the AIS to correlate missing or mutated alerts as long as the key types of alerts are reported. For instance, in the DDOS example, an intruder can directly attack without executing *Ping* but executing the similar process *traceroute* instead [7]. In this case, our DT-based AIS should be able to link *traceroute* to DDOS attack damage since any type of scanning process is understood as an apoptotic type of alert for DDOS attacks.

3.2 Strength of Reactions

Additionally, if the DT can quantify the degree of the immune response, DT-based AIS would be able to quantify the degree of overall alert detection strictness. For instance, false positive alerts of IDS are often caused by inappropriately setting of intrusion signatures or anomaly thresholds. Debar and Wespi [9] use a clustering algorithm to group a large number of alerts and manually extract a generalised alarm reflecting each alarm cluster. By doing so, they identify the root cause of each alarm cluster and discriminate false positive alert clusters from true positive alert clusters. The root cause is the most basic cause that can reasonably be identified and fixed [9]. According to the identified root causes, new intrusion signatures or anomaly thresholds are redefined by removing those causing root causes.

However, their work has not reported further impacts after intrusion signatures and anomaly thresholds are reset. Simple removal of intrusion signatures that cause the root causes might degrade true positive detection rate instead. Furthermore, continuous changes of network and system environments require constant updates of intrusion signatures and anomaly thresholds. Thus, it is important for IDS how to react to false positive alerts and true positive alerts dynamically. The key feature of the DT-based AIS would provide a possible solution for this issue. The DT-based AIS would adopt a similar way to two types of immune cell death signals affecting the activation of nearby APCs. Currently observed balances between two types of alerts would affect the IDS sensors' activation status by resetting intrusion signatures or anomaly thresholds. Then, these new settings will result in new balances between the two types of alerts. If the DT can explain that this kind of cascading reaction stabilises in a way so that the overall immune responses can converge to an ideal status at given time, the DT-based AIS would also be able to follow a similar mechanism to identify the most suitable intrusion signature and anomaly thresholds setting at given time.

3.3 Danger Zones

Furthermore, our study aims to investigate how the danger alerts reported from a sensor can be transmitted to other sensors in order to detect on-going intrusions. Once a sensor has generated the danger signals or alerts, the AIS can quantify the degree of alert correlations indicating the strength of possible intrusion scenarios. If the AIS has strong indications of possible intrusion scenarios, it can activate other sensors that are spatially, temporally or logically 'near' the original sensor emitting the danger signal. This process is similar to the activated APCs sending its immune response providing a self-nonself independent grounding. For instance, when the danger signal reports the strong possibility of a web server compromise, this signal can be sent to other web servers in the same network domain.

4 Summary and Conclusions

Our aim is to challenge the classical self-nonself viewpoint in AIS based IDS, and replace it by ideas from the DT. Existing systems using certain aspects of the HIS have been successful on small problems and have shown the same benefits as their natural counterparts: error tolerance, adaptation and self-monitoring. The DT is a new theory amongst immunologists stating that the natural immune system does not rely on self-nonself discrimination but identifies 'danger'. This is currently hotly debated by immunologists and far from widely accepted and has never before been applied to the IDS arena. It is our opinion that this theory is the key that will unlock the true potential of AIS by allowing us to build commercially viable systems that can scale up to real world problem sizes.

We intend to use the correlation of signals based on the DT. We believe the success of our system to be independent of the eventual acceptance or rejection of the DT by immunologist as the proposed AIS would achieve this by identifying key *types* of apoptotic and necrotic alerts and understanding the balance between these two types of alerts. In addition, the proposed AIS is extended by employing the APC activation mechanism explained by the DT. This mechanism has the advantage of detecting rapidly spreading viruses or scanning intrusions at an early stage.

References

1. Aickelin U, Cayzer S (2002), The Danger Theory and Its Application to AIS, 1st International Conference on AIS, pp 141-148.
2. Barcia R, Pallister C, Sansom D, McLeod J (2000), Apoptotic response to membrane and soluble CD95-ligand by human peripheral T cells, Immunology 101 S1 77.
3. Boulougouris G, McLeod J et al (1999), IL-2 independent T cell activation and proliferation induced by CD28. Journal of Immunology 163: 1809-1816.
4. Cayzer S, Aickelin U (2002), A Recommender System based on the Immune Network, Proceedings CEC, pp 807-813.
5. Cayzer S, Aickelin U (2002), Idiotypic Interactions for Recommendation Communities in AIS, 1st International Conference on AIS, pp 154-160.
6. Cuppens F (2001), Managing Alerts in a Multi Intrusion Detection Environment, the 17th Annual Computer Security Applications Conference.
7. Cuppens F et al (2002), Correlation in an Intrusion Process, Internet Security Communication Workshop (SECI'02).
8. Dain O, Cunningham R (2001), Fusing a Heterogeneous Alert Stream into Scenarios, Proceeding of the 2001 ACM Workshop on Data Mining for Security Applications, pp 1-13.
9. Dasgupta D, Gonzalez F (2002), "An Immunity-Based Technique to Characterize Intrusions in Computer Networks", IEEE Trans. Evol. Comput. Vol 6; 3, pp 1081-1088.
10. Debar H, Wespi A (2001), Aggregation and Correlation of Intrusion-Detection Alerts, the Fourth workshop on the Recent Advances in Intrusion Detection, LNCS 2212, pp 85-103.
11. Dennett N, Barcia R, McLeod J (2002), Biomarkers of apoptotic susceptibility associated with in vitro ageing, Experimental Gerontology 37, 271-283.
12. Esponda F, Forrest S, Helman P (2002), Positive and Negative Detection, IEEE Transactions on Systems, Man and Cybernetics.
13. F. Esponda, S. Forrest, and P. Helman (2002), Positive and Negative Detection, IEEE Transactions on Systems, Man and Cybernetics (Submitted).
14. Fadok et al (1998), Macrophages that have ingested apoptotic cells in vitro inhibit proinflammatory cytokine production through autocrine/paracrine mechanisms involving TGFb, PGE2, and PAF, Journal of Clinical Investigation 101(4), 890-898.
15. Gallucci S et al (1999), Natural Adjuvants: Endogenous activators of dendritic cells, Nature Medicine 5(11), pp 1249-1255.
16. Gallucci S, Matzinger P (2001), Danger signals: SOS to the immune system, Current Opinions in Immunology 13, pp 114-119.

17. Hirata et al (1998), Caspases are activated in a branched protease cascade and control distinct downstream processes in Fas-induced apoptosis, J Experimental Medicine 187(4), 587-600.
18. Hoagland J, Staniford S (2002), Viewing IDS alerts: Lessons from SnortSnarf, www.silicondefense.com/software/snortsnarf/
19. Hofmeyr S, Forrest S (2000), Architecture for an AIS, Evolutionary Computation, Vol. 7, No. 1, pp 1289-1296.
20. Holler et al (2000), Fas triggers an alternative, caspase-8-independent cell death pathway using the kinase RIP as effector molecule, Nature Immunology 1(6), 489-495.
21. Holzman D (1995), New danger theory of immunology challenges old assumptions, Journal Natl Cancer Inst, 87 (19): 1436-1438.
22. Inaba et al (1994), The tissue distribution of the B7-2 costimulator in mice, J Experimental Medicine 180, 1849-1860.
23. Kerr et al (1972), Apoptosis: Its significance in cancer and cancer therapy, British Journal of Cancer 26(4), pp 239-257.
24. Kim J (2002), Integrating Artificial Immune Algorithms for Intrusion Detection, PhD Thesis, University College London.
25. Kim J, Bentley P (1999), The Artificial Immune Model for Network Intrusion Detection, 7th European Congress on Intelligent Techniques and Soft Computing (EUFIT'99).
26. Kim J, Bentley P (2001), Evaluating Negative Selection in an AIS for Network Intrusion Detection, Genetic and Evolutionary Computation Conference 2001, 1330-1337.
27. Kim J, Bentley P (2002), Towards an AIS for Network Intrusion Detection: An Investigation of Dynamic Clonal Selection, the Congress on Evolutionary Computation 2002, pp 1015-1020.
28. Kuby J (2002), Immunology, Fifth Edition by Richard A. Goldsby et al.
29. Matzinger P (1994), Tolerance Danger and the Extended Family, Annual reviews of Immunology 12, pp 991-1045.
30. Matzinger P (2002), The Danger Model: A Renewed Sense of Self, Science 296: 301-305.
31. McLeod J (2000), Apoptotic capability of ageing T cells, Mechanisms of Ageing and Development 121, pp 151-159.
32. Morrison T, Aickelin U (2002), An AIS as a Recommender System for Web Sites, 1st International Conference on AIS, pp 161-169.
33. Ning P, Cui Y (2002), An Intrusion Alert Correlator Based on Prerequisites of Intrusions, TR-2002-01, North Carolina State University.
34. Ning, P, Cui Y, Reeves S (2002), Constructing Attack Scenarios through Correlation of Intrusion Alerts, 9th Conference on Computer & Communications Security, pp 245-254.
35. Sauter et al (2001), Consequences of cell death: exposure to necrotic tumor cells, Journal of Experimental Medicine 191(3), 423-433.
36. Stainford E, Hogland J, McAlerney J (2002), Practical Automated Detection of Stealthy Portscans, Journal of Computer Security, Vol. 10, Issues 1/2.
37. Todryk S, Melcher S, Dalgleish A et al (2000), "Heat shock proteins refine the danger theory" Immunology 99 (3): 334-337.
38. Valdes A, Skinner K (2001), Probabilistic Alert Correlation, RAID'2001, 54-68.
39. Vance R (2000), Cutting Edge Commentary: A Copernican Revolution? Doubts about the danger theory, j immunology 165 (4), 1725-1728.

A Danger Theory Inspired Approach to Web Mining

Andrew Secker, Alex A. Freitas, and Jon Timmis

Computing Laboratory, University of Kent, Canterbury, Kent, UK, CT2 7NF
{ads3,aaf,jt6}@ukc.ac.uk

Abstract. Within immunology, new theories are constantly being proposed that challenge current ways of thinking. These include new theories regarding how the immune system responds to pathogenic material. This conceptual paper takes one relatively new such theory: the Danger theory, and explores the relevance of this theory to the application domain of web mining. Central to the idea of Danger theory is that of a context dependant response to invading pathogens. This paper argues that this context dependency could be utilised as powerful metaphor for applications in web mining. An illustrative example adaptive mailbox filter is presented that exploits properties of the immune system, including the Danger theory. This is essentially a dynamical classification task: a task that this paper argues is well suited to the field of artificial immune systems, particularly when drawing inspiration from the Danger theory.

1 Introduction

Over the last few years, Artificial Immune Systems (AIS) have become an increasingly popular computational intelligence paradigm. Inspired by the mammalian immune system, AIS seek to use observed immune components and processes as metaphors to produce systems that encapsulate a number of desirable properties of the natural immune system. These systems are then applied to solve problems in a wide variety of domains [1]. There are a number of motivations for using the immune system as inspiration for data mining; these include recognition, diversity, memory, self-regulation, dynamic protection and learning [2].

Although some may assume AIS are only of use in computer security for virus detection and suchlike, AIS lend themselves particularly well to data mining, a strength that is in part due to a pattern matching process thought to trigger the natural immune response. In the past AIS have been turned to clustering and classification tasks with encouraging results. Hunt and Cooke [3] created an immune inspired algorithm to classify DNA sequences and the immune inspired classifier AIRS has been benchmarked on a number of standard datasets with impressive results [4, 5]. Timmis and Neal developed an AIS for clustering, AINE [6]. For a summary of immune inspired algorithms for data mining the reader is directed to the review chapter [7].

There are certain challenges associated with web mining, which we believe an AIS is particularly well suited to tacking. Baeza-Yates and Ribeiro-Neto [8] list a number of data-centric problems associated with web mining. These include the following, to which we add our thoughts on immune solutions:

J. Timmis et al. (Eds.): ICARIS 2003, LNCS 2787, pp. 156–167, 2003.

- **Distributed data** – The data on the web spans countless computers. The immune system is naturally distributed. Just like the internet this distribution provides the system with disposability and diversity.

- **High percentage of volatile data** – New computers and data can be added or removed from the internet easily; likewise immune cells are constantly undergoing cell death and reproduction. The ability for both to cope with this situation shows both are adaptive, resilient and robust.

- **Large volume** – The size of the web is incredible and is constantly growing, making it difficult for systems to mine. The immune system too is made from countless numbers of cells. As each type of cell has a specialised function and works independently the system functions efficiently.

- **Quality of data** – The ease with which anyone may publish to the web can raise questions regarding its quality. Errors and omissions are common. The immune system however is noise tolerant, such that absolute matching is not required to trigger a response. Such noise tolerance is essential to an algorithm mining low quality data. The learning characteristics of the immune system are invaluable in this case. The immune system quickly learns the new characteristics of invaders when they mutate, likewise a web mining system may learn to correctly classify documents even with errors, which may be thought of as mutated words.

- **Heterogeneous data** – There exists on the internet many different types of data, in many different languages and formats. The immune system too contains a huge number of different cells each with its own specialised function and is capable of recognising a very large number of different types of antigen.

We propose to extend the field of web mining with AIS by taking inspiration from an immunological theory called the Danger theory [9]. The application of this theory to AIS was identified and discussed in depth in [10]. In this paper the authors state, "it is the authors' intention that this paper stimulates discussion [about the Danger theory] in the research community" (p. 141). The ideas presented in this paper have indeed inspired discussion and as a result significantly influenced this work in which we try to identify the benefits of a Danger theory inspired system and relate these to a practical application. We continue discussion in this area by putting forward some more practical ideas pertinent to the production of such a system, and suggest some implementation details. We believe that by harnessing Danger theory principles a new strand of artificial immune systems may emerge. We believe that because of the difficulties associated with mining such a vast and ever-changing domain, the advantages of Danger theory may be most pronounced in the field of web mining and so concentrate on this topic area. With the Danger theory principles at its core, the final system may harness the principles of context dependent activation and automatic adaptation to changing user actions and preferences.

In the next section we discuss the background to the Danger theory including Danger theory immunology and a small literature review concerning the use of Danger theory and AIS. We then discuss web mining and briefly discuss why we believe our system may be productive in this domain. Section 3 continues by using an example of an adaptive mailbox as an illustration as to how Danger theory may be practically applied. Finally in section 4 we provide some concluding remarks about the Danger theory approach to AIS and web mining and the system we have described.

2 Background

2.1 The Danger Theory

It is acknowledged that the Danger theory is a relatively new area in the realm of artificial immune systems, so to aid the reader's understanding of this paper we would like to discuss some details of this theory. These details have been simplified and so for a more comprehensive review of this field the reader is directed towards the literature, such as [9, 11, 12, 13].

The Danger theory attempts to explain the nature and workings of an immune response in a way different to the more traditional and widely held self/nonself viewpoint. This view states that cells of the adaptive immune system are incapable of attacking their host because any cells capable of doing so are deleted during their maturation process. This view, although seemingly elegant and generally easy to understand has come under criticism as it fails to explain a number of observations. Examples of such may be the lack of immune response to injections of inert but foreign proteins, or the failure of the immune system to reject tumours even though nonself proteins are expressed. Matzinger argues a more plausible way to describe the immune response is as a reaction to a stimulus the body considers harmful, not a simple reaction to nonself. This model allows foreign and immune cells to exist together, a situation impossible in the traditional standpoint. Matzinger hypothesises that cells dying unnaturally may release an alarm signal which disperses to cover a small area around that cell, Antigen Presenting Cells (APCs) receiving this signal will become stimulated and in turn stimulate cells of the adaptive immune system. The term "danger area" was coined by Aickelin and Cayzer in [10] to describe this area, in which the alarm signal may be received by APCs. This simple explanation may provide reasons for the two anomalous observations cited. Foreign proteins in the injection are not harmful and so are ignored, likewise tumour cells are not undergoing necrotic cell death and therefore not releasing alarm signals, hence no immune reaction. The nature of these alarm signals is still under discussion but some possibilities have been empirically revealed. These include elements usually found inside a cell which are encountered outside (pre-packaged signals) or chemicals such as heat shock protein, which are synthesised by cells under stress (inducible signals) [14].

As these danger signals only activate APCs, these cells in turn stimulate B and T-cells into action according to the following rules:

- **Signal one** is the binding of an immune cell to an antigenic pattern or an antigen fragment which is presented by an APC.
- **Signal two** is either a "help" signal given by a T-helper cell to activate a B-cell, or a co-stimulation signal given by an APC to activate a T-cell.

This co-stimulation signal does not fit well in the traditional self/nonself view and also leads to the question "if a B-cell requires stimulation from a T-helper cell to become activated, what activates a T-helper cell?" As Matzinger in [11] states "perhaps for this reason co-stimulation was ignored from its creation by Laferty and Cunningham in 1974, until its accidental rediscovery by Jenkins and Schwartz in 1986" (p. 400). The danger model answers this question (often referred to as the *primer problem*) by stating that T-cells receive their co-stimulation signals from APCs, which in turn have been activated by alarm signals.

There is a criticism of the self/nonself view, which states the thymus is responsible for the negative selection of all autoreactive cells, that as the thymus provides an incomplete description of self, the selection process will impart only a thymus/nonthymus distinction on T-cells. With a few simple laws concerning the described two signal activation mechanisms applied to T-cells we may provide a simple yet plausible explanation of why autoreactive cells are found in the body, yet autoimmune disease is rare:

- A resting T-cell needs two signals to be activated (as described before).
- If a T-cell receives the first signal (a binding of its receptor to an antigen) without the second signal (co-stimulation from an APC) the T-cell is assumed to have matched a host antigen and will die by apoptosis.

Thus Danger theory allows autoreactive cells to roam the body, but if that cell is to bind to a host antigen in the absence of correct antigenic presentation by an APC, the cell will die instead of becoming activated. A number of functions originally the responsibility of the immune system are, under the danger model, actually the responsibility of the tissues. Firstly, by the second law above, simply by existing and expressing their own proteins, tissue cells induce immune tolerance towards themselves. Secondly, as an immune response is initiated by the tissues, the nature and strength of this response may also be dictated by the tissues. Thus different types of alarm signal may result in different types of response. It has long been known that in a certain part of the body an immune response of one class may be efficient, but the same class of response in another may severely harm the host. This gives rise to a notion that tissues protect themselves and use the immune system to do so, a proposition which is in stark contrast to the traditional viewpoint whereby it is the immune system's role to protect tissues.

There is still much debate in the immunological world as to whether the Danger theory is a plausible explanation for observed immune function, however we are not concerned with the plausibility of the biology. If the Danger theory is a good metaphor on which to base an artificial immune system then it can be exploited. The first steps to this are the identification of useful concepts and the application of these concepts to a suitable problem domain. It is these actions we wish to illustrate throughout the rest of this paper.

2.2 Danger Theory and Artificial Immune Systems

There are currently few AIS publications concerned with Danger theory, although the authors believe this is set to change in the coming years. Notable exceptions currently available are as follows. In the review paper [15] the author mentions Danger theory in a small section (p. 5). In this section it is stated that danger signals may ground the immune response but gives little further detail as to how or why this may occur. In [16] the author raises a number of issues concerning an immune-inspired fault detection system for a computer. In this conceptual paper the author identifies that once again a response can be grounded by the interception of a danger signal. It is suggested that these signals would be raised by dying computer processes and some interesting parallels are drawn between a cell dying by necrosis and a thread terminating abnormally with an error such as a segmentation fault (p. 288). However, we do believe that Danger theory and therefore an implementation is about more than reacting to a threat. We do not believe this paper to propose a danger inspired system, as there is no notion of a danger area surrounding this dying process, nor is there a notion of a context dependent or localised response.

We believe it is a potentially useful area to investigate for a number of reasons. Not least of which may be the increased scalability of the AIS. In the past, the scalability of such systems has been called into question as antigens are compared with all antibodies [17]. The danger area may be one possible solution to this. In the body the immune system may only become activated within the danger area, likewise we may only need to activate antibodies within some area of interest in an AIS. One other advantage may be to harness the role of the tissues and assign different responses to different contexts. We have given thought to the implementation of such ideas, although with no such system having been produced to date we have no literature to refer to for guidance. For example, unlike most AIS algorithms, the tissue cells play a large part in a Danger theory inspired system but how should the behaviour of these cells be implemented? For example, it may be helpful to implement a set of tissue cells in addition to the set of antibodies. Each individual cell may then react to a slightly different stimulus. Furthermore we may also ask how the signal released by these cells should be interpreted. Should a signal from one cell be enough to stimulate an immune response or should activation occur only after a number of cells have been stimulated? If this latter approach is chosen we may then consider an activation function for the immune system such that a certain concentration of signal over a given space or time will initiate a response.

Based on the biology of the Danger theory, we may identify a set of Danger theory characteristics. We believe that the implementation of the majority of characteristics in this set is what may set a true Danger theory inspired AIS apart from other immune inspired systems. This set would include a context dependent danger signal, a notion of a danger area and a localised response within that area.

3   A Practical Application of Danger Theory to Web Mining

Web mining [18, 19] is an umbrella term used to describe three different types of data mining where the data source is the web. These three activities can be summarised as: **Mining structure** - studying the topology of the web made by hyperlinks; **Mining usage** - discovering knowledge from the data users leave behind once they have visited a site in that site's weblogs and **Mining content** - extracting useful information from the content of web pages and the area in which we concentrate our studies. The strand of web mining we describe in section 3.1 is web content mining, which Linoff and Berry in [19] describe as "the process of extracting useful information from the text, images and other forms of content that make up the pages" (p. 22). We would extend this definition to cover classification of e-mail, as this process extracts information from the e-mail's text and structure for the purpose of class assignment, and e-mails are part of the internet environment. Section 3.2 briefly describes ideas involving the other two strands of web mining.

To our knowledge only a few AIS have been turned towards true web mining tasks. One is a web usage mining system as described in [20]. This aims to mine web logs to detect different user access patterns for a web server. Another is the only reference we have been able to find in the literature to an immune inspired system for text mining and therefore could be turned to web content mining. The papers [21, 22] detail an AIS concept learner for classification of HTML documents into two classes: those which were on a given topic or not on that topic. The algorithm was first tested on the UCI's 1984 Congressional voting records and then turned to classifying pages taken from the Syskill and Webert Web Page Ratings also from the UCI data repository [23]. This dataset consists of HTML pages, each on one of four different topics. The task was for this immune inspired system to predict if an unseen page was on a given topic or not when the system was trained using a number of example pages. The system was compared with a naïve Bayesian classifier and achieved a higher predictive accuracy in three out of four domains. The results showed that the system was relatively insensitive to the size of the training set which was in contrast to the Bayesian system with which it was compared.

Given these explanations we can now discuss our reasons for believing a Danger theory based immune algorithm is particularly suitable for a web content mining application. AIS have been shown to be an adaptive and robust computational paradigm. We feel this would be particularly suitable for a *dynamic* environment such as the internet. Internet content is ever-changing and so too are users' expectations. The Danger theory offers us the ability to initiate a response based on this context. To take an example suggested in [10] we could be searching for interesting documents on the internet. A danger zone may arise around an interesting document, possibly a spatial zone incorporating all pages within one hyperlink depth, such that all other documents within this zone are now considered more interesting – thus giving the notion of a localised response. As the users opinions on document interestingness change, so too will the danger signal. Some days we may release a stronger danger signal than others as users' preferences change about the data. This variable danger signal gives a perception of context dependency. Finally, using the notion that tissues may dictate the effector class of response the system may offer different responses to different types of data. Interesting pages on an academic site may be responded to in one way, whereas interesting pages on a commercial site may be responded to in quite another.

3.1 An Adaptive Mailbox

To illustrate the use of a Danger theory inspired approach to artificial immune systems, we propose an adaptive mailbox system which will accept or temporarily ignore incoming e-mail depending on a measure of predicted interestingness to the user at that moment in time. This is essentially a classification task, but one in which the class boundaries will change both as the user's preferences change and as the status of the mailbox itself changes. During this section we use a number of small sections of pseudocode to illustrate our example. In this pseudocode we use AB to refer to an initially empty set of artificial antibodies.

The system we propose works over two distinct stages. The first will be an initialisation and training stage with the second as a running stage. During this second stage the system will both sort incoming e-mail and use feedback from the user to drive the evolutionary processes natural to an AIS. During the first stage, a summary of which is given in Pseudocode 1, the system must generate an initial collection of antibodies, and so for a given amount of time the system may observe user actions when confronted with a new e-mail. If the user is to delete a message after viewing it for less than a set period of time (normalised by length) or without reading it at all, the e-mail is deemed uninteresting, the content of the e-mail will be processed and an antibody produced. The feature vector of the antibody may include a set of words, a set of features or a combination of the two. This choice may prove critical to the performance of the system, discussion of this may be found in [24]. At this point the system will clone and mutate the antibody with the aim of generalising this antibody set. This process will continue until the system contains an appropriate repertoire of antibodies, each representing a generalised example of an uninteresting e-mail. Interesting e-mails are ignored in this initialisation phase because the goal is to produce only antibodies for classifying uninteresting e-mail.

```
PROCEDURE Initialise_Train()
    WHILE (size of AB < a threshold)
       IF(user expresses disinterest in an e-mail)
          new_ab ← create antibody from e-mail
          add new_ab to AB
          FOREACH (ab ∈ AB)
             clone and mutate ab to maximise affinity
                with new_ab
             add best n clones to AB
```

Pseudocode 1. Initialisation and Training

When the repertoire of immune cells has reached a given size the system may run on new data as described in Pseudocode 2. The AIS will convert all incoming e-mail into a format such that affinity between it and antibodies can be evaluated. Conceptually therefore the e-mail is an antigen. The system makes a distinction between the terms antigen and e-mail, as follows. Antigen is the name used to refer to a processed e-mail which contains just a generalized representation of the original e-mail and the class assigned to the e-mail. The system starts initialising an antigen count to 0. This is the count of all e-mails that have been duly processed. When this count reaches a certain number (K) of antigens, we use the latest K antigens to perform clonal selection and mutation with the set of antibodies as described in the Update_Population procedure. Note that it is important that this procedure is performed only after we have a reasonable number of duly processed antigens, to avoid antibodies adapted to just one antigen and preserving generality. One of the main advantages of the immune inspired approach is this built in ability to adapt. The use of the clonal selection principle here has the effect of allowing our antibody set to change over time reflecting users changing preferences and the changing nature of the e-mail received. The clonal selection procedure will lead to an increase in the size of set AB over time and so to counter this the final line of this procedure will remove the w most unhelpful antibodies in the set AB.

The procedure Process_User_Feedback has the main goal of assigning a class (uninteresting or interesting) to the e-mail, based on the user's feedback, so that the affinity maturation of the antibodies is based on the class of the last K antigens.

Note that, at any given moment, there might be several e-mails waiting for the feedback from the user to be classified and duly processed into an antigen. The system keeps working in an asynchronous way, while those e-mails are waiting feedback from the user.

```
              PROCEDURE Continuous_adaptation()
                LOOP
                  antigen_count ← 0
                  receive incoming e-mail
                  Process_User_Feedback(email)
                ag ← preprocess e-mail into antigen
                  antigen_count ← antigen_count + 1
                  IF(antigen_count = K)
                    AG ← last K antigens
                    Update_Population(AG)
                    Antigen_count ← 0
                  compute degree of danger()
                  WHILE(danger is high)
                    compute temporal danger zone
                    AG ← all e-mails in the danger zone
                    FOREACH(ag ∈ AG)
                      FOREACH(ab ∈ AB)
                        compute affinity (ab,ag)
                      high_aff ← highest affinity value
                      IF(high_aff > a threshold)
                        move ag to temporary store

              PROCEDURE Process_User_Feedback(email)
                wait for feedback from user
                IF (user considers email uninteresting)
                  assign class uninteresting to email
                ELSE
                  assign class interesting to email

              PROCEDURE Update_Population(AG)
                FOREACH(ab ∈ AB)
                  FOREACH(ag ∈ AG)
                    compute affinity(ab,ag)
                    U ← {ag | ag's class is uninteresting}
                    I ← {ag | ag's class is interesting}
```

$$quality\_ab \leftarrow \sum_{i \in U} aff\big(ab,ag_i\big) - \sum_{j \in U} aff\big(ab,ag_j\big)$$

```
                  clone and mutate in proportion to
                    quality_ab
                  remove the w antibodies with the lowest
                    value of quality_ab
```

Pseudocode 2. Continuous adaptation

In the next part of the pseudocode, the system computes the degree of danger at the moment, which depends on the current status of the mailbox. So what may the nature of this danger signal be? The danger signal should signal something is wrong but there is still time to recover, and should come from something the antigens have little or no control over. There is also no reason why the danger signal must indicate danger in the real world; it could be a positive signal as long as it signals that something of significance to the system is taking place in a particular area. In this instance we considered several possibilities for such a danger signal, such as abnormal frequency and/or size of e-mail messages and a high number of unread messages or an abnormally full inbox. Although the system might work with a combination of danger signals, each of them requiring a somewhat different response, in this paper we focus on a single danger signal based on the idea that the mailbox has too many messages. Hence, this part of the pseudocode works as follows. First, the system computes the degree of danger. If the user has no messages waiting to be read then we may not have a danger signal at all. If however there are many unread messages a danger signal may be raised. Every time a new e-mail arrives the danger area should be re-evaluated based on the current state of the mailbox. Although in the natural immune system the danger area is spatial, in our system we are not so constrained. The nature of this danger area must be decided upon based on what we want it to signal or how we want to react to it. Hence in this example we propose a temporal danger zone, the size of which will vary according to a measured value of the danger signal. Thus unread messages in the users inbox which may have been let through previously may become candidates for removal on receipt of a danger signal. This temporal danger area will therefore stretch into the inbox's past and make the system even more adaptive: the larger the degree of danger, the larger the size of the danger area.

Once the danger area has been computed, the system has to decide, for each e-mail in that area, whether the e-mail is interesting or not. This decision consists of predicting the class of the e-mail without user feedback, based solely on the affinity between each email and the antibodies. Hence, the system computes the affinity between each e-mail in the danger area and each antibody. For each e-mail in the danger area, if the affinity between that e-mail and the most similar antibody is greater than a threshold, then the e-mail is considered uninteresting (since all antibodies represent uninteresting e-mails) and the e-mail is moved into temporary storage or otherwise hidden from the user. Otherwise the e-mail is considered interesting and e-mail remains in the inbox. This is an analogy to the natural situation as a recognition of an antigen by an antibody is signal one. There is a correspondence in the natural system between the release of a danger signal and the activation of APCs which in return supply the co-stimulatory signal to activate T-cells. Just the presence of danger in this context may therefore take the place of signal two.

The procedure `Process_User_Feedback()` works as follows. The expression of disinterest by the user may be measured by the time the user views the e-mail – normalized by the e-mail's length – or user's actions upon receipt of the e-mail, such as deleting it immediately or leaving it to read later. The exact details of how the system will interpret user actions are irrelevant for the purposes of this paper.

To end this section we refer back to the end of section 2.2 in which we identified a number of points we believe would set a Danger theory inspired AIS apart from immune inspired systems. For clarification and to illustrate that by our definition this system is truly danger inspired we may draw the parallels described in Table 1.

3.2 Other Web Mining Applications

We can further identify a number of areas in which such a system may be of use to a user whilst they are having dealings with the internet covering the remaining two strands of web mining. In the above example the mailbox is one tissue, the danger signal released by which provoke one type of immune response, but these ideas can be extended to different tissues we may encounter when using the internet. One such example could be turning the system to web usage mining. Consider a system used to mine the logs generated by user accesses to an academic webpage. A significant drop in accesses could trigger a danger signal. This may prompt the system to identify page accesses that have disappeared. The classes of these may point to developing situations such as a declining quality of publication or general disinterest in a given subject area. In this situation, the danger signal may only be raised if, other webpages hosted by the same department are not suffering such a fate, or the author has updated his site recently and so should be generating interest. This gives the danger signal the required context dependency.

Table 1. Comparison between Danger theory characteristics and the adaptive mailbox

Danger Theory	Adaptive mailbox
Tissue	Mailbox
Signal 1	High affinity between antibody and antigen (e-mail)
Signal 2	Receipt of danger signal
Source of danger	High number of unread messages
Danger area	Temporal (last K e-mails)
Immune response to danger	Move emails to temporary storage
Localised response	Only emails in the danger area are considered to be moved to temporary storage

Similarly a web usage mining system may be implemented with an e-commerce site in mind. A drop in the frequency of access to pages detailing certain products or services may point to a change in customer preferences similar to the manner above. In this case the immune response will be triggered and may begin to look for interesting information from competitors/associates websites, a principle described in [25]. This may give rise to information on new products or services as yet not detailed on the monitored site. The danger signal here has carried the information concerning what is going wrong. The different type of danger signal triggers a different response to that described in the previous section.

One final possibility is for the web mining system covers the domain of web structure mining. The system may monitor the local internet topology in which an academic or business related page is embedded. If the structure-mining system detects fewer and fewer pages or internet sites are linking to the one being monitored, the danger signal may once again be raised and in a similar manner to above. The adaptive AIS may then search for information on the internet which may enable the user to reverse this decline.

4 Conclusions and Further Work

In this conceptual paper we have discussed how immune inspired algorithms exhibit a similar set of desirable features to the natural immune system. We have also discussed the relatively new Danger theory and given examples as to how Danger theory principles may be used in the field of AIS. We believe that a Danger theory inspired approach to web mining could lead to the production of new and effective algorithms for knowledge discovery on the web. We believe the scalability of immune algorithms may be enhanced by initiating an immune response only when a local danger signal is present which may also yield an increase in result quality as the danger signal may be released in a context dependent manner.

Although the potential is clear, until a danger inspired AIS system is realized no firm claims can be made with regard to improvements over more traditional algorithms. However the area of danger inspired AIS algorithms is an exciting one. Our ultimate idea, combining artificial tissues capable of releasing artificial danger signals, is a significant paradigm shift for the field of artificial immune systems and with a relevant application already identified, one we are keen to pursue.

References

1. deCastro, L. N., & Timmis, J. (2002). *Artificial Immune Systems: A New Computational Intelligence Approach*: Springer.
2. Dasgupta, D. (1999). An overview of Artificial Immune Systems. In D. Dasgupta (Ed.), *Artificial Immune Systems and Their Applications* (pp. 3-21): Springer
3. Hunt, J. E., & Cooke, D. E. (1996). Learning using an artificial immune system. *Journal of Network and Computer Applications, 19*(2), 189-212.
4. Watkins, A. (2001). AIRS: A resource limited artificial immune classifier. Masters Thesis, Mississippi State University.
5. Watkins, A., & Timmis, J. (2002). Artificial Immune Recognition System (AIRS): Revisions and Refinements. *In proceedings of The First International Conference on Artificial Immune Systems (ICARIS 2002)* (pp 173-181), Canterbury, UK.
6. Timmis, J., & Neal, M. (2001). A resource limited artificial immune system for data analysis. *Knowledge Based Systems, 14*(3-4), 121-130.
7. Timmis, J., & Knight, T. (2002). Artificial Immune Systems: Using The Immune System as Inspiration for Data Mining. In H. A. Abbass, R. A. Sarker & C. S. Newton (Eds.), *Data Mining: A Heuristic Approach* (pp. 209-230): Idea Group Publishing.
8. Baeza-Yates, R. and Ribeiro-Neto, B. (1999). *Modern Information Retrieval.*: Addison Wesley Longman
9. Matzinger, P. (2002a). The Danger Model: A Renewed Sense of Self. *Science, 296*, 301-305.
10. Aickelin, U., & Cayzer, S. (2002). The Danger Theory and Its Application to Artificial Immune Systems. *In proceedings of The First International Conference on Artificial Immune Systems (ICARIS 2002)*(pp. 141-148), Canterbury, UK.
11. Matzinger, P. (1998). An Innate Sense of Danger. *Seminars in Immunology, 10*(5), 399-415.
12. Anderson, C., & Matzinger, P. (2000). Danger: The view from the bottom of the cliff. *Seminars in Immunology, 12*(3), 231-238.
13. Matzinger, P. (2002b). The Real Function of The Immune System or Tolerance and The Four D's. Retrieved 30/10/2002, 2002, from http://cmmg.biosci.wayne.edu/asg/polly.html
14. Gallucci, S., & Matzinger, P. (2001). Danger signals: SOS to the immune system. *Current Opinion in Immunology, 13*(1), 114-119.
15. Williamson, M. M. (2002). Biologically Inspired Approaches to Computer Security (*HP Labs Technical Reports HPL-2002-131*): HP Labs Bristol, UK. Available from: http://www.hpl.hp.com/techreports/2002/HPL-2002-131.html
16. Burgess, M. (1998). Computer Immunology. *In proceedings of The 12th Systems Administration Conference (LISA 1998)*, Boston, USA.
17. Kim, J., & Bentley, P. J. (2001, July 7-11, 2001). An Evaluation of Negative Selection in an Artificial Immune System for Network Intrusion Detection. *In proceedings of The Genetic and Evolutionary Computation Conference 2001 (GECCO 2001)* (pp. 1330-1337), San Francisco, USA.

18. Chakrabarti, S. (2003). *Mining the web (Discovering Knowledge from Hypertext Data)*: Morgan Kaufmann.
19. Linoff, G. S., & Berry, M. J. A. (2001). *Mining the web (Transforming Customer Data into Customer Value):* Wiley.
20. Nasraoui, O., Dasgupta, D., & Gonzalez, F. (2002). The Promise and Challenges of Artificial Immune System Based Web Usage Mining: Preliminary Results. *In proceedings of The SIAM Workshop on Web Analytics* (pp. 29-39), Arlington, VA
21. Twycross, J. (2002). An Immune System Approach to Document Classification (*HP Labs Technical Reports HPL-2002-288*): HP Labs Bristol, UK. Available from: http://www.hpl.hp.com/techreports/2002/HPL-2002-288.html
22. Twycross, J., & Cayzer, S. (2002). An Immune System Approach to Document Classification (*HP Labs Technical Reports HPL-2002-292*): HP Labs Bristol, UK. Available from: http://www.hpl.hp.com/techreports/2002/HPL-2002-292.html
23. Blake, C. L., & Merz, C. J. (1998). *UCI Repository of machine learning databases*. Retrieved 20 May 2003, from http://www.ics.uci.edu/~mlearn/MLRepository.html
24. Diao, Y., Lu, H., & Wu, D. (2000). A comparative study of classification based personal e-mail filtering. *In proceedings of The Fourth Pacific Asia Conference on Knowledge Discovery and Data Mining (PAKDD 2000)* (pp. 408-419), Kyoto, Japan.
25. Liu, B., Ma, Y., & Yu, P. S. (2001). Discovering unexpected information from your competitors' web sites. *In proceedings of The Seventh ACM SIGKDD International Conference on Knowledge Discovery and Data Mining (KDD 2001)* (pp. 144-153), San Francisco, USA.

Meta-stable Memory
in an Artificial Immune Network

Mark Neal

Department of Computer Science, University of Wales, Aberystwyth, UK
mjn@aber.ac.uk

Abstract. This paper describes an artificial immune system algorithm which implements a fairly close analogue of the memory mechanism proposed by Jerne [1] (usually known as the Immune Network Theory). The algorithm demonstrates the ability of these types of network to produce meta-stable structures representing populated regions of the antigen space. The networks produced retain their structure indefinitely and capture inherent structure within the sets of antigens used to train them. Results from running the algorithm on a variety of data sets are presented and shown to be stable over long time periods and wide ranges of parameters. The potential of the algorithm as a tool for multivariate data analysis is also explored.

1 Introduction

This paper presents an exploration of the capabilities of an unsupervised algorithm for generating networks of artificial recognition balls which capture structure and relationships within data sets. The algorithm represents the culmination of a series of attempts to produce a self-limiting, self-organizing, meta-stable network generation algorithm. The author believes that all of these goals have been satisfactorily achieved and has conducted extensive experiments to test this. A selection of these experiments are presented here using a simple graph-layout algorithm to present results, and principal component plots (PCA) to highlight equivalent structure within data sets. The algorithm also has the property of retaining its structure in the absence of any stimulation as was shown in [2], this is not explicitly shown here. The source code, a simple graph-layout program and a demonstration are available on request from the author.

2 Immune Network Theory

The immune network theory proposes that the B-cells in the body interact with each other to maintain the immune memory. The mechanism proposed is that B-cells which are capable of recognising similar (but not necessarily identical) pathogens are also capable of recognising and stimulating each other [1]. Thus a dynamic feedback mechanism can maintain parts of the immunological memory

J. Timmis et al. (Eds.): ICARIS 2003, LNCS 2787, pp. 168–180, 2003.

which are not frequently stimulated. Clearly however not all B-cells have sufficient stimulation to survive indefinitely and thus some will die out. In the human immune system T-cells both perform a surveillance role and interact with B-cells which complicates the mechanism somewhat. In our artificial immune system the role of T-cells is currently ignored. In the real immune system there are very large numbers of identical B-cells to deal with each type of infection. In an artificial system such repetition can be coded without representing all the identical cells individually. Fortunately the concept of a *recognition ball* which represents a region of antigen space that is covered by a particular type of B-cell can replace the repetition of individuals [3]. So our AIS consists of a network of artificial recognition balls (ARB) which are linked together if they are close to each other in antigen space (see [2] for an earlier version of the algorithm). Pathogens (data items) can be considered to be points in this antigen space, and thus proximity can be defined as a simple distance function.

3   The Artificial Immune Network Algorithm

The algorithm used here is a development (in fact a simplification) of an earlier algorithm presented in [2]. The new algorithm uses a very similar stimulation function and resource allocation mechanism, but the details vary in some important details. The algorithm now captures directly the ideas of *primary* and *secondary* response and is completely deterministic in its operation. The removal of the stochastic mutation operator was motivated by the wish to demonstrate the basic mechanisms and their important properties; namely the stability of the structures produced and the self-limiting and organizing growth of the networks.

3.1   The Network Affinity Threshold (NAT)

As in previous work the most important and sensitive control parameter for the algorithm is the NAT. This value dictates when ARBs in the network are to be connected. The rule is simply that if the distance between two ARBs is less than the NAT value then they are connected. Thus, simple Euclidean distance between the patterns represented by ARBs dictates the connectivity of the immune network. This is directly analogous to the concept of the *recognition ball* as presented in [3].

In this algorithm the NAT plays a further rôle, in that it provides a threshold for the cloning process. If an antigen is presented to the network which is further from the most stimulated ARB than the NAT dictates, then cloning is performed.

Thus the NAT is a measure of the distance in antigen shape-space beyond which recognition by an ARB is deemed to be insufficiently precise.

Fortunately, from the point of view of data-analysis, this measure has a direct meaning in terms of the data under examination. It is the Euclidean distance between items beyond which it is deemed appropriate to make a distinction. Although this may not be known in advance, it is often the case that some sensible estimate can be made in advance based on known cases. Even if it is not, however, there is a relatively easy route to determining useful values for the NAT, by running the algorithm several times on the data-set (see section 4).

3.2   The Algorithm

The algorithm is designed to run continuously, and does not have (or require) a stopping criterion. This was a fundamental goal when designing the algorithm and meant that the algorithm had to deal with the problem of *over-fitting* in some more intelligent way than by just halting the training process. The *culling* process combined with the selection of a suitable value for the *network affinity threshold* perform this rôle.

Network Initialization. Currently the network is initialized by taking a small set of arbitrarily chosen samples of the antigen set and creating ARBs which precisely recognise those antigens. The number of these ARBs in the initial network is made as small as possible. If too few ARBs are initially present then the algorithm culls all the ARBs in the network. This occurs when none of the ARBs are sufficiently connected or stimulated to form a stable memory structure. The process of determining the minimum number of ARBs that produces a non-empty network can be automated by simply taking one initial ARB and running the algorithm to see if the network dies off or not. If the network dies off then the algorithm is re-run with one more initial ARB and the process is repreated until the network survives. This process is not time consuming as the algorithm very quickly culls all the ARBs if there are not sufficient to maintain a population.

Stimulation. The stimulation level of an ARB is calculated using components analogous to those proposed by Jerne. These components are based on: affinity to the current antigen (positive contribution), and affinity to connected neighbours.
    These components can be summarised as follows:

1. Excitation, ps due to affinity to the current antigen:

$$ps = \frac{1}{1 + dis(p)}$$

2. Excitation, ns due to affinity to neighbours:

$$ns = \sum_{x=0}^{n} dis(x)$$

In both equations the function $dis(a)$ returns the Euclidean distance between the current ARB and the item a; and n represents the number of neighbours at the current ARB. These components are summed. The second component is based on the neighbours of the ARB, and there is no limit to the number of neighbours an ARB can have. Due to the way in which growth of the network proceeds, it is no longer necessary (or desirable) to normalise these neighbour contributions as was done in [2]. This is one of several simplifications to the algorithm which were undertaken, and a return to the function used in [4].

Cloning. Cloning is now only undertaken when expansion of the repertoire is required. This is determined by the fact that the most highly stimulated ARB (as calculated above) is further from the antigen pattern (as measured by Euclidean distance) than the distance dictated by the NAT. Thus there is now an explicit recognition of the difference between primary and secondary immune response: cloning is only undertaken when a primary response is required to expand the repertoire to cover an unrecognised antigen. Secondary response simply involves the stimulation of the relevant pre-existing parts of the network.

The cloning operation is also extremely simple. It consists of introducing into the network an ARB which precisely recognises the pattern which *caused* the primary response. There is currently no mutation operator used in the algorithm. Initial work included mutation, but subsequent experimentation showed that the networks produced without it were very similar to those produced with it. Whilst this is a significant deviation from the natural immune system which seems to rely on highly stochastic processes for repertoire expansion, it is not seen as central to the concept of a network memory mechanism for the immune system.

Resource Allocation. Since early in the development of the series of algorithms which have culminated in this work, the concept of limited resources has played a part. Initial work in [5] used a very brutal and simplistic approach which took little account of time and was reliant on an "epoch-based" learning regime. This algorithm uses a simple stimulation and decay mechanism for updating the resource level held by each ARB. Thus the level of resources held by each ARB is calculated on a rolling basis according to two mechanisms: first a simple geometric decay; second a boost to the resource level which is dependent on the stimulation level and resource level of the current ARB. It is worth pointing out that this means that all resource allocation and stimulation calculations are *local* to each ARB and do not require normalization or a central resource pool.

The decay mechanism can be expressed thus:

$$R_{decayed} = R_{current} \times decayrate$$

where *decayrate* is a scalar between zero and one. For this work a value of 0.99 was used in all cases; and $R_{current}$ is the resource level currently present at this ARB. The algorithm is robust to a wide range of values of the *decayrate* scalar. Further discussion can be found in section 3.3.

The resource level after each data presentation can be expressed as follows:

$$R_{new} = R_{curent} + (k \times (maxres - R_{decayed}) \times S)$$

where R_{new} is the new resource level for the ARB, k is a scalar between zero and one (a value of 0.0005 was employed throughout this work. *maxres* is a maximum resource level which any ARB can claim. Throughout this work the value was set at 1000.0. The algorithm is robust to a wide variety of values for these two scalars. For more detailed discussion of sensitivity of the algorithm to both of these scalars see 3.3.

Culling. ARBs are culled from the network when there resource level (as described above) falls below a threshold value. We call this threshold value *mortality* and throughout this work it was set at 1.0. The algorithm is robust to a wide variety of values of *mortality* (see section3.3).

3.3   Parameters and Value Selection

From the above, it can be seen that there are several scalars used to parameterise the algorithm. These are *decayrate, maxres, mortality* and *k*. All of these values are involved in the resource allocation process. Whilst a set of four parameters may seem daunting and dangerously "tweakable", they are in fact nowhere near as fiddly as they at first seem. In order to understand why this is so we must examine the resource allocation process in more detail, and the behaviour of typical networks of ARBs generated by the algorithm.

The resource decay mechanism is simple enough (see above). The resource boost mechanism is however a little more subtle. The level of boost given to an ARB's resource level is determined by a variety of factors:

Stimulation level(S): this ensures that ARBs which regularly recognise antigen patterns and/or are in a highly linked section of the network will accumulate more resources than ARBs which are not, and thus will survive longer.

Proximity to maximum resource level($maxres - R_{decayed}$): this ensures that ARBs which are already rich in resources will not go on claiming more and more without limit. Their resource level will geometrically approach the value *maxres*.

A small scalar(k): a small constant to ensure that ARBs with high stimulation levels do not achieve extremely high resource allocations very rapidly. This is desirable as it allows large values of *decayrate* and thus long time lags between the creation of ARBs and their ultimate survival or demise.

Extensive experimentation with the variables k, *maxres, mortality* and *decayrate* has shown that the ranges of values for these variables shown in table 1 produce very similar networks in all cases.

Table 1. Ranges of variables shown to produce very similar networks. Statistics were generated using Fisher's iris data.

Variable	Min	Network sizes	Max	Network sizes	Standard value
k	0.0001	39	0.001	33	0.0005
maxres	500	37	5000	32	1000
mortality	0.0	34	5.0	30	1.0
decayrate	0.90	34	0.999	35	0.99

This belief can be further reinforced when the mechanisms employed and the behaviour that they promote are considered. The boosting of resource level

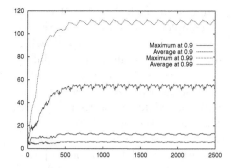
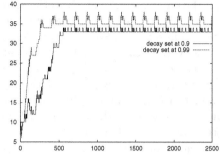

Fig. 1. Maximum and average stimulation levels present in the network throughout the evolution of the networks.

Fig. 2. Size evolution of networks with decay rates of 0.9 and 0.99. The meta-stable state size of both networks is very similar.

using an amount that reduces dependent on the current resource level is clearly going to strike a balance at some level when combined with a geometric decay function. So long as this equilibrium falls somewhere reasonably far away from both of the limiting values for the majority of the ARBs then the precise values of these two limits will have little effect on the networks produced. These two values are provided by *maxres* as an upper limit, and *mortality* as a lower limit. In a similar manner, the values of k and *decay* are in the first instance simply going to affect the level at which this balance is to be struck. Once again so long as these values are arranged to ensure that the resource levels at which most ARBs stabilise falls well away from the upper and lower limits then little effect will be observed. This effect can be seen in figure 1, which shows the maximum and average resource levels in the network produced for the iris data with two different values for *decayrate*. Although the values of the parameters and the average, maximum and minimum resource levels are all significantly different, the size evolution of the network is almost identical in all cases (see figure 2).

4   Forming Stable Memories of Data

In order to demonstrate the algorithm's behaviour, it has been tested extensively with a variety of data-sets. Results from three of these data-sets are presented here. The first of these is Fisher's iris data[1] [6] (which provides a trustworthy benchmark), the second is a larger data-set of much higher dimensionality which contains statistical information about a number of gene sequences[2] [7], and the third is the now well-explored Wisconsin breast cancer data set[3] [8]. The algorithm was used in all cases with all the standard parameter values from table 1. A wide range of values for the NAT were used in order to explore the structures

---

[1] this data-set contains 150 data items in four dimensions
[2] this data-set contains 1693 data items in 435 dimensions
[3] this data-set contains 699 data items in 9 dimensions

of all three data-sets. In all cases the algorithm was run until the network ceased to grow. That is not to say that the network completely stabilized, just that a meta-stable state of approximately constant size was attained. Graphs showing final network sizes show the median value for network size after meta-stability has been achieved.

In the cases of Fisher's iris data and the Wisconsin breast cancer data the way in which the data is clustered is presented as confusion statistics. These statistics are generated by taking each Bcell and using the class of the majority of the data items claimed by that Bcell as the "correct" class for that Bcell; and then counting the number of data items which do not fall into the majority class at that Bcell. Where there is an equal number of data items of the different classes, *all* of the data items are labelled as misclassified. The complete statistics are shown for a variety of networks at different NAT values.

Such data is not presented for the statistical sequence data due to the poor performance of the algorithm and the large number of classes (see section 4.2).

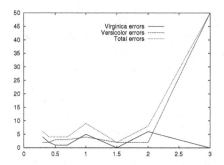

Fig. 3. Classification errors produced at various NAT values for the iris data.

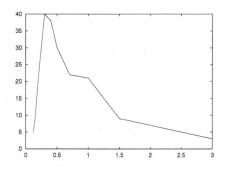

Fig. 4. Meta-stable network sizes reached at various NAT values for the iris data.

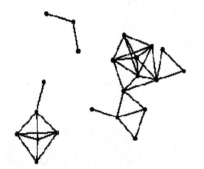

Fig. 5. Network produced by the algorithm at a NAT value of 0.7. We believe that qualitatively similar patterns can be discerned in the PCA plot and the network.

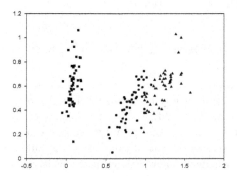

Fig. 6. PCA plot of first two principal components for Fisher's iris data. Squares represent setosa examples, circles represent virginica examples and triangles represent versicolor examples.

Table 2. Classification performance at various NAT values for Fisher's iris data.

Class	NAT	Correct	Incorrect	% Class Correct	% Total Correct
Setosa	0.7	50	0	100	
Virginica	0.7	49	1	98	
Versicolor	0.7	47	3	94	97.3
Setosa	1.0	50	0	100	
Virginica	1.0	45	5	90	
Versicolor	1.0	46	4	92	94
Setosa	1.5	50	0	100	
Virginica	1.5	50	0	100	
Versicolor	1.5	48	2	96	98.7
Setosa	3.0	50	0	100	
Virginica	3.0	50	0	100	
Versicolor	3.0	0	50	0	66.6

4.1   The Iris Data

The iris data has provided a useful benchmark data-set in previous closely related
work [2,5]. The data-set has the advantage of being relatively small and contains
simple, but interesting and non-trivial structure. See figure 6 for a principal component plot which captures the majority of the structure of the data-set. The
algorithm produces networks which separate the data into two distinct clusters.
This is as expected and as has been observed in previous versions of the algorithm. One of the networks produced by the algorithm presented here is shown in
figure 5. The network was generated with a NAT value of 0.7 and clearly shows
the separation of the data into well-defined clusters. The confusion statistics are
presented in table 2. The network can be seen to correctly classify 97.3% of the
data items at this NAT value. A better performance figure is acheived at a NAT
value of 1.5, however at this point the network produced is less informative in
structure, and captures much less detail of the structure inherent in the data.
From the perspective of the exploration of data in a data-mining context the
network produced at a NAT value of 0.7 is more appealing. In a similar manner
to the other parameters examined above it is reassuring to note that the precise
value of the NAT does not dramatically affect the performance of the algorithm.
    As observed in [9], it is interesting to note that one of the data classes tends
to dominate the structures produced by the algorithm. For the iris data it is the
Setosa class which is *always* correctly classified, and as the NAT increases the
Virginica class dominates at the expense of the Versicolor class. This effect is
not so damaging for this version of the algorithm however, as the network does
stabilise with all the components of the network present over a large range of
NAT values. This behaviour was not seen in previous versions of the algorithm
in which all but one region of the network eventually died.
    Thus for the iris data we can conclude that the algorithm performs very well
in terms of classification, and in terms of generating meaningful networks over
a good range of NAT values.

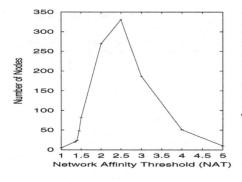

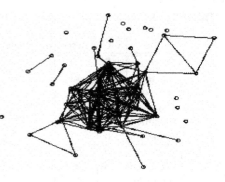

Fig. 7. Steady-state size of network generated at various NAT values for the statistical sequence data set.

Fig. 8. Network produced with NAT of 1.45 for the statistical sequence data. Qualitatively similar patterns can be seen in fig. 9.

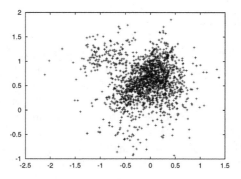

Fig. 9. PCA plot of first two principal components for the statistical sequence data. Compare with 8.

4.2   The Statistical Gene Sequence Data

This data set was chosen as it is quite large, and contains relatively little useful structure (see figure 9). The data set contains statistical information about the make-up of genetic sequences and labels which represent the functional class of the gene. There are 17 different functional classes represented in this data (although there are subdivisions within these also). The data was examined in order to test the performance of the algorithm, both for large data sets and for data sets which do not contain easily separable clusters. The performance of the algorithm with respect to the functional classes of the genes represented was, as expected, quite poor. The only functional class (class 29) which was reasonably separable can be seen as a more diffuse cloud of points above and to the left of the main clump in figure 9. This was reflected to an acceptable degree in the networks produced, and an example network generated at a NAT of 1.45 is shown in figure 8, the diamond-shaped structure attached to the upper-right of the network represents those data items belonging to class 29. It is worth saying that this relatively poor performance is not surprising when the PCA plot is examined: there is very little inherent structure for an unsupervised algorithm to capitalise on. In addition, when examined with standard single linkage cluster analysis (results not shown), it was very clear that there were no clear clumps of data that could be easily separated. When supervised algorithms such as C4.5 were applied to the data, much better classifications were possible. However it is not really sensible to compare performance with such supervised algorithms. Suffice it to say that there *is* sufficient information within the data to separate the classes reasonably effectively using supervised machine learning algorithms. This is stated simply to make clear that the data is worthy of examination, and that the algorithm presented here is restricted in just the same way as other unsupervised algorithms.

The data set provided a good test for the time complexity of the algorithm with a large data-set of high-dimensionality. The most useful network (with NAT of 1.45) was stable after 10000 data presentations (about 6 passes through the data set) and took 8 minutes to run on a 1.1GHz Celeron lap-top. For a data set of this size and a relatively modest computer system this is acceptable performance. The data set is available from [10].

4.3   The Wisconsin Breast Cancer Data

The Wisconsin breast cancer data is now well explored, and is a relatively easy data-set to classify to a fairly high accuracy. It is intermediate in size between the previous two data-sets and provides a further test of the suitability of the algorithm for separating relatively well-defined clusters of data. Unlike previous versions of the immune network algorithms, this algorithm retains segments representing both classes of data when it reaches its meta-stable state [9,11]. The final network represents the data in a way which reflects the structure seen in the PCA plot. This behaviour is also seen for the iris data (see above).

The network which was chosen as the most useful is that which was generated with a NAT value of 1.0. This network is shown in figure 12. For this data, this network is the best at classifying the data (see figure 11. In this case it is also the most appealing network to examine in the vizualization tool with a simple spring-embedder graph-layout algorithm [12].

5   Discussion

From the experiments that have been undertaken with various data sets it seems that the networks generated using this algorithm and displayed with a spring-embedder graph-layout algorithm have the following properties:

- There do not seem to be drastic changes in the networks produced for similar values of *any* of the parameters to the algorithm (including the NAT). The algorithm is quite insensitive to these parameters, although gross changes in the NAT will produce noticeably different networks.

Table 3. Classification performance at various NAT values for Breast Cancer data.

Class	NAT	Correct	Incorrect	% Class Correct	% Total Correct
Benign	0.05	432	12	97.3	
Malignant	0.05	226	13	94.6	96.3
Benign	0.7	428	16	96.4	
Malignant	0.7	232	7	97.1	96.6
Benign	1.5	430	14	96.9	
Malignant	1.5	230	9	96.2	96.6
Benign	2.0	432	12	97.3	
Malignant	2.0	216	23	91.4	94.9
Benign	4.0	442	2	99.5	
Malignant	4.0	166	73	69.5	89.0

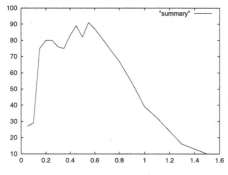

Fig. 10. Steady-state size of network generated at various NAT values for the Wisconsin Breast Cancer data set.

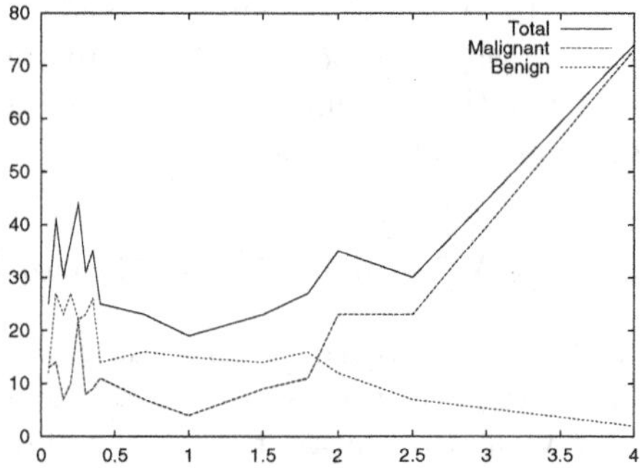

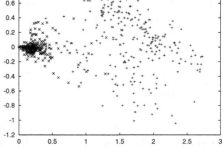

Fig. 11. Number of errors made in classifying the two classes for the Wisconsin Breast Cancer data set with increasing NAT value.

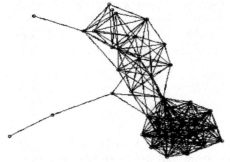

Fig. 12. Network generated with NAT of 1.0 for Wisconsin Breast Cancer data set. The Malignant examples appear in the sparse cluster at the top of the image. Compare with fig. 13.

Fig. 13. PCA plot for Wisconscin Breast Cancer data. × represents benign examples and + represents malignant examples. Note denser concentration of benign data points on the left of plot.

- Networks which perform well are often intuitively appealing and display structure that is inherent to the data as clusters in the network.
- Networks produced by the algorithm seem to pay more than a passing resemblance to the principal component plots of the first two most significant components. Obviously this will not necessarily be a direct mapping in two dimensions, but clusters which are apparent in the PCA plot will be distinguishable in the network layout and vice-versa. We make no claim for a theoretical basis for this observation.

These properties along with the self-organizing nature of the algorithm mentioned in the introduction indicate that we have obtained behaviour that reflects the ability to generate stable memory structures in the artificial immune networks generated. Furthermore these networks pick out structures inherent in the data and can be laid out in two dimensions for interactive examination when seeking to analyse data. Thus the algorithm forms a useful addition to the toolbox of the data-miner: the networks are intuitive to manipulate, easy to vizualize, retain relationships within the data, and perform a drastic dimensionality reduction. We are now satisfied that this algorithm represents a version with which we can usefully attempt some real data-mining problems, and the software (whilst still most definitely a prototype) is sufficiently developed to allow this.

6   Conclusion

A development of an unsupervised algorithm for generating artificial immune networks was presented. Evidence of its ability to extract useful structure from complex data-sets was presented. These results are now of a quality and reliablity that will allow the algorithm to be used in anger on some real data-mining problems. The software develolped is available on request from the author.

References

1. Jerne, N.K.: Towards a Network Theory of the Immune System. Ann. Immunol. (Inst. Pasteur) **C** (1979) 373–389
2. Neal, M.: An Artificial Immune System for Continuous Analysis of Time-Varying Data. In Timmis, J., Bentley, P., eds.: Proceedings of the First International Conference on Artificial Immune Systems (ICARIS), Canterbury, UK, UKC (2002) 76–85
3. Perelson, A.S.: Immune Network Theory. Imm. Rev. (1989) 5–36
4. Timmis, J.: Artificial Immune Systems: a novel data analysis technique inspired by the immune system (PhD Thesis). University of Wales, Aberystwyth (2000)
5. Timmis, J., Neal, M.: A Resource Limited Artificial Immune System. Knowledge Based Systems **14** (2001) 121–130
6. Fisher, R.A.: The use of multiple measurements in taxonomic problems. Annual Eugenics **II** (1936) 179–188
7. Clare, A.: Machine learning and data mining for yeast functional genomics (PhD Thesis). University of Wales, Aberystwyth (2003)

8. Mangasarian, O.L., Wolberg, W.H.: Cancer diagnosis via linear programming. SIAM News **23** (1990) 1,18
9. Knight, T., Timmis, J.: AINE: An immunological approach to data mining. In: Proc. of the IEEE International Conference on Data Mining. (2001) 297–304
10. Clare, A.: http://users.aber.ac.uk/compsci/Research/bio/dss/yeastdata/. University of Wales, Aberystwyth (2003)
11. Wierzchon, S., Kuzelewska, U.: Stable Clusters Formation in an Artificial Immune System. In Timmis, J., Bentley, P.J., eds.: Proceedings of the 1st International Conference on Artificial Immune Systems (ICARIS), University of Kent at Canterbury, University of Kent at Canterbury Printing Unit (2002) 68–75
12. Timmis, J.: aivis - artificial immune network visualisation. In: EuroGraphics UK 2001 Conference Proceedings, Univerisity College London., Eurographics (2001) 61–69

Improved Pattern Recognition
with Artificial Clonal Selection?

Jennifer A. White and Simon M. Garrett

Dept. of Computer Science, University of Wales, Aberystwyth, UK, SY23 3DB
{jaw00,smg}@aber.ac.uk

Abstract. In this paper, we examine the clonal selection algorithm CLONALG and the suggestion that it is suitable for pattern recognition. CLONALG is tested over a series of binary character recognition tasks and its performance compared to a set of basic binary matching algorithms. A number of enhancements are made to the algorithm to improve its performance and the classification tests are repeated. Results show that given enough data CLONALG can successfully classify previously unseen patterns and that adjustments to the existing algorithm can improve performance.

1 Introduction

Understanding the intricacies of the natural world has led to a creative explosion in artificial intelligence from the early origins of artificial neural networks, to genetic algorithms, swarm intelligence and Artificial Immune Systems (AIS).

The aim of this paper is to establish the suitability of the clonal selection algorithm, CLONALG, for pattern recognition, an application area for which it has been proposed but not tested. In order to validate the algorithm, a comparison will be made to Hamming distance classifiers. If successful the clonal selection algorithm could then be more aggressively tested with more complex classifiers. This work also aims to improve CLONALGs performance using a developmental algorithm to explore possible enhancements including population seeding between generations.

This paper is organised as follows: Section 2 describes the biological and artificial processes of clonal selection. Section 3 presents three hypotheses. Section 4 introduces the additional features added to CLONALG for the pattern recognition task and the alternative Hamming methods to which it will be compared. Finally in this section amendments are suggested to improve CLONALG recognition capabilities. Section 5 evaluates the set of methods over a number of different tasks, discussing the performance and suitability of each method for the task. Section 6 explores the findings from Section 5.

2 Background

The adaptive immune response is responsible for protecting a biological organism from previously unseen infectious microorganisms. Its power lies in its ability to

J. Timmis et al. (Eds.): ICARIS 2003, LNCS 2787, pp. 181–193, 2003.

identify and destroy any previously unseen invader using a relatively limited pool of resources. Adaptive immune cells, lymphocytes, can be split into two categories: B cells and T cells. The main role of B cells is to produce antibodies (B cell receptors). These are protein markers which can bind to an antigen, signaling that the cell should be destroyed. Although the body is capable of producing a wide variety of different types of antigen-specific receptors, the number that will respond to any given antigen is fairly low. In order to combat any invader successfully the body needs to produce an 'army' of antibodies capable of binding to the attacking antigen, this is the basis of Clonal Selection.

2.1   Clonal Selection

The Clonal Selection principle [3] is a form of natural selection. The antigen imposes a selective pressure on the antibody population by allowing only those cells which specifically recognize the antigen to be selected for proliferation and differentiation. In the selection stage, B cells with high affinity to the antigen are activated; they are then stimulated to proliferate producing large numbers of clones. In the final stage these clones can mutate and turn into plasma cells which secrete high numbers of antibodies or memory cells that retain the antigenic pattern for future infections. It is a general observation that the antibodies present in the memory response have, on average, a higher affinity than those of the early primary response [2]. The maturation of the immune response is a continuous process, in which the body will over a number of exposures build up a large collection of targeted memory cells that can act quickly to eliminate a pathogen. Although the maturation process produces a small number of high affinity matches it also produces a large number of low affinity B cells.

2.2   Artificial Clonal Selection

Research into AIS has led to the development of many of different algorithms, including a variety of clonal selection, immune network and negative selection algorithms. All of these methods seek to utilise the dynamic learning mechanisms of the immune system and apply this power to real world problems.

Much of the early work in the development of artificial immune systems was carried out using genetic and evolutionary computation techniques [6]. Indeed the two processes are very similar. The main distinction between the field of genetic algorithms and artificial immune systems is the nature of population development. In a genetic algorithm the population is evolved using crossover and mutation. However in the artificial immune system, as in evolutionary strategies, reproduction is asexual, each child produced by a cell is an exact copy of its parent. Both systems then use mutation to alter the progeny of the cells and introduce further genetic variation.

The computational model of the clonal selection principle, like many other artificial immune system models, borrows heavily from immunological theory but is not an exact copy of the immune system's behaviour. The main areas of clonal selection exploited by computer science are:

- **Diversity:** The population of cells available for the immune response can be sparsely distributed covering a wide area of the antigenic space.
- **Optimisation:** Selection and proliferation of high affinity cells produces a rapidly increasing population of high affinity matches useful in targeting and responding to secondary infection.
- **Exploration:** Mutation of cells to allow local exploration of the affinity landscape to achieve higher affinity matches to the invading antigen.
- **Replacement:** Cells that have a low affinity to the antigen being examined can be replaced, allowing global exploration of the affinity landscape.
- **Reinforcement Learning:** Repeated exposure to an antigenic stimulus can work as a method of reinforced learning. Memory cells may become increasingly more specific to that antigen and able to respond more quickly to a reoccurrence.

To create a secondary immune response a base population of antibodies is first immunised with a training set of antigens; these are the stimulus for the maturation of the immune response. The initial exposure, as in the natural immune system, creates a set of memory cells able to respond more swiftly to the second occurrence of the antigen. By setting a threshold of affinity for the cells with the antigen they are able to recognise not only the specific antigens for which they were immunized but also antigens that are structurally similar, this is known as the cross-reactive response [1]. This generalisation of knowledge is extremely advantageous for computing applications as it gives the system noise tolerance and greater flexibility.

CLONALG. The clonal selection algorithm, CSA, was first proposed by de Castro and Von Zuben in [4] and was later enhanced in their 2001 paper [5] and named CLONALG. The algorithm takes a population of antibodies and by repeated exposure to antigens, over a number of generations, develops a population more sensitive to the antigenic stimulus. The basic algorithm is:

1. Randomly generate an initial population of antibodies Ab. This is composed of two subsets Ab_m (memory population) and Ab_r (reservoir population).
2. Create a set of antigenic patterns Ag.
3. Select an antigen Ag_i from the population Ag.
4. For every member of the population Ab calculate its affinity to the antigen Ag_i using some affinity function (e.g. Hamming Distance).
5. Select the n highest affinity antibodies and generate a number of clones for each antibody in proportion to their affinity, placing the clones in a new population C^i.
6. Mutate the clone population C^i to a degree inversely proportional to their affinity to produce a mature population C^{i*}.
7. Re-apply the affinity function to each member of the population C^{i*} and select the highest score as candidate memory cell. If its affinity is greater than the current memory cell Ab_{mi}, then the candidate becomes the new memory cell.

8. Remove those antibodies with low affinity in the population Ab_r and replace them with new randomly generated members.
9. Repeat steps 3-8 until all antigens have been presented. This represents one generation of the algorithm.

One generation of the algorithm is complete when all antigens have been presented and all the steps have been carried out for each antigen. This algorithm retains only one memory cell for each antigen presented to it. The rate of clone production is decided using a ranking system [5]. The mutation of an antibody should be inversely proportional to the affinity of the antibody. Somatic hypermutation can be implemented in a number of different ways, such as multi-point mutation, substring regeneration and simple substitution [7]. In this paper the algorithm was implemented using multi-point mutation. This mutation method takes a proportion of randomly chosen attributes of the string and mutates them if a randomly generated control number is above a certain threshold. The method of mutation used in [5] has not been defined.

In the 2001 paper [5], De Castro and Von Zuben made the suggestion that CLONALG could be used for pattern recognition. They carried out a study using a set of 12 x 10 binary images as the target patterns, shown in Figure 1 and demonstrated that the process of selection and blind variation could produce memory cells with increased affinity.

Fig. 1. Data Set A: The binary character patterns to be learned. Each image is represented internally as a binary string of length 120 bits.

In biological immune system recognition, antigenic patterns are preserved by memory cells but what those patterns represent is not. In an artificial environment however it is possible to associate a memory cell with a particular pattern class, enabling them to perform classification tasks. The memory cell with the highest affinity to a newly presented pattern supplies that pattern's classification. Cells need only make an approximate match to classify a pattern, i.e. they must fall within a sphere of recognition in the affinity landscape. The outer limits of this sphere are defined by a threshold value below which binding will not take place. Although proposed in [5] the threshold is not implemented. Memory cells are generated but not tested on a recognition task.

If all that is required for pattern recognition is a memory cell which retains the pattern and a threshold to define the limits of recognition, then why use clonal selection at all? The method is computationally expensive, see Section 6, and provides a corrupted version of the pattern to be recognised for the memory cell. Indeed if the training set to be used consisted of single examples for different patterns then it would be more efficient to retain the pattern itself rather than generating a noisy version with clonal selection. The real strength of clonal selection for pattern recognition cannot be seen until considering multiple examples. What the memory cells can provide in this case is generalisation. They represent the common features of all the examples for a particular class of pattern. This has been explored using genetic algorithms by Forrest et al. in [6]. A generalist memory cell should preserve the key features of a pattern class and thus react strongly to those features if present in a new example. When using multiple examples clonal selection enables the data stored for recognition to be compressed, requiring only one memory cell per class of pattern and reducing the search time required for classification.

3 Hypotheses

H1. A Hamming distance measure using an exact copy of a pattern will recall correctly more images than CLONALG.

H2. A Hamming distance measure using an exact copy of a pattern will achieve significantly better results than CLONALG when classifying normalised data.

H3. A Hamming distance measure using an exact copy of a pattern will achieve significantly better results than CLONALG when classifying unnormalised data.

4 Methodology

This paper seeks to apply CLONALG to pattern recognition and assess its suitability for the domain. However, as the algorithm has never been applied to this task a before, a number of additional features have to be implemented.

4.1 Threshold Calculation

The threshold value defines the recognition boundary, providing a cut off point after which an example cannot be accurately classified. It is set at a level halfway between the affinity value expected for a successful match and the value expected for a random match. Each antigen presented is classified by the highest rated memory cell it matched. The threshold level is calculated in the same way for each of the methods tested.

4.2 Handling Multiple Examples of a Class

In [5] CLONALG evolves its memory cells from only single examples of each pattern class to be learned. To realise its full potential CLONALG must be able to develop memory cells from multiple different examples of each pattern class. This enables the evolution of generalist memory cells that represent the common features of the example set for each individual pattern class. As in the original algorithm the Hamming distance is used to establish the affinity of an antibody; the higher the score, the greater that antibody's affinity to the antigen presented:

$$\text{Total Affinity} = \sum_{j=1}^{n} \sum_{i=1}^{len} pos_i = Ab_i \oplus Ag_i^j. \tag{1}$$

Where Ab_i is the ith bit in the antibody Ab, Ag_i^j is the ith bit in the antigen pattern example Ag^j and n is the number of examples for a particular pattern class. len is the total length of an antibody/antigen and $\oplus$ represents the exclusive-OR operator.

This formula calculates the antibody's total affinity score over all the examples of a particular antigenic pattern class. The antibodies favoured for cloning should be those which best represent the common features of the antigen class.

4.3   Classification

CLONALG generates the memory cells which will be used in the pattern recognition task. The cells are then presented with a new set of patterns to be classified. The classification algorithm is as follows:

1. Select an antigen from the population to be classified.
2. Compare the antigen with each memory cell.
3. Calculate the percentage of accuracy (affinity/max)*100.
4. If percentage is > current highest, make the new candidate the highest.
5. If highest is > the threshold level, set classification to memory cell highest.
6. Add the result to the set of classifications.
7. Loop until all antigens have been presented.

For a successful identification the classification must match the specified antigen class. Antigens that score below the threshold value are deemed to be unclassified and are recorded as unknown.

4.4   Alternative Hamming Methods

The following methods perform basic pattern recognition using Hamming Distance and the threshold calculation in section 4.1 to classify examples. If CLONALG outperforms these simple methods then it would merit further study against more complex classifier systems.

Complete. This method is the most computationally expensive and least practical for real world applications. For the Complete method, every example for each class presented is stored as a memory cell. A large amount of memory storage is required for most problems and the time taken to perform the classification is expanded from $O(M)$, where M is the total number of memory cells to $O(M * N)$ where N is the total number of examples for each class.

Highest. This method compresses the number of cells required for a memory set down to the same number as used in CLONALG. In the Highest method only one pattern example is stored as a memory cell for each class. This cell is chosen by calculating the affinity total for a negative copy of each example in a class to all the other examples in the same class and selecting the example which has the highest total affinity. This method should choose the example pattern with the most complementary bits to all the others in its class and thus make for a more specific memory cell.

Lowest. This method also compresses the number of cells required for a memory set and as in Highest will only store one example from each class as a memory cell. This cell is chosen by calculating the affinity total for a negative copy of each example in a class to all the other examples in the same class and selecting the example which has the lowest total affinity. This method should choose the example pattern with the least complementary bits to all the others in its class and thus make for a more general memory cell.

Random. The final method selects a memory cell at random for each pattern class from the set of training examples for that class and uses a negative copy of this cell as its only representation of the class. The storage required is equivalent to CLONALG, Highest and Lowest.

4.5   Clonal Classification (CLONCLAS)

One potentially negative feature of CLONALG is that it fails to capitalise on the information generated by each clone population. Once a candidate memory cell has been selected, the remaining mutated clones are discarded, even though this population may contain a number of high affinity candidates. By preserving a larger proportion of the matured population, the algorithm could build from a stronger base of high affinity matches and should theoretically reach a optimal solution in fewer generations. However this also introduces a new danger of becoming stuck on a local minimum as the population becomes increasingly narrow in its focus. The replacement phase that introduces new randomly generated antibodies into the reservoir population should prevent this. Updating the reservoir population such that it tends towards an optimal point also requires some changes to the sequence of the algorithm. The amended clonal selection algorithm, CLONCLAS, is as follows:

1. Randomly generate an initial population of antibodies Ab. This is composed of two subsets Ab_m (memory population) and Ab_r (reservoir population).
2. Create a set of antigenic patterns Ag.
3. Select an antigen Ag_i from the population Ag.
4. For G generations.
   (a) Carry out steps 4-7 of CLONALG.
   (b) Replace the antibodies in Ab_r with the same number of antibodies from the sorted population C^{i*}.
   (c) Remove those antibodies with low affinity in the population Ab_r and replace with new randomly generated members.
5. Return to step 3 until all antigens have been presented.

5   Results

To examine the performance of CLONALG for pattern recognition a number of experiments were carried out. After a training period the algorithm is asked to classify sets of binary images. Each task is compared to a set of four alternative Hamming methods and the results examined. Finally alterations are made to the existing algorithm to try and improve its performance. This new algorithm, CLONCLAS, is then tested over the same tasks and the results compared. Each task is carried out ten times and the average of these runs is taken as the result. CLONALG and CLONCLAS are tested over 1, 5, 10, 50, 100 and 500 generations. Other running parameters for the experiments carried out include: $n = 5$, $d = 0.0$, and $\beta = 10$, as used in [5]. The complete set of images used in training and testing can be found at http://users.aber.ac.uk/jaw00/data.html.

5.1   Single Example

This test is designed to verify that the implementation of CLONALG is correct and that the results presented in [5] can be reproduced.

TASK 1.1. Each method is trained using data set A and is then tested on the same set. Data set A is the same set that is used in [5] and shown in Figure 1. After just five generations both CLONALG and CLONCLAS were able to successfully remember all of the training patterns. The Hamming methods were also able to classify all the patterns correctly. Both CLONALG and CLONCLAS's memory cells converge on the training patterns after 200 generations.

5.2   Normalised Examples

Data Set A is limited and does not provide sufficient examples for more complex tasks that require multiple examples of each pattern class to be learned. To overcome this, similar binary images of numbers were generated using standard text fonts. The second data set, data set B, is created by converting the pixel information into a string of binary data in a text file. Each class in data set B has ten different font variants of a character to be learned. The images underwent a normalising scaling process to ensure each example filled the image space.

TASK 2.1. This test is designed to verify that the implementation of CLON-ALG performs correctly for a multiple example task. Each method is trained using the training subset of data set B and tested using the same subset, to examine the effect of introducing more than one training example for each pattern class. This tests the algorithms' ability to generalise from multiple examples and to classify correctly those examples from the generalised memory cell. CLONCLAS produces a consistently higher rate of correct classifications than CLONALG for this task. CLONCLAS reaches a 87.5% accuracy in only fifty generations, CLONALG takes five hundred generations to reach this figure, as shown in Figure 3 (a) and (b). None of the Hamming methods, with the exception of Complete, are able to reach this level of accuracy. Highest gives the second best results with an accuracy of 81.2%. Results are shown in Figure 3.

TASK 2.2. This task tests the algorithms classification abilities on previously unseen data. Each method is trained and tested using disjoint subsets of data set B. Both CLONCLAS and CLONALG perform equally well given the previously unseen data to classify reaching an accuracy of 76.3% in only fifty generations. Highest and Random performed equally well from the Hamming methods each achieving 64% accuracy. Results are shown in Figure 4.

5.3   Unnormalised Examples

The third data set, C, is generated in the same way as set B but is not subject to the scaling process. This provided a unnormalised data set where the examples for a class are defined by only a small number of points within the image space.

TASK 3.1. For this task, each method is trained and tested using the disjoint subsets of data set C, to examine their ability to handle unnormalised distributed data. CLONCLAS performs on a similar though slightly better level than CLONALG. These methods are outperformed by the Highest Hamming method, which achieves an accuracy of 40%. Results are shown in Figure 5.

6   Discussion

CLONALG is a computationally expensive algorithm $O(M(N + N_cL)) + O(E^2M + T(ML))$ where M is the set of memory cells, N is the size of the total population, N_c is the size of the clone population, E is the number of examples for a pattern class, T is the number of test examples and L is the length of the antibody bit string. The algorithms success must be judged not only on the number of correct classifications but also on the efficiency with which these can be performed. The results are now revisited in the context of the hypotheses made in Section 3.

Hypothesis H1. In Task 1.1 CLONALG is able to correctly identify all the example patterns after only five generations. This however tests only recall and could be seen as a waste of processor resources as the simple Hamming methods perform the task with 100% accuracy in a much shorter time. Under these test conditions neither CLONALG nor the Hamming methods can compress the data so provide no improvements in storage capacity. The Hamming methods are considerably faster than both clonal selection algorithms running at only $O(E^2M + T(ML))$. For this task, hypothesis H1 is proved, although each method is capable of 100% accuracy the Hamming methods can achieve this level in a shorter time than both of the clonal selection algorithms. However in Task 2.1 CLONALG's real potential can be seen. This task is designed to test the algorithms abilities to generalise from a number of different examples of a class. Memory cells become templates of the features common to a class, as shown in Figure 2 (a), allowing the data required for recognition to be compressed.

Hypothesis H2. When recalling previously seen examples CLONALG is very successful, consistently improving its results as the number of generations increases. CLONCLAS however can reach similar success levels in a smaller number

(a) 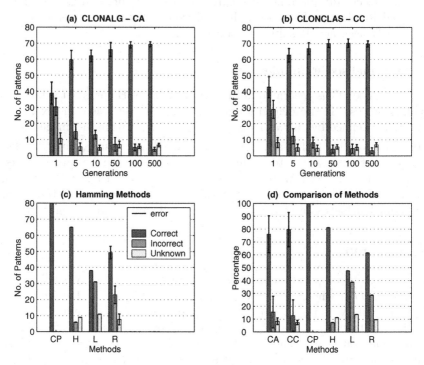 (b)

Fig. 2. Memory cells for a CLONALG run over 50 gen. on Task 2.1(a) and 3.1(b).

Fig. 3. TASK 2.1: The methods were trained on 10 different examples of each class and were tested using the same set of examples.

of generations, thus improving efficiency. Although Complete Hamming method achieves 100% accuracy, this method is memory greedy and is probably impractical for anything other than small numbers of examples. The memory cells developed by CLONCLAS between 5 and 50 generations are approximately $7-8\%$ higher affinity than those developed by CLONALG in this period. When reclassifying previously seen examples this increased affinity appears beneficial, as shown in Figure 3 (a) and (b). However when testing with unseen data CLONALG and CLONCLAS are more evenly matched, suggesting that the higher affinity memory cells developed by CLONCLAS may be over trained and provide no additional benefit when classifying unseen data, as shown in Figure 4 (a) and (b). The second hypothesis in Section 3 cannot be considered true as both the clonal selection methods achieve greater success than the practical Hamming methods, Highest, Lowest and Random.

Hypothesis H3. The final task tests the algorithms ability to generalise over unnormalised examples. The templates generated by CLONALG's memory cells, shown in Figure 2 (b), are limited by the lack of data describing each image.

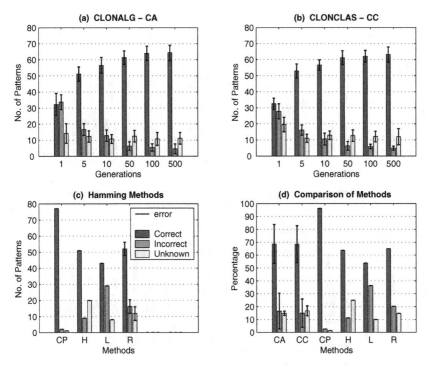

Fig. 4. TASK 2.2: The methods were trained on 10 different examples of each class and were tested using a set of 80 previously unseen examples.

For example in data set C, on average only 10% of the images 144 bits make up the character zero, compared with 45% in data set B. The results are significantly poorer with this data set for all the methods tested, with the exception of complete. For this data set the third hypothesis H3 holds true. The Hamming methods although not performing very well still significantly outperform the clonal selection algorithms.

Summary. CLONALG performs a global search for each example which is then reduced to a random local search in the cloning and mutation phase. This method produces good solutions from a small population but takes a reasonable number of generations to do so. CLONCLAS however, seeks to optimise the population by a directed walk in the search space for each example. By preserving the high affinity clones in the reservoir population each generation starts from a closer position to the optimal solution than the last. It is this directed method that enables CLONCLAS to reach a good solution more quickly than CLONALG. However this improvement is only slight and delivers no improvement in the classification of unseen data.

7   Conclusions

CLONALG has shown that it can given enough data make generalisations from examples and successfully classify previously unseen examples of its training

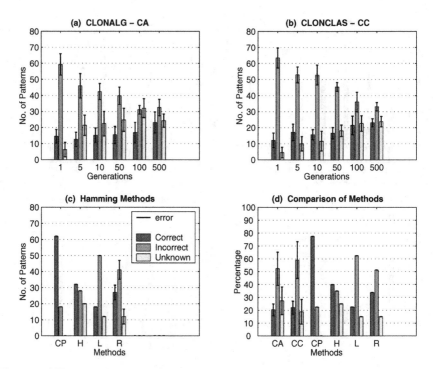

Fig. 5. TASK 3.1: The methods were trained on 10 different examples of each class and were tested using a set of 80 previously unseen examples.

classes. Its main weakness is the efficiency of the algorithm; the time taken to generate the memory cells can be considerable making it unattractive for application to time dependent real world problems. Steps have been made to reduce the training time through the implementation of CLONCLAS. Although the new algorithm has the same time complexity as CLONALG it is able to generate good candidate memory cells in a smaller number of generations, thus reducing the time required for learning. CLONCLAS is a work in progress, requiring further study in a number of areas including parameter sensitivity. Future works will also include a study into the development of dynamic stopping criteria for the training phase.

References

1. Gordon L. Ada and Sir Gustav Nossal. The clonal selection theory. *Scientific American*, 257(2):62–69, 1987.
2. Claudia Berek and Mike Ziegner. The maturation of the immune response. *Immunology Today*, 14(8):400–404, 1993.
3. F. M. Burnet. *The Clonal Selection Theory of Acquired Immunity*. Cambridge Press, Cambridge, 1959.

4. Leandro Nunes de Castro and Fernando J. Von Zuben. The clonal selection algorithm with engineering applications. In *Workshop Proceedings of GECCO'00, Workshop on Artificial Immune Systems and their Applications*, pages 36–37, Las Vegas, USA, July 2000.
5. Leandro Nunes de Castro and Fernando J. Von Zuben. Learning and optimization using clonal selection principle. *IEEE Transactions on Evolutionary Computation, Special Issue on Artificial Immune Systems*, 6(3):239–251, 2001.
6. Stephanie Forrest, Robert E. Smith, Brenda Javornik, and Alan S. Perelson. Using genetic algorithms to explore pattern recognition in the immune system. *Evolutionary Computation*, 1(3):191–211, 1993.
7. John E. Hunt and Denise E. Cooke. Learning using and artificial immune system. *Journal of Network and Computer Applications*, 19:189–212, 1996.

Appendix: Section 5 Results Graphs:

For each set of graphs: (a) Is CLONALG's classification success over 1,5,10,50,100 and 500 generations. (b) Is CLONCLAS's classification success over 1,5,10,50,100 and 500 generations. (c) Is the Hamming methods classification success, where CP = Complete, H = High, L = Low and R = Random. (d) Is the classification success for each method as a percentage of the number of examples. The values for CA = CLONALG and CC = CLONCLAS are the average results over all the generations sampled. The error bars indicate the standard deviation for each result.

Improving SOSDM:
Inspirations from the Danger Theory

Emma Hart and Peter Ross

Napier University, Scotland, UK
{e.hart,p.ross}@napier.ac.uk

Abstract. This paper presents improvements to SOSDM based on ideas gleaned from the Danger Theory of immunology. In the new model, antibodies emit a signal describing their current level of contentment – monitoring the total level of contentment in the system provides a mechanism for determining when an immune response should occur, i.e. when new antibodies should be produced. It also provides a method of detecting catastrophic changes in the environment, i.e. significant changes in input data, and thus provides a means of removing antibodies. The new system, dSOSDM, is shown to be more robust and better able to deal with dynamically changing databases than SOSDM.

1   Introduction

A growing body of literature has shown that the Artificial Immune System (AIS) paradigm is a viable metaphor for performing data-clustering, for example [4,5,8]. In particular, the most recent applications capitalize on the dynamic aspect of the immune metaphor to produce systems capable of clustering moving data. Such systems must necessarily be self-regulating, however experience has shown that they are often difficult to control. This paper introduces an extension to an existing system that allows it to self-regulate its own size, in response to a dynamically changing environment. The extensions are rooted in the relatively contentious Danger Theory.

Danger theory is a theory that has been proposed by Matzinger [7] as an alternative viewpoint to the classical self/non-self discrimination theory popular with a large faction of immunologists. The theory claims to counter certain objections to the classical viewpoint and takes the stance that the immune system does not discriminate between self and non-self, but 'some self from some non-self'. It is proposed that this occurs by the immune system responding to *danger* and not *non-self*. The theory is controversial – this paper does not defend or dispute its existence, nor does it attempt to *exactly* model any of the proposed biological mechanisms implicit in the theory. It is simply of interest because at a high level, some of its concepts can be adapted to improve the engineering of artificial systems.

The interested reader should refer to [7,2] for a detailed description of how she proposes the immune system utilises the notion of danger. The theory invokes many different types of immunological cell with a complex sequence of

J. Timmis et al. (Eds.): ICARIS 2003, LNCS 2787, pp. 194–203, 2003.

signals passing between them. However, a detailed analysis is unnecessary here in to order to understand how the theory can inspire the implementation of artificial systems. An extremely simplified explanation is as follows: if cells become damaged (for example due to attack by invading bacteria) then those cells emit a distress signal as they undergo lytic cell death. Antigen-presenting cells in the region of the cells emitting these signals capture any antigens in the neighbourhood, and then travel to the local lymph node where they present the captured antigen to lymphocytes. The immune system then responds, causing the stimulated antibodies within the danger zone to undergo clonal expansion. The nature of what exactly constitutes a danger signal is unclear and is the subject of much immunological research. It has been suggested that heat-shock proteins might be released as a cell dies, or that the sudden lack of synaptic contact with an antigen presenting cell might signal danger. However, in order to make use of the concept in artificial systems, it is sufficient to accept that such a signal can exist.

1.1   Danger Theory and AIS

The literature contains very few direct examples of the danger theory being utilised in Artificial Immune Systems. [3] implements a basic version of the idea in a computer immune system by using the signals generated by dying computer processes to indicate danger, and thus detect when a fault has occurred, though this is clearly only one of many possible danger signals that could be emitted by a computer immune system. [1] present a conceptual discussion on the use of danger theory in artificial systems, and attempt to ground the discussion by suggesting relevant application areas to which the theory could usefully be applied. However, their ideas tend to be directed towards systems which essentially implement some form of negative selection (for example to perform anomaly detection) and consider how danger theory can address weaknesses in such systems. In fact, they state that *"it is not obvious how the Danger Theory could be of use to data-mining problems ... because the notions of self and non-self are not used"*. However, in this paper we argue that the concepts embodied in the Danger Theory can be applied to models of the immune system in which there is no notion of self and non-self, so long as the AIS practitioner does not intend to faithfully replicate mechanisms observed in the biological system. This approach is of course common in probably all biologically inspired paradigms – neural networks cannot hope to faithfully model brains, nor ant-colony systems real colonies of ants, yet by taking inspiration from natural systems, successful artificial ones have been produced.

We suggest that two basic ideas can be gleaned from the Danger Theory which can be useful to many kinds of artificial immune system implementations:

1. cells can emit distress signals, which reflect their relationship with the current state of their immediate environment
2. cells can die an unnatural unprogrammed death (*lytic* cell death as opposed to *apoptosis*, natural cell death) if severely stressed

The new version of SOSDM implements both these ideas. First however, a brief description of the limitations of the current SOSDM and other AIS models is given.

2   Limitations of SOSDM and Other AIS Models

SOSDM was first presented in [5,6] as system for clustering dynamically changing data-sets. It is a self-organising system based on analogies with immunology and sparse-distributed memories – an overview of the algorithm is given in figure 1. This paper concerns step (6) of the algorithm – the original model dynamically adjusted the number of antibodies in its system through the use of an antibody-addition mechanism and an antibody-deletion mechanism. The former mechanism added antibodies to the system whenever *stagnation* of the system was detected – this was defined to occur whenever the number *and* type of antibody in the system had remained static over some pre-defined and fixed number of iterations. The antibody-deletion mechanism deleted antibodies from the system whenever their stimulation-level (relative to other antibodies in the system) was less than another pre-defined threshold. These methods have some unappealing aspects:

- Stagnation could occur simply because the system had discovered the best set of antibodies to cluster the data, and not because it had become 'stuck' in a local optima
- If unnecessary antibodies were added due to incorrectly detecting stagnation, the delete mechanism would have to be invoked several iterations later to remove such antibodies
- Determining a suitable threshold below which to delete antibodies was difficult – if not chosen carefully, severe oscillations occurred in which antibodies would be deleted then re-added a few iterations later, etc.

The literature shows that controlling the growth of an artificial immune system can often be problematic. In many proposed immune-network algorithms, for example [9], new antibodies are added to systems via a cloning mechanism, which needs to be carefully checked in order to produce networks of bounded size. Thus, the problem for such systems is not how to *add* antibodies but how to *delete* them from the system in order to prevent exponential growth of the network. Timmis [9] tackled this by introducing a resource allocation mechanism, in which a network had a finite number of arbitrary resources which it had to allocate to its members. Antibodies that do not obtain sufficient resource are removed. This work was further improved on by Neal [8] who simplified the resource allocation mechanism in an algorithm named SSAIS such that resources were not allocated centrally (which is contrary to the distributed nature of the biological immune system) but were dealt with locally by each node in the network. In the next section, we propose a mechanism by which both antibody addition and deletion can be controlled by an algorithm inspired from danger theory.

1. begin with a fixed number of antibodies A, randomly initialised.
2. present a subset s of the data-set visible at time t to the SOSDM
3. distribute the data in the set s to *each antibody* in the SOSDM, with a *strength* proportional to the *relative affinity* of the antibody for the data
4. compute the accumulated error at each antibody
5. update all antibody definitions depending on the total accumulated error at each antibody
6. add or delete antibodies if necessary
7. go back to step 2

Fig. 1. The SOSDM algorithm

3   Adding Danger to SOSDM

A key aspect of the SOSDM algorithm is that antigens become bound to an antibody if the affinity of the antibody for the antigen *relative* to all other antibodies in the system is greater than some threshold. Thus, it follows that all antigens bind to at least one antibody, even though the affinity between any given antigen-antibody pair may be very weak.

Inspired by the notions embodied in the danger-theory of immunology, we propose that an antibody accumulates a measure of the affinity between itself and all antigens it binds too. This quantity can be considered to be a measure of the current level of 'contentment' that the antibody is currently experiencing. The antibody transmits its current contentment level to the system – if the total level of contentment within the system consistently remains below a fixed threshold, then the system responds by producing a new antibody. Using the idea of contentment, we also model both natural and lytic cell death. If the system suddenly experiences a significant change in its overall level of contentment, cells undergo lytic death in response to the sudden 'shock'. This could happen for example if the data which the system is exposed to suddenly changes radically, for example if entire clusters disappear or clusters 'move'. If a cell has zero contentment, this indicates that it is not bound to any antigens and it undergoes natural cell death (i.e. the process is independent of the danger theory). The model is explained in detail below.

4   The New Model

Assume that an SOSDM immune system I contains N antibodies, a_i, each consisting of a binary string of length l, and X antigens (data-items), x_i, also of length l. Applying the SOSDM algorithm results in n_{a_i} antigens binding to an antibody a_i.

First, we measure the average *distress* of each antibody bit, $d(a_{ij})$ which is simply a cumulative measure of the error between the actual value of the antibody bit j and the value of corresponding antigen bit j of each antigen it binds.

$$d(a_{ij}) = \sum_{k=0}^{k=n_{a_i}} (|a_{ij} - x_{kj}|)/n_{a_i} \tag{1}$$

Then, once all data-items have been stored in the immune system, for each antibody a_i, the total number of bits whose average distress is greater than a threshold T_b (the distress-threshold) is calculated – D_{a_i}

$$D_{a_i} = \sum_{j=1}^{j=l} \begin{cases} 1 & if \quad d(a_{ij}) > T_b \\ 0 & otherwise \end{cases} \tag{2}$$

The *contentment* of an antibody, c_{a_i} is then defined as shown below, and reflects the percentage of contented bits in the antibody.

$$c_{a_i} = 1 - (D_{a_i}/l) \tag{3}$$

Thus, the average contentment of the whole immune system, c_I can also be calculated, simply as

$$c_I = \sum_{i=1}^{i=N} c_{a_i}/N \tag{4}$$

c_I is central to the new addition mechanism. The idea is to monitor the value of system contentment c_I and use it to signal to the immune system that it needs to produce new antibodies. In order to ignore the effects of any instability in the system from one iteration to the next due to random effects, we monitor the moving-average of c_I – $m(c_I)$ – and compare it to a threshold denoted T_s, the system-contentment threshold. If $m(c_I)$ is below this threshold, then a new antibody is added to the system, in order that it can try and increase its contentment level. The algorithm is shown in figure 2. Antibodies with contentment level equal to zero, i.e. that do not recognise any antigens, undergo the equivalent of natural cell death and are removed from the system. The algorithm allows the system to be in one of two states: *immature* or *matured*. Whenever a new antibody is added to the system, it enters a maturational phase to allow it to adjust to the new set of antibodies. This phase endures for a fixed number of iterations before the system is considered mature.

5   Experiments Using Static Data-Sets

An initial set of experiments was performed with the original SOSDM in order to analyse how the contentment parameter varied and hence determine suitable settings and sensitivities for the bit-threshold T_b and the system-threshold T_s. Typical results are reported for an experiment on a data-set known as the quarter-set, containing 200 binary data-items, each of length 64 bits, in which the data is equally divided into 4 clusters (see [5,6] for a detailed description of

> - At each iteration
>   - Calculate moving-average of system contentment c_I over previous m iterations, $m(c_I)$
>   * If $m(c_I) < T_s$ and the system is *not* immature, add a new antibody to the system
>   * Set system-phase to *immature* if an new antibody added
>   - If the system is *immature* phase
>   * Update number of iterations *immature* counter
>   * If immature counter equals maximum iterations allows in maturation, reset system phase to *matured*

Fig. 2. The new mechanism for antibody addition

this data-set). The original SOSDM algorithm was run in each from a starting point in which it contained two antibodies, and new antibodies were added at intervals of 20 iterations whenever stagnation was detected, up to a maximum of 4, as described in section 2. The deletion mechanism in SOSDM was turned off so that antibodies could only ever be added to the system for the purpose of these experiments. The moving average of the system contentment was calculated over 5 iterations of the algorithm.

5.1   Parameter Settings

The first experiments investigated the variation in the contentment parameter as the original SOSDM system was running. Figure 3(a) shows the variation in contentment of both the whole system and individual antibodies as the threshold T_b is varied. From these experiments, we concluded that a sensible value for the threshold parameter was 0.35 – if the parameter is set below this, it takes the system too long to achieve a stable level of contentment, and if it is much higher, the average contentment is always too high to make it a meaningful indicator of system performance. Figure 3(b) shows the variation in individual antibody contentment at the fixed threshold of 0.35. Further experiments showed that this choice of value was robust across the two other data-sets described in section 5.2.

Further experiments were performed using the quarter data-set, this time using $dSOSDM$ with T_b set to the chosen value of 0.35. Again, no deletion mechanism was included, to see if the addition mechanism alone could control the size of the systems produced. As above, the systems were initialised with 2 antibodies, however this time no limit was placed on the number of antibodies the mechanism could add. Figure 4 shows how the setting of the system-threshold parameter T_s affects the number of antibodies present in the final system after $dSOSDM$ had been applied for 200 iterations. The results are the average of 10 experiments for each value of T_s.

Figure 4 suggests that $0.5 < T_s < 0.6$ is a suitable value – the number of antibodies produced is then comparable to the known number of clusters (although

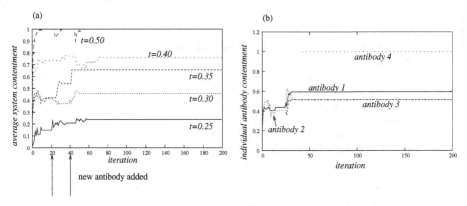

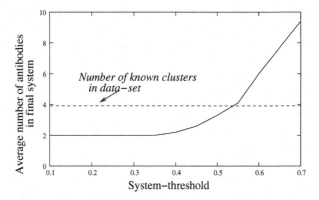

Fig. 3. (a) Variation in system contentment as the distress-threshold T_b is varied (b) Variation in individual contentment when $t = 0.35$

Fig. 4. Average number of antibodies obtained using dSOSDM as parameter T_s, the system-threshold, is varied

of course, due to the random method of generating the clusters, there may be more or less than exactly 4 clusters). Increasing the contentment threshold, i.e. requiring the average match between an antibody and its bound antigens to be higher, forces the system to find sub-clusters and hence add more antibodies. This parameter offers a simple way of tuning the specificity of the system – if specific trends wish to be identified in the data, the value can be increased, whereas a lower value identifies more general trends.

5.2   Results: Growing the AIS Using dSOSDM

Experiments were repeated using *half* and *eighth* data-sets, [5]. These binary data-sets are again artificially generated to contain two and eight known clusters respectively (although again, each cluster could contain sub-clusters due to the random generation process). dSOSDM was applied to both data-sets, and initialised with 2 random antibodies in each case. T_s was set to 0.55 and T_b to

Table 1. Comparison of the average number of antibodies used by SOSDM and
dSOSDM to cluster data-sets, and average accuracy of recall (*RA*) of data (standard
deviations in brackets)

Data	Expected No. clusters	# Clusters SOSDM	# Clusters dSOSDM	RA of string generalist	RA dSOSDM
half	2	2.29	2.30 (0.58)	48	49.38 (0.49)
quarter	4	6.75	3.99 (1.41)	40	43.38 (0.76)
eighth	8	10.06	10.18 (0.96)	36	42.85 (0.29)

0.35, the values found from experiments with the quarter data-set. The length
of the maturational period was set to 10 iterations. Again, dSOSDM did not
use any deletion mechanism and no limit was placed on the number of antibodies that could be added to the system. Table 1 shows the average number
of antibodies created by dSOSDM in each case (averaged over 100 runs of 200
iterations each). The table compares these results to those found using SOSDM
on the same data-sets, originally reported in [5]. Note that SOSDM required the
use of both addition and deletion mechanisms in order to control its size and
stability, but the simpler dSOSDM is either comparable or better in performance
in each case. The table also shows the average recall accuracy of each item in
the dataset which is indicative of the accuracy of clustering (see [5] for further
explanation).

6   Clustering Dynamically Changing Data

The original motivation behind SOSDM was to produce a system that could
dynamically cluster data, and thus react to changes in the environment. If new
clusters appear in the data-set, or clusters suddenly disappear, then the system
should be able to detect these changes and react accordingly, by adding new
antibodies or removing existing ones. Using the danger theory analogy, such
extreme changes in environment would cause severe stress or trauma to cells
which were previously content, causing them to undergo lytic cell death. Thus,
we model this in dSOSDM by monitoring the average change in cell contentment,
Δc_I between iteration (t) and iteration $(t + 1)$ for the system, according to
equation 5.

$$\Delta c_I = \frac{1}{N} \sum_{i=0}^{i=N} |c_{a_i}(t + 1) - c_{a_i}(t)| \qquad (5)$$

Note the use of the absolute value of the change in equation 5 as environmental changes could have a positive or negative effect on contentment, however,
even sudden positive changes are traumatic to the cells. If Δc_I changes by more
than some fixed parameter z then the environment that the system has been exposed is considered to have changed radically and *all* cells in the system undergo
lytic death. The consequence of this is that the system is effectively re-initialised
and therefore produces new, random, antibodies (the minimum number of antibodies required to be present in the system is always fixed at 2). The only caveat

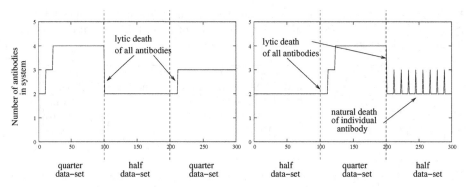

Fig. 5. Variation in numberof antibodies with dynamically changing data

to this is that if the system is still in a maturational phase, then catastrophic changes are ignored.

6.1   Experimental Results

Two set of experiments were performed with dynamically changing data: in experiment 1, the environment consisted of the quarter data-set for 100 iterations, this was replaced by the half data-set at iteration 101, and then again by the quarter data-set again at iteration 201. Experiment 2 reversed the order of presentation of the data-sets, i.e., first the half set, then the quarter set, etc. Initial experimentation showed that $z = 0.05$ was sufficient to cause the desired behaviour in the system. Figure 5 shows typical behaviour from both experiments over 300 iterations. Points at which lytic cell death occurred are marked. The left-hand figure shows antibodies being added to the system during the first 100 iterations to accurately cluster the quarter data-set with 4 antibodies – lytic death occurs when the data changes and the system is re-initialised with 2 new antibodies, and no further ones need to be added in order to cluster the half-set. At iteration 200, lytic death again occurs and 2 new antibodies are produced (therefore the total number in the system appears in the figure to remain constant), and a further antibody is added to more accurately cluster the quarter set. The right hand-figure basically shows the reverse – it is interesting to note in this figure that during exposure to the final half data-set, the system contentment is consistently just below the threshold T_s, resulting in the periodic addition of a new antibody. The new antibody does not succeed in recognising any antigens however, so is always removed due to natural cell death. dSOSDM is thus able to dynamically adjust to the correct number of clusters present in the data in each experiment.

7   Conclusion

Using ideas from Danger Theory, we have improved the original SOSDM algorithm to make it more able to deal with dynamically changing environments.

Simple experiments have shown that the immune systems produced do suffer un-controllable expansion and can react to changes in the environment. However, there is still much room for improvement – in particular we plan to modify the mechanism given in section 6 so that antibodies react *individually* to changes in their own contentment induced by their local environment, rather than transmit-ting values to a central controller. This is a simple modification to the system. This is more in keeping with the principles of the Danger Theory. Furthermore, more complex data-sets will be tested, and comparisons to conventional cluster-ing algorithms given.

References

1. U. Aickelin and S. Cayzer. The danger theory and its application to artifical immune systems. In J. Timmis and P Bentley, editors, *in Proceedings of the 1st International Conference on Artificial Immune Syste*, pages 141–148, 2002.
2. C.C. Anderson and P. Matzinger. Danger: The view from the bottom of the cliff. *Seminars in Immunology*, 12:231–238, 2000.
3. M. Burgess. Computer immunology. In *in Proceedings of LISA XII*, pages 283–297, 1998.
4. L.N. De Castro and F.J. Von Zuben. An evolutionary immune network for data clustering. In *Proceedings of the IEEE Brazilian Symposium on Artificial Neural Networks*, pages 84–89, 2000.
5. E. Hart and P. Ross. Exploiting the analogy between immunology and sparse dis-tributed memories: a system for clustering non-stationary data. In J. Timmis and P. Bentley, editors, *in Proceedings of the 1st International Conference on Artificial Immune Systems*, pages 49–58, 2002.
6. Emma Hart. *Immunology as a Metaphor for Computational Information Processing: Fact or Fiction*. PhD thesis, University of Edinburgh, 2002.
7. Polly Matzinger. Tolerance, danger and the extended family. *Annual Review Im-munology*, pages 991–1045, 1994.
8. M. Neal. An artificial immune system for continuous analysis of time-varying data. In J. Timmis and P. Bentley, editors, *Proceedings of 1st International Conference on Artificial Immune SYste,s (ICARIS)*, pages 76–85, 2002.
9. Jon Timmis and Mark Neal. A resource limited artificial immune system for data analysis. *Knowledge Based Systems*, 14(3-4):121–130, June 2001.

Artificial Immune Systems and the Grand Challenge for Non-classical Computation

Susan Stepney[1], John A. Clark[1], Colin G. Johnson[2],
Derek Partridge[3], and Robert E. Smith[4]

[1] Department of Computer Science, University of York
[2] Computing Laboratory, University of Kent
[3] Department of Computer Science, University of Exeter
[4] The Intelligent Computer Systems Centre, University of the West of England

Abstract. The UK Grand Challenges for Computing Research is an initiative to map out certain key areas that could be used to help drive research over the next 10–15 years. One of the identified Grand Challenges is *Non-Classical Computation*, which examines many of the fundamental assumptions of Computer Science, and asks what would result if they were systematically broken. In this discussion paper, we explain how the sub-discipline of Artificial Immune Systems sits squarely in the province of this particular Grand Challenge, and we identify certain key questions.

The UK Grand Challenges in Computing Research

The UK Computing Research Committee (UKCRC) is organising *Grand Challenges for Computing Research*, to discuss possibilities and opportunities for the advancement of computing science. It has asked the UK computing research community to identify ambitious, long-term research initiatives. The original call resulted in 109 submissions, which were discussed at a workshop in late 2002, and refined into a handful of composite proposals. (Further details, and how to get involved, can be found at [16]).

In this discussion paper, we explain how Artificial Immune Systems (AIS) sit squarely in the province of one of the resulting composite proposals: *Journeys in Non-Classical Computation*. First we summarise the Challenge itself [16], and then show where the sub-discipline of AIS falls within its remit, and the particular questions AIS raise and address. AIS provide excellent exemplars of non-classical computational paradigms, and provide a resource for studying *emergence*, necessary for a full science of complex adaptive systems.

We hope this discussion paper will encourage the AIS community to position and exploit their research within the wider Non-Classical Computation arena.

The Grand Challenge of Non-classical Computation

Some events permit huge increases in kinds and levels of complexity; these are termed *gateway events* [7]. Such events open up whole new kinds of phase space to a

J. Timmis et al. (Eds.): ICARIS 2003, LNCS 2787, pp. 204–216, 2003.

system's dynamics. Gateway events during evolution of life on earth include the appearance of eukaryotes (organisms with a cell nucleus), an oxygen atmosphere, multi-cellular organisms, and grass. Gateway events during the development of mathematics include each invention of a new class of numbers (negative, irrational, imaginary, ...), and dropping Euclid's parallel postulate.

A gateway event produces a profound and fundamental change to the system: once through the gateway, life is never the same again. We are currently poised on the threshold of a significant gateway event in computation: that of breaking free from many of our current "classical computational" assumptions. The corresponding Grand Challenge for computer science is **to journey through the gateway event obtained by breaking our current classical computational assumptions, and thereby develop a mature science of Non-Classical Computation.**

Journeys versus Goals

Many Grand Challenges are cast in terms of goals, of end points: "achieving the goal, before this decade is out, of landing a man on the moon and returning him safely to earth" [11], mapping the human genome, proving whether **P = NP** or not. We believe that a goal is not the best metaphor to use for this particular Grand Challenge, however, and prefer the metaphor of a *journey*.

The journey metaphor emphasises the importance of the entire process, rather than emphasising the end point. In the 17th and 18th centuries it was traditional for certain sections of "polite society" to go on "a Grand Tour of Europe", spending several years broadening their horizons: the experience of the entire journey was important. And in the Journey of Life, death is certainly not the goal! Indeed, an open journey, passing through gateway events, exploring new lands with ever expanding horizons, need not have an end point.

Journeys and goals have rather different properties. A goal is a fixed target, and influences the route taken to it. With an open journey of exploration, however, we are not able to predict what will happen: the purpose of the journey is discovery, and our discoveries along our journey will suggest new directions for us to take. We can suggest starting steps, and some intermediate way points, but not the detailed progress, and certainly not the end result.

Thinking of the Non-Classical Computation Challenge in terms of a journey, or rather several journeys, of exploration, we can today spy some early *way points*, as we peer through the gateway. As the community's journey progresses, new way points will heave into view, and we can alter our course to encounter these as appropriate.

Six Classical Paradigms to Disbelieve before Breakfast

Classical computing is an extraordinary success story. But there is a growing appreciation that it encompasses only a tiny subset of all computational possibilities.

Discoveries may emerge when an assumption that *this has to be the case* is found merely to be an instance of *this has always been the case*, and is changed. We wish to enable such discoveries by highlighting several assumptions that define classical computing, but that are not necessarily true in all computing paradigms. Researchers in many different fields are already challenging some these (for example, [8]), and we encourage the community to challenge more, in whatever ways seem interesting. In later sections we discuss alternatives in more detail. (Some of the categories arguably overlap.)

1 The Turing Paradigm

classical physics: states have particular values, information can be can be freely copied, information is local. Rather, at the quantum level states may exist in superpositions, information cannot be cloned, and entanglement implies non-locality.

atomicity: computation is discrete in time and space; there is a before state, an after state and an operation that transforms the former into the latter. Rather, the underlying implementation realises intermediate physical states.

unbounded resources: Turing machines have infinite tape state, and zero power consumption. Rather, resources are always constrained.

substrate as implementation detail: the machine is logical, not physical. Rather, a physical implementation of one form or another is always required, and the particular choice has consequences.

universality is a good thing: one size of digital computer, one size of algorithm, fits all problems. Rather, a choice of implementation to match the problem, or hybrid solutions, can give more effective results.

closed and ergodic systems: the state space is pre-determined. Rather, the progress of an interactive computation may open up new regions of state space in a contingent manner.

2 The von Neumann Paradigm

sequential program execution. Rather, parallel implementations already exist.

fetch-execute-store model of program execution. Rather, other architectures already exist, for example, neural nets, FPGAs.

the static program: the program stays put and the data comes to it. Rather, the data could stay put and the processing rove over it.

3 The Output Paradigm

a program is a black box: it is an oracle abstracted away from any internal structure. Rather, the computation's *trajectory* can be as interesting, or more interesting, than its final result.

a program has a single well-defined output channel. Rather, we can chose to observe other aspects of the physical system as it executes.

a program is a mathematical function: logically equivalent systems are indistinguishable. Rather, correlations of multiple outputs from different executions, or different systems, may be of interest.

4 The Algorithmic Paradigm

a program maps the initial input to the final output, ignoring the external world while it executes. Rather, a system may be an ongoing adaptive process, with inputs provided over time, with values dependent on how it interacts with the open unpredictable environment; identical inputs may provide different outputs, as the system learns and adapts to its history of interactions; there is no prespecified endpoint.

the computer can be switched on and off: computations are bounded in time, outside which the computer does not need to be active. Rather, the computer may engage in a continuous interactive dialogue, with users and other computers.

randomness is noise is bad: most computer science is deterministic. Rather, nature-inspired processes, in which randomness or chaos is essential, are known to work well.

5 The Refinement Paradigm

incremental transformational steps move a specification to an implementation that realises that specification. Rather, there may be a discontinuity between specification and implementation, for example, bio-inspired recognisers.

binary is good: answers are crisp yes/no, true/false, and provably correct. Rather, probabilistic, approximate, and fuzzy solutions can be just as useful, and more efficient.

a specification exists, either before the development and forms its basis, or at least after the development. Rather, the specification may be an emergent and changing property of the system, as the history of interaction with the environment grows.

emergence is undesired, because the specification captures everything required, and the refinement process is top-down. Rather, as systems grow more complex, this refinement paradigm is infeasible, and emergent properties become an important means of engineering desired behaviour.

6 The 'Computer as Artefact"Paradigm

computation is performed by artefacts: computation is not part of the real world. Rather, in some cases, nature "just does it", for example, optical Fourier transforms.

the hardware exists unchanged throughout the computation. Rather, new hardware can appear as the computation proceeds, for example, by the addition of new resources. Also, hardware can be "consumed", for example, a chemical computer consuming its initial reagents. In the extreme, nanites will construct the computer as part of the computation, and disassemble it at the end.

the computer must be on to work. Rather, recent quantum computation results [9] suggest that you don't even need to "run" the computer to get a result!

Doubtless there are other classical paradigms that we accept almost without question. They too can be fruitfully disbelieved.

There is a gulf between the maturity of classical computing and that of the emerging non-classical paradigms. For classical computing, intellectual investment over many years is turning craft into science. To fully exploit emerging non-classical computational approaches we must seek for them such rigour and engineering discipline as is possible. What that science will look like is currently unclear, and the Grand Challenge encourages exploration.

The Real World: Breaking the Turing Paradigm

Real World as Its Own Computer

The universe doesn't need to compute, it just does it. We can take the *computational stance*, and view many physical, chemical and biological processes *as if* they were computations: the Principle of Least Action "computes" the shortest path for light; water "computes" its own level; evolution "computes" fitter organisms (evolution of bacterial resistance is evolution of real bacteria against an increasingly strong "data set" of attacks to the bacterial "population"); DNA and morphogenesis "computes" phenotypes; the immune system "computes" antigen recognition.

This natural computation can be more effective than a digital simulation. For example, the real world performs quantum mechanical computations exponentially faster than can classical simulations [6].

Real World as Our Computer

Taking the computational stance, we may exploit the way the world works to perform "computations" for us. We set up the situation so that the natural behaviour of the real world gives the desired result.

There are various forms of real world sorting and searching, for example. Centrifuges exploit differences in density to separate mixtures of substances, a form of gravitational sorting. Vapours of a boiling mixture are richer in the components that have lower boiling points; distillation exploits this to give a form of thermal sorting. Chromatography provides a chemical means of separation. Other kinds of computations exist: for example, optics performs Fourier transforms.

Real World as Analogue Computer

We may exploit the real world in more indirect ways. The "computations" of the "real world as our computer" are very direct, yet often we are concerned with more abstract questions. Sometimes we can harness the physical world to provide the results that we need: we may be able to set up the situation so that there is an *analogy* between the computation performed by the real world, and the result we want.

There is an age-old mechanism for finding the longest stick of spaghetti in an unruly pile, exploiting the physics of gravity and rigidity: we can use this to sort by setting up an analogy between spaghetti strand length and the quantity of interest.

Classical computing already exploits physics at the level of electron movements. But there are other ways of exploiting nature.

Analogue computing itself exploits the properties of electrical circuits as analogues of differential equations (amongst other analogues).

DNA computing encodes problems and solutions as sequences of bases (strands) and seeks to exploit mechanisms such as strand splitting, recombination and reproduction to perform calculations of interest. This can result in vast parallelism, of the order of 10^{20} strands.

Quantum computing presents one of the most exciting developments for computer science in recent times, breaking out of the classical Turing paradigm. As its name suggests, it is based on quantum physics, and can perform computations that cannot be effectively implemented on a classical Turing machine. It exploits interference, many worlds, entanglement and non-locality. Newer work still is further breaking out of the binary mind-set, with multiple-valued *qudits*, and continuous variables.

Real World as Inspiration

Many important techniques in computer science have resulted from simulating (currently very simplified) aspects of the real world. *Meta-heuristic search* techniques draw inspiration from many areas, including physics (simulated annealing), evolution (genetic algorithms, genetic programming), neurology (artificial neural networks), immunology (artificial immune systems [5]), and social networks (ant colony optimisation [2]).

In the virtual worlds inside the computer, we are no longer constrained by the laws of nature. Our simulations can be other than the way the real world works. For example, we can introduce novel evolutionary operators to our genetic algorithms, novel kinds of selection algorithms to our artificial immune systems, and even, as we come to understand the embracing concepts, novel kinds of complex adaptive systems themselves. The real world is our inspiration, not a restriction.

Reality based computing techniques have proved successful, or look promising, yet the science underpinning their use comes nowhere near matching the science of classical computing. Given a raft of nature-inspired techniques we would like to get from problem to solution efficiently and effectively, and we would like to reason about the performance of the resulting systems. But this falls outside the classical refinement paradigm.

Massive Parallelism: Breaking the von Neumann Paradigm

Parallel processing (Cellular Automata, etc) and other non-classical architectures break out of the sequential, von Neumann, paradigm.

Under the classical computational assumptions, any parallel computation can be serialised, yet parallelism has its advantages.

Real-time response to the environment. The environment evolves at its own rate, and a single processor might not be able to keep pace. (Possibly the ultimate example of this will be the use of vast numbers of nanotechnological assemblers (nanites) to build macroscopic artefacts. A single nanite would take too long, by very many orders of magnitude.)

Better mapping of the computation to the problem structure. The real world is intrinsically parallel, and serialisation of its interactions to map to the computational structure can be difficult. Parallelism also permits colocation of each hardware processor and the part of the environment with which it interacts most. It then permits colocation of the software: software agents can roam around the distributed system looking for the data of interest, and meeting other agents in a context dependent manner. For example, artificial antibodies can patrol the network they are protecting.

And once the classical computational assumptions are challenged, we can see that serialisation is not necessarily equivalent.

Fault tolerance. Computation requires physical implementation, and that implementation might fail. A parallel implementation can be engineered to continue working even though some subset of its processors have failed. A sequential implementation has only the one processor.

Interference/interaction between devices. Computation requires physical implementation, and those implementations have extra-logical properties, such as power consumption, or electromagnetic emissions, which may be interpreted as computations in their own right (see later). These properties may interfere when the devices are running in parallel, leading to effects not present in a serialised implementation. (Possibly the ultimate example of this is the exponentially large state space provided by the superposed parallel qubits in a quantum computer.)

The use of massive parallelism introduces new problems. The main one is the requirement for decentralised control. It is just not possible for a single centralised source to exercise precise control over vast numbers of heterogeneous devices. Part of this issue is tackled by the sister Grand Challenges in *Ubiquitous Systems* [16], and part is addressed in the later section, on open processes.

In the Eye of the Beholder: Breaking the Output Paradigm

The classical paradigm of program execution is that an abstract computation processes an input to produce an output. This input-output mapping is a logical property of the computation, and is all that is important: no intermediate states are of interest, the computation is independent of physical realisation, and different instances of the computation yield precisely the same results.

Computation, however, is in the eye of the beholder. Algorithms are implemented by physical devices, intermediate states exist, physical changes happen in the world, different devices are distinguishable. Any information that can be observed in this physical world may be used to enrich the perceived computation [4].

Logical Trajectory Observations. An executing algorithm follows a trajectory through its logical state space. (Caveat: this is a classical argument: intermediate quantum computational states may be in principle unobservable.) Typically, this trajectory is not observed (except possibly during debugging). This is shockingly wasteful: such logical information can be a computational resource in its own right. For example, during certain types of heuristic search the trajectory followed can give more information about a sought solution than the final "result" of the search itself.

Physical Trajectory Observations. An executing algorithm is accompanied by physical changes to the world: for example, it consumes trajectory-dependent power as it progresses, and can take trajectory-dependent time to complete. Such physical resource consumption can be observed and exploited as a computational resource, for example, to deduce features of the logical trajectory. (For example, recent attacks on smart cards have observed such things to deduce secret key information [3].)

Differential Observations. An executing algorithm is realised in a physical device. Physical devices have physical characteristics that can change depending on environmental conditions such as temperature, and that differ subtly across logically identical devices. So one can observe not merely the output of a single execution, but a set of outputs from a family of executions, from multiple systems, from different but related systems, and perform differential analyses.

Higher-Order Observations. These are observations not of the program execution itself, but of the execution of the program used to design (the program used to design…) the program.

Open Processes: Breaking the Algorithmic Paradigm

In the classical paradigm, the ultimate goal of a computation is reaching a fixed point: the final output, the "result" of the computation, after which we may switch off the computer. The majority of classical science is also based around the notion of fixed-point equilibrium and ergodicity (the property that a system has well defined spatial and temporal averages, as any state of the system recurs with non-zero probability).

Many modern scientific theories consider systems that lack repetition and stability: they are *far-from-equilibrium* and *non-ergodic*. The most obvious non-ergodic, far from equilibrium system is life itself, characterised by perpetual evolution (change).

Consider the most basic of chaotic systems: the logistic process:

$$x_{t+1} = Rx_t(1 - x_t)$$

The behaviours of various logistic processes as a function of the parameter R form the well-know bifurcating, chaotic *logistic curve* (see, for example, figure 21 of [12]). For small values of R, these logistic processes have a fixed point attractor. As R increases, the attractor becomes period two, then four, then eight. This *period doubling* continues, and the values of R where each doubling occurs get closer together. For $R > 3.569945671…$ the logistic process's attractor goes through an infinite number of values (except for a few "islands" of order, of attractors with multiples of odd periods). There is a phase transition from order (the region of period doubling) to chaos ("random" behaviour). The phase transition point at $R = 3.569945671...$ is the so-called *edge of chaos*.

Consider a discretised process whose underlying (continuous) dynamics are those of the logistic equation, and imagine taking samples of length L bits. Construct an automaton machine that represents the process, for a given L. There is a clear phase transition (a peak in the machine size versus the entropy of the bit sequence) as we move from the period doubling region to the chaotic region. At the phase transition, the machine size versus the length of the sequence L *expands without bound*. That is, at the edge of chaos, the logistic machine requires an infinite memory machine for accurate representation: there is a leap in the level of intrinsic computation going on.

At the edge of chaos, we can add new resources (computational or physical) and get results that are neither redundant (as in the structured period doubling regime) nor random (as in the chaotic regime). Within the classical paradigm, such conditions would be anathema, indicating unceasing variety that never yields "the solution". But in life-like systems, there is simultaneously sustained order, and useful innovation. New matter can be brought into such systems and used in ways that are neither redundant nor random. In this setting, emergence of the unforeseen is a desirable property, rather disruptive noise.

Computing often attempts to exploit the biological paradigm: cellular automata, evolutionary computation, recurrent networks (autocatalytic, neural, genomic, cytokine immune system, ecological webs, ...), social insect and agent-based systems, DNA-computing, and nanite-systems that build themselves. The implementations in most of these cases, however, are locked into themselves, *closed*, unable to take on new matter or information, thus unable to truly exploit emergence.

Open systems are systems where new resources, and new *kinds* of resources, can be added at any time, by external agency, or by the actions of the system. (For example, an immune system might have inoculation material introduced by an external agent, or evolve a new kind of immune cell.) These new resources can provide *gateway events*, that fundamentally alter the character of the system dynamics, by opening up new kinds of regions of phase space, allowing new possibilities.

Computational systems are beginning to open themselves to unceasing flows of information (if not so much to new matter). The openness arises, for example, through human interactivity as a continuing dialogue between user and machine [15], through unbounded networks, through robotic systems with energy autonomy. As computers become ubiquitous, the importance of *open systems physics* to understanding computation becomes crucial.

Artificial Immune Systems, and the Grand Challenge

The Inspiration and the Analogy

AIS are relatively recent example of using the real world as computational inspiration. One such inspiration for AIS runs something like: the vertebrate immune system fights infection by recognising and attacking *non-self*; can an analogous computational system be used to detect, diagnose, and fight computer intrusions (from hacker attacks to computer viruses)?

In addition to this obvious security metaphor, many other AIS application areas have been developed, to cover more general *anomaly detection*, optimisation, fault tolerance, and general purpose machine learning applications such as recognition and classification.

The Models

There are two main classes of models for AIS: the population-based (or selection) model, and the network model (see [5] for details), which have impacts on different areas of the main Challenge.

The Population-Based Model

The population-based model is computationally inspired by the processes during early maturation of immune cells, before they are released into the lymphatic system. It uses some particular algorithm (positive, negative, clonal, ...) to select a set of *recognisers* (supervised learning) or *classifiers* (unsupervised learning), of self or non-self (details depending on the precise algorithm).

This model fits well with the other bio-inspired soft learning systems, such as neural nets and genetic algorithms. The major contributions to the Grand Challenge are in the area of *breaking the refinement paradigm.*

In all these soft learning approaches, there is a discontinuity between the problem statement and the bio-inspired solution. With both NNs and AISs, the solution is distributed over the entire system. Each artificial antibody may recognise several different antigens: the specific response to a particular antigen is a global property of all the antibodies. The complex response emerges from the simpler behaviour of individual parts.

The way point questions specific to AIS include:

- What are the effect of aspects and parameters of the selection algorithm on the outcome and applicability of the algorithms?
- Can we observe the computational trajectory taken during selection and recognition to get useful information?

The immune system population-based model forms an excellent exemplar for breaking the refinement paradigm. The challenge is to develop a *science of non-classical refinement*, that permits quantitative reasoning about *all* bio-inspired algorithms, including AISs, in both a bottom up and top down manner:

- *understanding* and *predicting* the global recognisers and classifiers that emerge from a collection of local non-specific agents
- a means to *design* and *implement* appropriate sets of recognisers or classifiers for particular applications, in a rigorous (but possibly non-incremental) way
- *quantitative description methods* that enable rigorous reasoning about the behaviour of AISs, such that they can be used reliably in critical applications

Taking inspiration and input from all the bio-inspired learning algorithms, major way points on the Non-Classical Computation journey are

- a *general theory of learning systems* that includes neural, evolutionary, and immune systems as special cases
- use of the general theory to develop *more effective kinds* of learning systems, inspired by, but not based upon, any known biological processes

The Network Model

The immune system network model is computationally inspired by the biological processes used to maintain a dynamic "memory" of immune responses, in a system where the lifetime of individual immune memory cells is on the order of weeks, yet the memory itself persists on the order of years or decades.

The immune system network model forms a superb exemplar for *breaking the output paradigm*. It is one of many dynamic network models that occur in biological and social systems, from Kauffman's autocatalytic networks [10], and genomic control networks, through dynamical models of neural networks, to ecological food webs, and social and technological networks. All these subject areas could benefit from better networks models. Much of the existing mathematical network theory is restricted to static, homogeneous, structured, closed networks, since these are the simplest, most tractable models to work with. However, these are not realistic models of biological networks. Antibodies rove around the body (network, system, ...) looking for the anomalies, and new kinds of attacks call for new kinds of defence. The challenge is to develop a pragmatic theory of *dynamic, heterogeneous, unstructured, open networks* [13].

- *Dynamic*: the network is not in steady state or equilibrium, but is far from equilibrium, governed by attractors and trajectories. (*Swarm networks* may offer insights to this kind of dynamics [2])

- *Heterogeneous*: the nodes, the connections, and the communications can be of many different types, including higher order types.

- *Unstructured*: the network connectivity has no particular regularity: it is not fully regular, or fully connected, or even fully random. Clearly there need to be *some* kinds of regularity present, but these are likely to be of kinds that cannot be reasoned about in terms of simple averages or mean field notions; they are more likely have fractal structure. Some recent advances in *Small World* networks offer intriguing new insights [1][14].

- *Open (metadynamic)*: the structures are unbounded, and the components are not fixed: nodes and connections may come and go; new *kinds* of nodes and connections may appear.

A general theory of such networks would have application well beyond AISs. Such a theory is a basic requirement of complex systems development in general, one application of which is pervasive, or ubiquitous, computing (the subject of another Grand Challenge [16]). Such a theory a necessary way point for answering such challenging questions as

- *Computation as a dynamical process.* What are the various attractors of a dynamical computation? How can we encourage the system to move to a "better" attractor? How can we map the route through intermediate attractors that it should take?

- *Computation at the edge of chaos.* What are it capabilities? How can we hold a system at the edge, far from equilibrium, to perform useful computations? How can we make it self-organise to the edge?
- *Designed emergence.* How can we design (refine) open systems that have desired emergent properties? And do not have undesired emergent properties?
- *Open systems science.* What are the fundamental properties of open systems? How can we predict the effect of interventions (adding new things, or removing things) to the system? How can we understand the effect of a gateway event that opens up new kinds of regions of phase space to a computation? How can we design a system such that gateway events, natural changes to phase space, can occur endogenously?

The Biological Models

Like many biologically inspired computational ideas, the computer science and the biology are developing in parallel. The natural immune system, in particular, is an exceedingly complicated and not well understood biological mechanism. The current discipline of AIS may have been *inspired* by the biology, but it is painfully clear that AISs are but a pale shadow of the vast complexity and subtlety of the natural immune system. Computer scientists, mathematicians, and immunologists working together can ask, and answer, some deep and interesting questions. For example:

- How might we use the real immune system, and other real physical and biological systems, for computation?
- To what extent is the working of the immune system, and other biological systems, dictated by the physical substrate? Can all putative "immune" responses be realised on all substrates? Do some diseases exploit *computational* constraints of the immune system to defeat it?
- How can we use models to decide which parts of the biology are necessary for correct robust functioning, which parts are necessary only because of the particular physical realisation, and which parts merely contingent evolutionary aspects?
- How can we use nature inspired computation to build "better than reality" systems? What are the computational limits to what we can simulate?

Conclusions

AIS do not break all the classic computational paradigms: for example, they do not (yet?) use concepts from quantum physics. However, they do challenge some of the major paradigms. The population-based model is a good exemplar for examining alternatives to the refinement paradigm, and the network model is an excellent exemplar for examining open network dynamics and emergence, necessary for a full science of complex adaptive systems.

Classical physics did not disappear when modern physics came along: rather its restrictions and domains of applicability were made explicit. Similarly, the various forms of non-classical computation will not supersede classical computation: they will augment and enrich it. And when a wide range of tools is available, we can pick the best one, or the best combination, for each job. For example, it might be that

216 S. Stepney et al.

using a quantum algorithm to reduce a search space, and then a meta-heuristic search to explore that, is more effective than using either algorithm alone. AISs form one of a whole array of novel approaches to computation that are becoming available. It is important that these separate areas are not seen as independent. Rather, their results and insights should provide valuable groundwork for the overarching challenge, to produce **a fully mature science of all forms of computation, that unifies the classical and non-classical paradigms**.

References

1. A.-L. Barabasi. *Linked: the new science of networks*. Perseus, 2002.
2. E. W. Bonabeau, M. Dorigo, G. Theraulaz. *Swarm Intelligence*. OUP, 1999
3. S. Chari, C. S. Jutla, J. R. Rao, P. Rohatgi. *Power analysis*. In A. McIver, C. Morgan, eds. *Programming Methodology*. Springer, 2003.
4. J. A. Clark, S. Stepney, H. Chivers. Breaking the model (submitted)
5. L. N. de Castro, J. Timmis. *Artificial Immune Systems*. Springer, 2002.
6. R. P. Feynman. Simulating Physics with Computers. *Int. J. Theor. Phys.* 21(6/7) 1982.
7. M. Gell-Mann. *The Quark and the Jaguar*. Abacus, 1994.
8. T. Gramss, S. Bornholdt, M. Gross, M. Mitchell, T. Pellizzari. *Non-Standard Computation*. Wiley, 1998.
9. R. Jozsa: Characterising Classes of Functions Computable by Quantum Parallelism. *Proc. R. Soc. Lond.* A 435, 1991.
10. S. A. Kauffman. *The Origins of Order*. OUP, 1993.
11. J. F. Kennedy. Announcement to the US Congress. 25 May, 1961.
12. H.-O. Peitgen, P. H. Richter. *The Beauty of Fractals*. Springer, 1986.
13. S. Stepney. Critical Critical Systems. In *Formal Aspects of Security, FASeC'02*. LNCS vol 2629, Springer, 2003.
14. D. J. Watts. *Small Worlds*. Princeton University Press, 1999.
15. P. Wegner. Why interaction is more powerful than algorithms. *CACM*, 40(5) 1997.
16. UK Grand Challenges in Computing Research Website.
    http://umbriel.dcs.gla.ac.uk/NeSC/general/esi/events/Grand_Challenges

A Paratope Is Not an Epitope: Implications for Immune Network Models and Clonal Selection

Simon M. Garrett

Department of Computer Science,
University of Wales, Aberystwyth, UK, SY23 3DB
smg@aber.ac.uk

Abstract. Artificial Immune Systems (AIS) research into clonal selection and immune network models has tended to use a single, real-valued or binary vector to represent both the paratope and epitope of a B-cell; in this paper, the use of alternative representations is discussed. A theoretical generic immune network (GIN) is presented, that can be used to explore the network dynamics of several families of different B-cell representations at the same time, and that combines features of clonal selection and immune networks in a single model.

Keywords: Paratope, epitope, Artificial Immune Systems (AIS), critical evaluation, Clonal Selection (CS), Immune Network Models.

1 Introduction

A vertebrate's body is continually under attack from pathogen that can cause various illnesses. Fortunately, each pathogen has portions of its surface that are antigenic; i.e. they can elicit an immune response. This occurs when parts of the pathogen's antigen molecules, known as *epitopes*, are bound to *paratopes* that are present at the tips of the Y-shaped *antibodies*—protein structures produced in vast numbers by the vertebrate's B-cells. The action of paratope-epitope binding causes the structure hosting the epitope to be repressed and causes the paratope's B-cell to be stimulated. However, some, such as Jerne (1974), have suggested that B-cells have epitopes that allow them to be repressed by other B-cells, and that this interaction between B-cells forms a *network* of repression and stimulation.

A common assumption in artificial immune system (AIS) research is that the paratope and epitope regions of a B-cell can be simplified to a single vector of binary or real-valued numbers. In this paper we will call this the 'Single Vector Assumption'. While it will be confirmed that the Single Vector Assumption is a valuable metaphor and/or modelling representation (if a rather artificial one), alternative B-cell and antigen representations will be discussed, and *a priori* suggestions will be made about the usefulness of the dynamics of the models that such representations entail. All the common *clonal selection* and *immune network* AIS algorithms (described below) make the Single Vector Assumption and produce powerful results (de Castro and Von Zuben, 2000; de Castro and Von Zuben, 2001; Knight and Timmis, 2001). E.g. in one form, de Castro and

J. Timmis et al. (Eds.): ICARIS 2003, LNCS 2787, pp. 217–228, 2003.

Von Zubens's AINET is able to perform multimodal optimisation as well as, if not better than, existing methods, and in a similar form it is also able to localise even interlinked clusters. However, alternative B-cell and antigen representations do exist, and they seem to offer alternative computational possibilities. For example, the formative paper by Farmer et al. (1986), uses *two* binary vectors to represent a B-cell—one for the paratope of the B-cell and the other for its epitope—and it was shown that the dynamics of the resulting system was very similar to a classifier system (Holland, 1976).

It seems obvious, therefore, that different representations of antibodies and antigen (or at least their epitopes) can lead to very different B-cell dynamics, and this is true whether the aim is to obtain a model or metaphor of some aspect of the immune system. Several forms of representational difference will be discussed, including numbers of paratopes and epitopes, and types of interactions between these paratopes and epitopes. A generic algorithm is suggested that encompasses all these varieties in a single, analysable algorithm.

This conceptual paper is structured as follows: Section 2 briefly introduces and contrasts the main approaches to artificial immune networks, and to a lesser extent, clonal selection. Readers who desire a more general immunological background are referred to the excellent paper by Perelson and Weisbuch (1997). Section 3 sets out several representations of B-cells and antigen and suggests some of the dynamics of a populations of such elements on the basis of formal reasoning and existing experimentation. Section 4 draws together aspects of these new models, and the various vector representations of a B-cell and antigen, to give a generic immune network (GIN). Two types of GIN are presented, a cellular automata version and a synchronised population version. Section 5 makes some final conclusions and suggests further work.

Finally, to avoid confusion later, the following terms are explicitly defined: 'Representation' = an artificial, simplified analogue of some aspect of reality. 'Model' = one or more represented elements, interacting in a manner that bears resemblance to observed, real-world system dynamics. 'System' = the interacting collection of real-world entities being observed.

2   Background Concepts

2.1   Clonal Selection, CLONALG and AINET

Natural clonal selection (Burnet, 1959) occurs to the degree that a B-cell matches an antigen. A strong match causes a B-cell to be cloned many times, and a weak match results in little cloning. These 'clones' are mutated from the original B-cell at a rate inversely proportional to the match strength: a strongly matching B-cell mutates little and thus retain its match to the antigen, to a slightly greater or lesser extent, and a weakly matching cell mutates much more.

These immunological processes of clonal selection (and affinity maturation) have been used for inspiration in AIS, the most common abstraction being CLONALG (de Castro and Von Zuben, 2000). A form of clonal selection underlies most, if not all, immune network models, although it is not explicitly developed in all of them. CLONALG currently exists in two similar but distinct forms—one for optimisation and one for pattern matching—but in both cases the B-cell is implemented as a single real-valued vector, and no two B-cells are allowed to interact. In the pattern matching version of CLONALG, a set of *memory cells* may also be kept that 'remember' previously found patterns or solutions.

CLONALG has been modified by adding antibody-antibody interaction to give AINET (de Castro and Von Zuben, 2001), indeed de Castro has shown that AINET subsumes CLONALG and produces better optimisation and pattern recognition. However, the B-cell representation remains a single vector—there is no differentiation between epitopes and paratopes. B-cells that are strongly stimulated by both antigen and antibody interactions (which are calculated separately) are stored as memory cells, resulting in a population of memory cells locations that effectively map out clusters in data in an unsupervised manner. Moreover, by statistical analysis, these clusters can be arranged hierarchically. The addition of antibody-antibody interaction has clearly changed/improved the dynamics of the system radically, when compared to a system with no network (i.e. CLONALG).

2.2   The 'Farmer Model' Immune Network

Alternatively, the immune network model of Farmer et al. (1986), which followed Jerne's network principle, represents a B-cell with both a paratope and an epitope binary vector, and an antigen as a single binary vector. Consider a set of antigen and a set of antibody *types*, where 'antibody type' means a concentration of antibodies that share the same binding features; then the m_{ij} matching affinities are defined as,

$$m_{ij} = \sum_{k=1}^{rng} G\Big(\sum_{n=1}^{l} e_i(n+k) \oplus p_j(n) - s + 1 \Big), \qquad (1)$$

where '$\oplus$' is the complementary XOR operator; k is the offset, measured in bits, between the paratope and epitope; $e_i(n)$ is the n'th bit of the epitope; $p_j(n)$ is the n'th bit of the paratope, and s is a threshold since $G(x) = x$ if $x > 0$ and $G(x) = 0$ otherwise. The number of bits in a string, $l = min(len(e_i), len(p_j))$, $rng = l - s, s \leq l$. Therefore, the value of k is in the range $-rng \leq k \leq rng$. Note that the variable rng has been deduced here from Farmer et al. (1986) to clarify k's range. Also note that Equation 1 is *not* symmetric because m_{ij} means "epitope i binds with paratope j," and m_{ji} means "epitope j binds with paratope i."

Equation 1 was then used in a differential equation for modelling the concentrations of antibody types. Given N antibody types, with concentrations $\{x_1, \ldots, x_N\}$ and n antigen types, with concentrations $\{y_1, \ldots, y_n\}$, the change in concentration of a given x_i was modelled as,

$$\frac{dx_i}{dt} = c\Big[\sum_{j=1}^{N} m_{ji}x_i x_j - k_1 \sum_{j=1}^{N} m_{ij}x_i x_j + \sum_{j=1}^{n} m_{ji}x_i y_j \Big] - k_2 x_i. \qquad (2)$$

The $x_i x_j$ and $x_i y_j$ elements model the probability that a paratope and epitope will be close enough to attempt to bind, since high concentrations of either increases this probability. The first term in Equation 2 models the stimulation of an antibody type's paratope by the epitope of another antibody type. The second term indicates the repression of an antibody type due to its epitope binding with the paratope of another antibody type. The third term models the stimulation of an antibody type by binding with the epitope of an antigen. The constant k_1 indicates a possible inequality between the simulation and repression terms. The equation ends with $k_2 x_i$ (where $k_2 > 0$), a 'death term' that removes a proportion of x_i antibodies. Farmer et al advise that the value of k_2 is adjusted until constant population size is obtained, as in the natural immune system, although this is far from easy in practice. Finally, c is a rate constant, common in kinetic equations, that depends on the number of collisions per unit time and the rate of antibody production stimulated by a collision.

The 'Farmer model', and later work in this form of network (e.g. De Boer et al. (1992)), show that there are alternative, useful B-cell representations. Due to its complexity, however, AIS research has generally modelled Jerne's immune network assumption in the style of cellular automata, with discrete elements representing B-cells (de Castro and Von Zuben, 2001), or groups of B-cells, e.g. AINE (Knight and Timmis, 2001).

2.3   The 'Timmis-Neal' Model Immune Network

Timmis and Neal's early work, e.g. (Timmis et al., 2000), made several changes to the Farmer model. They preferred a single real-valued B-cell representation in place of the functionally unrelated epitope and paratope vectors, and changed from a continuous to a discrete model, which necessitated a *similarity* measure in place of the *complementary* measure of the Farmer model. This 'Timmis-Neal model' also introduced the idea of a network affinity threshold (NAT), used to limit the connections between two antibodies to those that are the strongest, to control the density of the network. There have been various Timmis-Neal algorithms, but the central equations are generic and are generalised here as follows. The similarity measure is,

$$m(x,y) = H\left(\sqrt{\sum_{n=1}^{l}(x(n) - y(n))^2}\right), \tag{3}$$

(i.e. l-dimensional Euclidean distance) such that $m(x,y) = H(x)$ if $H(x) \leq NAT$, or $m(x,y) = 1$ otherwise. The results of $m(x,y)$ are normalised to fall on or within the unit sphere, i.e. $0 \leq m(x,y) \leq 1$. Using the same form as the Farmer model, the dynamics of the Timmis-Neal model can be defined by,

$$sl = 1 + \sum_{j=1}^{N}(1 - m(x_i, x_j)) - \sum_{j=1}^{N} m(x_i, x_j) - \sum_{j=1}^{n} m(x_i, y_j),$$
$$\text{if } sl > \theta \text{ then } x_i = x_i + k(sl), \text{ else } x_i = x_i. \tag{4}$$

with the NAT scalar selecting only those antibodies that are close enough to each other. The resulting network can be used to indicate clusters in a data set in an unsupervised manner, so even though the equations of motion are similar to the Farmer model, the change in representation has significantly changed the nature of the network dynamics.

2.4 Immunological Modelling and Immune Networks

In contrast to AIS work, which develops useful data analysis and optimisation methods by abstraction from immunological process, *computational immunology* models immune processes to allow 'what if' questions about the biology of immunological processes. Clearly, B-cell representation also matters here.

Many immunologists reject Jerne's immune network theory—at least as a controlling feature of the immune system—and prefer simpler theories of interactions between B-cells. For example, Kleinstein and Seiden (2000)'s work, that attempts to simulate all the key features of the adaptive immune system, models a B-cells with a single paratope, without epitopes and without antibody-antibody interaction. In other words they consider clonal selection and affinity maturation sufficient for antigen control. However, some immunological models do contain an antibody network component. The Farmer model is one obvious example that is an immune model as well as an AIS approximation of a classifier system. This work was further developed, particularly by Perelson (De Boer et al., 1992; Stadler et al., 1994; Smith et al., 1996). Building on work by Stewart and Varela (1991), Bersini and Calenbuhr (1997) have also developed a model that shows the oscillatory behaviour or the immune network. Despite their system requiring many parameters to be "tuned" until the desired behaviour was found, they state that the behaviour was then robust to changes in parameters and that the values of the parameters were biologically tenable.

Vertosick and Kelly (1991) discuss the possibility of *multiple* epitopes in the context of the immune system as a neural network. Their work also includes a valuable insight into the mechanism of immune memory, under the representational assumption that a B-cell forms a complementarily interacting paratope-paratope network. Therefore, they say, there exist layers of idiotypes and anti-idiotypes, because the paratope and its epitope are considered to be functionally related. Vertosick and Kelly make two other assertions: (i) because each layer of recognition is imprecise there is a tree-like branching structure to the network (like a restricted form of neural network), and (ii) an antigen's multiple epitopes are each part of the whole epitope "image" of that antigen. In this sense they speak of an "artificial retina" where parts of the immune network recognise different features or attributes of a whole. They relate this to the Oudin-Cazenava enigma (Oudin and Cazenava, 1971).

Taken together, these works highlight the importance of the choice of representation, and the form of antibody-antibody network that is allowed, if any. It would seem that an investigation of alternative types of representation in clonal selection and immune networks would be useful, not just for new AIS algorithms but also for new computational immunology models.

3   Investigating Alternative Network Dynamics

Given the previous review it is clear that there are many possible representations of B-cells and antigen, and many methods of forming interactions between them. Table 1 shows some of the possibilities, given four variables that can affect network dynamics. In more detail, these are:

1. *The Number of Epitopes on the Antigen:* namely, one epitope, 'E', or more than one, 'E...E', indicated above each column.
2. *The Number of Epitopes on the Antibody:* namely none, one epitope, 'E', or more than one, 'E...E', indicated to the side of each row.
3. *The Number of Paratopes on the Antibody:* namely one paratope, 'P', or two, 'PvP' (i.e. in a v-formation), indicated for a block of three rows.
4. *The Type of Network Binding Interaction Between the Antibodies:* namely, 'none', paratope-paratope ('P-P'), paratope-epitope ('P-E') and both 'P-P' and 'P-E' allowed at the same time—the network's type is indicated within each cell of the table. Of course, each of these types of network may be partially- or fully-interconnected, and in this sense 'none' is any of these networks when the degree of interconnectedness is reduced to zero.

Table 1. A table of the types of immune network available (see text for more details)

	paratope	epitope	Antigen Representation E	Antigen Representation E.E
Antibody Representation	P	no E	CLONALG=*none*; AINET=*P-P*; AIRS=*P-P*	
Antibody Representation	P	E	'Farmer model'=*P-E*	
Antibody Representation	P	E...E		Vertosick and Kelly=*P-P*
Antibody Representation	PvP	no E		
Antibody Representation	PvP	E		
Antibody Representation	PvP	E...E		Natural Immune System=*P-E* or *both*?

Types of Antibody-Antibody Network Interaction:
none = no network   P-P = paratope-paratope
P-E = paratope-epitope   both = both types of network interaction

In addition to these four variables, and the degree of network, there is the question of whether matching should be *complimentary-* or *similarity-*based. This point will not be addressed in detail here since it mainly applies to binary vectors, and because it is (surprisingly) not that important in most cases. We will speak in general terms of 'matching' rather than 'similarity' or 'complementarity.'

The real immune system is arguably best modelled at the location indicated in Table 1, and some of the existing AIS and immunological modelling systems are also shown. It is clear that there is generally a large gap in complexity between AIS models and models that might more accurately model B-cell-antigen interactions, and this is because a model should be as simple as possible while still exhibiting the same dynamics of the system it is modelling (Ockham's razor). The question is therefore, 'are there any B-cell and antigen representations that might offer interesting dynamics that are *not* currently observed in existing models.' Some possibilities are now described, based on the four variables above.

3.1   Number of Epitopes (Antigen and Antibody)

As mentioned above, the work of Vertosick and Kelly (1991) suggests that a multiple epitope approach may allow elements of a whole entity to be recognised. Since all the E in 'E...E' are different, the various antibodies bound to each in 'E...E' will probably have different paratopes too, giving rise to Vertosick and Kelly's multiple recognition effect. However, another effect of a multiple epitope representation is to increase the chance that each antigen or antibody will be strongly matched at one of its epitopes, and therefore suppressed.

3.2   Number of Paratopes

When an antibody has just one paratope it can bind to just one epitope at a time, but when it has two paratopes, one paratope can bind to an antigen and the other to an antibody that has a similar epitope to the antigen. When P-P binding is assumed, this can have the effect of re-presenting the antigen to the immune system, amplifying its presence as shown below, and making the eradication of the antigen likely to be faster. This is true whether matching is by similarity or by complementarity.

```
        [E3]                <- Antigen
        [E2]
        [E1]=[P1 E4]        <- Antibody-Antigen binding
           ] E5]            <- Antibody A
   [E7 P2]=[P1 E6]          <- P-P binding
   [E8  [                   <- Antibody B
   [E9 P2] <- Antibody B's paratope is similar to E1
```

3.3   Types of B-cell Network Interaction

Network-Free Systems When there is no network, as is the case with CLON-ALG, no two antibodies can directly interact, although there may be an indirect effect due to population-fitness dynamics—in other words a fit antibody can indirectly kill of an unfit antibody. This leads to a proliferation of the same high-quality antibodies, instead of promoting diversity. The lack of diversity does not matter as much as it does with a GA because CLONALG can always mutate from a converged state if the fitness function should change, but it does mean that there is a delay before diversity is restored enough for it to converge on the new maximum or maxima. Since there is no direct network, either a similarity or complementarity measure can be used with the same overall effect. Network-free systems are static when there are no antigens presents. This is not true of the following network paradigms.

Paratope-Paratope (P-P) Networks The Timmis-Neal and AINET P-P networks result in a strong form of positive feedback. Given an antibody, ab_1, that has strongly bound to an antigen and cloned many times, any other antibody ab_2 that binds this antibody will: (i) be similar to it, and (ii) reinforce the overall strength of binding to this antigen for the whole population of B-cells because ab_2 will also clone. In the case of the Timmis-Neal model there is a slight negative feedback—due to the closeness of ab_1 and ab_2 in the state space, see Equation 4—but this is not enough to overcome the overall positive feedback because even if antibody ab_1 is killed off by ab_2, it has been simultaneously replaced by ab_2! Therefore, both the Timmis-Neal model and AINET quickly form networks that represent the clusters in the antigen data set, in a manner rather like shrink-wrapping an object. This is clearly very useful, but it may not represent the behaviour of the immune system, which is also useful. As well as being found in found in AINET and AINE, the (P-P) network is found in the immunological literature (see Lydyard et al. (2000)).

Paratope-Epitope (P-E) Networks When the paratope and epitope of an antibody are not functionally the dynamics are very different. Consider the case where an antibody, ab_1, has strongly matched to an antigen, ag (either complementary or similarity matching will do), and as a result has produced many near-clones of itself. Both the paratopes and epitopes of ab_1's clones will be very similar to ab_1, because ab_1 is a close match to ag, and therefore if the B-cell population contains another antibody, ab_2, that binds reasonably strongly to the epitopes of antibodies like ab_1 then it too will clone, and begin to suppress the ab_1 antibodies. This is good because it prevents redundancy in the set of antibodies. Of course, now there is a larger than average population of ab_2 antibodies that are controlling the the ab_1 antibodies, and this population is also liable to be controlled in the same way by another antibody, ab_3. Therefore the effect of the paratope-epitope immune network is to prevent any one type of antibody from dominating the population. The Farmer model attempted to capture these dynamics in terms of concentrations, which was possible because natural clonal selection tends to produce exact copies of a particular antibody, but it did not describe the mutation dynamics well. This form of network encourages diversity by means of negative feedback, or even 'frustration' and near-chaos (Bersini and Calenbuhr, 1997), giving fascinating dynamics.

Both P-P and P-E Networks Chemically, there is no reason to assume that the natural immune system must have the dynamics of *either* a 'P-P' network *or* a 'P-E' network, so a network that allows both types of binding is probably biologically most accurate. In an artificial setting, such a network also suggests interesting dynamical properties. Not only can all the dynamics above be obtained, by controlling the amount of each type of network interaction, extra dynamics are likely as a result of the varied ways that the B-cells can interact with each other and with the antigen. This has yet to be investigated.

4   Method

In principle one might create a model for each of the possible models in Table 1, however this would be tedious and time consuming. As an alternative, more general solution, a Generic Immune Network (GIN) is presented, in two forms, that can exhibit the dynamics of any of the network dynamics (resulting from any of the B-cell representations just discussed) including clonal selection.

A GIN has several benefits. Firstly, if it were fully analysed for its dynamics (for example, by qualitative reasoning (QR) (Kuipers, 1984)) then every specialisation of a GIN, such as CLONALG, would exhibit a subset of the behaviours observed from the GIN. Secondly, by beginning with a GIN and then later specialising to a simpler implementation, it is likely that fewer false assumptions will be designed in. To some extent this approach has been taken by Stadler et al. (1994) who model an immune network with replicator equations. They claim that any immune system can be modelled by a set of m-dimensional replicator equations; however, they do not set out to model generic B-cell representations, as discussed here. Moreover 2^n replicator equations are required. For reasons of simplicity, therefore, we prefer the models below.

Two suggestions are made for the style of the GIN. It may be a population-based method in which the dynamics are synchronised, or it may be a stochastic, asynchronous cellular automata-style system where each cell has its own internal state and changes from state to state as required, and meets other cells in a random manner. Both styles appear to produce similar results: the cellular automata version is shown below and the synchronised population version follows.

4.1   A Cellular Automata GIN

1. Choose the values of $|P_1|$ and $|P_2|$, the sizes of two populations.
2. Define an initial population P_1 of B-cell objects that have either one or two random, identical paratope regions, and between 1 and e_1 epitopes, and set their initial fitness to zero.
3. Define an initial population P_2 of antigen objects that have between 1 and e_2 epitopes. (If the GIN implementation is being used to optimise a function then the values of the epitopes are incidental: it is the matching/fitness function that will matter.)
4. While termination condition not met:
   (a) Randomly choose a $p_i \in P_1$.

(b) Randomly choose a $p_j \in sub(P_1, k1) \cup sub(P_2, k2)$, where $k1, k2$ are constants that define the size of a stochastic subset of the population, given by the $sub()$ function.

(c) Assess the match between p_i and p_j according to some matching function $m = M(p_i, p_j)$, ensuring that p_i and p_j have free paratopes or epitopes for matching to occur. If the GIN is being used to optimise a function then the matching function should be a fitness or cost function.

(d) If $m > as$, where as is an affinity scalar, then consider the two entities to be bound and change the internal state of the entities to reflect this fact. Also reduce the number of free binding sites. Set a binding strength value, bsv, that is functionally related to the value of m. Add m to the fitness of p_i and subtract it from the fitness of p_j.

(e) If the fitness of a random, unbound $p_j \in P_1 \cup P_2 < 0$, then delete it from its population.

(f) Randomly choose a bound pair and halve their bsv; if now $bsv < as$ then consider the two entities to have separated, and change their internal states, including the number of free binding sites, to reflect this fact.

(g) Randomly choose an unbound B-cell and perform clonal selection and affinity maturation by creating clones in proportion to its fitness, and by mutating each clone inversely proportionally to its fitness.

(h) Delete a random d percent of the non-bound P_1 population (cell death).

(i) Either create a random c percent members of P_1 (cell creation), or enough new population members to keep the population size constant.

There are twelve parameters in this algorithm, two of which are functions: population sizes 1 and 2; e_1 and e_2, the number of epitopes; the number of evaluations; $k1$ and $k2$, the subset proportion constants that control the degree of networking; the choice of matching function; as, the affinity scalar; the choice of binding strength function; d, the percent of the population to die, and c, the percent/number of new members to add to the population.

4.2   A Synchronised Population GIN

The synchronised version is identical for steps 1–3, and has step 4 as follows:

4. While termination condition not met:

(a) For each member of $p_i \in P_1$ take each $p_j \in P_1 \cup P_2$, and match them if a random number in $[0,1) > nk$, the network proportion scalar, which controls the degree of network connectivity.

(b) Assess the match between each p_i and its list of p_j according to some matching function $m = M(p_i, p_j)$. Since there is no internal state in this GIN scheme, we just chose an epitope for binding at random, and the number of paratopes makes no difference. If the GIN is being used to optimise a function then the matching function should be a fitness or cost function. Sum the values of m for each p_j to give $msum$.

(c) Add $msum$ to the fitness of p_i and subtract each m individually from the fitness of the appropriate p_j.

(d) Order the population by fitness and perform clonal selection on the top t percent by creating clones in proportion to fitness, and by mutating each clone inversely proportionally to its fitness.

(e) Either create a random c percent members of P_1 or enough new population members to keep the population constant. In evolutionary computing terms, these are random immigrants. Consider the mutated clones and the new population members to be the new population, P_1', all having a fitness of zero.

Clearly the dynamics will be different since the second type of GIN can not properly implement multiple paratopes due to lack of memory.

There are ten parameters in this algorithm, one of which is a function: population sizes 1 and 2; e_1 and e_2 the number of epitopes; number of evaluations; nk, the network proportion scalar; the matching function; as, the affinity scalar; t, the top percent of the population to clone, and c, the percent/number of new members to add to the population.

Currently a B-cell only survives for one generation; this partly makes it clear that the results are not at all due to elitist convergence and partly simplifies the algorithm. This does not lead to much discontinuity between generations since the clones will be similar to their parents.

Note that in the synchronised population GIN there is only one evaluation operation and one sorting operation per generation. This makes it more efficient than other clonal selection algorithms such as CLONALG, which it approximates when $nk = 0$. However, since the cellular automata GIN does not require the population to be sorted at any point, it is even more scalable than the synchronised population GIN that does require sorting, typically it is the difference between $O(N)$ and $O((N/P)logN + N) = O(NlogN)$, where N is the number of evaluations and P is the size of the population.

5   Conclusions and Further Work

It has been shown that it is theoretically possible to unify several of the variable features of both immune networks and clonal selection into a GIN. This can provide a valuable test-bed for AIS ideas, and a useful tool for immune modelling. Furthermore it could be formally analysed to give given a set of behaviours that would be a superset of the behaviours of all simpler models. Simpler immune network models could be developed more quickly and reliably since they would spring from a well-defined, well-formed GIN.

Both forms of GIN ('cellular automata' and 'synchronised population') have been instantiated and are currently being tested in two applications, ARPEN-'A' and ARPEN-'B' (Adjustable Relationship Paratope-Epitope Network). This work needs to be developed further before being reported.

Some of the ideas mentioned in the literature discussed above could be of great use here, particularly the use of replicator equations (Stadler et al., 1994) and an analysis of frustrated and chaotic systems (Bersini and Calenbuhr, 1997).

References

Bersini, H., Calenbuhr, V., 1997. Frustrated chaos in biological networks. J. Theor. Biol. 188, 187–200.

Burnet, F. M., 1959. The Clonal Selection Theory of Acquired Immunity. Cambridge University Press.

De Boer, R. J., Kevrekidis, I. G., Perelson, A. S., 1992. Immune network behavior II: From oscillations to chaos and stationary states. Only the long abstract could be obtained for this paper.

de Castro, L. N., Von Zuben, F. J., 2000. The clonal selection algorithm with engineering applications. In: Proceedings of GECCO'00, Workshop on Artificial Immune Systems and Their Applications. pp. 36–37.

de Castro, L. N., Von Zuben, F. J., 2001. AINET: An artificial immune network for data analysis. In: Abbass, H. A., Sarker, R. A., Newton, C. S. (Eds.), Data Mining: A Heuristic Approach. Idea Group Publishing, USA, Ch. XII, pp. 231–259.

Farmer, J., Packard, N., Perelson, A., 1986. The immune system, adaptation and machine learning. Physica D 22, 187–204.

Holland, J. H., 1976. Escaping brittleness: The possiblities of general purpose learning algorithms applied to parallel rule-based systems. In: Michalski, R. S., Carbonell, J. G., Mitchell, T. M. (Eds.), Machine Learning 2. Kaufman, pp. 593–623.

Jerne, N., 1974. Towards a network theory of the immune system. Annals of Immunology 125, 373–389.

Kleinstein, S. H., Seiden, P. E., July/August 2000. Simulating the immune system. Computing in Science and Engineering , 69–77.

Knight, T., Timmis, J., 2001. AINE: An immunological approach to data mining. In: Cercone, N., Lin, T., Wu, X. (Eds.), IEEE International Conference on Data Mining. San Jose, CA. USA, pp. 297–304.

Kuipers, B., 1984. Commonsense reasoning about causality: Deriving behavior from structure. Artificial Intelligence 24, 169–204.

Lydyard, P. M., Whelan, A., Fanger, M. W., 2000. Instant Notes in Immunology. BIOS Scientific Publishers Ltd.

Oudin, J., Cazenava, P., 1971. Similar idiotopic specificities in immunoglobin fractions with different antibody functions or even without detectable antibody function. Proc. Natn. Acad. Sci. 68, 2616–2620.

Perelson, A. S., Weisbuch, G., 1997. Immunology for physicists. Rev. Modern Phys. 69, 1219–1267.

Smith, D. J., Forrest, S., Perelson, A. S., 1996. Immunological memory is associative. In: Int. Conference of Multiagent Systems. Kyoto, Japan, pp. 62–70, workshop Notes, Workshop 4: Immunity Based Systems.

Stadler, P. F., Schuster, P., Perelson, A. S., 1994. Immune networks modelled by replicator equations. J. Math. Biol. 33, 111–137.

Stewart, J., Varela, F. J., 1991. Morphogensis in shape space. Elementary metadynamics in a model of the immune network. J. Theor. Biol. 153, 477–498.

Timmis, J., Neal, M., Hunt, J., 2000. An artificial immune system for data analysis. Biosystems 55 (1/3), 143–150.

Vertosick, F., Kelly, R., 1991. The immune system as a neural network: A multi-epitope approach. Journal of Theoretical Biology 150, 225–237.

Revisiting the Foundations of Artificial Immune Systems: A Problem-Oriented Perspective

Alex A. Freitas and Jon Timmis

Computing Laboratory
University of Kent
Canterbury, CT2 7NF, UK
{A.A.Freitas,J.Timmis}@kent.ac.uk

Abstract. Since their development, AIS have been used for a number of machine learning tasks including that of classification. Within the literature, there appears to be a lack of appreciation for the possible bias in the selection of various representations and affinity measures that may be introduced when employing AIS in classification tasks. Problems are then compounded when inductive bias of algorithms are not taken into account when applying seemingly generic AIS algorithms to specific application domains. This paper is an attempt at highlighting some of these issues. Using the example of classification, this paper explains the potential pitfalls in representation selection and the use of various affinity measures. Additionally, attention is given to the use of negative selection in classification and it is argued that this may be not an appropriate algorithm for such a task. This paper then presents ideas on avoiding unnecessary mistakes in the choice and design of AIS algorithms and ultimately delivered solutions.

1 Introduction

Artificial Immune Systems (AIS) are a relatively new computational intelligence paradigm [5]. As in other computational intelligence paradigms, the main goal is to design effective problem-solving algorithms, rather than to model a biological phenomenon. Intuitively the design of an AIS algorithm should be strongly determined by the kind of problem that the algorithm will try to solve. However, this is not always the case in the AIS literature. In some cases we can observe a certain mismatch between the design of the algorithm and the problem being solved by the algorithm. This paper illustrates a number of these mismatches and suggests ways to remove them, and a problem-oriented perspective is advocated for designing and applying AIS algorithms.

It should be noted that AIS algorithms are normally designed to be generic algorithms. Hence, the criticism presented in this paper is not intended to be a criticism to the design of current generic AIS algorithms nor as a criticism of the AIS paradigm as a whole. Rather, the core idea of our criticism is that, when applying a generic AIS

J. Timmis et al. (Eds.): ICARIS 2003, LNCS 2787, pp. 229–241, 2003.

algorithm to a well-defined and specific problem, the algorithm typically needs to be adapted to specific characteristic of the problem at hand, a new AIS algorithm more suitable to that problem must be designed.

Before we proceed, it is necessarily to specify the scope of this paper. The field of AIS is too big to be revisited as a whole in a single conference paper. Hence, this paper focuses on one kind of application of AIS, which allows us to focus the discussion on important issues in the design of AIS algorithms for that kind of application. The selected application involves classification and other related tasks involving prediction, which is sometimes referred to as supervised learning. In the classification task the goal is to predict the class of an example (a record, or data instance), given the values of a set of attributes – called the predictor attributes – for that example. The motivation for focusing in this task is two-fold. First, this is an important task in the context of computational intelligence, and it has been extensively studied in several fields such as machine learning [15], data mining [23] and pattern recognition. Second, this task has been less studied in the field of AIS, where only recently an AIS algorithm specifically designed for classification has been proposed [22], [21]. Hence, there is a strong need for a comprehensive discussion on important issues in the design and application of AIS algorithms for classification and related tasks.

In order to organize the sequence of ideas and arguments presented in this paper, we decided to follow the high-level structure of the framework for engineering AIS algorithms proposed by [5]. According to this framework, the design of an artificial immune system contains three basic elements, namely:

a) a representation for the components of the system – in this paper we are mainly interested in the representation of antibodies and antigens in the context of the classification task;

b) an affinity measure, which quantifies the interactions between components of the system – in this paper we are mainly interested in affinity functions measuring the similarity between an antibody and an antigen, in the context of classification;

c) an immune algorithm – in this paper we are particularly interested in analyzing the effectiveness of the negative selection algorithm for the classification task.

The remainder of this paper is organized as follows. Section 2 briefly reviews the concept of inductive bias, a key concept in classification. Section 3 discusses issues in the choice of antibody/antigen representation. Section 4 discusses issues in the choice of affinity functions. Section 5 discusses issues in the use of the negative selection algorithm for classification. Finally, section 6 summarizes the paper.

We emphasize that the issues involving the negative selection algorithm are considered only in section 5. Sections 3 and 4 are independent of any AIS algorithm.

2 A Review of the Concept of Inductive Bias

This section briefly reviews the important concept of inductive bias, which will support the discussions about issues in the choice of antibody/antigen representation and affinity functions to be presented in later sections of this paper.

As pointed out by [12], given a set of observed facts (data instances), the number of hypotheses – e.g. classification rules - that imply these facts is potentially infinite. Hence, a classification algorithm *must* have an *inductive bias*. An inductive bias can be defined as any (explicit or implicit) basis for favoring one hypothesis over another, other than strict consistency with the data being mined – see [14], [15]. Note that without an inductive bias a classification algorithm would be unable to prefer one hypothesis over other consistent ones. In machine learning terminology, a classification algorithm without an inductive bias would be capable of performing only the simplest kind of learning, namely rote learning.

We emphasize here a well-known fact about classification. Any bias has a *domain-dependent* effectiveness. Since every classification algorithm has a bias, the performance of a classification algorithm strongly depends on the application domain. In other words, claims such as "classification algorithm A is better than classification algorithm B" should only be made for a given (or a few) application domain(s). This has been shown both theoretically – see [18], [17] – and empirically – see [13].

There are two major types of inductive bias, namely representation bias and preference bias [15], [7]. Representation bias is associated with the knowledge representation used by the algorithm. For instance, suppose the algorithm's knowledge representation consists of rule conditions expressed in prepositional logic – where each condition is an attribute-value pair such as *Income > 50,000* – but not in first-order logic. Then the algorithm will not be able to discover rule conditions involving relations between two attributes, such as *Income > Expenditure*.

Preference bias is associated with the evaluation function used by an algorithm to measure the quality of a candidate hypothesis. In the Instance-Based Learning (IBL) paradigm [1], also called nearest neighbours or lazy learning, preference bias is determined mainly by the distance function used to measure the distance between a pair of examples (data items). This is directly relevant for the discussion of AIS algorithms in this paper, because many AIS algorithms also have to use some kind of distance function to measure the "affinity" between an antibody and an antigen, as will be discussed in the next sections.

3   Issues in the Choice of Antibody/Antigen Representation

We follow [5] in assuming the general case in which each antibody Ab (a "pattern detector") is represented by an L-dimensional vector $\mathbf{Ab} = <Ab_1, Ab_2, ..., Ab_L>$, and each antigen Ag (a data item, or record, to be classified) is represented by an L-dimensional vector $\mathbf{Ag} = <Ag_1, Ag_2, ..., Ag_L>$, where L is the length (i.e., the number of coordinates) of the vectors.

At least three basic kinds of representations can be used.

Binary representations – In this case the matching between an antibody and an antigen is typically based on computing the number of bits that are the same (or different, depending on whether we want to measure similarity or distance) in a pair of vectors **<Ab, Ag>**.

Continuous (numeric) representations – In this case the coordinates of the antibody and antigen vectors are either real-valued or integer-valued, and the matching between an antibody and an antigen is typically based on a distance metric such as the Euclidean distance or the Manhattan distance – the differences between these distance metrics will be discussed later.

Categorical (nominal) representations – In this case the coordinates of the antibody and antigen vectors are categorical or nominal values, such as the values *female* and *male* of the attribute *Gender*. It is important to distinguish categorical representations from continuous one because in the former there is no notion of "order" between the values, unlike continuous representations. Note that in general binary representations can be considered a particular case of categorical ones.

Finally, hybrid representations are possible and *intuitively desirable* when coping with data sets having attributes of different data types. (Note that this also holds in evolutionary algorithms for data mining [7].) This point does not seem fully appreciated in the AIS literature, where sometimes a single kind of data representation is artificially used, and as a result the data has to be somehow "adapted" to the AIS algorithm (see below), rather than adapting the algorithm to the data. Intuitively, the latter would be more natural – and probably more effective. In some cases, the approach of "adapting" the data to the algorithm will even throw away some potentially relevant data just because the algorithm cannot handle that data. For instance, [4] apply a negative selection algorithm to a multidimensional personnel data containing both categorical and numeric data. However, instead of using a hybrid categorical/numeric representation and take all the attributes into account, they simply ignore categorical attributes and work only with numeric attributes. This approach seems unnatural and, from a problem-oriented point of view, it does not seem very effective, since it throws away potentially relevant attributes.

This could be avoided by using a hybrid categorical/numeric antibody and antigen representation, with a correspondingly adapted affinity measure. In particular, an affinity measure for categorical attributes will be discussed in subsection 4.3. That measure could be used in a number of AIS algorithms that currently handle only continuous attributes, and not categorical attributes. This includes AIRS, which, although designed for classification, seems to have the limitation – in its current version [22] – of coping only with continuous attributes.

4   Issues in the Choice of Affinity Functions

4.1   Affinity Functions for Binary Antibody/Antigen Representation

When using binary representation, a natural and simple affinity function is the well-known Hamming distance (or its complement), which counts the number of bit positions with the same value (1 or 0) in the antibody and antigen being matched. Other affinity functions have also been used, in particular the r-contiguous bits rule.

An antibody Ab and an antigen Ag are said to match under the r-contiguous bits rule if Ab and Ag have the same bit value in at least r contiguous bit positions. Ideally, the use of this affinity function (or any other affinity function) should be justified taken into account the data being mined, but this is not usually the case in the literature. The r-contiguous bits rule or its variants are often used without any specific justification for this choice [3], [4], [19]. When a justification is presented, it is usually the fact that this rule is more *biologically plausible* than the Hamming distance [9], [5] (p. 70). We do not find this argument satisfactory, for two related reasons.

First, for the general case, we do not think that this particular metaphor with biology is desirable in AIS algorithms for analysing data. Why not? Because in this case the metaphor involves a *physical* (rather than *logical*) characteristic of the natural immune system. As a rule of thumb, AIS algorithms should use metaphors based on logical (rather than physical) characteristics of the natural immune system, which intuitively tend to be more generic and so more appropriate as an inspiration to design AIS algorithms for analysing data in a virtual data space. In the particular case in question, in the natural immune system a contiguous, position-dependent matching makes sense, because the lymphocytes and antigens have a contiguous genetic material in physical 3-D space. However, in data mining and machine learning the artificial lymphocytes and antigens are *virtual* entities, and the AIS algorithm does a search in an *abstract* data space. In this kind of space it is usually more natural to consider that the attributes (or features) represented by lymphocytes and antigens are not ordered, so that the notion of contiguousness is not a natural one, of course unless this is dictated by the application area. This point is further discussed in the next paragraphs.

Second, the argument ignores the data set being mined. The choice of a particular affinity function determines a part of the inductive bias of the AIS algorithm. As mentioned in section 2, the fact that the effectiveness of an inductive bias is entirely data set-dependent is well established in the machine learning and data mining communities. So, the choice of an affinity function should be made by taking into account the data set being mined and the problem being solved. It is important to understand that r-contiguous bits rule have a *positional bias*. For instance, in [9] each lymphocyte represents a "data-path triple" describing a connection between computers, consisting of 3 values: the source IP address, the destination IP address and the service (or port) by which the computers communicate. These 3 values are represented by a single 49-bit string. Let B_{source}, B_{dest} and B_{serv} be the (sub)strings of bits used to represent the values of those 3 variables, respectively. Hence, each lymphocyte is a string obtained by concatenating those 3 (sub)strings. There are 6 different permutations of those (sub)strings that can be used to form the string representing a lymphocypte, namely: $<B_{source}, B_{dest}, B_{serv}>$, $<B_{source}, B_{serv}, B_{dest}>$, $<B_{dest}, B_{source}, B_{serv}>$, $<B_{dest}, B_{serv}, B_{source}>$, $<B_{serv}, B_{source}, B_{dest}>$, $<B_{serv}, B_{dest}, B_{source}>$. Since the r-contiguous bits rules takes the position of the bits into account, the result of the algorithm – i.e., the evolved detectors, the true positive and false positive rate, etc. – will be different for each of those 6 permutations. This is an inductive bias, since this difference in the results has nothing to do with consistency with the data. It is a side-effect of different, arbitrary choices of (sub)string permutations.

The problem is by no means restricted to this particular application domain/data set. It is much more generic. The basic problem is that in tasks related to classification and anomaly detection each detector or pattern recognizer evolved by an AIS – corresponding to a candidate solution to the underlying problem – usually represents a *set* of attributes (features), in the mathematical sense of a set, i.e., an *unordered* collection of elements without duplications. Hence, the position of attributes is irrelevant, from the point of view of the machine learning or data mining algorithm. Indeed, the vast majority of classification algorithms treat the attributes of the data as a set, and they obtain results that are independent of the order of the attributes in the file or internal data structure used by the program. Hence, they do not have the positional bias associated with the r-contiguous bits rule. This is *not* to say that we should always remove positional bias, since any bias has a domain-dependent effectiveness (section 2). Hence, the decision on whether or not to use an affinity function with a positional bias should be made by taking into account the data set being mined.

4.2   Affinity Functions for Continuous Antibody/Antigen Representation

When dealing with numeric data, the majority of the AIS literature uses the Euclidean distance (or its complement, if measuring similarity) as the affinity function, as specified in formula (1). It is interesting to note that, in general, this choice of affinity function is not justified in the literature. Presumably, authors of AIS algorithms implicitly assume that the Euclidean distance is a "natural" or "default" distance metric. Sometimes authors mention that other distance metrics – such as the Manhattan distance, specified in formula (2), where "$|x|$" denotes the absolute value of x – could be used as well, but without discussing the pros and cons of these two distance metrics.

$$Dist(Ab, Ag) = (\sum_{i=1}^{L} (Ab_i - Ag_i)^2)^{1/2} \quad (1) \qquad\qquad Dist(Ab, Ag) = \sum_{i=1}^{L} |Ab_i - Ag_i| \quad (2)$$

An exception is the AIS textbook of [5] (p. 65), where the authors make the following comment: "Although no report of the latter [Manhattan distance] has yet been found in the literature, the Manhattan distance constitutes an interesting alternative to Euclidean distance, mainly for parallel (hardware) implementation of algorithms based on the shape-space formalism."

We agree with the basic idea of this comment, but we would like to add two comments. First, the Manhattan distance tends to be computationally more efficient than the Euclidean distance even in sequential (non-parallel) implementations, since the former involves no exponentiation or square root operation. Second, we believe that it is important to go further in the analysis of the pros and cons of these two distance metrics. In addition to the issue of computational efficiency, there is an important issue of effectiveness. These two distance metrics have different *inductive biases*, and so they tend to be effective for different kinds of data set. To understand this point, let us consider the very simple example shown in Figure 1, involving a two-dimensional data set. Antigen Ag is at the origin (coordinates <0,0>) of the graph, antibody Ab₁ is at coordinates <4,4>, and antibody Ab₂ is at coordinates <6,1>. Now, which of the two antibodies is "closer" (i.e., has higher affinity to) the antigen Ag? The answer depends on the choice of distance metric. Let Dist(Ag, Ab) be the distance between antigen Ag and antibody Ab. If we use the Euclidean Distance we have:

$$\text{Dist(Ag, Ab}_1) = (4^2 + 4^2)^{1/2} = 5.66 \quad \text{and} \quad \text{Dist(Ag, Ab}_2) = (6^2 + 1^2)^{1/2} = 6.08$$

On the other hand, if we use the Manhattan distance we have:

$$\text{Dist(Ag, Ab}_1) = 4 + 4 = 8 \quad \text{and} \quad \text{Dist(Ag, Ab}_2) = 6 + 1 = 7.$$

Hence, the nearest antibody to antigen Ag is Ab_1 according to the Euclidean distance, but it is Ab_2 according to the Manhattan distance.

Why did the two distance measures lead to such a different result? Because they have different inductive biases. In particular, the Euclidean distance overemphasizes (by comparison with the Manhattan distance) large differences in the values of one or few individual attributes (coordinates). Intuitively, this makes this distance more sensitive to noisy data. That is, a single error in the value of one coordinate in the antibody or antigen vectors can be considerably amplified by the Euclidean distance formula. By contrast, the Manhattan distance tends to be more robust to noisy data, in the sense that errors in the value of one or few attributes will have relatively little impact (by comparison with the Euclidean distance) in the computation of the distance between an antibody and an antigen.

To summarize, the choice between Euclidean distance or Manhattan distance (or any other affinity function) should not be done in an arbitrary way. This is an important choice, having an influence not only in the computational efficiency but also (and usually more importantly) in the effectiveness of the algorithm, and this choice should be done by taking into account characteristics of the data being mined.

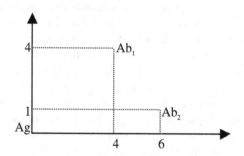

Fig. 1. Euclidean distance vs. Manhattan distance – a very simple example

4.3 An Affinity Function for Categorical Antibody/Antigen Representation

The antibody/antigen representation and corresponding affinity functions of AIS algorithms usually focus on either binary or continuous (numeric) representations. From a machine learning/data mining viewpoint, this is a significant limitation, since many real-world data sets contain categorical attributes.

Hence, it is important to review here a distance measure specifically designed for coping with categorical attributes, which could be used as an affinity function in AIS algorithms where the antibodies and antigens contain categorical data. To the best of our knowledge, this measure has not been used yet in the AIS literature. This measure is called Value Difference Metric [20], [11], and it is defined by formula (3):

$$\text{Dist}(Ab_i, Ag_i) = \sum_{c \text{ in } C} (Pr(c|Ab_i) - Pr(c|Ag_i))^2 \qquad (3)$$

where $\text{Dist}(Ab_i, Ag_i)$ is the distance between the values of the i-th attribute of the antibody Ab and antigen Ag being matched, C is the set of classes (values of the class attribute), c denotes the c-th class, and $Pr(c|Ab_i)$ – or $Pr(c|Ag_i)$ – denotes the empirical conditional probability that the class of an example (data instance) is c given that the example has the value Ab_i – or Ag_i – for its i-th attribute. That is, $Pr(c|Ab_i)$ is the ratio of the number of training examples having class c and i-th attribute value Ab_i divided by the number of training examples having i-th attribute value Ab_i. $Pr(c|Ag_i)$ is computed in the analogous way. Note that the above formula measures similarity between values of a single categorical attribute, so of course it must be applied once for each categorical attribute in the antibody/antigen representation.

The rationale for the above formula is to measure the "distance" between two categorical values as a function of the difference between the class probability distributions associated with the two values. That is why the index c in the summation symbol ranges over all classes in the set C.

5   Issues in the Use of Negative Selection for Classification

In this section we revisit the use of the negative selection algorithm in classification and related tasks, which has been a popular application of this kind of algorithm. The negative selection algorithm was originally proposed as an anomaly-detection (or change-detection) algorithm in the application domain of computer security [6]. It is based on a metaphor with the process of negative selection of T-cells in the thymus, where T-cells that match self are eliminated [5]. Hence, the mature T-cells leaving the thymus will not, in general, match self, and will therefore match only non-self.

The basic idea of the negative selection algorithm – shown at a high level of abstraction in the pseudocode of Figure 2 – is simple. The algorithm uses, as input, a set of "normal" examples, called the *self*. It iteratively generates – at random – immature T-cells and tries to match them with all the examples in the self. If a T-cell matches at least one example in the self it is discard, otherwise it is promoted to a mature T-cell and it is output by the algorithm. This iterative process is repeated until a stopping criterion is satisfied, such as sufficient coverage of the non-self space has been achieved. Once this "training phase" (originally called "censoring") is over, the set of mature T-cells are used to monitor changes or anomalies in the data in a "testing phase" (originally called "monitoring phase"). That is, each new example (data item) is compared with each mature T-cell. If the example matches a mature T-cell an anomaly or change has been detected, so that the example is considered to be a *non-self* example. Otherwise the example is considered to be a *self* example.

Input: a set of "normal" examples (data items), called *the self* (*S*)
Output: a set of "mature" T-cells that do not match any example in *S*
REPEAT
  Randomly generate an "immature" T-cell (detector)
  Measure the affinity (similarity) between this T-cell and each example in *S*
  IF the affinity between the T-cell and at least one example in S is greater than
    a user-defined threshold
  THEN discard this T-cell
  ELSE output this T-cell as a "mature" T-cell
UNTIL stopping criterion

Fig. 2. Pseudocode of the Negative Selection Algorithm

In the previous discussion we have used the terms training and testing set to cast the negative selection algorithm as a kind of classification algorithm, which is often done in the AIS literature. (Note that we are *not* defending such casting, we will rather criticize it.) More precisely, the algorithm is often used to classify examples into two classes, the *self* class and the *non-self* class. In conventional machine learning terminology, non-self examples are called positive examples (since the goal of the mature T-cells is to detect these examples) and the self examples are called negative examples. Indeed, under this framework the performance measure of the algorithm typically involves the true positive (TP) rate – i.e., the number of positive (non-self) examples correctly detected by the mature T-cells divided by the total number of positive examples – and the false positive (FP) rate – i.e., the number of negative (self) examples wrongly detected by the mature T-cells divided by the total number of negative examples. The goal is, of course, to maximize the TP rate and to minimize the FP rate. Some examples of this use of the negative selection algorithm and its variations/extensions can be found in [3], [8], [2], [10].

Let us now present a critical review of the use of the negative selection algorithm for classification and related tasks. First, the algorithm is inefficient and time-consuming, as a vast number of random detectors need to be discarded before the required number of competent detectors is obtained. Second, it should be noted that the negative selection algorithm (in its basic form) has just one means of generating detectors: at random. As pointed out by [5], p. 78, this means that the generation of detectors is not adaptive and it does not use any information in the set of self examples to guide the search. In other words, in essence the algorithm – in its basic, original form – performs a type of random search.

Furthermore, we would like to point out that the negative selection algorithm has no mechanism to minimize the danger of overfitting and oversearching – which are important mechanisms in a classification algorithm [15]. In essence, overfitting occurs when the classification algorithm learns a model that is adapted to idiosyncrasies of the training set that are unlikely to occur in an unseen test set. A related problem is oversearching [16], which occurs when the algorithm considers too many hypotheses and finds a hypothesis that reflects a spurious ("fluke") relationship, again unlikely to be true in an unseen test set.

In order to mitigate some of these limitations, the original version of the algorithm has been extended by several authors to make it adaptive. For instance, [8] proposed to use a genetic algorithm (GA) to evolve detectors in the form of IF-THEN rules covering the non-self space. [2] also proposed to use a GA as a form of affinity maturation for antibodies, although in this work the use of the GA is considered an optional aspect of the antibody life cycle, since it is very computationally expensive. Despite these advances, in general the algorithms developed in these projects are still based on one idea which is at the core of the negative selection algorithm, namely the fact that the "training" (censoring) phase of the algorithm uses only examples of one class (the self), rather than examples of two classes (self and non-self). On the other hand, the "testing" (monitoring) phase must use both self and non-self examples. After all, when monitoring new examples (say, new data packets, or new network connections), each example can be either a self (e.g., non-attack) or non-self (e.g., a network attack), and we do not know which is the true class of the example when it is being classified. This is the whole point of the classification task: the algorithm has to classify examples in the test set without knowing the true class of the example. Classification involves prediction, and the above-mentioned TP and FP rates are measures of predictive accuracy.

Now, the extended versions of the negative selection algorithms discussed in [3], [8], [2] use a test set containing both self and non-self examples – as they should, of course – but use a training set containing only self examples – due to the fact that the core of those algorithms is the negative selection algorithm, trained only on self examples, as mentioned earlier. This raises the question of how effective these algorithms are, by comparison with more conventional classification algorithms that use a training set containing data from all the classes – i.e., both self and non-self. This is an open question at present, because unfortunately, in general comparison between these two kinds of algorithms are not reported in the literature.

To summarize, if the task being solved is classification, where we want to predict the class of examples in a test set that is completely separated from the training set, the conventional approach is to use a training set containing examples of all the classes that occur in the test set. The use of the negative selection algorithm goes against this approach, because it uses only examples of one class for training. Intuitively, this would reduce the predictive accuracy of the algorithm on the test set. Therefore, in classification or other prediction tasks the use of the negative selection algorithm does not seem to be the best approach; in principle, it would seem better to use an AIS algorithm which was specifically developed for classification, such as the AIRS algorithm [22], [21].

We emphasize that the criticism in this section refers to the use of the negative selection algorithm in classification, and *not* to the use of this algorithm in a simpler anomaly-detection task, as initially proposed by [6].

6   Summary and Future Research

In this paper we have presented an application-oriented criticism of artificial immune systems (AIS) and their use in the classification task. The motivation for this criticism is that in the AIS field this task has often been used by using generic AIS algorithms, which have not been tailored for this task. Clearly, the design of generic AIS algorithms is important, but it is also important to recognize that specific applications, such as classification, have specific requirements that have to be incorporated into the design of an AIS algorithm applied to this task.

More precisely, the classification-related issues discussed in this paper were divided into three broad groups, corresponding to the three basic elements of the AIS framework proposed by [5], namely representation, affinity function and immune algorithm.

Concerning representation, we have emphasized the importance of using hybrid antibody/antigen representations that can represent both categorical and continuous data, since both these data types are commonplace in real-world data sets. By contrast, the AIS algorithms currently being used for classification typically use either a binary or a continuous representation, and they tend to ignore categorical attributes, which limits their application.

Concerning affinity functions, most AIS algorithms for classification use functions such as Hamming distance, the r-contiguous rules and the Euclidean distance. Clearly, this choice of functions is heavily influenced by the choice of representation – binary or continuous. We pointed out that these representations have specific inductive biases that are often ignored in the AIS literature, and these biases must be considered when choosing a particular affinity function. No inductive bias is the best across all data sets. Hence, from a problem-oriented perspective, the choice of the affinity function should be made by taking into account both the inductive bias of the affinity function and the characteristics of the data being mined. We have also drawn attention to the Value Difference Metric, a distance function specifically designed for categorical attributes. This distance metric is often used in the Instance-Based Learning (IBL) field, but it seems that it has never been used yet in the AIS field. The use of this affinity function in AIS algorithms (possibly combined with another affinity function for continuous attributes), in conjunction with the use of a categorical (or hybrid categorical/continuous) representation for antibodies and antigens, would considerably facilitate the application of AIS algorithms to data sets containing categorical attributes, which are quite common in the context of the classification task.

Concerning the immune algorithm, we have criticized the use of the negative selection algorithm (a generic AIS algorithm) in classification. More precisely, we have pointed out that the algorithm generates detectors in a random – rather than data-driven – fashion and that it has no mechanism to minimize the danger of overfitting and oversearching in the context of the classification task. The root of the problem is that the negative selection algorithm – even in its extended versions that render it more adaptive – essentially relies on a training set containing examples of a single class, whereas in classification it is important to train the algorithm in examples of all the classes that will occur in the test set.

Hence, the main contribution of this paper can be regarded as bringing concepts and principles of machine learning and data mining into the AIS field, in order to support the design of AIS algorithms that are more adapted to the classification task. In particular, among the several well-established machine learning paradigms often used in the classification task [15], the IBL paradigm seems to have a lot to offer to the AIS field, and this potential should be explored in future research.

In addition to the above example of the Value Difference Metric, another important potential contribution of the IBL paradigm to the AIS field is the use of weighted-attribute distance metrics [1]. In most classification applications, different attributes have different degrees of relevance for predicting the class attribute, which strongly suggests that AIS algorithms should be extended to use affinity functions where different attributes have different weights in the distance formula.

References

1. D.W. Aha. (Ed.) *Artificial Intelligence Review – special issue on lazy learning, 11(1-5)*, June 1997.
2. K.P. Anchor, P.D. Williams, G.H. Gunsch, and G.B. Lamont. The computer defense immune system: current and future research in intrusion detection. *Proc. Congress on Evolutionary Computation (CEC-2002)*. IEEE Press.
3. J. Balthrop, F. Esponda, S. Forrest and M. Glickman. Coverage and generalization in an artificial immune system. *Proc. Genetic and Evolutionary Computation Conf. (GECCO-2002)*, pp. 3-10. Morgan Kaufmann, 2002.
4. D. Dasgupta and N.S. Majumdar. Anomaly detection in multidimensional data using negative selection algorithm. *Proc. Congress on Evolutionary Computation (CEC-2002)*, pp. 1039-1044. IEEE Press.
5. L.N. de Castro and J. Timmis. *Artificial Immune Systems: a new computational intelligence approach*. Springer, 2002.
6. S. Forrest, A.S. Perelson, L. Allen and R. Cherukuri. Self-nonself discrimination in a computer. *Proc. IEEE Symp. On Research in Security and Privacy*, pp. 202-212. 1994.
7. A.A. Freitas. *Data Mining and Knowledge Discovery with Evolutionary Algorithms*. Springer, 2002.
8. F.A. Gonzalez and D. Dasgupta. An immunogenetic technique to detect anomalies in network traffic. *Proc. Genetic and Evolutionary Computation Conf. (GECCO-2002)*, pp. 1081-1088. Morgan Kaufmann, 2002.
9. S.A. Hofmeyr and S. Forrest. Immunity by design: an artificial immune system. *Proc. Genetic and Evolutionary Computation Conf. (GECCO-1999)*. Morgan Kaufmann, 1999.
10. J. Kim and P.J. Bentley. Towards an artificial immune system for network intrusion detection: an investigation of dynamic clonal selection. *Proc. Congress on Evolutionary Computation (CEC-2002)*. IEEE Press.
11. T.W. Liao, Z. Zhang, C.R. Mount. Similarity measures for retrieval in case-based reasoning systems. *Applied Artificial Intelligence, 12*, 267-288. 1998.
12. R. W. Michalski. A theory and methodology of inductive learning. *Artificial Intelligence 20, 1983, 111-161*.
13. D. Michie, D.J. Spiegelhalter, and C.C. Taylor. *Machine Learning, Neural and Statistical Classification*. New York: Ellis Horwood.
14. T.M. Mitchell. The need for biases in learning generalizations. *Rutgers Technical Report, 1980*. Also published in: J.W. Shavlik and T.G. Dietterich (Eds.) *Readings in Machine Learning, 184-191*. Morgan Kaufmann, 1990.
15. T.M. Mitchell. *Machine Learning*. McGraw-Hill, 1997.

16. J.R. Quinlan and R. Cameron-Jones. Oversearching and layered search in empirical learning. *Proc. 14th Int. Joint Conf. on Artificial Intelligence (IJCAI-95)*, 1019-1024. Morgan Kaufmann, 1995.

17. R.B. Rao, D. Gordon, and W. Spears. For every generalization action, is there really an equal and opposite reaction? Analysis of the conservation law for generalization performance. *Proc. 12th Int. Conf. on Machine Learning,* 471-479. Morgan Kaufmann.

18. C. Schaffer. A conservation law for generalization performance. *Proc. 11th Int. Conf. on Machine Learning, 259-265.* Morgan Kaufmann.

19. S. Singh. Anomaly detection using negative selection based on the r-contiguous matching rule. *Proc. 1st Int. Conf. on Artificial Immune Systems (ICARIS-2002),* pp. 99-106. University of Kent at Canterbury, UK, Sep. 2002.

20. G. Stanfill and D. Waltz. Towards memory-based reasoning. *Communications of the ACM, 29(12),* 1213-1228, Dec. 1986.

21. A.B. Watkins and L. Boggess. A resource limited artificial immune system classifier. *Proc. Congress on Evolutionary Computation (CEC-2002).* IEEE Press.

22. A. Watkins and J. Timmis. Artificial Immune Recognition System (AIRS): revisions and refinements. *Proc. 1st Int. Conf. on Artificial Immune Systems (ICARIS-2002),* pp. 173-181. University of Kent at Canterbury, UK, Sep. 2002.

23. I.H. Witten and E. Frank. *Data Mining: practical machine learning tools and techniques with Java implementations.* Morgan Kaufmann, 2000.

Complementary Dual Detectors
for Effective Classification

Hyi Taek Ceong[1], Young-il Kim[2], Doheon Lee[3,*], and Kwang-Hyung Lee[3,**]

[1] Department of Computer Science, Yosu National University, Republic of Korea
htceong@info.yosu.ac.kr
[2] Division of Computer Science, Department of EECS, KAIST, Republic of Korea
cutty@bioif.kaist.ac.kr
[3] Department of BioSystems, KAIST, Republic of Korea
{dhlee,khlee}@bioif.kaist.ac.kr

Abstract. In this paper we introduce a method of using a pair of complementary negative detectors. When both self and non-self antigens are given, we can build a pair of complementary negative detectors using self and non-self antigens respectively and augment the results given by the detectors. When self or non-self antigens change over time, antibodies of a negative detector that gives a false positive error for the change, are used to fill the holes of the other negative detector giving a false negative error. They try to adapt to the change in complementary ways.

1 Introduction

Natural immune systems have the ability to adaptively learn, to memorize, and to recognize self and non-self to defend the body from possibly harmful foreign pathogens. An artificial immune system(AIS) is a computational system based on the metaphors of the natural immune system [1]. Recently, there has been a lot of researches on AIS and its applications [1, 5, 8, 10, 11]

Negative detectors are pattern matching systems that detect the changes of protected strings by storing strings negatively selected with respect to the strings to be protected [2]. Since the introduction of negative detectors, interest in negative detection has been growing, especially for applications in which noticing anomalous patterns is important, like computer security and computer virus detection [5].

Chao and et al. [3] outlined features of an information immune system(IIS) that could help people deal with the glut of data. As discussed in [3], negative detectors and negative selection could be used to censor unwanted information. Unlike anomaly detection or change detection, in most information systems, we can assume we have both self and non-self examples, for examples, filtering news group articles or emails.

---

* Corresponding author
** This work was supported by the Korea Science and Engineering Foundation (KOSEF) through the Advanced Information Technology Research Center(AITrc).

J. Timmis et al. (Eds.): ICARIS 2003, LNCS 2787, pp. 242–248, 2003.
© Springer-Verlag Berlin Heidelberg 2003

In this paper we introduce a method of using a pair of complementary negative detectors by using both self and non-self antigens. Antibodies of a negative detector that gives a false positive error, can be used to fill the holes that the antibodies of the other negative detector do not detect, thus giving a false negative error.

2   Related Works

2.1   Immune Systems

Immunity is composed of both non-specific (innate immunity) and specific components (adaptive immunity). They work together in an interactive and cooperative way resulting in a more effective way than either could be alone. The adaptive immunity is of great interest in most AISs [10].

Adaptive immune system has four distinctive properties: specificity, diversity, memory, and self/non-self recognition. Functionally, an immune response consists of two interrelated events: recognition of antigen and response to that antigen, generation of effector cells and molecules. Antigen-presenting cells, B lymphocytes, and T lymphocytes are the primary cells of the immune response. For basic immune system information, read [10].

In the immune system, T cells go through a maturation process in the thymus. In the thymus T cells are censored against the normally occurring peptide patterns of the body(self). T cells that react with self are deleted in the thymus(negative selection). Only those T cells that survive this censoring operation are allowed to mature [4].

Clonal selection theory gives a model to explain the adaptive immunity [10]. On the surface of B cells, there are surface receptors that can bind to an antigen. When exposed to an antigen, a small group of B cells which bind to the antigen recognizes it. Coupled with a costimulatory signals from helper T cells, these B cells are stimulated. This simulation causes the B cells to proliferate and mature into effector cells(plasma cells and memory cells). The plasma cells secret antibodies specific for the antigen and often the secreted antibodies have higher affinity to the antigen(affinity maturation). The memory cells do not secret antibodies, but when they encounter the same antigen again, they proliferate more rapidly and mature into effector cells producing high affinity antibodies. During proliferation, the B cells go through the hyper somatic mutation. The hyper somatic mutation gives chances to develop B cells that can produce higher affinity antibodies to the antigen. However, the mutation may occur to develop B cells that are reactive to self antigens. These B cells go through a negative selection. They are either destroyed, inactivated or they go through receptor editing. B cells then go through a positive selection, only those B cells that have high affinity to the antigen are selected from cell death.

2.2   Negative Detectors

Antibodies that bind to antigens are called the complementary antibodies. Antigens can be represented as the complementary antibodies in a shape space [10].

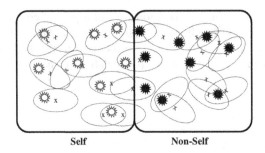

Fig. 1. Antibodies are represented as X marks and elipsoides represent the recognition region of the antibodies. White and black marks represent the complementary antibodies of self and non-self antigens.

Figure 1 shows the relation of the complementary antibodies of antigens and the recognition region of antibodies. The antigens whose complementary antibodies lie within this region are recognized by the antibody. Affinity of an antigen and an antibody can be calculated by using a similarity measure between the complementary antibody of the antigen and the antibody. Often, inverse of distance measures like hamming distance or euclidian distance are used [10].

Negative detectors are antibodies that recognize to non-self antigens and they are built with only given the self-antigens. Negative detectors are negatively selected with respect to the self-antigens. Because all negative detectors are negatively selected with respect to the self antigens, no false positive error can occur. Negative detectors are used for computer virus detection [8] and intrusion detection [5]. Forrest and et al. [2] have applied models of T cell maturation process to detect changes of computer systems. They used negative detectors to detect change of computer systems. It is difficult to build negative detectors that cover all non-self antigens [6]. There can be holes that if an antigen falls in the holes, it causes false negative errors [7].

Negative detection approach has several advantages [4]: First it has been successfully used in both engineering application and by naturally occurring biological systems. Second, if we assume a closed world, then the information can be classified in self and non-self sets. Third, it allows the detection process to be completely distributed.

3   Complementary Negative Detectors

Unlike anomaly detection or change detection, in most information systems, we can assume we have both self and non-self examples. For example, when filtering news group articles, we always have the articles that a user reads(self), and the other articles that the user does not read(non-self) and when filtering emails, we have mails that a user keep in mail boxes(self), and mails that the user classify as spam mails(non-self). After having enough such self and non-self examples, we can use them to build a pair of complementary negative detectors.

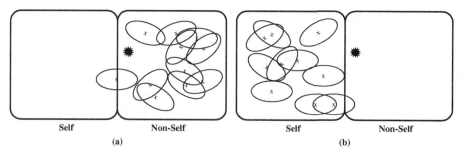

Fig. 2. The black mark shows a complementary antibody of a non-self antigen. (a) ND1 gives a false negative error.(b) ND2 gives the correct answer.

Complementary negative detectors are two detectors built by using self and non-self antigens, they detect either non-self or self antigens respectively. Negative Detector I (ND1) is a negative detector detecting non-self antigens and Negative Detector II (ND2) is a negative detector detecting self antigens. Given two sets of self and non-self antigens. Let Ab_+ be the set of the complementary antibodies of the self antigens, and Ab_- be that of the non-self antigens. We build ND1 using Ab_+ only, and ND2 with only Ab_- using negative selection [2]. Figure 2 shows a pair of complementary negative detectors, ND1 and ND2.

The final detection result can be augmented from ND1 and ND2. Since ND1 and ND2 do not give false positive errors, the final result is either that ND1 and ND2 agree with each other, or that ND1 and ND2 do not agree. If ND1 and ND2 do not agree, ND1 or ND2 is giving a false negative error.

Figure 2 gives an example of this disagreement. In this case, ND1 gives a false negative error while ND2 gives the correct answer. This is because the antibodies of ND1 do not cover the shape space correctly. This type of errors can be reduced if we can use both Ab_+ and Ab_-. In the example shown in Figure 2, we can use Ab_- to make ND1 better tuned. Ab_{ND1} and Ab_{ND2} are the set of antibodies for ND1 and ND2 respectively. For each complementary antibody(ab) in Ab_-, build a set of antibodies that recognize ab. This can be done by cloning ab with mutation, i.e., CloneMutate($\{ab\}$, Ab_-). Apply negative selection to this clones with respect to Ab_+. Update Ab_{ND1} using them. The pseudo code is given in Algorithm 1.

Algorithm 1

1. Build Ab_+ and Ab_- from self antigens and non-self antigens respectively.
2. Build ND1 using Ab_+.
   $Ab_{ND1} = \emptyset$,
   For each $ab \in Ab_-$, if ND1 do not agree with ND2,
   $Ab_{ND1} = Ab_{ND1} \cup$ NSelection(CloneMutate($\{ab\}$, Ab_-), Ab_+)
3. Build ND2 using Ab_-.
   $Ab_{ND2} = \emptyset$,
   For each $ab \in Ab_+$, if ND1 do not agree with ND2,
   $Ab_{ND2} = Ab_{ND2} \cup$ PSelection(CloneMutate($\{ab\}$, Ab_+), Ab_-)

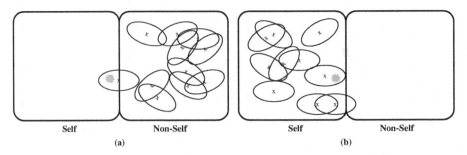

Fig. 3. Gray mark represents the complementary antibody of a new antigen. (a) ND1 gives a false positive error.(b) ND2 gives the correct answer.

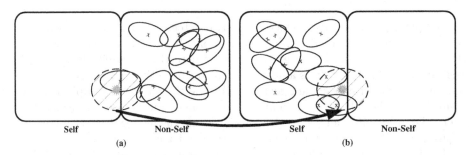

Fig. 4. Gray mark represents the complementary antibody of a new antigen. The region filled with lines shows the result of CloneMutate(PSelection(Ab_{ND1}, $\{ab\}$), $\{ab\}$). (a) ND1 gives a false positive error.(b) ND2 gives a false negative error.

PSelection() and NSelection() perform positive and negative selection on the first parameter with respect to the second parameter. CloneMutate() performs cloning with mutation elements in the first parameter are cloned according to their matching results to the second parameter, and mutation is applied to them inverse proportional to the matching result to the second parameter like CLON-ALG [10].

Negative detectors are built offline. They can not deal with the changes if self antigens changes over time. If a new antigen is introduced as shown in Figure 3 to ND1, it can give a false positive error. Ab_{ND1} has to be updated properly. Or if a new antigen cause an error shown in Figure 4, we can use Ab_{ND1} to fill the holes of Ab_{ND2}. As noted in [11], it is advisable in a distributed setting to choose a different rule for each machine, so each will have a different set of holes which are likely covered by some other machines. But if we can make use of non-self antigens, we can use antibodies of the pair of complementary negative detectors to cover holes. Antibodies of a negative detector that gives a false positive error, can be used to fill the holes that the antibodies of the other negative detector do not detect, thus giving a false negative error.

Suppose there is an orcle to tell if the detection results given by ND1 and ND2 are correct or not. In the case of email, for example, user's action can be considered as the oracle. If the oracle reports an error for the detection made by complementary negative detectors, the complementary negative detectors try to adapt Ab_{ND1} and Ab_{ND2}. The pseudo code is given in Algorithm 2.

Algorithm 2

1. Build ND1 and ND2 using algorithm1
2. If the orcale signals an error for the result given by ND1 and ND2 for a new antigen, ag,
   (a) let ab be the complementary antibody of ag.
   (b) If ab is Self, $Ab'_+ = Ab_+ \cup \{ab\}$ and $Ab'_- = Ab_- $ - PSelection($Ab_-, \{ab\}$), otherwise $Ab'_- = Ab_- \cup \{ab\}$ and $Ab'_+ = Ab_+ $ - PSelection($Ab_+, \{ab\}$).
   (c) For each cases,
      i. ND1 is false positive and ND2 is false negative
         $Ab_{ND1} = Ab_{ND1} \cup$ NSelection(CloneMutate($\{ab\}$, Ab_{ND1}),
         Ab'_+) $Ab_{ND2} = Ab_{ND2} \cup$ NSelection(CloneMutate(PSelection(Ab_{ND1}, $\{ab\}$), $\{ab\}$), Ab'_-)
      ii. ND1 is false negative and ND2 is false positive
         $Ab_{ND1} = Ab_{ND1} \cup$ NSelection(CloneMutate(PSelection(Ab_{ND2}, $\{ab\}$), $\{ab\}$), Ab'_+)
         $Ab_{ND2} = Ab_{ND2} \cup$ NSelection(CloneMutate($\{ab\}$, Ab_{ND2}), Ab'_-)
      iii. ND1 is false positive and ND2 is correct
         $Ab_{ND1} =$ NSelection(Ab_{ND1}, Ab'_+)
      iv. ND1 is correct and ND2 is false positive
         $Ab_{ND2} =$ NSelection(Ab_{ND2}, Ab'_-)
      v. ND1 is false negative and ND2 is correct
         $Ab_{ND1} = Ab_{ND1} \cup$ NSelection(CloneMutate($\{ab\}$, Ab_-), Ab'_+)
      vi. ND1 is correct and ND2 is false negative
         $Ab_{ND2} = Ab_{ND2} \cup$ NSelection(CloneMutate($\{ab\}$, Ab_+), Ab'_-)
3. $Ab_+ = Ab'_+$ and $Ab_- = Ab'_-$.

As shown in Algorithm2, when an error occurs, Ab_{ND1}, Ab_{ND2}, Ab_+ and Ab_- are updated accordingly. Then are updated according to the error types.

For example, if ND1 gives a false positive error and ND2 gives a false negative error, shown in Figure 4, then ND2 is updated using antibodies in ND1. It first searches for antibodies that recognize the ab in Ab_{ND1} and clone them with mutation. This can be written as (CloneMutate(PSelection(Ab_{ND1}, $\{ab\}$), $\{ab\}$)). Then applies negative selection to them with respect to the Ab_-. By cloning PSelection(Ab_{ND1}, $\{ab\}$), it searches for the antibodies that are near to the antibodies that recognize ab in ND1, however, it is a false positive error for ND1. On the other hand, ND2 gives a false negative error. ND2 failed to detect ab which is falsely detected by ND1. By negatively selecting PSelection(Ab_{ND1}, $\{ab\}$) with respect to Ab_-, they are used to cover the holes not deteced by ND2.

4   Discussion

In this paper, we presented a sketch of idea of using a pair of complementary negative detectors when we can use both self and non-self antigens. Negative detectors assumed that only self antigens are known [2]. However, when we can make use of both self and non-self antigens. We can build a pair of complementary negative detectors and augment them. Also, we presented how we can use the pair of complementary negative detectors to adapt to error cases by using antibodies of complementary detectors. Antibodies of a negative detector that gives a false positive error, are used to fill the holes that the antibodies of the other negative detector do not detect, thus giving a false negative error.

There are many cases when we are not restricted to only self-antigens. Many classification applications assume they have both positive, and negative examples when they train classifiers. For examples, in spam mail filtering, they often use black list of sender information, or phrase and URL information in the body content of emails. They use rule base systems to describe spam mails. It's, in a sense, a positive detection. When building negative detectors, we should be able to incorporate existing detection schemes. For example, we can use non-self antigens to generate negative detectors more efficiently as in Algorithm 1 and Algorithm 2, this way we can ensure the generated detectors covers the non-self antigens we know.

References

1. J. Timmis and M. Neal, "Investigating the Evolution and Stability of a Resource Limited Artificial Immune System", *Proc. of the Genetic and Evolutionary Computation Conference,* Workshop on Artificial Immune Systems and Their Applications, pp.40-41, (2000).
2. S. Forrest, A. Perelson, L. Allen and R. Cherukuri, "Self-Nonself Discrimination in a Computer", *Proc. of the 1994 IEEE Symposium on Research in Security and Privacy,* Los Almitos, CA:IEEE Computer Society Press, (1994).
3. D. Chao and S. Forrest, "Information Immune System", *Proc. of ICARIS 2002,* Editors: J. Timmis and P.J. Bentley, pp132-140, (2002).
4. F. Esponda, S. Forrest, and P. Helman, "A Formal Framework for Positive and Negative Detection Schemes", http://www.cs.unm.edu/ immsec/publications/Positive and Negative Detection.pdf
5. M. M. Williamson, "Biologically inspired approaches to computer security", *Tech. Rep. HPL-2002-131,* HP Laboratories, June (2002).
6. M. Ayara, J. Timmis, R. De Lemos, L. deCastro and R. Duncan, "Negative Selection: How to Generate Detectors", *Proc. of ICARIS 2002,* Editors: J. Timmis and P.J. Bentley, pp89-98, (2002).
7. S. Wierzchon, "Generating Optimal Repertoire of Antibody Strings in an Artificail Immune System", *M. A. Klopotek, M. Michalewicz, and S. T. Wierzchon, eds: Intelligent Information Systems. Advances in Soft Computing Series of Physica-Verlag/Springer Verlag,* Heidelberg/ New York (2000).
8. IBM, http://www.research.ibm.com/antivirus/, (2002)
9. "Mail Abuse Prevention System: Definition of SPAM", http://mail-abuse.org/standard.html
10. L. de Castro and J. Timmis, *Artificial Immune Systems: A New Computational Ingelligence Approach,* Springer (2002)
11. P. D'haeseleer, S. Forrest and P. Helman, "An Immunological Approach to Change Detection: Algorithms, Analysis and Implications", *Proc. of IEEE Symposium on Research in Security and Privacy,* Oakland, CA, (1996).

The Crossover Closure
and Partial Match Detection

Fernando Esponda, Stephanie Forrest, and Paul Helman

Department of Computer Science
University of New Mexico
Albuquerque, NM 87131-1386
{fesponda,forrest,helman}@cs.unm.edu

Abstract. The crossover closure generation rule characterizes the generalization achieved by artificial immune systems using partial match detection. The paper reviews earlier results and extends the previously introduced notion of crossover closure to encompass additional match rules. For concreteness, the discussion focuses on r-chunks matching, giving alternative ways that detectors can be used to implement the crossover closure.

1 Introduction

Much of the success of artificial immune systems (AIS) and other learning systems depends on the choice of representation. In an AIS it is common to represent information using a population of detectors, analogous to immune cells in the body. A matching criterion is typically defined that determines for any given detector how closely it matches a certain data item. This is analogous to receptor/ligand binding in the immune system. We refer to this as *partial match detection*, that is, detection of a concept class based on partial matching rules. In this paper, we focus on a particular class of match rules, which have formed the basis of several earlier AIS implementations. We are interested in the properties of the match rule itself, independently of how it is employed in an immune system framework. For example, many of the results we present apply both to *positive detection* and *negative detection* systems, and can be used to examine tradeoffs between these two detection schemes. In an earlier paper, we developed an extensive formal framework for analyzing positive and negative detection under various matching criteria [12]. Much of this paper is devoted to summarizing those earlier results, illuminating their importance for artificial immune systems and extending them to cover a more general set of conditions.

The paper adopts some terminology from the machine learning literature, and accordingly, the problem addressed by the paper is described as follows: Given a collection of instances drawn from some concept class, where the instances are represented as attribute vectors or strings, we wish to derive some means for inductively determining the underlying concept (or in the case of negative detection, the counter concept(s)). The resulting characterization must be flexible enough to accommodate both concept drift and distributability.

J. Timmis et al. (Eds.): ICARIS 2003, LNCS 2787, pp. 249–260, 2003.
© Springer-Verlag Berlin Heidelberg 2003

Although the paper adopts a machine learning perspective, our approach draws its inspiration from an important component of the immune system. In the immune system a collection of lymphocytes are deployed throughout the body to monitor the well-being of an organism. Lymphocytes are equipped with receptors able to bind peptides on the surface of cells, and if such a binding occurs an immune response may be initiated. T-cells, in particular, are subjected to a selection process before they are released into the body, which ensures they will recognize only nonself peptides[1]. Analogously, the proposed system is comprised of a set of *detectors*, the counterpart of lymphocytes. Whenever a new string (instance) is observed, a detector determines if the instance refers to it or not, i.e., if they bind. This said, we are interested in establishing a scheme whose generalization is readily understood and analyzed. In doing this we will be in a better position to establish mechanisms and policies to control it. In this paper we set forth the crossover closure generation rule as a learning paradigm and review a match rule and two detection schemes that implement it.

In the following sections, we first give a brief overview of related work. Then, we define a small extension of the crossover closure, giving an example and some motivation. We then review several variants of contiguous bits matching rules, introducing two new variants. In section 5, we summarize the detection schemes most relevant to the paper, and in section 6, we describe some of the interesting properties of the various r-chunks decompositions. Section 6.1 reviews our earlier results on overlapping fixed-size windows, and section 6.2 gives new results on nonoverlapping fixed size windows. We then discuss the significance of these results and conclude with a summary of the paper.

2   Related Work

The r-chunks match rule, on which our paper focuses, was introduced in [3, 12]. It is a simplification of the r-contiguous bits (rcb) match rule [13, 28, 29], which has been used in many artificial immune system projects. Modeling projects incorporating this rule include [13, 14, 28, 29], and application projects using the rule include [2, 5–8, 15, 18, 26, 30]. Many formal studies of immune algorithms are based on systems employing r-contiguous bits, e.g. [9, 10, 31–33].

The problem discussed in this paper, broadly stated, has been studied in the machine learning and statistical learning literature, often under the term "one-class learning". In [23, 24] some theoretical results for learning without counter-examples are given. A review of unsupervised learning, of which many AISs are an example, is presented in [22]. Ref. [1] discusses a variety of instance-based learning algorithms, and a survey of on-line learning algorithms can be found in [4]. Finally a comprehensive explanation of the theoretical underpinnings of classification and learning in general, can be found in [11, 16, 25, 27].

---

[1] Although T-cells undergo both positive and negative selection in the thymus, this detail is not directly relevant to this paper, as we are ignoring the role of MHC in peptide presentation.

3   The Crossover Closure

Consider a sample S (for *self*) of strings taken from a concept class RS (real self) which we wish to characterize. We adopt a simple categorical division into "similar to S" versus "dissimilar from S" and distinguish these categories by means of a *generation rule* which attempts to characterize the underlying set RS from which S is likely drawn. It has been shown experimentally that this interpretation of the detection task often captures sufficient detail of process behavior to provide effective detection [19, 20].

Definition: A generation rule Q is a mapping from a set S of length l strings to a set $Q(S)$ of length l strings containing S.

We focus our attention on a generation rule that is both simple to analyze and intuitively appealing, the crossover closure. The crossover closure was introduced in [12], where it was restricted to contiguous *windows* of attributes. Here, we remove this restriction and extend it to a set of features. The basic idea of the crossover closure is as follows: Given examples of some concept class represented as a vector of features, the crossover closure is a hypothesis stating that only some combinations of the observed features define instances of the concept class.

Consider a simple example of the concept *vehicle*, exemplified by the following instances (S), where each row of the table corresponds to a single instance:

Wheels	Color	Max. Speed (mph)
4	red	100
2	black	200

Under the crossover operator the following are also valid instances of the class vehicle:

Wheels	Color	Max. Speed (mph)
4	black	100
4	red	200
4	black	200
4	red	100
2	black	100
2	red	200
2	black	200
2	red	100

Formally, given a set S of strings, and a fixed $1 \leq r \leq l$, the crossover closure $CC(S)$ of S is defined in terms of its features as:

$$CC(S) = \{u \in U | (\forall features\ w)(\exists s \in S)\ u[w] = s[w]\} \tag{1}$$

where U is the set of possible strings and $u[w]$ is the projection of string u onto feature w. In words, a string u of length l is in the crossover closure of S if and only if each of u's features exactly matches the corresponding feature of some member of S. In the above example, instances of the concept *vehicle*

are represented as strings with three features: *Wheels, Color* and *Max. Speed.*
A string containing any combination of the sampled values for these features is
part of the crossover closure. When S is such that $CC(S) = S$ we say that S
is *closed* under crossover closure. In general, we understand a feature to be any
combination or function of attributes of the instance vectors, and not necessarily
a specific attribute. This broader interpretation of "feature" is the sense in which
this definition of crossover closure extends our earlier definition.

An interesting motivation and justification for this rule stems from the similarities it has with some well known relational database operations [12]. The
join operator and the crossover closure are closely related, under some partial
match rules, leading us to believe that the crossover closure may be a useful
characterization for many practical data sets.

The name "crossover closure" was partially inspired by the crossover operation in genetic algorithms (GA) [21]. However, these notions do not exactly
correspond, as the crossover discussed here depends on what a feature is defined
to be. For the example presented above, in which features are nonoverlapping,
the crossover closure corresponds exactly to the set of possible strings that can
be generated (from an initial population S) using the GA crossover operator
alone. However, other decompositions such as the one discussed in Sect. 6.1 do
not exactly correspond to the traditional one point (or multi-point) crossover
operator. In the overlapping case (Sect. 6.1), the crossover closure is a proper
subset of the possible strings generated by the GA's crossover operator.

4   R-Chunks Matching

As outlined in Sect. 1, an AIS is typically composed of a collection of detectors
or agents. The detectors are independent in the sense that each binding event
is determined locally by each detector on its own, even if the classification of
a string is ultimately resolved by some combination of matches. Thus, we are
interested in match rules between detectors and data than are local, but which
correspond in the aggregate to the crossover closure.

Further, a detector should be as simple as possible since we want its operation
to be efficient in generation time, storage requirements, and run-time (cost of
determining a match). Recall from the above that the instances from which the
learning process is to take place are represented as attribute vectors or strings. In
this context, a natural way to represent a detector is also as a string and to use
string matching as the method of detection. In what follows, we give examples
of a class of partial matching rules, some of which correspond to the crossover
closure generation rule. The variations appear to be interesting because they
open the possibility of more efficient algorithms for some AIS applications.

All of the rules studied in the following sections are derived from the r-
contiguous bit matching rule (rcb) introduced in [17, 28, 29]. A detector under
rcb is a string of length l, and is said to match another string, of the same length,
if it has at least r consecutive bits in common. One simplification of rcb, which
corresponds exactly to the crossover closure, is known as r-*chunks*. In r-chunks
matching, only r contiguous positions are specified, rather than fully specifying

all l attributes of a string. Thus, an r-chunks detector can be thought of as a string of r bits, together with its starting position within the string, known as its *window*. An r-chunks detector d is said to match a string x if all the symbols of d are equal to the r symbols of x in the window specified by d. More formally, if d is an r-chunk on window w, the matching rule considered is:

$$dMx \leftrightarrow x[w] = d \ .$$

where dMx denotes that detector d matches string x and $x[w]$ is the projection of string x onto window w. Therefore, an r-contiguous bit detector can be decomposed into $l - r + 1$ overlapping r-chunks detectors, as the following figure illustrates. Let $d = 1101$ be an r-contiguous bit detector with $l=4$, $r=2$ and $d[1], d[2], d[3]$ the corresponding r-chunk detectors:

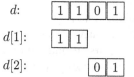

Interesting variants of the *overlapping window* r-chunks rule can be constructed, and we are currently exploring such variants and their properties. For example, we can require that the windows not overlap (the *nonoverlapping* variant) as shown in the following figure.

A second variant can be constructed by relaxing the assumption that r is fixed, although we do not study it in this paper.

It was shown in [12] that the r-chunks and the rcb match rules are not equivalent in terms of the languages they recognize. However, the result depends on the details of how the match rules are deployed, a topic addressed in the next section. In particular, under certain detection schemes (Sect. 5), it was shown that the r-chunks match rule corresponds exactly to the crossover closure and that rcb rules do not. To simplify the discussion of the crossover closure (eq.1), we focus on the special case when a feature is understood to be the r attributes encompassed by a window, and we consider the overlapping and nonoverlapping variants in sections 6.1 and 6.2 respectively.

5   Detection Schemes

In [12], a taxonomy of detection schemes was given in terms of the languages—the set of strings—that a detection scheme is able to recognize. This taxonomy is constructed along two dimensions. The first specifies whether detectors are tailored to match strings in self or nonself, denoted as P or N respectively. Many AIS systems use the idea of *negative detection*, in which a set of detectors is generated that recognizes the complement of self (known as nonself). Various claims have been made by several research groups about the efficacy of this detection scheme, and in particular, how it compares with a more traditional *positive detection* approach to pattern recognition, in which a representation of the positive instances is stored explicitly.

The second dimension specifies how many matches are required to determine the membership of a string. We considered two options, one in which a single match suffices and a second in which we require a detector to match in each window, although we note the possibility of intermediate schemes. We refer to these as disjunctive matching (D) and conjunctive matching (C) respectively. Let Υ be a set of r-chunk detectors:

- Negative Disjunctive Detection $Scheme_{ND}$:
  $Scheme_{ND}(\Upsilon)$ is the set of strings x in U such that $(\forall features\ w)(\nexists d \in \Upsilon)(dMx)$.
- Positive Conjunctive Detection $Scheme_{PC}$:
  $Scheme_{PC}(\Upsilon)$ is the set of strings x in U such that $(\forall features\ w)(\exists d \in \Upsilon)(dMx)$.

Consider, for instance, the following sets of positive detectors: $\Upsilon_1 = \{01, 11\}$ detectors meant to match the first two bits in a string and $\Upsilon_2 = \{10, 11\}$ detectors for the last two bits. Under $Scheme_{PC}$ only strings that are matched by a Υ_1 detector in their first window *and* a Υ_2 detector in their second window will be considered part of the language: $Scheme_{PC}(\Upsilon_1 \cup \Upsilon_2) = \{010, 011, 110, 111\}$. Now consider the case where Υ_1 and Υ_2 are negative detectors. Then a string matched in its first window by a Υ_1 detector *or* in its second window by a Υ_2 detector will be considered outside the language: $Scheme_{ND}(\Upsilon_1 \cup \Upsilon_2) = \{000, 001, 100, 101\}$. Although these two examples do not result in identical sets it turns out that the class of languages recognized by $Scheme_{ND}$ and $Scheme_{PC}$ is identical, and is exactly the class of sets closed under crossover closure when r-chunks matching is used [12].

6   R-Chunks Decompositions

In this section we discuss two decompositions based on the r-chunks match rule under the detection schemes of the previous section. We will examine the overlapping and nonoverlapping variants in terms of the size of their detector sets and the size of the generalization they induce (the crossover closure).

6.1   Overlapping Fixed Size Windows

In the following two sections we summarize some properties of $Scheme_{PC}$ and $Scheme_{ND}$ under the r-chunks match rule when a sliding window decomposition is used. Given a set of instances S it is straightforward to compute exactly how many distinct detectors can be generated. For $Scheme_{PC}$, it requires counting the number of distinct patterns for each of the t windows that comprise the strings in S, whereas for $Scheme_{ND}$, enumerating the distinct patterns that are not present in each window will result in the number of detectors. We are interested in how the number of detectors behaves as a function of the window size r and the number of training instances. In the following, we consider the case when S is a random, uniformly generated collection of strings defined over some finite alphabet $\mathbb{A}$. In such a scenario, the expected number of positive detectors E_{pos} and the expected number of negative detectors E_{neg} are given by:

$$E_{pos} = tE_r \tag{2}$$

$$E_{neg} = t(\mathbb{A}^r - E_r) \tag{3}$$

where $E_r \approx \mathbb{A}^r - \mathbb{A}^r(1 - \mathbb{A}^{-r})^{|S|}$, $t = l - r + 1$ is the number of windows.

With these formulas it is possible to determine when one scheme is beneficial over the other with regards to the number of detectors they require. For this purpose, it suffices to compute the number of strings in S for which both schemes yield the same number of detectors (i.e., when $E_{pos} = E_{neg}$), and note that a sample smaller than this value will require fewer detectors for the positive scheme, and fewer negative detectors if the sample exceeds it. Both schemes have an equal number of detectors when:

$$|S| \approx (0.693)\mathbb{A}^r \ . \tag{4}$$

Note that this value depends only on the choice of r and the cardinality of the alphabet and not on the actual string length.

A detector set generated in this manner is highly likely to be redundant. That is, it will likely contain some detectors whose removal would not change the recognized language recognized. Redundancy might be a desirable feature, especially if detectors are to be distributed. However, it is important to understand how much redundancy is present and address the related question of finding an efficient detector set. Intuitively, redundancy arises from the fact that for some strings a match in window i implies a match in window $i + 1$. For example, for $l = 3$ and $r = 2$ consider the following sample $S = \{000, 101\}$. The implied generalization consists of strings $CC(S) = \{000, 101, 001, 100\}$. Clearly, the positive detectors for window 1, $\{00, 10\}$, match every string in the closure, and only such strings. Thus, it is unnecessary to check for a match in window 2. It is easily verified that the same holds if negative detectors are used, the case most relevant to AIS. The following two equations eliminate this source of redundancy from the detector set when an binary alphabet is used:

$$E_{minN} = 2^r - E_r + (l - r)(E_r - 2(E_r - E_{r-1})) \tag{5}$$

$$E_{minP} = E_r + (l - r)(E_r - 2(E_r - E_{r-1})) \ . \tag{6}$$

The size of the sample S for which E_{minN} and E_{minP} yield the same number of detectors is the same as with the full repertoire (4).

The Crossover Closure and Its Expected Size. In order to examine the size of the crossover closure as a function of the sample size $|S|$ and window size r, a similar assumption is made as in the preceding section, namely we consider the case of a random sample of strings over a binary alphabet. This problem can be mapped into a graphical representation, a directed acyclic graph (DAG), where each level contains nodes corresponding to the positive detectors derived from S for each of its windows. Nodes in consecutive levels are connected if the detectors to which they correspond overlap (crossover) i.e., this is if they match in their common $r - 1$ positions. Take, for instance, a self set S comprised of the following two strings $S = \{0101, 1111\}$ with $l = 4$, $r = 2$, which can be represented by the following DAG:

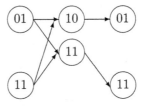

In this example, where $r = 2$, there is only one bit position that overlaps between adjacent windows and whose symbols must match for the corresponding nodes to be connected. Thus, nodes whose label ends with symbol 1 are connected to nodes in the next level with label starting with symbol 1, and nodes that end in 0 are connected to nodes that start with 0. Under this representation, the crossover closure is exactly the set of strings formed by traversing the graph from level 1 to level t (the number of windows) $CC(S) = \{0101, 1111, 0111, 1101\}$.

In order to compute the number of strings in the closure, note from the DAG that the number of paths departing from a given node doubles if it has two outgoing edges, i.e., if the corresponding detector crosses-over with two detectors in the following window. The closed form solution for the expected number of paths in such a graph and hence the size of the crossover closure is given by:

$$CC(t) = E_r(\bar{o})^{(t-1)} \tag{7}$$

where E_r is the expected number of positive detectors given by (2), $\bar{o}$ is the expected outdegree of each node[2] and t is the number of windows.

The size of the generalization, $CC(S)$, can be determined by the size of S or by the size of the detector set (obtaining an estimate for $|S|$ from either (3) or (2) and substituting in (7)). It is important to note that the actual size will depend on the structure of the specific self set. Nevertheless, the analysis provides insight into its behavior and enables us to ascertain the impact of allowing novel strings into the sample. This can be useful for determining, in a dynamic scenario, when (or at what rate) detectors should be added or deleted from the working set.

---

[2] For an estimate of the out degree see [12].

6.2   Nonoverlapping Fixed Size Windows

As noted in Sect. 4 the r-chunks match rule does not necessarily require the use
of a sliding window nor is it restricted to a fixed window size. As an illustration
of another matching scheme for which the crossover closure is the characteristic
generalization, we discuss an alternative decomposition based on the r-chunks
match rule.

This decomposition restricts detector creation to non-overlapping windows
but maintains a fixed size for each window. For simplicity we assume that r
exactly divides l. In the case of positive detection, all distinct patterns in nonoverlapping windows are potential detectors as are all absent patterns potential
negative detectors. It is straightforward to see that the generalization implied
by this design is the crossover closure of the strings in the training sample S
(according to (1)). In fact its size is easier to compute than with the sliding
window model and is simply the product of the number of detectors for each
window:

$$CC(S) = \prod_i |\Upsilon[i]| \tag{8}$$

where $\Upsilon[i]$ is the set of detectors for the ith window.

Likewise the number of detectors can be obtained as the sum of the number
of detectors for each window:

$$\sum_i |\Upsilon[i]| \; . \tag{9}$$

If we consider, as we did above, a random sample of strings S, the expected
number of detectors is simply tE_r for positive detectors and $t(\mathbb{A}^r - E_r)$ for negative detectors, where E_r is given by (2) and $t = \frac{l}{r}$ is the number of windows.
Interestingly, the tradeoff point between negative and positive detectors is the
same as with the sliding window model (4). Lastly, the number of strings encompassed in the generalization follows directly from (8): $CC_r(S) = (E_r)^t$. Figure 1
plots the size of the crossover closure of the two decompositions reviewed in this
paper.

7   Discussion

It is difficult if not impossible to determine in general what the best generation
rule is and how best to represent a detector that implements it. However, having
a clear understanding of what the generalization is allows us to exert more precise
control over its performance, balancing its benefits and shortcomings. The results
presented in this paper still leave some questions unanswered. In particular,
how is r to be determined? Although the above analysis might provide some
guidelines for setting this parameter in terms both of the size of the detector set
and the size of the generalization, implicit in this rule is the prior assumption
that important attributes are contiguous within the string. In order to improve
and adjust classification performance as well as the space requirements, it will
be necessary to define a mechanism that is able to change the relative position of

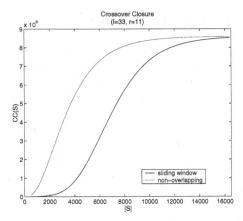

Fig. 1. The crossover closure as a function of the size of a random sample of binary strings for both the sliding window and non-overlapping decompositions

attributes within the string and an algorithm for finding suitable arrangements. One such mechanism, permutation masks, has been proposed before but was used as a means of reducing the size of the generalization [12, 17]. However, this mechanism naturally alters the contiguity of bits and hence can be used for finding better decompositions. What remains is to design an algorithm for finding a good permutation. This is the focus of our current research.

These are only the first steps toward building an AIS with a firm formal footing. It remains to establish what are the policies and mechanisms that will permit the tracking of a shifting self and the distribution of detectors. These are important issues as they are some of the potential benefits that an immune inspired design might have over other paradigms.

8   Conclusion

In this paper we explored the crossover closure generation rule as a learning model for artificial immune systems. We discussed two detection schemes, together with a match rule that implements this generalization. A summary of theoretical results regarding the partial matching rule described in this work was presented, including results for the size of the detector set and the size of the generalization as a function of its parameters and the sample size. We described a positive detection scheme for which detectors are customized to match instances of self and a negative detection scheme where they match instances of nonself. We reviewed how both schemes partition the instance space equivalently and some of the tradeoffs involved in using one scheme over another.

Acknowledgments

The authors gratefully acknowledge the support of the National Science Foundation (grants ANIR-9986555 and DBI-0309147), the Office of Naval Research (grant N00014-99-1-0417), Defense Advanced Projects Agency (grant AGR F30602-00-2-0584), the Intel Corporation, and the Santa Fe Institute. F.E. thanks Consejo Nacional de Ciencia y Tecnología (México) (grant 116691/131686) for its financial support.

References

1. D.W. Aha, D. Kibler, and M.K. Albert. Instance-based learning algorithms. *Machine Learning*, (6):37–66, 1991.
2. M. Ayara, J. Timmis, R. de Lemos, L. N. de Castro, and R. Duncan. Negative selection: How to generate detectors. In J Timmis and P J Bentley, editors, *Proceedings of the 1st International Conference on Artificial Immune Systems (ICARIS)*, pages 89–98, University of Kent at Canterbury, September 2002. University of Kent at Canterbury Printing Unit.
3. J. Balthrop, F. Esponda, S. Forrest, and M. Glickman. Coverage and generalization in an artificial immune system. In *Proceedings of the Genetic and Evolutionary Computation Conference (GECCO-02)*, pages 3–10, 2002.
4. Avrim Blum. On-line algorithms in machine learning. In *Online Algorithms*, pages 306–325, 1996.
5. D. W. Bradley and A. M. Tyrrell. The architecture for a hardware immune system. In D. Keymeulen, A. Stoica, J. Lohn, and R. S. Zebulum, editors, *The Third NASA/DoD Workshop on Evolvable Hardware*, pages 193–200, Long Beach, California, 12-14 July 2001. IEEE Computer Society.
6. D. W. Bradley and A. M. Tyrrell. A hardware immune system for benchmark state machine error detection. In *Proceedings of the Congress on Evolutionary Computation 2002 (CEC2002)*, Honolulu, Hawaii, May 2002.
7. D. W. Bradley and A. M. Tyrrell. Immunotronics: Novel finite state machine architectures with built in self test using self-nonself differentiation. *IEEE Transactions on Evolutionary Computation*, 6(3):227–238, June 2002.
8. D. Dasgupta, editor. *An agent based architecture for a computer virus immune system*. GECCO 2000 Workshop on Artificial Immune Systems, 2000.
9. P. D'haeseleer. An immunological approach to change detection: theoretical results. In *Proceedings of the 9th IEEE Computer Security Foundations Workshop*. IEEE Computer Society Press, 1996.
10. P. D'haeseleer, S. Forrest, and P. Helman. An immunological approach to change detection: algorithms, analysis and implications. In *Proceedings of the 1996 IEEE Symposium on Computer Security and Privacy*. IEEE Press, 1996.
11. R.O. Duda, P.E. Hart, and D.G. Stork. *Pattern Classification*. John Wiley and Sons, 2001.
12. F. Esponda, S. Forrest, and P. Helman. A formal framework for positive and negative detection schemes. *IEEE Transactions on Systems, Man and Cybernetics Part B: Cybernetics*, In press.
13. J. D. Farmer, N. H. Packard, and A. S. Perelson. The immune system, adaptation, and machine learning. *Physica D*, 22:187–204, 1986.
14. S. Forrest, B. Javornik, R. Smith, and A. Perelson. Using genetic algorithms to explore pattern recognition in the immune system. *Evolutionary Computation*, 1(3):191–211, 1993.
15. S. Forrest, A. S. Perelson, L. Allen, and R. CheruKuri. Self-nonself discrimination in a computer. In *Proceedings of the 1994 IEEE Symposium on Research in Security and Privacy*, Los Alamitos, CA, 1994. IEEE Computer Society Press.

16. T. Hastie, R. Tibshirani, and J. Friedman. *The Elements of Statistical Learning: Data Mining, Inference, and Prediction.* Springer, 2001.
17. S. Hofmeyr. *An immunological model of distributed detection and its application to computer security.* PhD thesis, University of New Mexico, Albuquerque, NM, 1999.
18. S. Hofmeyr and S. Forrest. Immunity by design: An artificial immune system. In *Proceedings of the Genetic and Evolutionary Computation Conference (GECCO)*, pages 1289–1296, San Francisco, CA, 1999. Morgan-Kaufmann.
19. S. Hofmeyr and S. Forrest. Architecture for an artificial immune system. *Evolutionary Computation Journal*, 8(4):443–473, 2000.
20. S. Hofmeyr, A. Somayaji, and S. Forrest. Intrusion detection using sequences of system calls. *Journal of Computer Security*, 6:151–180, 1998.
21. J.H. Holland. *Adaptation in Natural and Artificial Systems.* The University of Michigan Press, 1975.
22. A.K. Jain, M.N. Murty, and P.J. Flynn. Data clustering: A review. *ACM Computing Surveys*, 31(3):264–323, 1999.
23. N. Japkowicz. Are we better off without counter-examples? In *Proceedings of the First International ICSC Congress on Computational Intelligence Methods and Applications (CIMA-99)*, pages 242–248, 1999.
24. N. Japkowicz. *Concept-Learning in the Absence of Counter-Examples: An Autoassociation-Based Approach to Classification.* PhD thesis, University of New Jersey, New Brunswick, NJ, 1999.
25. M.J. Kearns and U.V. Vazirani. *An Introduction to Computational Learning Theory.* MIT Press, 1994.
26. J. Kim and P. J. Bentley. An evaluation of negative selection in an artificial immune system for network intrusion detection. In *Proceedings of the Genetic and Evolutionary Computation Conference (GECCO)*, pages 1330–1337, San Francisco, CA, 2001. Morgan-Kauffman.
27. T.M. Mitchell. *Machine Learning.* McGraw-Hill, 1997.
28. J. K. Percus, O. Percus, and A. S. Perelson. Probability of self-nonself discrimination. In A. S. Perelson and G. Weisbuch, editors, *Theoretical and Experimental Insights into Immunology*, NY, 1992. Springer-Verlag.
29. J. K. Percus, O. Percus, and A. S. Perelson. Predicting the size of the antibody combining region from consideration of efficient self/non-self discrimination. *Proceedings of the National Academy of Science*, 90:1691–1695, 1993.
30. S. Singh. Anomaly detection using negative selection based on the r-contiguous matching rule. In Jonathan Timmis and Peter J. Bentley, editors, *Proceedings of the 1st International Conference on Artificial Immune Systems (ICARIS)*, pages 99–106, University of Kent at Canterbury, September 2002. University of Kent at Canterbury Printing Unit.
31. S. T. Wierzchon. Discriminative power of the receptors activated by k-contiguous bits rule. *Journal of Computer Science and Technology*, 1(3):1–13, 2000.
32. S. T. Wierzchon. Generating optimal repertoire of antibody strings in an artificial immune system. In M. A. Klopotek, M. Michalewicz, and S. T.Wierzchon, editors, *Intelligent Information Systems*, pages 119–133, Heidelberg New York, 2000. Physica-Verlag.
33. S. T. Wierzchon. Deriving concise description of non-self patterns in an artificial immune system. In S. T. Wierzchon, L. C. Jain, and J. Kacprzyk, editors, *New Learning Paradigms in Soft Computing*, pages 438–458, Heidelberg New York, 2001. Physica-Verlag.

A Randomized Real-Valued
Negative Selection Algorithm

Fabio González[1,2], Dipankar Dasgupta[2], and Luis Fernando Niño[1]

[1] Depto. de Ing. de Sistemas, Universidad Nacional de Colombia, Bogotá, Colombia
[2] Division of Computer Science, The University of Memphis, Memphis TN 38152
{fgonzalz,dasgupta}@memphis.edu, lfnino@ing.unal.edu.co

Abstract. This paper presents a real-valued negative selection algorithm with good mathematical foundation that solves some of the drawbacks of our previous approach [11]. Specifically, it can produce a good estimate of the optimal number of detectors needed to cover the non-self space, and the maximization of the non-self coverage is done through an optimization algorithm with proven convergence properties. The proposed method is a randomized algorithm based on Monte Carlo methods. Experiments are performed to validate the assumptions made while designing the algorithm and to evaluate its performance.

1 Introduction

The negative selection (**NS**) algorithm is one of the most widely used techniques in the field of artificial immune systems. It is primarily used to detect changes in data/behavior patterns by generating detectors in the complementary space (given normal samples). In the original version of the NS algorithm [8], the detectors are used directly to classify new data as self (normal) or non-self (abnormal). Subsequent works have shown the feasibility of combining the NS algorithm with classification algorithms [11]; in this case, the generated detectors are used by the classification algorithm to learn high-level anomaly detection functions. Regardless of how the detectors are used, a good coverage of the non-self space is important for the anomaly detection process.

This paper focuses on the problem of efficient generation of detectors when a real-valued representation of the self/non-self space is used. Other important issues concerning the NS algorithm are discussed elsewhere (positive vs negative detection [6,9], representation and matching rules [10,12], applications[3]), and thus they are not considered in this paper.

González et al. [11] proposed a Real-Valued Negative Selection (**RNS**) algorithm based on heuristics that try to distribute the detectors in the non-self space in order to maximize the coverage. This algorithm uses a real-valued representation for the self/non-self space that differs from the binary representation used in original negative selection algorithms [5,8]. This higher-level representation provides some advantages such as increased expressiveness, the possibility of extracting high-level knowledge from the generated detectors, and, in some cases, improved scalability [9,11]. However, this algorithm lacks the theoretical support of the binary negative selection algorithm [5,6]. The main difficulties due to the lack of theoretical support include:

J. Timmis et al. (Eds.): ICARIS 2003, LNCS 2787, pp. 261–272, 2003.

- The number of detectors needed to cover the non-self space, as well as the radius of each detector, are not known in advance; hence, it is necessary to determine them by a trial-and-error procedure.
- There is no guarantee that the algorithm will converge to an optimal or close-to-optimal space coverage with minimum overlap.

This paper proposes a randomized RNS algorithm (**RRNS**) based on some mathematical models, which can provide specific criteria to setup the algorithmic parameters and to assess the expected performance. The proposed algorithm is based on two main ideas:

- To estimate the volume of the self space, which, by complementarity, is also an approximation of the volume of the non-self space. Using this volume, it is possible to calculate how many hyper-spherical detectors (of a given radius) are needed to cover the non-self space.
- To use a well known optimization algorithm, simulated annealing [13,16], to find a good distribution of the detectors that maximizes the coverage of the non-self space.

The algorithm is called *randomized* because it is based on an important class of randomized algorithms known as Monte Carlo methods [2,7,14]. Specifically, it uses *Monte Carlo integration* to estimate the volume of the self (and non-self) space and *simulated annealing* [13,16] to optimize the distribution of detectors in the non-self space.

It is to be noted that this is not the first time that simulated annealing has been used in an artificial immune algorithm. De Castro and Von Zuben [4] proposed a technique to initialize feed-forward neural network weights, where the basic idea is to represent the network weights by detectors which correspond to n-dimensional real-valued vectors. The detectors are dispersed in the space by maximizing an energy function that takes into account the inverse of the inter-detector affinity. De Castros's approach is substantially different from the one proposed here; his approach does not use the concept of self/non-self distinction, and its main goal is producing diversity instead of performing anomaly detection.

2   Randomized Real-Valued Negative Selection Algorithm (RRNS)

Similar to the RNS algorithm, the objective of this algorithm is to generate a set of hyper-spherical detectors that cover the non-self space. The algorithm primarily consists of two steps: first, it generates an initial set of detectors; second, it optimizes the distribution of this set to maximize the non-self coverage. The input to the algorithm is a set of samples from the self set, S'; the allowed variability in the self set, r_{self}; the detector radius, r_{ab}; and a set of parameters, Π. The global structure of the algorithm is shown in Figure 1.

Accordingly, the algorithm is implemented with two main functions: Calculate-Init-detector-Set (described in Section 2.1), which estimates the volume of the non-self space in order to produce a good initial set of detectors, and Optimize-detector-Distribution (details in Section 2.2), which distributes the detectors uniformly in the non-self space based on simulated annealing optimization. These two functions will be discussed in the following sections.

RR-Negative-Selection(S', r_{self}, r_{ab}, Π)

   S' : set of self samples
  r_{self} : self variability threshold
   r_{ab} : detector radius
   Π : additional parameters

1: $D \leftarrow$ Calculate-Init-detector-Set(S', r_{self}, r_{ab})
2: $D' \leftarrow$ Optimize-detector-Distribution(D, r_{ab}, S', r_{self})
3: Return D'

Fig. 1. Randomized real-valued negative selection (RRNS) algorithm.

2.1 Determining the Number of Detectors

Let V_d be the volume covered by an individual detector and let $V_{\text{non-self}}$ be the volume of the non-self space. A rough approximation of the number of detectors can be given by:

$$num_{ab} = \frac{V_{\text{non-self}}}{V_d}. \tag{1}$$

Note that this is a very optimistic approximation since it does not take into account the fact that, in general, it is impossible to cover a given volume with spherical detectors without allowing some overlapping. If overlapping is allowed, the effective covering volume is not anymore the volume of the hypersphere that defines a detector, but a smaller value. We define the covering volume of a detector as the volume of the inscribed hypercube. The main reason to choose this definition is that there is a straightforward way to cover an n-dimensional region using hypercubes without holes.

According to the previous discussion, the effective volume covered by a detector d with radius r is defined as:

$$V_d = \left(\frac{2r}{\sqrt{n}} \right)^n. \tag{2}$$

Using Equations (1) and (2), it is possible to calculate a good approximation of the number of detectors with a given radius needed to cover the non-self space. This will require, however, the knowledge of the volume of the non-self space, which will be addressed in the remaining part of this section.

Calculating the volume of the self (non-self) set. The self/non-self space, U, corresponds to the unitary hypercube, $[0, 1]^n$. Clearly, the volume of the self/non-self space is equal to 1.0; therefore, the volume of the non-self space is defined as:

$$V_{\text{non-self}} = 1 - V_{\text{self}}.$$

In most cases, the input to the NS algorithm is a subset of the self set. Thus, in general, the entire volume of the self space is not known. We assume a model of the self set, $\widehat{S}$, that is defined in terms of a set of self samples, S'. The basic assumption in this definition is that an element that is *close enough* to a self sample is considered as self. The closeness is specified formally by a variability threshold, r_{self}, that defines the minimum distance between a self sample and an element x, such that x can be considered part of the self set. The model of the self set, $\widehat{S}$, is defined as follows:

$$\widehat{S} := \left\{ x \in U \mid \exists s \in S', \|s - x\| \le r_{\text{self}} \right\}.$$

We define V_{self} as the volume of $\widehat{S}$, which is calculated as:

$$V_{\widehat{S}} := \int_U \chi_{\widehat{S}}(x)dx,$$

where $\chi_{\widehat{S}}$ corresponds to the characteristic function of the set $\widehat{S}$ defined by

$$\chi_{\widehat{S}}(x) := \begin{cases} 1 \text{ if } x \in \widehat{S} \\ 0 \text{ if } x \notin \widehat{S} \end{cases}.$$

It is possible to produce an estimate of $V_{\widehat{S}}$ using random sampling. The basic idea is to generate a sequence $\{x_i\}_{i=1..m}$ of random samples uniformly distributed in U. The expected value of $\chi_{\widehat{S}}(x_i)$ is

$$\mathrm{E}\left[\chi_{\widehat{S}}(x_i)\right] = \int_U \chi_{\widehat{S}}(x)dx = V_{\widehat{S}};$$

therefore, an estimate of $\mathrm{E}\left[\chi_{\widehat{S}}(x_i)\right]$ is also an estimate of $V_{\widehat{S}}$. As it is well known, a good estimate of the mean of a random variable (expected value) is the mean of a set of samples; so, we use the average of $\left\{\chi_{\widehat{S}}(x_i)\right\}_{i=1..m}$ as an estimate, $\widehat{V_{\widehat{S}}}$, of the self volume:

$$V_{\widehat{S}} \approx \widehat{V_{\widehat{S}}} = \frac{\sum_{i=1}^m \chi_{\widehat{S}}(x_i)}{m}. \tag{3}$$

The estimation of a defined integral by averaging a set of random samples is known as *Monte Carlo integration* [2,14]. The main advantage of this method, in contrary to other non-probabilistic methods, is that it is possible to calculate an interval of confidence for the estimated integral. Using the *central limit theorem* [1], it is possible to calculate such interval of confidence as:

$$Pr\left(|\widehat{V_{\widehat{S}}} - V_{\widehat{S}}| < 3\sqrt{\frac{\widehat{V_{\widehat{S}}} - \widehat{V_{\widehat{S}}}^2}{m}}\right) \approx 0.998. \tag{4}$$

Algorithm to calculate an initial set of detectors. Now that we know how to calculate the area of the self (non-self) space, it is straightforward to calculate the number of detectors that are needed to cover the non-self space and to generate an initial set of detectors located in the non-self space. The pseudo-code of this algorithm is given below (Figure 2).

The algorithm receives (as input) samples from self (S'), the variability radius of the self (r_{self}), the radius of each detector (r_{ab}), the maximum allowed error (ϵ_{max}), and a minimum number of iterations that have to be performed (m_{min}). The purpose of the last parameter, m_{min}, is to produce a good initial estimate of the error (ϵ) by enforcing a minimum number of iterations. This prevents a premature stop of the algorithm due to

Calculate-Init-detector-Set(S', r_{self}, r_{ab}, ϵ_{max}, $init\_iter$)

> S' : set of self samples $\qquad$ ϵ_{max} : maximum allowed error
> r_{self} : self variability threshold $\quad$ m_{min} : initial number of iterations
> $\qquad$ r_{ab} : detector radius $\qquad\qquad$ n : dimension of the self/non-self space

1: $num\_hits \leftarrow 0$
2: $m \leftarrow 0$
3: Repeat
4: $\quad m \leftarrow m + 1$
5: $\quad x \leftarrow$ uniformly distributed random sample from $[1,0]^n$
6: $\quad y \leftarrow$ Nearest-Neighbor(S', x)
7: $\quad$ If $\|x - y\| \leq r_{self}$
8: $\quad$ Then $num\_hits \leftarrow num\_hits + 1$
9: $\quad$ EndIf
10: $\quad \widehat{V_S} \leftarrow \frac{num\_hits}{m}$ $\quad \triangleright$ Eq. 3
11: $\quad \epsilon \leftarrow 3\sqrt{\frac{\widehat{V_S} - \widehat{V_S}^2}{m}}$ $\quad \triangleright$ Eq. 4
12: Until $m \geq m_{min}$ and $\epsilon \leq \epsilon_{max}$
13: $num_{ab} \leftarrow \left\lfloor \frac{1 - \widehat{V_S}}{\left(\frac{2r_{ab}}{\sqrt{n}}\right)^n} \right\rfloor$ $\quad \triangleright$ Eq. 2
14: $D \leftarrow \emptyset$
15: Repeat
16: $\quad x \leftarrow$ uniformly distributed random sample from $[1,0]^n$
17: $\quad y \leftarrow$ Nearest-Neighbor(S', x)
18: $\quad$ If $\|x - y\| \geq r_{self}$
19: $\quad$ Then $D \leftarrow D \cup \{x\}$
20: $\quad$ EndIf
21: Until $|D| = num_{ab}$
22: Return D

Fig. 2. Algorithm to calculate an initial detector set.

a poor initial estimation of ϵ. Notice that the algorithm can be easily modified to receive as input the number of detectors instead of the detector radius (r_{ab}). In that case, line 13 (Figure 2) must be replaced by

$$r_{ab} \leftarrow \sqrt[n]{\frac{1 - \widehat{V_S}}{num_{ab}}} \cdot \frac{\sqrt{n}}{2}. \qquad (5)$$

2.2 Improving the Detector Distribution

We describe a procedure to improve the distribution of detectors produced by the Calculate-Init-detector-Set algorithm (Figure 2) in order to optimize the coverage of the non-self space.

The problem of finding a set with good distribution of detectors can be stated as an optimization problem as follows:

Maximize:

$$V(D) = Volume\{x \in U \mid \exists d \in D, \|x - d\| \leq r_{ab}\}, \qquad (6)$$

restricted to:

$$\{s \in S' \mid \exists d \in D, \|s - d\| \leq r_{ab}\} = \emptyset \text{ (not covering of self)}, \tag{7}$$

where,
D : set of detectors with a fixed cardinality, num_{ab},
r_{ab} : detector radius, and
S' : input self set.

The function defined in Equation (6) represents the amount of the self/non-self space covered by a set of detectors, D, which corresponds to the volume covered by the union of hyper-spheres associated with each detector. The restriction specified in Equation (7) tells that no detector should match any self point.

The evaluation of the function $V(D)$ can be a costly process; in fact, the only practical way to compute it is to use a Monte Carlo integration method similar to the one used in the previous section (2.1). Instead, we will use a simplified version of this optimization problem, which we will show, experimentally, to be an equivalent.

Next we describe an optimization algorithm to solve this problem. The technique uses a very well known Monte Carlo based optimization method, *simulated annealing*, which is adapted to solve this particular problem.

Simulated annealing. The simulated annealing technique was initially proposed by Kirkpatrick et al. [13] borrowing inspiration from the physical annealing of solids. The physical process can be described as follows: a solid is heated to a high temperature, then, it is slowly made to cool down until some desired properties of the solid are obtained; these properties are related to a low energy state.

In the algorithm, the energy corresponds to the function to minimize, $C(s)$, whose domain is the space of states of a system. The system is randomly perturbed by moving it from the current state, s_i, to a new state, s_j. If $C(s_j) < C(s_i)$, the transition is accepted; otherwise, its acceptance is defined by a random process. The probability of accepting this transition is a function of the temperature: the higher the temperature, the higher the probability of accepting a worse state. This step is repeated a number of times until the system reaches *thermal equilibrium*. This perturbation process is known as the Metropolis algorithm [14,15], and it belongs to a broader class of algorithms called Monte Carlo methods [14].

In our particular problem, we are searching for a set of detectors that optimizes the coverage of non-self space. In consequence, the configuration of the system is given by the coordinates of the detector set. Notice that the number of detectors is fixed (based on the estimate produced by Calculate-Init-detector-Set, Figure 2), no detectors are created or eliminated in this algorithm.

The original function to optimize corresponds to the volume covered by the detector set (Equation (6)); however, to calculate it can be very costly. Therefore, we need another function which is easier to calculate, and such that its optimization corresponds to the optimization of the covered volume. Intuitively, to maximize the coverage produced by a set of detectors, it is necessary to reduce their overlapping, i.e., to increase the inter-detector distance. The following equation defines an approximate measure of overlapping between two detectors:

$$\text{Overlapping}(d_i, d_j) = e^{\frac{-\|d_i - d_j\|^2}{r_{ab}^2}}. \tag{8}$$

The maximum value, 1, is reached when the distance between the two detectors is 0. When the distance is equal to $2r_{ab}$, the value of the function is very close to 0. Notice that this function can be interpreted as the matching function of the detector.

Based on Equation (8), the amount of overlapping of a set, $D = \{d_1, \ldots, d_{num_{ab}}\}$, of detectors is defined as

$$\text{Overlapping}(D) = \sum_{i \neq j} e^{\frac{-\|d_i - d_j\|^2}{r_{ab}^2}}, \quad i, j = 1, \ldots num_{ab}. \tag{9}$$

Now, the question is if minimizing $Overlapping(D)$ is the same as maximizing $V(D)$ (Equation (6)). In general, it is not true; however, we will show in the next section that in the practice they are equivalent.

The original optimization problem includes a restriction that prevents detectors from covering the self (Equation (7)). Simulated annealing does not provide a direct way to include such restrictions; therefore, it is necessary to include a term in the cost function that penalizes configurations which violate this restriction. Then, the function to optimize is defined as follows:

$$C(D) = \text{Overlapping}(D) + \beta \cdot \text{SelfCovering}(D), \tag{10}$$

where, the second term corresponds to the penalization factor for violating the self-covering restriction, and is defined by

$$\text{SelfCovering}(D) = \sum_{s \in S'} \sum_{d \in D} e^{\frac{-\|d - s\|^2}{\left(\frac{r_{ab} + r_{self}}{2}\right)^2}}. \tag{11}$$

Notice that this function is based on the same principle used to define the *Overlapping* function (Equation (9)). Each individual term on the sum measures the amount of matching between a detector and a self element.

The term β in Equation (10) specifies the relative importance of self-covering with respect to the inter-detector overlapping. It controls the amount of penalization in the cost function caused by violating the self-covering restriction.

An advantage of this cost function is that in each step of the algorithm it is not necessary to calculate all the terms in Equations (9) and (10). It is only required to evaluate the terms that involve the detectors affected by the transition (detector movement).

Optimization algorithm for detector distribution. The detector distribution algorithm is shown in Figure 3. The main inputs to the algorithm are the initial detector set (generated by the Calculate-Init-detector-Set algorithm, Figure 2), D; the set of self samples, S'; and the number of iterations, num_{iter}. The shape of detectors (and self elements) is determined by the detector radius, r_{ab}, and the self variability threshold, r_{self}, respectively. The number of iterations on the inner loop (lines 5 to 20) is controlled by the parameter, η_{min}, which expresses the minimum number of accepted transitions as a percentage of

Optimize-detector-Distribution(D, r_{ab}, S', r_{self}, num_{iter}, η_{coef},, α, α_{pert}, β)

$D = \{d_1, \ldots, d_{num_{ab}}\}$: initial detector set η_{min} : minimum accepted transitions %
S' : set of self samples α : Temperature decay rate
num_{iter} : number of iterations α_{pert} : Neighborhood radius decay rate
r_{ab} : detector radius β : Self covering importance coefficient
r_{self} : self variability threshold

1: $r_{pert} \leftarrow 2 \cdot r_{ab}$
2: $T \leftarrow$ Calculate-Init-T(D, r_{ab}, S', r_{self}, r_{pert}, β)
3: For $i \leftarrow 1$ to num_{iter}
4:    $\eta \leftarrow 0, steps \leftarrow 0$
5:    Repeat
6:      $index \leftarrow$ random element $\{1, .., num_{ab}\}$
7:      $d \leftarrow$ random element $\{v \in [0,1]^n \mid \|d_{index} - v\| \le r_{pert}\}$
8:      $\Delta C \leftarrow$ Calculate-Cost-Difference(D, $index$, d, r_{ab}, S', r_{self}, β)
9:      If $\Delta C < 0$
10:     Then ▷ accept transition
11:        $\eta \leftarrow \eta + 1$
12:        $d_{index} \leftarrow d$
13:     Else
14:        If $e^{\frac{-\Delta C}{T}} >$ random $[0,1)$
15:        Then ▷ accept transition
16:           $\eta \leftarrow \eta + 1$
17:           $d_{index} \leftarrow d$
18:        EndIf
19:     EndIf
20:   Until $\eta \ge \eta_{min} \cdot num_{ab}$ or $steps > 2 \cdot \eta_{min} \cdot num_{ab}$
21:   $T \leftarrow \alpha \cdot T$
22:   $r_{pert} \leftarrow \alpha_{pert} \cdot r_{pert}$
23: EndFor
24: Return D

Fig. 3. Algorithm to optimize the distribution of detectors in order to improve the coverage of non-self space.

the number of detectors. The temperature decay rate, α, and the neighborhood radius decay rate, α_{pert}, control how the temperature and the neighborhood radius are going to be changed in each iteration of the outer loop. Finally, the parameter β specifies the relative importance of covering self points when calculating the cost function.

3   RRNS Experimentation

3.1   Overlapping vs Non-self Coverage

Section 2.2 formulates the problem of detector distribution as an optimization problem corresponding to maximizing the non-self volume covered by a set of detectors ($V(D)$, Equations (6) and (7)). The Optimize-detector-Distribution algorithm (Figure 3) solves a modified optimization problem: to minimize the function $C(D)$ defined by Equation (10). This function is composed of two terms: one measures the amount of overlapping

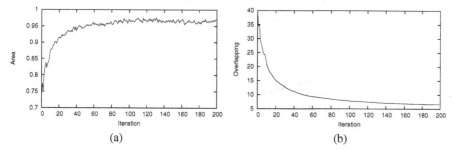

(a)   (b)

Fig. 4. The RRNS is applied to spread a set of detectors in an unitary square. (a) Progress in the area covered by the detectors. (b) Evolution of the inter-detector overlapping calculated using Equation (9).

between detectors and the other penalizes the covering of self points. The main assumption is that minimizing $C(D)$ is approximately equivalent to maximizing $V(D)$. The intuition behind this assumption is that the lesser the overlapping of a set of detectors, the larger the volume they can cover.

Figure 4 shows the evolution of the area covered by a set of detectors and their overlapping, when the Optimize-detector-Distribution (Figure 3) is applied to an initial set of random detectors in a unitary square. The overlapping, which is the objective function minimized by the algorithm, goes down with the successive iterations. This means that the detectors are moving apart resulting in an increase in the area covered by them, as shown in Figure 4(a). The area curve is not as smooth as the overlapping curve; this can be explained by the fact that the area is estimated (using Monte Carlo integration, $\epsilon = 0.01$), whereas the amount of overlapping is calculated exactly.

This experiment suggests that, in fact, the algorithm is able to maximize the area covered by minimizing the inter-detector overlapping. However, this experiment in a 2-dimensional space is not significant enough to evaluate the algorithmic performance. In order to build a stronger experimental evidence, we performed the following experiment: a random set of detectors is generated close to the center of the unitary hypercube, then the function Optimize-detector-Distribution (Figure 3) is applied for a given number of iterations, the volume covered and the inter-detector overlapping (Equation (9)) are measured; this process is repeated 30 times, each time starting with a new random set of detectors (around the center).

Figure 5 shows the overlapping-versus-volume graphics corresponding to the data generated by the experiment for space dimension 5 and 10. It is easy to see that there is a clear inverse relationship between the volume covered by a set of detectors and their inter-detector overlapping. As it is shown in Figure 5, the relationship is not necessarily linear; however, it does not affect the algorithmic performance as the results demonstrate that the volume increases monotonically while the amount of overlapping decreases.

3.2   RRNS vs RNS

An interesting question is: how does the new algorithm (RRNS) compare to the previous algorithm (RNS) in terms of the optimization of the volume covered by the set of

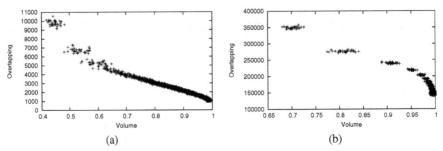

Fig. 5. The graphics show the overlapping-versus-volume relation for a set of detectors produced by the successive application of Optimize-detector-Distribution function (Figure 3). (a) Dimension = 5. (b) Dimension = 10.

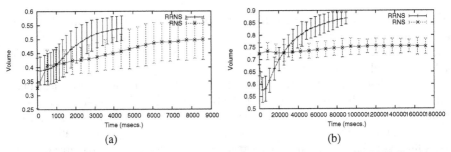

Fig. 6. Evolution of the non-self covered volume against the time for RNS and RRNS algorithms. (a) 2-dimensional data set; (b) 4-dimensional data set.

detectors? It is important to take into account that the RNS algorithm was not developed to optimize explicitly the volume or the overlapping. The RNS algorithm is based on heuristic rules that try to move the detectors away from each other and from the self points. An indirect result of this is an increase in the non-self space covered by the set of detectors. Therefore, we expect the RRNS algorithm to perform better than the RNS algorithm in terms of the optimization of the volume covered by the generated set of detectors.

To perform a comparison, we used two data sets based on the Mackey-Glass time series (as described in [9]) having two and four features respectively. Notice that the RRNS is able to calculate the detector radius if the number of detectors is given (Equation (5)); this is not the case for RNS. Therefore, to make a meaningful comparison, we used the detector radius calculated by the RRNS algorithm as input to the RNS algorithm.

Both algorithms are run for a fixed number of iterations. After each iteration, the volume covered by the set of detectors is calculated using a Monte Carlo integration method similar to the one described in the Calculate-Init-detector-Set algorithm (Figure 2). In this case, the value of the error is $\epsilon=0.005$. The process is repeated 30 times (i.e. 30 experiments). Figure 6 shows the evolution of the covered volume for each algorithm and for both data sets.

The points in the curve represent the average volume of 30 experiments, and the length of vertical lines correspond to three times the standard deviation. In both cases, the covered volume increases in successive iterations. The RRNS algorithm produces a larger covering volume, as was expected because of its optimization components. The results are encouraging , which suggest that the theoretical foundation of the RRNS also provides a more efficient coverage of the non-self; however, a more extensive testing (with different data sets) is needed in order to assess the real strength of the RRNS algorithm.

4   Conclusions

This paper presented a NS algorithm to generate detectors in a real-valued non-self space, called Randomized Real-Valued Negative Selection (RRNS) algorithm. The algorithm is based on Monte Carlo simulation techniques; this gives it the appellative of *randomized*. The algorithm improves the RNS algorithm by providing a mathematical support that facilitates:

- the production of a good estimate of the number of detectors (of a given radius) needed to cover the non-self space, and
- the provision of a guarantee, at least theoretically, that the algorithm can converge to an optimal configuration.

The RRNS algorithm appears to be better than the RNS algorithm in providing a theoretical basis for analyzing its performance. However, this does not mean to claim that it can produce better empirical results. In some cases, heuristic algorithms outperform other algorithms with better theoretical foundation. Preliminary experiments presented in this paper suggest that the RRNS algorithm can offer an improved performance. It is necessary, however, to perform extensive experimentation to measure the real strength of the RRNS algorithm as well as the impact of the improved non-self coverage on the anomaly detection performance.

References

1. H. D. Brunk. *An Introduction to Mathematical Statistics*. Blaisdell Publishing Co., 1965.
2. Computational Science Education project. Introduction to monte carlo methods. Oak Ridge National Laboratory, 1995.
3. L. N. de Castro and J. Timmis. *Artificial Immune Systems: A New Computational Approach*. Springer-Verlag, London, UK, 2002.
4. L. N. De Castro and F. J. Von Zuben. An immunological approach to initialize centers of radial basis function neural networks. In *Proc. of CBRN'01 (Brazilian Conference on Neural Networks)*, pages 79–84, 2001.
5. P. D'haeseleer, S. Forrest, and P. Helman. An immunological approach to change detection: algorithms, analysis and implications. In J. McHugh and G. Dinolt, editors, *Proceedings of the 1996 IEEE Symposium on Computer Security and Privacy*, pages 110–119, USA, 1996. IEEE Press.
6. F. Esponda, S. Forrest, and P. Helman. A formal framework for positive and negative detection schemes. Draft version, July 2002.
7. G. S. Fishman. *Monte Carlo. Concepts, algorithms, and Applications*. Springer-Verlag, 1996.

8. S. Forrest, A. Perelson, L. Allen, and R. Cherukuri. Self-nonself discrimination in a computer. In *Proceedings IEEE Symposium on Research in Security and Privacy*, pages 202–212, Los Alamitos, CA, 1994. IEEE Computer Society Press.

9. F. González and D. Dagupta. Neuro-immune and self-organizing map approaches to anomaly detection: A comparison. In J. Timmis and P. J. Bentley, editors, *Proceedings of the 1st International Conference on Artificial Immune Systems (ICARIS)*, pages 203–211, Canterbury, UK, Sept. 2002. University of Kent at Canterbury Printing Unit.

10. F. Gonzalez, D. Dasgupta, and J. Gomez. The effect of binary matching rules in negative selection. In *Proceedings of the Genetic and Evolutionary Computation Conference (GECCO)*, July 2003.

11. F. González, D. Dasgupta, and R. Kozma. Combining negative selection and classification techniques for anomaly detection. In D. B. Fogel, M. A. El-Sharkawi, X. Yao, G. Greenwood, H. Iba, P. Marrow, and M. Shackleton, editors, *Proceedings of the 2002 Congress on Evolutionary Computation CEC2002*, pages 705–710, USA, May 2002. IEEE Press.

12. P. Harmer, G. Williams, P.D.and Gnusch, and G. Lamont. An Artificial Immune System Architecture for Computer Security Applications. *IEEE Transactions on Evolutionary Computation*, 6(3):252–280, June 2002.

13. S. Kirkpatrick, C. D. Gelatt, and M. P. Vecchi. Optimization by simulated annealing. *Science, Number 4598, 13 May 1983*, 220(4598):671–680, 1983.

14. J. S. Liu. *Monte Carlo Strategies in Scientific Computing*. Springer-Verlag, 2001.

15. N. Metropolis, A. W. Rosenbluth, M. N. Rosenbluth, A. H. Teller, and E. Teller. Equation of state calculations by fast computing machines. *Journal of Chemical Physics*, 21:1087–1092, 1953.

16. P. J. M. van Laarhoven and E. H. L. Aarts. *Simulated Annealing: Theory and Applications*. D. Reidel Publishing Company, 1987.

Dynamic Function Optimisation: Comparing the Performance of Clonal Selection and Evolution Strategies

Joanne H. Walker and Simon M. Garrett

Department of Computer Science,
University of Wales, Aberystwyth, UK, SY23 3DB
{jnw,smg}@aber.ac.uk

Abstract. This paper reports on novel work using clonal selection (CS) for dynamic function optimisation. A comparison is made between evolution strategies (ES) and CS, for the optimisation of two significantly different dynamic functions at 2, 5 and 10 dimensions. Firstly a sensitivity analysis was performed for both the CS and the ES for both fitness functions. Secondly the performance of the two algorithms was compared over time. The main finding of this work is that the CS optimises better than the ES in problems with few dimensions, although the ES optimises more slowly. At higher dimensions however, the ES optimises both more quickly and to a better level.

Keywords: Artificial immune systems, critical evaluation, clonal selection, evolution strategies.

1 Introduction

The problem of dynamic optimisation relates to a large set of real-world problems in which the location of the global and local optima of a state space change over time. Often genetic and evolutionary computation (GEC) methods, and artificial immune system (AIS) methods address the simpler problem of finding one or more static optima—avoiding this extra level of complexity—however, it is important to consider dynamic of optimisation since many optimisation tasks are dynamic to some extent.

This paper begins to compare the performance of the clonal selection AIS (CS) and evolution strategies (ES) on two dynamic optimisation tasks. The aim is to begin to assess the weaknesses and strengths of both methods (No Free Lunch theorem not withstanding (Wolpert and Macready, 1997)) so that the appropriate method may be chosen for a given task. Both these methods share common algorithmic features but there are also significant differences.

The paper is structured as follows. Section 2 introduces ES and CS, and discusses previous work using GEC for dynamic function optimisation. In Section 3 the methodology is stated. In Section 4 the results of the experiments are presented and discussed in terms of the relative performance of the ES and the CS. Finally, in Section 5, some conclusions are drawn.

J. Timmis et al. (Eds.): ICARIS 2003, LNCS 2787, pp. 273–284, 2003.

2   Background

2.1   Evolution Strategies

ESs share similarities with genetic algorithms (GAs). The original ES algorithm used a single parent which produced one offspring per generation by mutation alone. The offspring would then replace its parent in the next generation, if it had a better fitness (Back and Schwefel, 1993). The mutation step size is defined by a Gaussian distributed random number with a mean of zero and a standard deviation that is encoded on a different part of the chromosome. The standard deviation of the Gaussian distribution is itself mutated in each generation – there is an extra gene on an ES chromosome which encodes the standard deviation, and after mutation the new standard deviation is given by:

$$sp\prime = sp * A_i$$

where A_i is *alpha* or $1/alpha$ depending on the value of an equally distributed random number E. The value of *alpha* is usually set at 1.3.

The parts of the chromosome which encode the solution are called the object parameters and the parts with the mutation step size are called the strategy parameters, there is usually a strategy parameter for each object parameter. This allows the ES to be self-optimising in its performance, to the extent that the genes can mutate at different rates, making the ES an ideal optimisation method for dynamic functions (Fogel, 1995; Back and Schwefel, 1993).

2.2   Clonal Selection and CLONALG

Natural clonal selection (Burnet, 1959) occurs to the degree that a B-cell matches an antigen. A strong match causes a B-cell to be cloned many times, and a weak match results in little cloning. These 'clones' are mutated from the original B-cell at a rate inversely proportional to the match strength: a strongly matching B-cell mutates little and thus retains its match to the antigen.

The immunological processes of clonal selection (and affinity maturation) have been used for inspiration in AIS, the most common abstraction being CLON-ALG (de Castro and Von Zuben, 2000). Clonal selection also underlies all immune network models. CLONALG currently exists in two similar but distinct forms—one for optimisation and one for pattern matching—but in both cases the B-cell is implemented as a single real-valued vector, and no two B-cells are allowed to interact. In pattern matching CLONALG, a set of *memory cells* may also be kept that 'remember' previously found patterns or solutions.

2.3   Dynamic Function Optimisation

Within the evolutionary algorithms literature there has been a significant amount of work in dynamic function optimisation, almost all of which is based around GAs. However the authors are aware only of one study which has looked at using AIS methods for dynamic function optimisation (Gaspar andCollard, 1999).

Three main approaches to dynamic function optimisation by GEC methods have been defined by Branke (1999) as: (1) React to changes in the environment by triggering change in the operation of the GEC; this change is usually detected by the corresponding change in fitness. (2) Maintain diversity throughout the run, so that the EA is always ready to respond to changes to the environment. (3) Remember good past solutions so that they can be used again if necessary. A more recent review can be found in (Walker, 2003; Garrett and Walker, 2002), a selection of significant work is now discussed.

Methods Using Triggered Change. Cobb and Grefenstette used a method they called "triggered hypermutation" which was based on a GA. Triggered hypermutation was designed to increase the diversity of the population when the environment changed, so that the population could spread out to new parts of the search space before converging again on the global optimum.

In (Cobb, 1990) a mutation rate of 0.001 was used unless the average fitness of the population worsened over time, at which point the mutation rate was increased to 0.5 until the time-average fitness levelled off or improved. However, Grefenstette (1992) pointed out that triggered hypermutation will not work in all kinds of dynamic environment. Firstly, if the environment changes significantly and the new optimum, or optima, in the search space are not close enough to previous ones, hypermutation cannot introduce enough diversity to overcome this. Also, if the search space includes new peaks of optimum performance but the old peaks remain, then hypermutation would not be triggered at all.

Methods Which Maintain Diversity in the Population. In (Grefenstette, 1992) Cobb's triggered hypermutation was replaced by a "partial hypermutation" step. This step occurred in every generation, and involved a proportion of the population being replaced by random individuals. Grefenstette called the new algorithm the "random immigrants GA". In a comparison between the performance of a standard GA, triggered hypermutation and random immigrants (Cobb and Grefenstette, 1993), it was found that in dynamic environments with large scale changes random immigrants performed best, and also caused less disruption in stable environments.

A method using sub-populations was introduced by Oppacher and Wineberg (1999), called the "shifting balance GA" (SBGA). The SBGA had a "core" population, and "colonies" which explored different parts of the fitness landscape. These colonies were forced to keep away from the core population's fitness space, but also performed local hill-climbing to avoid exploring poor parts of the landscape. Crossover mates were chosen from within sub-populations. Good colony members periodically migrated to the core, providing it with increased diversity and allowing it to quickly adapt when the environment changed. The SBGA was found to out-perform a standard GA in dynamic environments.

Another method using sub-populations has been presented by Garrett and Walker (2002), called Evolutionary Random Search (ERS). ERS combined ideas from random mutation hill-climbing, (Mitchell et al. 1993) and GEC. In ERS the sub-populations were called "shipwrecks", and unlike other methods, the members of the shipwrecks changed each generation. All members of the shipwreck were mutated twice, once with a small standard deviation and once with a large standard deviation, and then certain individuals were crossed over. The best resulting children of the shipwreck were then returned to the population. It was found that ERS performed very favourably in comparison to both Random Mutation Hill-Climbing Mitchell et al. (1993) and genetic algorithms.

Memory-Based Methods. Multiploidy is often used to implement implicit memory, where a phenotypic trait is represented by more than one gene, any of which can be chosen to be expressed. The gene that is expressed can be chosen in various ways, usually by some form of dominance, i.e. one gene is dominant over another, and will therefore always be expressed over that other. An example of the use of multiploidy is the "structured GA" (sGA) (Dasgupta and McGregor, 1992), where each chromosome was a hierarchical structure of genes, and genes at each level could activate or deactivate genes at the level below themselves, a gene was only expressed if it was active. This meant that information in a chromosome could remain present in the population without being expressed, and that it could be retrieved later. It was found that when tested on a dynamic problem the sGA performed better than a simple GA.

Case-based reasoning approaches have also been investigated by a number of researchers. Eggermont et al. (2001) used a system with a memory of past successful solutions which a GA could access whenever the environment changed. After each generation the best chromosome was added to memory, then when the environment changed the chromosomes in memory were re-evaluated and the best in the current environment reintroduced into the population. It was found that adding this case-based memory to the GA improved its performance in dynamic environments.

AIS and Dynamic Function Optimisation. Gaspar and Collard (1999) compared the performance of an AIS network model to a variety of genetic algorithm methods on a dynamic optimisation problem. They found that their AIS algorithm performed better than all but two of the GAs – a "hybrid GA" and one using hypermutation (Gaspar and Collard, 1999).

Gaspar and Collard's work is the first to perform a comparison between GEC methods and AIS for dynamic function optimisation. The work described here differs from theirs in three main ways. Firstly, this paper concentrates on comparing simple implementations of an ES and CS, rather than Gaspar and Collard's network model. In this paper the ES and CS parameters were set only after a thorough examination of their performance over the whole range of settings (this was possible because of the few parameters used); this allowed the algorithms to be compared when they both were performing at their best. Finally, rather than quickly comparing AIS to a range of GEC methods, this paper makes a detailed examination of the difference in performance ES and CS on two, very different fitness functions, over a range of dimensionalities, enabling some important conclusions to be drawn, and some general predictions about their performance to be made.

3   Methodology

3.1   The Dynamic Functions

The optimisation tasks to be solved were 2-, 5- and 10-dimensional versions of two equations, the "peak" function and the "circles" functions. These were both made more difficult to optimise by increasing the number of dimensions, from 2, to 5 to 10, since this reduces the density of points in the fitness space. In all cases the space searched by the methods below is limited to an $0 \le x_i < 10$ square/hypercube.

Peak function:
The peak function was as follows:

$$f = (\mathbf{x}) = 1/5.\frac{sin(5(\sum_{i=1}^{N}(x_i - xf_i)^2)^1/2}{5(\sum_{i=1}^{N}(x_i - xf_i)^2)^1/2}$$

where f defines the fitness at a point in space represented by the genes of an individual/chromosome, and $N \in \{2, 5, 10\}$.

Circles function:
The circles function was as follows:

$$f = min(E(1, \boldsymbol{x}), E(3, \boldsymbol{x}))$$

Where E is the shortest euclidean distance between the circle of a radius in the first parameter, and the point $\boldsymbol{x}$, the second parameter, and $x \in \{2, 5, 10\}$. This function creates two concentric circles in the fitness landscape, one with a radius of 1, and the other with a radius of 3.

These two functions were chosen because they have significantly different fitness landscapes: the peak function has a central global optimum, surrounded by several ripples that were suboptima and the circles function contained two equal global optima (the two circles).

3.2   Algorithms

Both the ES and CS algorithms were made up of parents, offspring and *random immigrants* (new, random population members added each generation). As seen in Section 2, Grefenstette used the concept of random immigrants to add diversity. This is a familiar concept for CS, since CLONALG introduces a number of new population members each generation, and random immigrants have also been incorporated into a basic ES.

Both the ES and CS had a population size of 33, which can be further described in terms of the number of parents (p_n), number of offspring (c_n) and number of random immigrants (ri_n). Sensitivity tests were undertaken to decide the exact composition of the population, which are described below. In each generation, the whole population (parents, offspring and random immigrants) was ranked by performance, the best p_n chromosomes were mutated until c_n

new offspring had been produced; then ri_n random immigrants were created and replaced the worst individuals in the population. No recombination operators were used in the ES.

For both the ES and the CS, each population member encoded a single co-ordinate in the search space, so that the number of genes in an individual was the same as the dimensionality of the fitness functions. In the ES, there were also corresponding strategy parameters for each object parameter.

The number of *fitness evaluations* was fixed at as close to 1000 as possible for the two algorithms so that each would perform the same amount of work. One fitness evaluation refers to a single calculation of fitness. This concept of fitness evaluations was used, rather than number of generations, because in the CS the size of a population changed over the course of a generation.

The position of the global optimum of the fitness functions (and corresponding local optima) moved randomly after each 1000 fitness evaluations, this was done 20 times, so that in total each algorithm run comprised of (20 * 1000) fitness evaluations.

3.3   Experimental Procedure

ES and CS tests were undertaken so that Walker, who has previously used ES undertook the ES tests, and Garrett, who has experience of CS undertook the CS tests. This helped to ensure that each experimentor was trying to get the best results they could.

Sensitivity Tests. These experiments aimed to find out how sensitive ES and CS are to the population composition, and to find out what the best settings were. The sensitivity tests involved running the ES and CS with different numbers of random immigrants, parents and offspring, with both fitness functions, at 2, 5 and 10 dimensions. The proportion of random immigrants introduced each generation was varied between 0 and 0.9, and the proportion of the remaining population made up of parents was varied between 0.1 and 1 for the ES and between 0 and 1 for the CS (it is not possible to have zero parents in an ES).

In all these experiments the fitnesses of all the chromosomes in the best performing generation were averaged and used in the analysis in Section 4.1.

Comparative Tests. Once the best population parameters had been determined for the ES and CS for the different fitness functions and dimensionalities, they were used in further runs using those functions and dimensionalities. In this case the data that was saved for analysis in Section 4.2 were the fitnesses of the best chromosome in each generation. In addition, the gene values of each population member in the last generation of the 2 dimensional versions of both fitness functions were saved.

4   Experimental Results

In this section the results from the sensitivity tests are presented first, followed by a comparison of the performance of ES and CS on the dynamic functions.

Table 1. Summary of the findings of the sensitivity tests, the best proportions of random immigrants and parents in the population for the 2 fitness functions at 2, 5 and 10 dimensions. ri_n refers to the proportion of random immigrants in the population; p_n refers to the proportion of parents in the remaining population.

Peak function		
	ES	CS
ri_n	Between 0.4 and 0.7 of population, widening as dimensionality reduces	Little effect
p_n	Between 0 and 0.2	Around 0.3 at low dimensions, and 0.4 to 0.5 at high
Cicles function		
ri_n	Little effect at low dimensions, between 0.3 and 0.8 at high	Less than 0.2 parents, best around 0.1; with more parents, best over 0.2
p_n	Little effect at low dimensions, best over 0.2 at high	Around 0.3 to 0.4

Note that in all the graphs, a lower value indicates a better performance, as the fitness value from the peak function has been inverted to match the result from the circle function, so that they can both now be thought of as *cost* functions.

4.1 Sensitivity Results

In this section, only the results from the peak fitness function are included, however the discussion refers to both sets of results. Figure 1 shows the performance of the ES and CS on the peak function at 2, 5 and 10 dimensions. The results of these tests on both the peak and circle functions, in terms of optimum population composition, are summarised in Table 1.

It can be seen from the variations in landscape in the plots that both the CS ES were sensitive to changes in the population composition, in terms of both the proportion of random immigrants, and of parents vs. offspring. In addition, as the number of dimensions was increased from 2 to 5 to 10 the sensitivity of both the ES and CS increased, with smaller areas of optimality within the plots.

The ES was more sensitive to the number of random immigrants, especially at higher dimensions, than was the CS, shown by the greater change in landscape along the y-axis compared to the CS plots. This indicates that the use of random immigrants in an ES can more significantly improve its performance at high dimensions.

Both the ES and CS were more sensitive to the number of parents vs. offspring than to the proportion of random immigrants in the population. The CS showed the greatest impact, with a clear gradient along the x-axis, for instance in Figure 1b, with the best values falling at around 30 to 40% (of the population minus the number of random immigrants).

4.2 Comparative Tests

For each fitness function and dimension the best chromosome in each generation was recorded, and in Figure 2 a representative set of these results for the peak function are plotted, comparing the ES and CS results in each case.

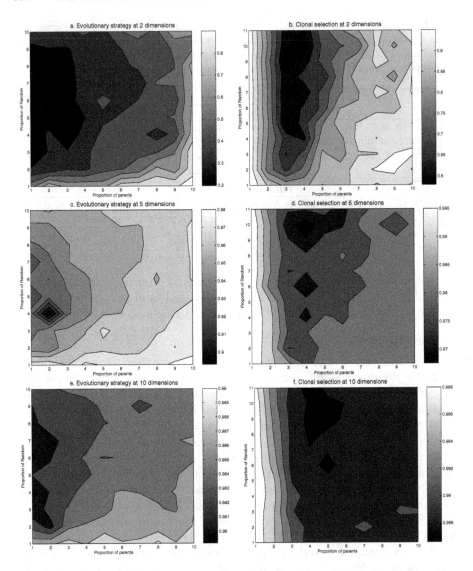

Fig. 1. Results from the sensitivity tests on the ES and CS for fitness function 1, showing the average fitness of the best performing generation over the range of population parameter settings. Darker (lower) areas indicate better performance.

It can be seen, that as would be expected, as the number of dimensions increased, and therefore the size of the search space increased dramatically, there was a significant worsening of performance, for both the ES and CS (note the different y-axis scales on the 2 and 10 dimensional plots.

For both the peak and circles functions, at 2 dimensions, the CS performed better overall than the ES, shown for the peak function in Figures 2 a and b. The ES optimised more quickly than the CS, shown by the almost squared shapes in

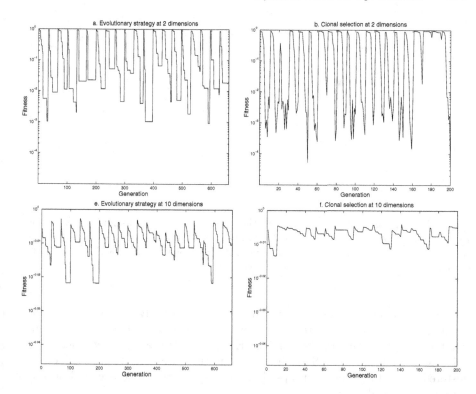

Fig. 2. A representative set of results, comparing the ES and CS ability to optimise the dynamic peak function. As before, a lower value indicates a better performance, and each change in performance indicates when the global has moved.

the graph, compared to the points on the CS plots. However, the ES tended to level off at a worse value than that found by the CS. Also, the CS rarely levelled off before the fitness landscape changed again, which indicates that with a more slowly changing function, it would be able to reach even better levels of fitness.

It was found that at 5 and 10 dimensions, however, the ES performed better than the CS for both functions, with the level reached almost consistently better than that found by the CS (Figures 2 c and d).

In addition to the performance of the populations of the ES and CS, the gene values of each individual in the last generation were recorded so that the state of the population at the end of the run could be analysed. Figure 3 shows the gene values for the best run of the ES and CS on both functions for 2 dimensions. In these plots, a greater scattering of values indicates more variation in the population, which is valuable when optimising a dynamic function. Clustering indicates that many individuals are located around an optimum, a sign that the algorithm has been successful in locating the current global best.

In Figure 3 it can be seen that for the peak function, in the ES there is a cluster towards the bottom right of the plot, with a sparse scattering throughout

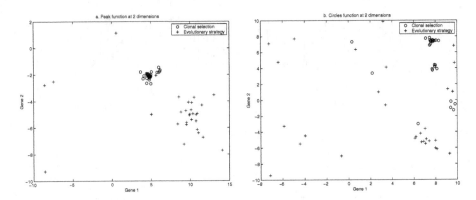

Fig. 3. A comparison of the locations in the search space of the individuals from the final generation of the ES and CS, in the 2 dimensional versions of the peak and circles functions. N.B. the positions of the global optima are not the same for the ES and CS as they were determined randomly at run time.

the rest of the space. The CS genes are even more tightly clustered, with the remaining individuals scattered over a much smaller area. This pattern holds true for the circles function—where the ES' gene values are clearly much more widely scattered than the CS'. Interestingly, in this case, the CS' gene values are clustered around 3 points, perhaps these correspond to previous global optima or to areas of local optima?

The wider scattering of individuals, even after 1000 fitness evaluations, in the ES may explain why the ES was able to optimise faster than the CS when the landscape changed—with individuals located in more parts of the landscape, it is more likely that one of them will be close to the new optimum. However, the CS was still able to optimise to a better level in the 2 dimensional cases, showing that it is a powerful optimisation method. At higher dimensions however, it appears that the advantage of higher population diversity enabled the ES to perform better.

5   Conclusion

This work is the first to have used CS for dynamic function optimisation, despite the importance of this type of application, and the plethora of evolutionary approaches that have been devised. Two dynamic functions, which posed different challenges for the CS, were investigated at 3 dimensionalities. Furthermore, this work has compared CS's performance to an ES for the same functions. This work begins to suggest which search spaces are better suited to CS rather than evolutionary methods.

In addition to opening a new field of application for CS, this paper has undertaken an analysis of the best set of population parameters for the functions optimised, which has shown how sensitive CS is to the number of random individuals introduced each generation, and the ratio of parents to offspring, when it is used for dynamic functions.

It has been found that both the ES and CS are sensitive to the composition of their population, with both being most sensitive to the proportion of random immigrants. Significantly, it has also been found that an ES can optimise more quickly than CS, but that at low dimensions, although it is slightly slower, CS reaches a better level of than the ES before the environment changes again. With higher dimensional landscapes however, CS performed worse that the ES.

The reasons for these differences are not clear, although the higher population diversity of the ES may indicate why it can perform better than CS at higher dimensions.

This preliminary work looking at the use of AIS methods for dynamic function optimisation will be continued in the future. The next step will be to experiment to find out if the conclusions made in this paper hold true in the more general case. The reasons for the differences in performance between the CS and ES will also be further investigated, as this should provide insights into ways that both approaches can be improved. Another important step will be to apply CS to some real world dynamic functions.

References

Back, T., Schwefel, H.-P., 1993. An overview of evolutionary algorithms for parameter optimization. Evolutionary Computation 1 (1), 1–23.

Branke, J., 1999. Evolutionary approaches to dynamic optimization problems – a survey. In: Wu, A. (Ed.), GECCO Workshop on Evolutionary Algorithms for Dynamic Optimization Problems. pp. 134–137.

Burnet, F. M., 1959. The Clonal Selection Theory of Acquired Immunity. Cambridge University Press.

Cobb, H., 1990. An investigation into the use of hypermutation as an adaptive operator in genetic algorithms having continuous, time dependent nonstationary environments. NRL Memornadum Report 6760 (NCARAI report AIC-90-001).

Cobb, H., Grefenstette, J., 1993. Genetic algorithms for tracking changing environments. In: Genetic Algorithms: Proceedings of the 5th international conference ICGA93. pp. 523–530.

Dasgupta, D., McGregor, D., 1992. Nonstationary function optimisation using the structured genetic algorithm. In: Proceedings of Parallel Problem Solving from Nature (PPSN-92). pp. 145–154.

de Castro, L. N., Von Zuben, F. J., 2000. The clonal selection algorithm with engineering applications. In: Proceedings of GECCO'00, Workshop on Artificial Immune Systems and Their Applications. pp. 36–37.

Eggermont, J., Lenaerts, T., Poyhonen, S., Termier, A., 2001. Raising the dead; extending evolutionary algorithms with a case-based memory. In: Proceedings of 2nd European Conference on Genetic Programming (EuroGP'01).

Fogel, D. B., 1995. Evolutionary Computation - Towards a New Philosophy of Machine Intelligence. IEEE Press, New York.

Garrett, S., Walker, J., 2002. Combining evolutionary and 'non'-evolutionary methods in tracking dynamic global optima. In: Genetic and Evolutionary Computation Conference, GECCO 2002. pp. 359–366.

Gaspar, A., Collard, P., 1999. From GAs to artificial immune systems: Improving adaptation in time dependent optimization. In: Proceedings of the Congress on Evolutionary Computation. Vol. 3. IEEE Press, Mayflower Hotel, Washington D.C., USA, pp. 1859–1866.

Grefenstette, J., 1992. Genetic algorithms for changing environments. In: Proceedings of Parallel Problem Solving from Nature 2. pp. 137–144.

Mitchell, M., Holland, J., Forrest, S., 1993. When will a genetic algorithm outperform hill climbing? Neural Information Processing Systems 6, 51–58.

Oppacher, F., Wineberg, M., 1999. The shifting balance genetic algorithm: Improving the GA in a dynamic environment. In: The Proceedings of the Genetic and Evolutionary Computation Conference GECCO-99. pp. 504–510.

Walker, J., 2003. Experiments in evolutionary robotics: investigating the importance of training and lifelong adaptation by evolution. Ph.D. thesis, Department of Computer Science, University of Wales, Aberystwyth.

Wolpert, D. H., Macready, W. G., 1997. No Free Lunch Theorems for Optimization. IEEE Transactions on Evolutionary Computation 1 (1), 67–82.

The Effect of Antibody Morphology
on Non-self Detection

Johan Kaers[1], Richard Wheeler[2], and Herman Verrelst[1]

[1] Data4s Future Technologies,
Ambachtenlaan 13G, 3001 Heverlee, Belgium
{johan.kaers,herman.verrelst}@data4s.com
[2] Edinburgh Research and Innovation Ltd.
1-7 Roxburgh Street, Edinburgh EH8 9TA, Scotland
richard.wheeler@ed.ac.uk

Abstract. Anomaly detection algorithms inspired by the natural immune system often use the negative selection metaphor to implement non-self detection. Much research has gone into ways of generating good sets of non-self detectors or antibodies and these methods' time and space complexities. In this paper, the antibody morphology is defined as the collection of properties defining the shape, data-representation and data-ordering of an antibody. The effect these properties can have on self/non-self classification capabilities is investigated. First, a data-representation using fuzzy set theory is introduced. A comparison is made between the classification performance using fuzzy and m-ary data-representations using some benchmark machine learning data-sets from the UCI archive. The effects of an antigen data reordering mechanism based on Major Histocompatibility Complex (MHC) molecules is investigated. The population level effect this mechanism can have by reducing the number of holes in the antigen space is discussed and the importance of data order in the r-contiguous symbol match-rule is highlighted. Both are analysed quantitatively using some UCI data-sets.

1   Introduction

Anomaly detection algorithms based on the biological immune system have been applied to a variety of problems, including virus detection [7], network intrusion detection [12] [11] and hardware fault tolerance [3]. The T-cell maturation process is used as an inspiration for algorithms that produce a set of *change detectors* or *antibodies*. A *censoring* process removes a *detector* when it *matches* with a cell or *data-string* of the *self* from a large space of possible detectors. The remaining ones are then used to determine if an incoming data-string or *antigen* is part of the self or not. The time and space complexities of these algorithms have been extensively analysed and variations inspired on other immunological phenomena [14] and evolutionary computing [16] [10] have been proposed [12].

One common property is that they all use a binary or m-ary symbol string data-representation. In the biological immune system however, recognition between receptors and antigens is based on their three-dimensional shapes and

J. Timmis et al. (Eds.): ICARIS 2003, LNCS 2787, pp. 285–295, 2003.

other physical properties [15]. Following the biological structure of the antibody-antigen binding process more closely could enable us to transpose the performance and adaptability of the natural immune system onto these computer algorithms. Therefore we investigate in this paper some modifications of the shape, data-representation and data-ordering of artificial antibodies. We will refer to these properties as the *antibody morphology*. They are analysed from the machine learning viewpoint and evaluated according to their usefulness as tools to enhance the classification capabilities.

The Artificial Life hypothesis is used because we assume that it is possible to model the biological immune system as a complex system of many interacting components. Similar to work in Artificial Chemistries [6] we abstract from natural molecular processes to investigate the fundamental dynamics of the complex system. An antibody morphology that uses Fuzzy Set Theory [20] is introduced. It captures the graded nature of the physical antibody/antigen match process and allows the non-self detection algorithms to handle data-sets with complex symbolic structures.

The paper is organized as follows. Section 2 looks at a data-representation inspired by fuzzy set theory and shows how the r-contiguous symbol matching rule can be modified accordingly. This fuzzy morphology is applied to some data-sets and statistically compared with the m-ary one. In section 3, the effect of using a data reordering method inspired by the *Major Histocompatibility Complex* (MHC) molecules is analysed. The importance of the data-order for the matching process is highlighted and the problem of *holes* in the non-self space is addressed by taking advantage of the population level effects resulting from using the MHC method. Section 4 contains the results and details of the various experiments using standard machine learning data-sets from the UCI repostiry [2].

1.1   Antibody Generation

Algorithms that generate antibodies make assumptions about their internal data-representation and therefore are tied to the antibody morphology. From the ones known in the literature [1], the *linear*, *greedy* and *binary template* algorithms build most heavily on the assumption of the binary (or m-ary [19]) string morphology. The ones based on generating random antibodies and/or genetic mutation operators (e.g. *exhaustive*, *NSMutation*) are more easily extended to arbitrary morphologies. The only requirement they have is that the morphology should allow for the generation of random antibodies and that a self to antibody matching scheme is present. Because of this independence of morphology, the *exhaustive* algorithm introduced by Forrest, Perelson et al. in [7] is used in the experiments included in section 4.

1.2   Machine Learning

Throughout the paper, non-self detection is considered as a 2-class classification problem, discriminating between self and non-self classes. The data-sets used in the statistical analysis of the classifiers in section 4, are taken from the UCI Machine Learning archive [2]. These benchmark data-sets have well known properties and are widely used throughout the machine learning community, allowing comparisons with different types of classifiers [8].

2   Fuzzy Antibodies

The binding strength or *affinity* between an antigen and an antibody in the biological immune system depends on the physical and chemical forces acting at the binding site [15]. In the immune response, effective antibodies are the ones that bind tightly to an antigen and do not let go. In this section we capture the graded character of antibody-antigen affinity by modifying the bit-string morphology to include elements of fuzzy set theory. Other work also combines elements of artificial immune systems and fuzzy set theory. [13] shares our classifier point of view but uses another immune system model and another type of learning algorithm (AINE). [5] presents a hybrid function approximation algorithm that uses localized fuzzy models. [18] uses immune network theory and fuzzy soft-computing techniques for control and diagnosis of dynamical systems.

2.1   Data Fuzzification

Fuzzy set theory is used in various machine learning algorithms to cope with the inherent complexity often present in real-life datasets. It provides an intuitive means to represent data backed by a strong mathematical theory. As such, we use it here to extend the binary (and m-ary) string morphologies.

The *self set* S consists of a number N_s of independent data-strings of length l

$$s \in S = (x_1, \ldots, x_l)$$

where all x_i are values belonging to the *attribute* A_i. All attributes A_i have a number (n_i) of *fuzzy membership functions* or *FMFs* F_{ij} associated with them. The domain of these functions differs depending on the format and type of data the attribute is linked with. Every F_{ij} converts a value x_i to a *fuzzy membership value* between 0 and 1 that signifies a degree of membership to the function. In addition to this, a *match threshold* th_i is defined for every attribute.

The literature contains a large number of meaningful ways to define FMFs for various types of data. For example :

– *Continuous numbers*
   If the data is numeric and continuous from a given interval, the axis can be divided into a number of equal sub-intervals, each receiving one FMF. In this paper, we use triangle-shaped FMFs, centred in the middle of their sub-intervals. The amount of *overlap* between the triangles is determined by a parameter. A value of 1 means only its own sub-interval is covered, values > 1 and < 2 that the neighbouring intervals are partially covered, > 2 that further intervals are also covered. Figure 1 shows this kind of set-up for values from $[0, 100]$ and overlap $= 1.5$.

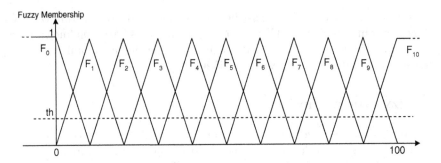

Fig. 1. The axis is divided up into overlapping domains by the FMFs. F_1 - F_9 cover the region between 0 and 100. F_0 and F_{10} capture everything outside this range. The dashed line is the fuzzy threshold for this attribute.

- *Categorical data*
  If the data is taken from a fixed set of unrelated symbols, every symbol gets an FMF that is 1 for that symbol and 0 for all the others. The FMFs reduce to identity functions, one for each symbol.
- *Textual data*
  Often, text data is structured in a way that allows meaningful fuzzy functions to be defined. e.g. an FMF acting on a date field can produce higher fuzzy membership values when the date is closer to a fixed moment in time. Spelling errors can be handled using an FMF based on digram matching [17].

2.2   Fuzzy Matching

The *r-contiguous symbol* match rule that is used to determine if an antibody matches an antigen or self string is modified as follows. Assume the data contains l values. An antibody or detector d is a string of FMFs

$$d = (F_{1j_1}, \ldots, F_{lj_l}) \quad \forall i = 1 \ldots l : 1 \leq j_i \leq n_i$$

A string is said to *match* if there are r (the *match length*) contiguous positions where the data applied to the corresponding FMF exceeds it's fuzzy threshold. Call $a = (a_1, \ldots, a_l)$ the data-string.
a matches $d \Leftrightarrow$

$$\exists p, \forall q : p \leq q \leq p + r - 1 : F_{qj_q}(a_q) \geq th_q$$

Figure 2 illustrates this matching process with a data-string of length 5 and a match length of 3.

When all attributes are categorical with symbols 0 and 1 and the match threshold is set to 1, this set-up corresponds to the binary string morphology. The m-ary morphology is attained when all attributes are categorical with m categories, again with the match threshold set to 1. The thresholds define the

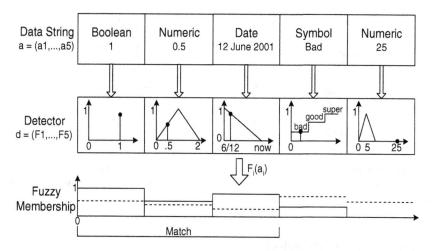

Fig. 2. Antigen - Fuzzy Antibody match with $l = 5$ and $r = 3$. The data is evaluated with the detector's FMFs (F_i) and compared to the fuzzy thresholds (dashed lines). The Fuzzy Membership Values at positions 1,2 and 3 exceed the thresholds. Therefore, there is a match.

specificity of a match. Low thresholds will result in a more approximate view on the data while higher ones constrain matching to more narrowly defined regions. The tuning of the FMF/Threshold combinations will therefore have a direct impact on the detection performance.

An immune response algorithm can take into account the *match affinity f* defined by

$$0 \le f = \sum_{q=p}^{p+r-1} F_q j_q(a_q) - \sum_{q=p}^{p+r-1} th_q \le r \tag{1}$$

that measures how strong the match between an antibody and an antigen is.

Section 4.2 gives some results obtained using this method together with all relevant details about the data-sets and algorithm parameters.

3   Major Histocompatibility Complex

Major Histocompatibility Complex or *MHC* molecules play the role of antigen presentation agents in the biological immune system. They bind to parts of antigens and display these at the cell surface where they can be recognized by T-cells. There is a high degree of variability in the MHC molecules between individuals, each mounting a slightly different immune response. This increases the population level immunity against diseases [15]. In this section, we look at a possible implementation of the MHC system and how it affects classification performance.

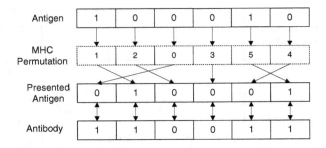

Fig. 3. Antigen presentation using a MHC permutation mask. The bits of the antigen are re-orderder according to the permutation mask before being matched to the antibody.

3.1   Population Level Effects

When using the r-contiguous match rule, there are always parts of the non-self space that are undetectable for any antibody. These *holes* in the non-self space occur where any detector for the hole will also match some self string and therefore is an undesirable one. This phenomenon was investigated in [4] and Hofmeyr [11] was the first to use the analogy with MHC molecules to combat this problem. By using a random permutation mask to produce a different data-representation in a number of local antibody sets, the holes also differ in every location. The likelihood that an antigen will fall in the cross-section of all local holes is lower than for the individual locations separately. Combining the local antibody sets can therefore result in a higher performance that cannot be attained with a single set. In section 4.3 this effect is illustrated using a synthetic data-set containing random bit-strings.

3.2   Attribute Order

Transposing the MHC system to the Artificial Immune System domain, it can be said to form a bridge between the data-representations of the antigen and the antibody. When using a string morphology (m-ary of fuzzy), the MHC molecules can be implemented as a permutation mask as first suggested in [11]. In this set-up, antigen data-strings are broken down into their components whose order is re-arranged according to the permutation mask before being presented to an antibody. Figure 3 illustrates this process.

When using the r-contiguous symbol match rule, the order of the attributes in the data-string is important. Per definition, the self/non-self patterns have to occur between attributes no further than r symbols apart. MHC permutations can therefore potentially destroy or enable the ability to capture the significant patterns in the data-set. When there are no dependencies between the attributes in the string, the re-arranging will not affect classification performance. In section 4.3 we illustrates this using some data-sets.

Table 1. The data-sets and the size of the self- and antibody-sets derived from them. Length of the data-strings and the match-length used in r-contiguous matching.

Data-set	#Self	#Non-self	#Antibodies	Length	Match Length
Data-Sets and Algorithm Parameters					
Iris	50	100	300	4	2
Cancer	458	241	1000	9	3
Hepatitis	123	32	75000	20	4
Zoo Animals	41	59	100	16	7
Mushrooms	4208	3916	50000	21	8
Random Bit-String	100	-	200	32	8

4   Results

All test were performed on a number of benchmark data-sets from the UCI machine learning database archive [2]. Continuous attributes were discretized for the m-ary symbol representation by dividing the interval of possible values into m equal sub-intervals and assigning a symbol to each one. For the fuzzy data-representation these same sub-intervals were used to space the overlapping Fuzzy Membership Functions as outlined in section 2.1

4.1   Data-Sets

The goal of the Iris data-set is to predict the type of iris plant using instances of 4 continuous attributes. This 3-class problem was converted to a 2-class one by grouping the "versicolor" and "virginica" types into 1 class. The Cancer and Hepatitis data-sets deal with medical diagnosis data. The Cancer data-set has 10 continuous attributes that are used to determine benign or malignant classes. The Hepatitis set uses 15 boolean and 5 continuous attributes to predict the survival of a patient. The Zoo Animals data-set classifies, using 15 boolean and 1 categorical attribute, a number of animals into 7 classes. We grouped together the non mammal classes, so the task became to distinguish between mammals and non mammals. The Mushroom set has 22 categorical values that define whether a mushroom is edible or poisonous. Finally, "Random Bit-String" is a data-set of 100 32-bit random bit-strings.

4.2   Fuzzy Morphology Results

Using the settings of table 1 we configured experiments to determine the classification error of Artificial Immune Systems using the m-ary and fuzzy morphologies. The results in table 2 were obtained from 10 runs of 10-fold cross validation. The number of continuous attributes is given, as well as the number of intervals in which they were discretized. We used the set-up of overlapping FMFs as outlined in section 2.1. The fuzzy threshold was set to 0.01 for these

Table 2. Summary of classification errors on UCI repository data-sets using different antibody morphologies.

Classification Error					
Data-set	**Continuous**	**Intervals**	**Overlap**	**Error**	**Variance**
Iris	4	8	1.0	0.14899	0.09623
Iris	4	8	2.0	0.11744	0.03183
Cancer	9	10	1.0	0.08108	0.01449
Cancer	9	10	3.0	0.03567	0.00588
Hepatitis	4	5	1.0	0.20129	0.01257
Hepatitis	4	5	1.5	0.21415	0.02483
Zoo Animals	0	-	-	0.047	0.09597
Mushrooms	0	-	-	0.02093	0.00832

Table 3. Comparison between m-ary and fuzzy morphologies on data-sets.

Morphology Comparison				
Data-set	**M-ary**	**Fuzzy**	**Winner**	**Significance**
Cancer	0.05912	0.03945	Fuzzy	98.14664%
Iris	0.14094	0.12081	Fuzzy	92.72657%
Hepatitis	0.20315	0.21496	(M-ary)	62.47845%

attributes and to 1.0 for the categorical attributes. Therefore the morphology reduces to the m-ary one when the fuzzy overlap is set to 1.0 (rows 1 and 3).

The figures in table 2 seemed to indicate that fuzzy morphology can result in lower error-rates (row 2 < row 1 and row 4 < row 3). To confirm this, we performed paired t-tests of 30 runs of 10-fold cross-validation between a classifier using the m-ary (overlap 1.0) and one with the fuzzy morphology. Table 3 shows the average classification errors over the 30 runs for both morphologies and the outcome of the t-test. The *winner* column is the morphology with lowest average classifcation error and the *significance* column shows how certain we can be of this results according to the t-test. Given the results we can conclude that the data-sets that are dominated by continuous attributes (Iris and Cancer) could attain a lower classification error using the fuzzy morphology. The Hepatitis data-set did not show a significant difference in classification error when using the fuzzy morphology.

4.3   MHC Results

In order to illustrate the population level effects of MHC re-ordering we set up the following experiment using the Random Bit-String data-set as self set. One antibody set of 200 antibodies was generated without MHC reordering, while another one was split up in 4 sub-sets of 50 antibodies, each with a different random MHC permutation mask. All matching operations for these 4 sub-sets

Table 4. Comparison between classifiers without MHC re-ordering and with MHC re-ordering.

MHC Comparison				
Data-set	**No MHC**	**MHC**	**Winner**	**Significance**
Random Bit-String	0.3051	0.1548	MHC	99.99877%
Iris	0.1312	0.1083	MHC	99.93038%
Cancer	0.0335	0.0389	(No MHC)	56.31424%

took into account the attribute re-ordering caused by their MHC permutation masks as illustrated in 3. For 1000 iterations bit-strings from the self set were picked at random and modified in 1 bit before being matched against both antibody sets. If a set failed to detect the change, the classification error was increased. This experiment was repeated 30 times and the classification errors from both sets used as input for a paired t-test. Table 4 shows that the statistical significance that the MHC set is better is very high. Since the data consists of random bit-strings, there is no significance in the order of the data-string, and the positive effect can be attributed to the population level effects discussed in section 3.1.

Other data-sets were investigated in a similar fashion. The Iris set was used to train an antibody set of 300 antibodies and another one containing 3 sub-sets of 100 antibodies with different MHC permutations. The Cancer set was tested with one set of 1000 versus 3 sub-sets of 333 with MHC. As in the previous section, 10-fold cross-validation was used and the classification errors of 30 such experiments were used in a paired t-test. The Iris set shows a significant difference favouring the classifier using MHC, while the Cancer set does not show a significant difference. We can conclude that for some sets the data-order and hole reducing effects of the MHC re-ordering are significant, whereas in other cases they show no positive or negative effect on the classification performance.

5 Conclusions

In this paper we looked at properties related to the data-representation and data-ordering of antibodies, collectively called the antibody morphology. We introduced an alternative way of representing antibodies based on fuzzy set theory and showed how the r-contiguous symbol match rule can be adapted accordingly. Using the fuzzy morphology we trained a number of classifiers on data-sets from the UCI archive. Paired t-tests confirmed that using a properly tuned fuzzy morphology can have positive effect on the classification performance.

We discussed how a data-reordering mask inspired by MHC molecules can reduce the effect of holes in the antigen space and emphasized that the ordering of attributes has to take into account the specific properties of the data-set. Using data-sets of random bit-strings, the population level effect in the MHC re-ordering was shown to have a significant effect on the classification performance.

We illustrated that depending on the inherent self/non-self patterns present in the data, the order in which the attributes occur can have an impact on the classification performance and therefore MHC reordering can influence the classification performance and robustness.

More research into methods to predict these effects and guide the MHC permutation process are needed to optimally benefit from them. Currently the authors are working on more formal ways to characterize the ideal data order inside the antibodies. Also, algorithms are being investigated that can inductively derive the optimal morphology and match parameters given an arbitrary data-set.

Acknowledgments

This work has been supported by Data4s Future Technologies, Leuven, Belgium. The authors would like to thank Prof. Peter Ross for the useful comments. Richard Wheeler would like to thank Marco Dorigo for his support and consideration.

References

1. M. Ayara, J. Timmis, R. de Lemos, L. de Castro, R. Duncan *Negative Selection: How to Generate Detectors*, in Proceedings of the 1st International Conference on Artificial Immune Systems (ICARIS), 2002, p89-98.

2. C.L. Blake, C.J. Merz, *UCI Repository of machine learning databases*, http://www.ics.uci.edu/mlearn/MLRepository.html, Irvine, CA: University of California, Department of Information and Computer Science, 1998.

3. R. O. Canham, A. M. Tyrrell, *A Multilayered Immune System for Hardware Fault Tolerance within an Embryonic Array*, in Proceedings of the 1st International Conference on Artificial Immune Systems (ICARIS), 2002, p3-11.

4. P. D'haeseleer, S. Forrest, P. Helman. *An immunological approach to change detection : Algorithms, analysis and implications*, in Proceedings of the 1996 IEEE Symposium on Research in Security and Privacy, pages 110-119, IEEE Computer Society Press, Piscataway, New Jersey.

5. Y. Diao, M. Passino. Immunity-Based Hybrid Learning Methods for Structure and Parameter Adjustment, IEEE Transactions on Systems, Man and Machine, July 2000.

6. P. Dittrich, J. Ziegler and W. Banzhaf. *Artificial Chemistries - A Review*, Artificial Life VII, 3, 2001, p225-275.

7. S. Forrest, A. S. Perelson, L. Allen, R. Cherukuri, *Self-nonself discrimination in a computer.*, in Proceedings of the 1994 IEEE Symposium on Research in Security and Privacy, Los Alamitos, CA : IEEE Computing Society Press, 1994.

8. Z. Frederick, *A Comprehensive Case Study: An Examination of Machine Learning and Connectionist Algorithms*, Masters Thesis, Brigham Young University, 1995

9. P. Helman, S. Forrest, *An efficient algorithm for generating random antibody strings*, Technical Report CS-94-07, The University of New Mexico, Albuquerque, NM, 1994.

10. R. R. Hightower, S. Forrest, A. S. Perelson, *The Evolution of Emergent Organiza-
    tion in Immune System Gene Libraries*, Proc. of the 6th Int. Conference on Genetic
    Algorithms, L. J. Eshelman (ed.), Morgan Kaufmann, 1995, p344-350.
11. S.A. Hofmeyr, *An Immunological Model of Distributed Detection and its Applica-
    tion to Computer Security*, Ph.D. Thesis, University of New Mexico, May 1999
12. J. Kim, P. Bentley, *An Artificial Immune Model for Network Intrusion Detection*,
    Proceedings of the 7th European Congress on Intelligent Techniques - Soft Com-
    puting (EUFIT'99). Aachen, Germany. September 13-19, 1999.
13. O. Nasraoui, F. González, and D. Dasgupta, *The Fuzzy Artificial Immune System:
    Motivations, Basic Concepts, and Application to Clustering and Web Profiling.* In
    IEEE International Conference on Fuzzy Systems, pages 711-716, Hawaii, HI, 13
    May 2002. IEEE.
14. M. Oprea, S. Forrest, *Simulated Evolution of Antibody Gene Libraries under
    Pathogen Selection*, Proc. of the IEEE conference on Systems, Man and Cyber-
    netics, 1998.
15. P. Parham, *The Immune System*, Garland Publishing/Elsevier Science, 2000
16. A. S. Perelson, R. Hightower, S. Forrest. *Evolution and Somatic Learning in V-
    Region Genes*, Research in Immunology 147, 1996, p202-208.
17. U. Pfeifer, T. Poersch and N. Fuhr. *Searching proper names in databases*, in Pro-
    ceedings of HIM95: Hypertext-Information Retrieval and Multimedia, Konstanz,
    Germany, pages 259–275. Universitatsverlag Konstanz, 1995.
18. N. Sasaki, Y. Dote. *Diagnosis and Control for Multi-Agent Systems using Immune
    Networks*, Artificial Neural Networks in Engineering (ANNIE 2002), November
    2002.
19. S. Singh, *Anomaly Detection Using Negative Selection Based on the r-contiguous
    Matching Rule*, Proceedings of the 1st International Conference on Artificial Im-
    mune Systems (ICARIS), 2002, p99-106.
20. L. Zadeh, *Fuzzy sets*, Inf. Control 8, 338-353, 1965.

The Immune System as a Cognitive System: New Perspectives for Information Technology Society

Claudio Franceschi

"L. Galvani" Interdisciplinary Center for the study of Bioinformatics, Biophysics and Biocomplexity, University of Bologna, Bologna, Italy
clafra@alma.unibo.it

Survival and maintenance in living organisms, from invertebrates to mammals, are assured by a variety of evolutionary conserved mechanisms. From this point of view, a critical role is played by cognitive systems, capable of acquiring and elaborating information from the environment (external world), as well as from the internal milieu (internal world).

Three biological systems, the immune system (IS), the nervous system (NS), and the endocrine system (ES), evolved to play such a fundamental role for complex living organisms. These systems are deeply interconnected among them, and share some basic architectural and organisational characteristics, despite having specific peculiarities.

The lecture will highlight the major characteristics of the IS as a whole stressing the fact that the IS is constituted by a very large number of heterogeneous interacting cells, which can be considered as the main components of a real world complex network, in the context of the danger/damage signals perspective. Indeed, when an organismal damage is going to occur, because of infections or stressing events pushing the body out of the physiological working range, danger/damage signals are delivered inside the system triggering the appropriate immune response.

The response as a whole is in fact a temporal and spatial coordination between mechanisms belonging to the two major IS subsystems, the innate and the clonotypic ones. In the case of foreign antigens (pathogens) danger signals are delivered as molecules detected by Toll-like receptors while damage signals as "alarming" cytokines due to local inflammatory processes. Thus, it is the association of foreign molecular patterns owned by pathogens with the danger and/or damage molecular signals that is able to trigger the immune response, allowing to put forward the concept that the innate IS is sensitive to and perceives the context.

Key molecular elements for building the immunological context are cytokines. Cytokines, regulatory molecules of immune phenomena, are locally produced and handled by the interacting immune cells (macrophages, T and B lymphocytes, among others) during immune responses (cytokine field hypothesis), in order to indirectly induce functional status changes in the immune cells themselves. Their role can be considered as fundamental during the establishment and maintenance of the following immunological processes:

J. Timmis et al. (Eds.): ICARIS 2003, LNCS 2787, pp. 296–297, 2003.
© Springer-Verlag Berlin Heidelberg 2003

1. The cascade of different pattern recognition processes involving the innate as well as the clonotypic immunity, during which molecular patterns shared by different antigens, stimulating the innate IS, work as a prerequisite for the subsequent effective recognition of individual and specific patterns of the same antigens by cells of the clonotypic IS compartment. A key role in all the quoted mechanisms, being the antigen recognition process at the basis of the structural capabilities of the IS at any time of its ontogenetic evolution, is played by the proteasome and its changes with age. The proteasome is the cellular "machinery" (organelle) devoted to chop self and foreign proteins for showing the resulting antigenic fragmented peptides to the appropriate immune cells.

2. The temporal and spatial dynamics of various network systems, corresponding to different levels of system description where elements, cell pools, cells and/or molecules have as main characteristics promiscuity and/or redundancy. Among others we can mention:

    i.   the two-layer connected network, in which one layer has the peculiarities of elements and mechanisms of the innate IS and the other of the clonotypic IS;

    ii. a multi-layer connected network, inspired to the interaction among the IS, the ES and the NS;

3. The self antigen stimulation (internal activity of the IS), the exogenous antigen stimulation (acute antigenic stress), and the immunological noise (fluctuating chronic exogenous antigenic stress), which can act separately or jointly to eventually give rise to the IS long time scale evolution (immunosenescence) by influencing:

    i.   the type of connectivity of the IS, envisaged as a dynamical network evolving over short and long time scales. Such a connectivity is tightly bound to the phenomenon of the expansion of specific cell clones, which has different weights over short and long time scales, taking into account the limitation of the Immunological Space;

    ii. the realization and maintenance of immunological memory in presence and absence of antigens.

All these major characteristics of the IS can inspire new and innovative models, useful for other branches and disciplines of computer science, information technology and artificial intelligence. From this point of view the graph theory approach applied to real world complex systems deserves particular attention.

Author Index

Lecture Notes in Computer Science

For information about Vols. 1–2688
please contact your bookseller or Springer-Verlag

Vol. 2726: E. Hancock, M. Vento (Eds.), Graph Based Representations in Pattern Recognition. Proceedings, 2003. VIII, 271 pages. 2003.

Vol. 2727: R. Safavi-Naini, J. Seberry (Eds.), Information Security and Privacy. Proceedings, 2003. XII, 534 pages. 2003.

Vol. 2728: E.M. Bakker, T.S. Huang, M.S. Lew, N. Sebe, X.S. Zhou (Eds.), Image and Video Retrieval. Proceedings, 2003. XIII, 512 pages. 2003.

Vol. 2729: D. Boneh (Ed.), Advances in Cryptology – CRYPTO 2003. Proceedings, 2003. XII, 631 pages. 2003.

Vol. 2731: C.S. Calude, M.J. Dinneen, V. Vajnovszki (Eds.), Discrete Mathematics and Theoretical Computer Science. Proceedings, 2003. VIII, 301 pages. 2003.

Vol. 2732: C. Taylor, J.A. Noble (Eds.), Information Processing in Medical Imaging. Proceedings, 2003. XVI, 698 pages. 2003.

Vol. 2733: A. Butz, A. Krüger, P. Olivier (Eds.), Smart Graphics. Proceedings, 2003. XI, 261 pages. 2003.

Vol. 2734: P. Perner, A. Rosenfeld (Eds.), Machine Learning and Data Mining in Pattern Recognition. Proceedings, 2003. XII, 440 pages. 2003. (Subseries LNAI).

Vol. 2735: F. Kaashoek, I. Stoica (Eds.), Peer-to-Peer Systems II. Proceedings, 2003. XI, 316 pages. 2003.

Vol. 2740: E. Burke, P. De Causmaecker (Eds.), Practice and Theory of Automated Timetabling IV. Proceedings, 2002. XII, 361 pages. 2003.

Vol. 2741: F. Baader (Ed.), Automated Deduction – CADE-19. Proceedings, 2003. XII, 503 pages. 2003. (Subseries LNAI).

Vol. 2742: R. N. Wright (Ed.), Financial Cryptography. Proceedings, 2003. VIII, 321 pages. 2003.

Vol. 2743: L. Cardelli (Ed.), ECOOP 2003 – Object-Oriented Programming. Proceedings, 2003. X, 501 pages. 2003.

Vol. 2744: V. Mařík, D. McFarlane, P. Valckenaers (Eds.), Holonic and Multi-Agent Systems for Manufacturing. Proceedings, 2003. XI, 322 pages. 2003. (Subseries LNAI).

Vol. 2745: M. Guo, L.T. Yang (Eds.), Parallel and Distributed Processing and Applications. Proceedings, 2003. XII, 450 pages. 2003.

Vol. 2746: A. de Moor, W. Lex, B. Ganter (Eds.), Conceptual Structures for Knowledge Creation and Communication. Proceedings, 2003. XI, 405 pages. 2003. (Subseries LNAI).

Vol. 2747: B. Rovan, P. Vojtáš (Eds.), Mathematical Foundations of Computer Science 2003. Proceedings, 2003. XIII, 692 pages. 2003.

Vol. 2748: F. Dehne, J.-R. Sack, M. Smid (Eds.), Algorithms and Data Structures. Proceedings, 2003. XII, 522 pages. 2003.

Vol. 2749: J. Bigun, T. Gustavsson (Eds.), Image Analysis. Proceedings, 2003. XXII, 1174 pages. 2003.

Vol. 2750: T. Hadzilacos, Y. Manolopoulos, J.F. Roddick, Y. Theodoridis (Eds.), Advances in Spatial and Temporal Databases. Proceedings, 2003. XIII, 525 pages. 2003.

Vol. 2751: A. Lingas, B.J. Nilsson (Eds.), Fundamentals of Computation Theory. Proceedings, 2003. XII, 433 pages. 2003.

Vol. 2752: G.A. Kaminka, P.U. Lima, R. Rojas (Eds.), RoboCup 2002: Robot Soccer World Cup VI. XVI, 498 pages. 2003. (Subseries LNAI).

Vol. 2753: F. Maurer, D. Wells (Eds.), Extreme Programming and Agile Methods – XP/Agile Universe 2003. Proceedings, 2003. XI, 215 pages. 2003.

Vol. 2754: M. Schumacher, Security Engineering with Patterns. XIV, 208 pages. 2003.

Vol. 2756: N. Petkov, M.A. Westenberg (Eds.), Computer Analysis of Images and Patterns. Proceedings, 2003. XVIII, 781 pages. 2003.

Vol. 2758: D. Basin, B. Wolff (Eds.), Theorem Proving in Higher Order Logics. Proceedings, 2003. X, 367 pages. 2003.

Vol. 2759: O.H. Ibarra, Z. Dang (Eds.), Implementation and Application of Automata. Proceedings, 2003. XI, 312 pages. 2003.

Vol. 2761: R. Amadio, D. Lugiez (Eds.), CONCUR 2003 - Concurrency Theory. Proceedings, 2003. XI, 524 pages. 2003.

Vol. 2762: G. Dong, C. Tang, W. Wang (Eds.), Advances in Web-Age Information Management. Proceedings, 2003. XIII, 512 pages. 2003.

Vol. 2763: V. Malyshkin (Ed.), Parallel Computing Technologies. Proceedings, 2003. XIII, 570 pages. 2003.

Vol. 2764: S. Arora, K. Jansen, J.D.P. Rolim, A. Sahai (Eds.), Approximation, Randomization, and Combinatorial Optimization. Proceedings, 2003. IX, 409 pages. 2003.

Vol. 2765: R. Conradi, A.I. Wang (Eds.), Empirical Methods and Studies in Software Engineering. VIII, 279 pages. 2003.

Vol. 2766: S. Behnke, Hierarchical Neural Networks for Image Interpretation. XII, 224 pages. 2003.

Vol. 2769: T. Koch, I. T. Sølvberg (Eds.), Research and Advanced Technology for Digital Libraries. Proceedings, 2003. XV, 536 pages. 2003.

Vol. 2777: B. Schölkopf, M.K. Warmuth (Eds.), Learning Theory and Kernel Machines. Proceedings, 2003. XIV, 746 pages. 2003. (Subseries LNAI).

Vol. 2783: W. Zhou, P. Nicholson, B. Corbitt, J. Fong (Eds.), Advances in Web-Based Learning – ICWL 2003. Proceedings, 2003. XV, 552 pages. 2003.

Vol. 2786: F. Oquendo (Ed.), Software Process Technology. Proceedings, 2003. X, 173 pages. 2003.

Vol. 2787: J. Timmis, P. Bentley, E. Hart (Eds.), Artificial Immune Systems. Proceedings, 2003. XI, 299 pages. 2003.

Vol. 2789: L. Böszörményi, P. Schojer (Eds.), Modular Programming Languages. Proceedings, 2003. XIII, 271 pages. 2003.

Vol. 2796: M. Cialdea Mayer, F. Pirri (Eds.), Automated Reasoning with Analytic Tableaux and Related Methods. Proceedings, 2003. X, 271 pages. 2003. (Subseries LNAI).